D1539505

Building e-Commerce Sites
with the .NET Framework

Jason Bentrum and James Whatley

A Division of Macmillan USA
201 West 103rd St., Indianapolis, Indiana, 46290 USA

Building e-Commerce Sites with the .NET Framework

Copyright © 2002 by Sams Publishing

International Standard Book Number: 0-672-32169-6

Library of Congress Catalog Card Number: 2001086060

Printed in the United States of America

First Printing: September 2001

04   03   02   01   4   3   2   1

Trademarks

Warning and Disclaimer

EXECUTIVE EDITOR
Shelley Kronzek

DEVELOPMENT EDITOR
Songlin Qiu

MANAGING EDITOR
Charlotte Clapp

PROJECT EDITOR
Carol Bowers

COPY EDITOR
Chuck Hutchinson

INDEXER
Rebecca Hornyak

PROOFREADER
Marcia Deboy

TECHNICAL EDITOR
Kevin Price

TEAM COORDINATOR
Pamalee Nelson

INTERIOR DESIGNER
Anne Jones

COVER DESIGNER
Aren Howell

PAGE LAYOUT
Octal Publishing, Inc.

Contents at a Glance

Table of Contents

PART V   Appendixes

Dedication

*To my loving wife Tonya. Without your love, support,
and understanding, this book would not have been possible.*

—Jason Bentrum

*I would like to dedicate this book to my new wife Jenna; without her never-ending support, I would
not have achieved this challenging endeavor. I also would like to say a special thank you
to my Mom and Dad; without their guidance and wisdom, I would not be where I am today.*

—James Whatley

Acknowledgments

First, I'd like to thank James Whatley and Michael Abdelmalek. Without their help, this book would not have been possible. They are two of the brightest, most talented developers I have ever met.

I would also like to thank Bill Brown for his continued support during this endeavor. Bill was always there to encourage and help me when I felt like I couldn't go on.

I've learned so much from so many people that it would be difficult to thank all of the people who influence me and made this endeavor possible, but here is a shot at it. In the beginning, there were Eric Fritsche and Chris Rogers who helped me get my career going. Between Eric's vision and Chris's tutelage, I worked on some of the most exciting projects and learned the most I've learned to date.

More recently, Barry Bloom, Bob Tabor, David Findley, Garth Hughes, Venkat Rangaswamy, Daryl Myrick, Gary Hartley, Chris Beck, and David Sipos have taught me more than I ever would have been able to learn on my own. They are all the best of the best, and it has been a privilege and an honor to work with them.

A special thanks to James Worrell for creating the MyGolfGear.NET look and feel. James's talent and creativity are second to none.

Last, but not least, I'd like to thank the editorial team at Sams. This book would not have been possible without the hard work and dedication of Shelley Kronzek, Songlin Qiu, Carol Bowers, and Kevin Price.

Tell Us What You Think!

As the reader of this book, *you* are our most important critic and commentator. We value your opinion and want to know what we're doing right, what we could do better, what areas you'd like to see us publish in, and any other words of wisdom you're willing to pass our way.

As an Executive Editor for Sams Publishing, I welcome your comments. You can fax, email, or write me directly to let me know what you did or didn't like about this book—as well as what we can do to make our books stronger.

Please note that I cannot help you with technical problems related to the topic of this book, and that due to the high volume of mail I receive, I might not be able to reply to every message.

When you write, please be sure to include this book's title and author as well as your name and phone or fax number. I will carefully review your comments and share them with the author and editors who worked on the book.

Fax: 317-581-4770

Email: feedback@samspublishing.com

Mail: Shelley Kronzek
         Executive Editor
         Sams Publishing
         201 West 103rd Street
         Indianapolis, IN 46290 USA

Introduction

The presence of the Internet has been growing at an unbelievable rate over the past five years. With this rapid growth, portions of the developer community started moving into the world of Web development. During this time frame, developers were using tools that were originally created for building Windows-type applications. All types of companies, both new and existing, started jumping to the Internet with e-Commerce applications. Now, with the emergence of .NET, developers have a tool that was created from the ground up with the Internet in mind. This book focuses on building a business-to-consumer (B2C) e-Commerce site using Microsoft's .NET Framework.

Who Is This Book's Intended Audience?

This book is mainly geared toward developers. We expect the developer audience to be made up both of new developers to the .NET Framework as well as .NET developers who have been using .NET since its early stages. All the code in this book is in C#.

What Do You Need to Know Before Reading This Book?

Having some type of programming background should be the minimum requirement. This background could include Visual Basic and even some scripting languages. We don't go over the basics of programming. Also, some knowledge of Web development is helpful but not necessary.

What Will You Learn from This Book?

This book will provide you with a foundation necessary to develop an e-Commerce application using the .NET Framework. You will learn about various ASP.NET features available to build a robust, yet scalable, Web site. This includes but is not limited to state management in ASP.NET, datasets, and user controls. We also discuss the database that supports the site and components that manage or manipulate an order.

What Software Will You Need to Complete the Examples Provided with This Book?

Your system must meet some requirements to run the code provided with this book. First, you will need to install the Microsoft .NET SDK, which is available for download at Microsoft's Web site at http://msdn.microsoft.com. Although we used Microsoft VisualStudio.NET as an "editor," it is not required.

What's on the Web Site?

The chapter-by-chapter source code that is described in this book is available on the Sams Web site at `http://www.samspublishing.com/`. Enter this book's ISBN in the Search box and click Search. When the book's title is displayed, click the title to go to a page where you can download all the source code in a chapter-by-chapter zip file.

The Case Study's e-Commerce Web Site: MyGolfGear.NET

This book is a case study on how the MyGolfGear.NET e-Commerce site was designed, developed, and deployed. It depicts in detail how each part of the site was developed using the .NET framework and walks through the code necessary to implement all the features of the site.

MyGolfGear.NET has the basic functionality that you would expect an e-Commerce site to provide, such as a product catalog, shopping cart, and the normal checkout pages. In addition, the site contains some rich features including but not limited to cross selling and up selling of products, a product search, a wish list, a product spotlight, user registration, and support for gift certificates.

The site is fully functional and can be found online at `http://www.MyGolfGear.net`. We recommend that you visit the site often while reading the book to try out the different features that you are learning how to code.

How Is This Book Organized?

To organize the great deal of information covered in this book, we have divided it into four main sections. The following list describes these sections:

- Part I: Foundations

  In this section, we discuss the foundation for building an e-Commerce application using the .NET Framework. This section includes an overview of .NET as well as the planning that went into the creation of the MyGolfGear.NET e-Commerce site.

- Part II: Building the B2C Storefront

  This section focuses on the storage, retrieval, and maintenance of our product catalog.

- Part III: Building Advanced Features

  This section discusses areas where we added more functionality to the e-Commerce site to make it more appealing to its users. These enhancements include discounts, featured products, product reviews, wish lists, gift certificates, product information e-mail, cross selling, and up selling.

This section also discusses key parts of an e-Commerce site such as building the shopping cart, the checkout process, and order status.

- Part IV: Delivering and Keeping the Site Going

    The main focus of this section is on the tasks that are required after coding is complete. These tasks include optimizing and debugging, securing the site, and finally deploying the site.

- Appendixes

    The appendixes included in this book are a C# Language Reference, VB.NET Language Reference, the ASP.NET Object Model, and finally an ADO.NET Quick Reference.

Conventions Used in This Book

The following typographic conventions are used in this book:

- Code lines, commands, statements, variables, and any text you type or see onscreen appears in a `mono` typeface.
- Code that we wanted to emphasize appears in an *`italic mono`* typeface.
- *Italics* highlight technical terms when they're being defined.
- The drop-down arrow is used before a line of code to signify that the author meant for the continued code to appear on the preceding line.
- The book also contains Notes, Tips, and Cautions to help you spot important or useful information more quickly. Some of them are helpful shortcuts to help you work more efficiently.
- Some code listings have line numbers in them. We used them to make sure that you know which line of code is being described.
- Some chapters end with a Self Instruction section. Here, we will give you instructions on how to enhance the code that was just described in detail.

From the Authors

When deciding how we wanted to approach the subject of building B2C e-Commerce sites, we thought about the qualities we look for in books *we* buy. Every time we discussed it, two things always came up: code samples and real-world situations. We think readers will benefit from this approach because we tried to look at it from the developer's perspective.

Additionally, we felt this subject matter lent itself naturally to a case study approach. James and I have spent most of our careers building applications like the one discussed in this book and think that sharing our experience in this way will maximize what you take away. We hope you find this book useful and enjoyable to read. We welcome your comments, criticisms, corrections, and suggestions for improving this book. We can be reached via our email addresses at

Jason@TechnicalLead.com and James@TechnicalLead.com.

Foundations

IN THIS PART

Business-to-Consumer e-Commerce Overview

IN THIS CHAPTER

Objectives

- Understand current e-Commerce trends

- Understand, at a high level, what B2B e-Commerce is

- Learn about common B2C features, architecture, and the steps involved in creating a B2C e-Commerce application

The Internet has enjoyed enormous growth over the past few years. In large part, this growth can be attributed to consumers' enthusiasm for buying goods and services online. According to Emarketer.com's March 2001 B2C report, consumer e-Commerce sales in the U.S. will grow from $60 billion in 2000 to $428 billion by 2004.

To stay competitive in this new economic environment, companies that do business on the Internet are looking for better, more cost-effective ways to develop and maintain their online presence. The current tools and techniques for designing, developing, deploying, and maintaining robust, scalable, and highly available e-Commerce applications have many shortcomings. The .NET Framework and new suite of .NET enterprise servers address these shortcomings.

Microsoft's .NET Framework makes it easy to quickly build secure, scalable e-Commerce applications. This chapter discusses the current Microsoft technologies used to build commerce sites and current business trends. It introduces the .NET Framework as a solution to the problem of creating highly available, secure commerce sites, and it discusses e-Commerce from a technical perspective.

Current e-Commerce Trends

It's safe to say that in the not-too-distant future, most business will be e-Business in one form or another. Startup dot.coms may be on the decline, but the so-called "click-and-mortar" businesses are quickly taking control. Based on a report from Jupiter Media Metrix, 8 of the 10 fastest-growing retail sites on the Internet are traditional companies. More and more, consumers and business operators are relying on the Internet and other electronic means to improve their positions in the marketplace. Consumers can take advantage of auctions and easier price comparisons, and businesses can improve their position in the marketplace by being able to offer 24-hour shopping and customer support.

In general, e-Commerce is divided into two main areas: business-to-business (B2B) and business-to-consumer (B2C).

> **NOTE**
>
> Some would suggest a third type of e-Commerce that's common today is consumer-to-consumer (C2C). In this case, consumers buy and sell products and services from each other like they do on Web sites such as eBay. To my mind, this is really just a special case of B2B e-Commerce, with the consumers acting as their own businesses.

B2B e-Commerce is exactly what it sounds like—companies buying goods and services from other companies via the Internet or other electronic avenues. The business-to-business market is dwarfing the business-to-consumer (B2C) market. According to the Gartner Group, B2B e-Commerce is expected to grow to $7.29 trillion in the next few years. A comprehensive discussion of B2B e-Commerce is beyond the scope of this book; entire books are dedicated to the topic.

B2C e-Commerce is the exchange of goods and services from businesses to the public. Amazon.com and Buy.com are two of the most popular and well-known B2C e-Commerce sites today. As the name suggests, B2C e-Commerce will be the focus of this book. The technical discussions will focus around a working, but otherwise fictitious, Web site called MyGolfGear.NET at `http://www.MyGolfGear.NET`.

Business-to-Business e-Commerce

Business-to-business (B2B) e-Commerce is the use of the Internet and other electronic means to exchange goods and services. B2B e-Commerce usually means different things to different companies, but in general, companies engage in B2B e-Commerce to aid their supply chain management (SCM) or for Maintenance, Repair, and Operations (MRO).

> **NOTE**
>
> *Supply chain management (SCM)* is the process of acquiring goods and services directly related to a business' finished product. For instance, computer manufacturers buy memory and processors from other vendors to build their finished product.
>
> *Maintenance, Repair, and Operations (MRO)* are supplies consumed in the course of manufacturing or creating a product but aren't part of the end result. For example, they are office supplies or computer equipment.

By procuring goods and services based on aggregated catalogs and supplier offerings, businesses can reduce costs and lessen the risk of customers ordering out-of-stock products. By participating in B2B e-Commerce transactions, businesses can reduce costs and increase the efficiency of their acquisition processes.

B2B e-Commerce is complicated and worthy of an entire book's attention. Therefore, this book will limit its discussion of e-Commerce to the business-to-consumer model.

A Technical Overview of Business-to-Consumer e-Commerce

As stated earlier, business-to-consumer (B2C) e-Commerce is simply the electronic exchange of goods and services from businesses to consumers. From a technical perspective, B2C sites require a catalog, shopping cart, and payment processing mechanism, at a minimum. More typically, though, B2C e-Commerce sites encompass a wide range of advanced, value-added features. Many of these advanced features will be more fully discussed in their own chapters later in the book. For now, here's a brief overview of many of the features that shoppers are likely to find on a typical site.

e-Commerce functions such as giving repeat customers recommendations based on previous purchases are based on the concept of personalization, or *user profiles*. As part of the checkout process, shopper information can be prepopulated into the checkout forms if the shopper has previously registered or bought something from the site. This information may include—but isn't limited to—name, home phone number, work phone number, shipping address, billing address, and e-mail address.

To accomplish personalization, as described here, you need some way to *authenticate* users. That is, you must be able to recognize and verify that the patrons are indeed who they say they are. Later, this book will discuss in detail the ins and outs of Web site security, along with user authentication.

To display product details to your visitors, you need a *catalog*. At the very heart of this catalog is an organized, often hierarchical data store of product details. To create a catalog, you first need to have the appropriate information pertaining to each product stored in a database.

To maintain the relationship between your users and the products they want to buy, you need to give them a *shopping basket*. Online shoppers need to be able to add and delete items from the shopping basket, as well as view the quantity ordered, as they move throughout site. At any point, shoppers should be able to view and alter the contents of their shopping basket, and then resume shopping or proceed to check out. You also can allow shoppers to save their shopping baskets so that they can leave the site, return later, and resume shopping.

If you want to get paid for the goods and services your customers are requesting, you need a way to securely and verifiably transfer money from an account of your users' choice to your own. When shoppers check out, they need to verify or change the items and quantities they ordered before proceeding with their purchases.

When you're offering goods for sale electronically, usually you are responsible for shipping the products directly to your customers. You'll need some way of calculating the cost of shipping and adding it to the price of your users' purchases.

Current tax laws regarding Internet commerce are too complicated to adequately discuss in this book. Therefore, my coauthor and I built MyGolfGear.NET based on the simple premise that when a business has a physical presence (a storefront, warehouse, or distribution center) in a state, often that business is required to charge sales tax for the sale of goods online.

In addition to the core functionality discussed in this section, be sure to note that you need to build administrative functionality into your B2C e-Commerce site to make it an ongoing success.

One primary piece of site functionality that needs administrative tools is the catalog. An administrator should be able to add, delete, and modify products and their associated information. Administrators also may need to add, modify, and delete shopper information, or shoppers themselves, from the customer database.

If you're going to support more advanced features, such as product specials or featured items, it is a good idea to implement administrative functionality to support the addition, deletion, and modification of such specials and promotions.

An Overview of the MyGolfGear.NET B2C Architecture

This book is primarily centered on how we wrote the code necessary to develop MyGolfGear.NET, a scalable, robust B2C e-Commerce site. Discussing the actual implementation and physical location of each piece of the design is not possible. Instead, you will be able to correlate functionality discussed in this book with an actual, working B2C e-Commerce site (`http://www.MyGolfGear.NET`). Therefore, most of the book will discuss the logical design features.

Whenever possible, however, the book will suggest how to physically segment similar applications, given a best-case scenario. When we designed the B2C e-Commerce site, we used a classic *n*-tier design. We segmented the application into three basic layers: a presentation layer (also called the user interface layer), business layer, and data services layer. Each layer can be segmented further—*n* tiers as opposed to just three tiers.

The user interface tier is made up of visual elements that the user will interact with. In addition to providing the code that determines the site's look and feel, the user interface tier is also responsible for managing the way users navigate the site. The user interface, or presentation layer, was implemented almost entirely using ASP.NET. We took advantage of all the basic ASP.NET functionality, as well as many of the more advanced features such as templates, repeaters, and custom user controls. You can see all this functionality at the MyGolfGear.NET site.

The business tier of the site is made up of multiple tiers itself. You'll learn about the actual segmentation later in the book. For now, the business tier is made up of .NET business components implemented in C#. (A VB.NET version will be available for download from TechnicalLead.com.) In addition to the .NET components we developed, we took advantage of the ASP.NET code-behind functionality. The purpose of the business tier(s) is to provide logical separation and segmentation of the shopping basket, the order-processing pieces, shipping and tax calculations, and personalization features, as well as most of the other advanced functionality.

We used several types of data in the data tier while developing the B2C storefront. The most obvious is a database of product information for the catalog. In addition to the database that will store the catalog, we store and transmit data in the form of XML for other parts of the site. Finally, several data-access components will be implemented to retrieve data from the various data sources.

Steps Involved in Creating a B2C e-Commerce Application

Building a robust, scalable B2C e-Commerce application involves several steps. I like to break up the process as follows:

- Clarifying the vision
- Planning and designing
- Developing the application
- Testing and piloting
- Planning for security
- Planning the architecture
- Deploying the application
- Administering the application

Clarifying the Vision

Although the envisioning phase is often complete—or at least well under way—by the time developers are brought onto a project, this step is still worth mentioning. Basically, in this step, the business goals, shopper goals, and overall business requirements are defined. Depending on the size and structure of the organization driving the development of the project, the scope of the envisioning step may vary greatly.

Planning and Designing

The next (and most often neglected) step in creating Web-based applications like the storefront is the planning and designing phase. In this phase, you'll more fully define, on a technical level, what you're going to build and how you're going to build it. The most common artifacts to come out of this phase are design documents and a project plan.

Developing the Application

Most of the discussion will be about the development phase. In this phase, you write the code and assemble the necessary pieces to build the storefront. The actual development of the storefront will consist of implementing the user interface, business, and data services tiers. Also, you'll test and pilot the application before moving on to the deployment phase.

Testing and Piloting

After you pilot the site with a select group of users, you move to the deployment phase. After you receive and incorporate the pilot members' feedback into the site, you need to deploy the application to the production environment. This step can be as simple as copying files to a Web server and running a couple of SQL scripts on your database server, or as complex as copying Web files (HTML, ASPX, ASP, and so on) to multiple Web servers, copying and configuring remote components to application servers, and setting up and configuring a new SQL Server database. This case study will be as simple as possible while still illustrating the most important aspects.

NOTE

A *pilot* is somewhat analogous to a beta. After a new site undergoes testing, it's sometimes common to allow a select group of users early access to verify usability and help flush out any remaining bugs.

Planning for Security

As part of every phase in the development of a site, you need to think about security. In general, you need to consider authentication and authorization in conjunction with one another. Specifically, you'll delve into authentication, which simply means discovering who a particular user is and verifying that person's identity against a secure source. After you deal with ways to identify users, you must develop a way to authorize the use of specific functions of your site. In other words, you need a way to determine what actions a particular user is allowed to take.

Planning the Architecture

Before you can get too far into the development of your e-Commerce site, you must consider certain architectural issues. The one question that has been weighing heavily on my mind since I first began exploring the .NET Framework is how, specifically, to architect distributed applications created with the .NET Framework. Many of us have grown accustomed to developing three physically separate tiers for our *n*-tier applications. Therefore, we have to address the issue of where the middle tier resides. Do we implement the middle tier entirely as Simple Object Access Protocol (SOAP) Web services, interoperate with COM+ component services, take advantage of some of the other remoting capabilities in the rich .NET Framework library, or only separate the middle tier logically? Perhaps the best answer is that this book will consider each option as you implement specific pieces of functionality. With any luck, you'll find the best solution and maybe find a way to use each option.

Deploying the Application

After the code is written, security is implemented, and physical architecture is decided on, it's time for deployment. At this point, all the components, Web pages, and database objects and data need to be moved to a production environment. You can do so in several ways, and Chapter 21, "Deploying the Site," will cover each of them in more detail. In short, the options are as follows:

- Copy the files manually
- Create a VisualStudio.NET Setup and Deployment Project
- Use Microsoft's new Application Center

Each option has pros and cons. Copying the files manually is inexpensive (free) and requires no training. However, it's tedious and error prone. Components and pages can be forgotten or incorrectly installed.

Creating a VisualStudio.NET Setup and Deployment Project is fairly simple and seems to be reliable. However, it does require some training, and resources can be forgotten or overlooked.

Application Center looks very promising, especially for deploying applications to larger environments, but it's not without its own faults. It isn't cheap and requires at least some training and experience to get the most out of it.

NOTE

Using Application Center's content deployment feature is pretty straight forward. Taking advantage of some of its other features, such as one of its three supported load balancing strategies, will take practice.

Administering the Application

When the application is up and running, administering it will become necessary. e-Commerce applications need to have product information updated, orders researched or retrieved, and users' information managed. The best policy is usually to build such functionality into the site. Later chapters cover in detail how administrative functionality was built into MyGolfGear.NET.

Current Tools for Developing B2C Applications

Today, you can use many different development tools to create all the features mentioned previously. One of the most common combinations is Microsoft's Active Server Pages, Visual Basic 6.0, and SQL Server. This combination is popular for good reason. The tools are easy to use, easy to understand, and reasonably inexpensive. They aren't perfect, though.

I can think of at least a few reasons to consider developing Internet applications with .NET instead of some of the other tools available today:

- ASP is based on interpreted scripting languages and Visual Basic is compiled, but it still gets executed via a runtime library. Using the .NET Framework allows non-C++ programmers to produce compiled and therefore faster executing code.

- The only available inheritance with COM is interface-based inheritance. The only way to get implementation inheritance is to use C++ or Java, something most VB developers aren't willing to do.

- Deploying a complicated ASP- and COM-based application can be very tricky. Components have to be registered, and new versions can't run along with old ones. In other words, if you change an interface to a component, your application will break.

The team at Microsoft had a good idea when it came up with Site Server Commerce Edition, which provides a good framework and a set of reusable components for quickly building e-Commerce Web sites. Unfortunately, the previous versions of Commerce Server, prior to Commerce Server 2000, suffered from poor performance when order sizes were very large. They were problematic because the Dictionary and OrderForm objects were implemented as linked lists; therefore, iterating through order items was costly.

Commerce Server 2000 addresses most of these performance issues but still isn't based on the .NET Framework. It does provide a nice set of tools and a decent framework to help you get started, but it still suffers from being based on COM components and Scripted Active Server Pages. The same problems encountered with using only ASP and COM objects apply here as well. These shortcomings are eliminated in the new .NET framework through the increased scalability and availability of the Common Language Runtime (CLR).

Java has made the transition from a novelty used to write applets to a viable server-side programming platform. With the introduction of Java Server Pages (Sun's answer to ASP?), Web developers have an object-oriented, platform-independent way to create robust, scalable Internet applications. The biggest downside to using Java as your primary development language for building e-Commerce sites is the inferior set of development tools.

The .NET Framework addresses the shortcomings of the current toolset. It enables non-C++ programmers to produce compiled code; supports true separation of user interface elements such HTML tags and code; supports built-in caching; and provides object-oriented language support for implementation inheritance. It also provides a rich set of extendable classes from which to build on, supports multiple languages, and enables easier deployment.

Summary

This chapter covered a wide range of topics and gave you a good indication of what the rest of this book will cover. It talked about the current trends in e-Commerce, and it gave a high-level outline of the common features of today's B2C e-Commerce sites. It discussed the current tools used for developing Internet applications and outlined some of the areas where they fall short. Finally, it talked briefly about what makes a good B2C architecture and some of the steps necessary to develop a robust, secure B2C e-Commerce application.

The next chapter will provide a brief overview of the .NET Framework. Specifically, it will cover the Common Language Runtime, self-describing components, assemblies, application domains, the Common Type System, cross-language interoperability, the managed execution of code, and the mechanics of ASP.NET page execution.

.NET Overview

IN THIS CHAPTER

Objectives

- Understand what the .NET Framework is

- Learn about the Common Language Runtime and how .NET components are packaged

- Understand the execution flow of .NET components and ASP.NET pages

The purpose of this book isn't to teach you object-oriented programming, or even to guide you step-by-step through the .NET Framework. Rather, it's meant to illustrate how to build a robust business-to-consumer (B2C) e-Commerce site using the .NET Framework.

Having said that, let me also say that building Internet applications with .NET is different in many ways from building Internet applications with other tools, such as Visual Basic 6.0 and ASP 3.0. Therefore, before we discuss how we built MyGolfGear.NET, we should discuss some of the basics of the .NET Framework.

The .NET Framework

Microsoft's .NET initiative includes the .NET Framework, which is a new development and implementation platform. The .NET Framework was developed with the Internet in mind from the very beginning, so it fits nicely into the overall .NET goal of allowing for the creation of software as a service.

The .NET Framework is at the core of the .NET "big picture." You can think of this big picture as being made up of layers of building blocks and services. These layers include end-user clients, Visual Studio.NET, other applications, and Web Services; the .NET Framework itself; Windows operating systems; open Internet protocols such as XML, SOAP, WAP, DISCO, and HTTP; the .NET Enterprise Servers such as SQL Server 2000, Commerce Server 2000, and Application Center 2000; and other building block services. Figure 2.1 illustrates this relationship.

The .NET Framework includes a new execution environment and a rich and powerful class library that arguably provides more out-of-the-box functionality than any class library to date. The rest of this chapter describes much of the internal functionality provided by this new execution environment.

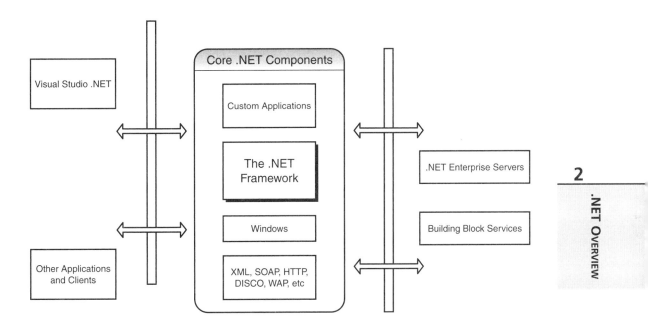

FIGURE 2.1
The .NET Big Picture.

The Common Language Runtime

So, what exactly is the Common Language Runtime (CLR)? It is the .NET runtime environment for managing the execution of code.

Before we get into some CLR specifics, it's important that we discuss some of its goals. CLR's designers wanted to provide a system that would allow for simplified development and deployment, multilanguage support, and side-by-side execution of different versions of the same components, all the while improving performance and scalability.

The CLR allows for simplified development in many ways. The most important is by allowing developers to write less and reuse more. What do I mean by that?

The .NET Framework provides a rich set of reusable classes, from `Array` to `XMLWriter` and hundreds in between. The CLR provides for *implementation inheritance*, so developers can extend the already robust .NET Framework by simply deriving their own classes from any one of the hundreds of extendable classes just mentioned.

What's more, the CLR enables you to take advantage of this reuse in any supported language. You can create a class in one language and extend that class by using any other supported .NET language. In other words, objects can be written in different languages and still communicate with each other as though they were written in the same language.

In the COM world, you can create a component with one language—C++, for instance—and call that component from another component, or application, written in another language, such as Visual Basic. The difference, however, is that data types aren't always exposed compatibly. Also, in this example, VB developers can't easily extend the functionality of the C++ component.

Cross-language inheritance and data type compatibility are made possible because the .NET compilers use a common type system defined by the CLR that adheres to rules about defining new types and using the built-in types.

The CLR also simplifies development by removing the need to develop "plumbing code." This is especially true for C++ developers who, in the COM/COM+ world, had to worry about implementing IUnknown and IDispatch. Developers no longer need to worry about GUIDs, HRESULTS, or Type Libraries (of course, the Active Template Library (ATL) and Microsoft Foundation Classes (MFC) don't suffer from this problem but have some of their own). With the CLR, you no longer need to worry about reference counting, dynamic binding, or type safety.

Simplified deployment is another important goal of the CLR. Because you don't need to register .NET components, you can install applications by simply copying all appropriate files. If application assemblies are split into multiple files, applications can take advantage of the .NET Framework's capability to download only code that it needs to execute. In other words, users can take advantage of incremental downloads. Different versions of the same component also can run side by side, thus allowing you to update existing components while avoiding "*DLL hell.*"

> **NOTE**
>
> The term *DLL hell* refers to DLL versioning conflicts that occur when an application installs a version of a component that is not backward compatible with previously installed versions.

The code that you write and compile to take advantage of this runtime environment is called *managed code*. As I've mentioned, some advantages of writing managed code are enhanced security, cross-language inheritance and exception handling, versioning, developer services such as debugging and profiling, automatic memory management, enforcement of code access security, and access to rich metadata. The CLR also provides automatic memory management by handling object layout and managing object references. *Managed data* is the term used to describe objects whose lifetimes are managed this way. Having the runtime environment manage memory allocation for you reduces the risk of memory leaks and other common programming errors. Writing managed code allows you to use managed or unmanaged data.

Depending on the languages you are familiar with, you will notice the benefits of the Common Language Runtime's functionality in different ways. For instance, if you are a C++ developer, you can use managed extensions to C++. If you do, you will probably be most affected by the cross-language interaction and inheritance and automatic memory management, so you will no longer need to worry about reference counting. Also, because .NET components are self describing, Interface Definition Language (IDL) is no longer needed. If you are a Visual Basic developer, you will likely be most impressed by the performance improvements and the addition of many new, powerful language features such as inheritance, structured exception handling, and the ability to create free-threaded applications.

Self-Describing Components

To take advantage of these services, the runtime requires *metadata* to be emitted by compilers. Metadata provides type information and information about references. All this information is stored with your code. The runtime uses this metadata to locate and load classes, enforce security, generate native code, resolve method invocation, and set up runtime context boundaries.

All managed components contain information, in the form of metadata, about every component, resource, and dependency they were built with. .NET components don't rely on the System Registry for versioning information. Each .NET component carries with it its identity (including name, version, culture, and public key), what types are exported, what types are references, and any security permissions it needs to run. In other words, it has everything it needs. Therefore, it is much less likely that your code will break because of a dependency not being met. Registration and state information is no longer kept in the Registry. Instead, information about dependencies and types you define is kept with the code in the component. This makes replicating and registering your components much easier.

Metadata is used in a number of places, such as type viewers (like ILDASM), documentation tools, debuggers and profilers, and classes that use reflection. Perhaps the most important place metadata is used is in assemblies.

> **NOTE**
>
> *ILDASM*—short for Intermediate Language Disasembler—is a tool that ships with the .NET Framework. It parses .NET DLLs and EXEs to show their metadata in a human-readable form.

Assemblies

As I've mentioned, when you write .NET code and compile it to Microsoft Intermediate Language (MSIL), metadata is created and kept with the resulting code. But where exactly is it kept? The CLR uses *assemblies* for packaging metadata and code. All executable code must be associated with an assembly. So, an assembly is just a collection of .NET interfaces, classes, and resources such as images and other files. The CLR also provides APIs for script engines to use when executing scripts. It does so by creating dynamic assemblies, which are like an in-memory version of assemblies. They aren't typically saved to disk, although they can be.

Assemblies are said to form "logical" DLLs. Assemblies form basic units for reuse, distribution, versioning, scoping, and permissions. They are self-describing because of the metadata discussed earlier. This metadata contains scope and reference information, which is kept in *manifests* inside assemblies. In the .NET world, applications are made up of assemblies much like applications are made up of DLLs today. Assembly manifests can be kept in either a Portable Executable (PE) file, such as a DLL or EXE, or in a standalone file.

Figure 2.2 shows the .NET Framework tool ILDASM, which is being used to look at the `System.Web.dll`. You can see some of the metadata associated with the `System.Web` assembly. Notice the `.assembly` and `.assembly extern` commands, which identify the assembly and its external dependencies.

FIGURE 2.2

A manifest contains the metadata associated with an assembly.

Most often assemblies are created by .NET language compilers, like those available in the Microsoft .NET Framework SDK. Another, less common way to create assemblies is to use the .NET API `Reflection.Emit` method to create dynamic assemblies.

Basically, assemblies contain four main elements: the manifest, or the actual metadata about the assembly; the MSIL code; metadata about the types used in the assembly; and any resources.

Assemblies can package their information in two ways. One way, as Figure 2.3 illustrates, is to house all the assembly information in one file.

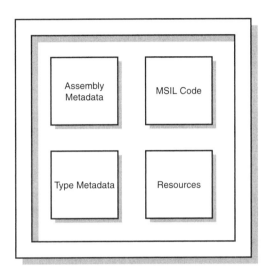

FIGURE 2.3
A single DLL containing all the assembly's information.

Alternatively, an assembly's information may be spread across multiple files, as illustrated in Figure 2.4. You can choose to split up your assemblies like this to ease large downloads. The .NET Framework will download a file only when it's referenced. So, if you have some infrequently referenced code or large resource files, splitting them into their own files will increase download efficiency.

Because an assembly's version number is part of its name, the runtime can store multiple versions of the same assembly in the *global assembly cache*. This allows the runtime to load the appropriate assembly at runtime.

NOTE

The *global assembly cache* is a machine-wide code cache that stores assemblies specifically designed to be shared by multiple applications on the same computer.

The global assembly cache can also be used for other reasons. For instance, it can be used to boost performance because the runtime can find assemblies faster if they are in the global assembly cache.

File security is another reason the global assembly cache might be used. Only users with administrative privileges can delete files from the global assembly cache.

Side-by-side versions are also made possible by the global assembly cache. Multiple copies of assemblies with the same name but different version numbers are kept in the global assembly cache.

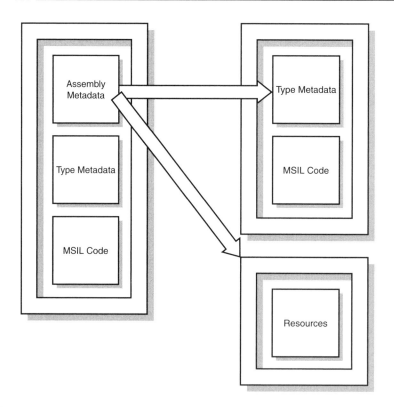

FIGURE 2.4

Multiple files being used for assembly information.

The most important things you, as a developer, need to remember about assemblies are as follows:

- They allow different versions of the same component to run side by side.
- They are the unit of deployment for .NET applications.

- An assembly's manifest contains versioning information about its own code as well as resources. It also contains scope information.
- Assemblies are the level at which permissions are granted.
- They contain the code that the runtime executes.

Application Domains

Application domains are the CLR's unit of processing and security policy enforcement. They also provide for isolation between applications. Application domains are lightweight enough that many can run in a single Win32 process.

It's not uncommon for runtime environments to provide application isolation. Applications need protection from faults that may occur in other applications. Applications often need to be independently stopped and debugged as well. This type of isolation also prevents code in one application from accessing code in another application. In other words, isolation protects against possible security holes.

In most contemporary operating systems, isolation is achieved by using process boundaries. Typically, a process runs only one application and is responsible for the scope and resources available for that application. This means, for instance, that a pointer in one process is meaningless in the scope of another process.

CLR guarantees fault isolation between applications because it can safely assume that code is type-safe and verifiable. In Win32 computing, fault isolation is achieved at the process level, which is much more expensive than the static type verification used by the CLR. In this way, the CLR's application domains are analogous to the Win32 process.

The CLR creates an application domain for each application. Applications running in a single process are separated by application domains. Application domains can take advantage of an XML configuration file by discovering security and other attributes at runtime. It's the combination of application domains and their configuration files that creates application isolation.

An assembly's permissions are directly influenced by the way it is loaded into application domains. Direct calls can't be made between objects in different application domains. In other words, the code loaded into one application domain can't directly access the code loaded in another application domain.

Common Type System

The .NET Framework, which is built in an object-oriented fashion, supports several different data types. The CLR-supported types are defined by the *common type system,* which also defines how types interact with each other as well as how they are persisted in metadata.

The .NET Framework provides support for primitive types such as integers and characters as well as classes and interfaces and other types to derive your own types from.

Every type in the common type system is derived from the Object class. All primitive types or value types are derived from the class ValueType, which in turn is derived from the Object class. Figure 2.5 shows the basic layout of the type system and some of the important parts of the object hierarchy.

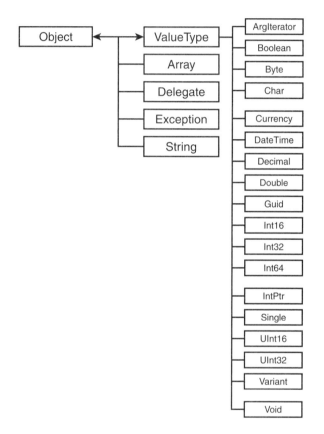

FIGURE 2.5

The CLR common type system. This is by no means a comprehensive diagram.

If you use ILDASM to look at the String class, notice that it's *sealed*. In other words, you can't derive your own type from the String class. Figure 2.6 shows what this looks like with ILDASM.

FIGURE 2.6
The sealed String class.

Notice that the Array class with ILDASM is not sealed (see Figure 2.7). You could create your own class, maybe a Vector class, and derive it from class Array. Notice also, as I mentioned earlier, the Array class is derived from the Object class.

FIGURE 2.7
The nonsealed Array class.

Cross-Language Interoperability

In most programming environments, code written in one language can communicate with code written in another language only if established binary standards are followed. For example, you could write a COM DLL in C++, create an instance of it, and call methods on it from a component written in Visual Basic. Your ability to do so is possible, however, only because both pieces of code follow the COM binary standard. The downside of this type of interaction is that these two separate components can't share functionality via simple inheritance. With the .NET Framework, you can write classes in two different languages that fully interact with each other. For instance, an object written in C# can call methods and properties on an object written in VB.NET. That same C# object could even inherit functionality directly from the VB.NET object.

> **NOTE**
>
> I'm using C# for the examples throughout this entire book. Microsoft designed the C# language specifically for writing managed code. Keep in mind that although the sample code shown throughout the book is in C# and the explanations are geared toward C#, the concepts apply to any language that supports the Common Language Runtime.

Listing 2.1 shows a simple C# class called Box. This class has three public properties—Length, Width, and Height—as well as a single method that prints those properties to the system console. Class Box also contains a default constructor as well as a constructor that takes, as parameters, values for initializing the public properties. For brevity, the fields have been made public. Also, both constructors contain calls to the Print method.

LISTING 2.1   The Box Class Written in C#

```
public class Box{
    public Double Length;
    public Double Width;
    public Double Height;

    public Box(){
        Length=0;
        Width=0;
        Height=0;
        Print();
    }
```

LISTING 2.1   Continued

```
    public Box(Double dLength, Double dWidth, Double dHeight){
        Length=dLength;
        Width=dWidth;
        Height=dHeight;
        Print();
    }

    public void Print(){
        System.Console.WriteLine("Length=" + Length.ToString());
        System.Console.WriteLine("Width=" + Width.ToString());
        Console.WriteLine("Height=" + Height.ToString());
    }
}// End of Class
```

If you create a driver class that creates an instance of the Box class, like the one in Listing 2.2, you get the expected outcome. In other words, when you create an instance of the class, the values you pass in the constructor are printed out.

LISTING 2.2   Using a Constructor for the *Box* Class

```
public class BoxDriver{
    public static void Main(String[] args){
        Box oBox = new Box();
        Console.WriteLine();
        Box oBox2 = new Box(10,20,30);
    }
}
```

Now imagine that you want to create a Car class inherited from the above Box class, and you want to do so in VB.NET. Listing 2.3 shows a simple example along with a simple driver module called Test that creates an instance of the Car class. When you run the driver, the default constructor from the Box class prints 0s when the Car class is instantiated.

LISTING 2.3   VB.NET Simple Inheritance

```
Public Class Car : Inherits Box
    Private iAxils as Integer

    Property Axils as Integer
        Get
            Axils = iAxils
        End Get
        Set
            iAxils = Value
```

LISTING 2.3 Continued

```
      End Set
   End Property
End Class

Public module Test
   public sub Main()
      Dim oCar as New Car
   End Sub
End module
```

NOTE

The use of the term *driver program* is meant to be synonymous with test program and has nothing to do with the fact that some of the sample classes are Car classes.

Another important aspect of language interoperability is exception handling. The .NET Framework enables you to handle exceptions the same way across different languages. For example, if you throw an exception in one language, you can catch that exception and handle it in any other .NET language. Listing 2.4 shows a simple class called Foo. The constructor intentionally causes a divide-by-zero exception.

LISTING 2.4 Throwing a *new* Exception

```
using System;
public class Foo{
   public void Go(){
      throw new Exception("A bogus exception.");
   }
}
```

Now look at a *driver program* written in VB.NET. Listing 2.5 shows a simple module called Test. It simply tries to create an instance of the Foo class written in C#. When you compile and try to run the test module, you can catch the newly created error. Running this driver module results in the display of the message A bogus exception.

LISTING 2.5 The VB.NET Test Harness

```
Imports System
Public Module Test
   public sub Main()
      Try
```

LISTING 2.5   Continued

```
      Dim oFoo as New Foo
      oFoo.Go
    Catch e as exception
      Console.WriteLine (e.Message)
    End Try
  End Sub
End Module
```

As of this writing, more than 15 languages already support the CLR. The .NET Framework comes with the Microsoft-supported VB, C#, C++, and JScript. Some third-party supported languages available are COBOL, Pascal, SmallTalk, Perl, and Python. So, how can all these different languages effectively communicate with each other? All .NET languages are based on a Common Language Specification.

The Common Language Specification

The cross-language compatibility discussed in the preceding section is possible because objects created in different .NET languages agree on a common set of types and features. These common types and features are spelled out in the *Common Language Specification* (CLS). So, if you write code that uses only CLS features, that code is guaranteed to run seamlessly with code written in any other CLS-compliant language. The CLS specifies primitive types such as Boolean, character, integer (16-, 32-, and 64-bit), Single, and Double, as well as classes such as the base Object and String along with many others. When you write code that strictly adheres to the CLS and uses only the features spelled out by the CLS, it's said to be *CLS-compliant*.

To write CLS-compliant applications, you must consider the definitions of your public classes, the public members of those classes, and, because of inheritance, the definitions of members accessible to subclasses of your components. The parameters to these public members and sub-classable members also must adhere to the CLS. In other words, if you want to write a CLS-compliant class, you need to make sure that all public methods in that class adhere to the CLS, as well as any method that you allow to be extended. One more way of saying that last part is that you cannot write a class that contains protected members that don't adhere to the CLS.

You still have plenty of room in your private classes and private methods of your public classes, local variables, and so on to use language features outside the CLS. If you are sticking to C# (as I am for the examples in this book) or even VB.NET, CLS-compliance will come virtually automatically. If, however, you are using managed extensions for C++ or some other third-party supported language, keeping CLS compliance in mind will be important when writing your code, especially if you are creating a framework or class library intended to be used by .NET developers.

Managed Execution

After you write your code, a .NET compiler compiles it into the MSIL and the component's metadata is generated. MSIL is the instruction set that .NET programs are compiled into. MSIL, which is CPU-independent, contains the instructions for loading and calling the objects' methods. Besides the instructions for loading and calling methods, MSIL also contains myriad other instructions, such as instructions for memory access, control flow, arithmetic operations, and exception handling. Cross-language integration is possible because of the combination of metadata and the common type system built into the CLR.

Part of this compilation process involves verification of the MSIL and metadata to determine whether it's truly type-safe. In other words, the .NET Framework verifies that your code will access only the memory it's authorized to access. This process ensures isolation of objects from each other and safety from corruption. The goal of this verification process is to ensure that type references are compatible, that only the appropriate methods are called on an object, and that the authenticity of components and resources being executed is ensured.

Because MSIL can't be executed directly, it's converted into CPU-specific native code at runtime by a just-in-time (JIT) compiler. The .NET Framework allows developers to create a single set of MSIL code that can be JIT-compiled on different machines with different CPU architectures. Bear in mind that although you can write platform-specific API calls, you need to write .NET friendly code to take full advantage of CLR's platform independence.

The reason for JIT compilation is that some code may never get called during execution. The idea is, rather than expend valuable time and resources converting all the MSIL into native code, the runtime converts only the portions of code that are called and saves the resulting native code away for subsequent calls. So, basically, MSIL isn't compiled every time a given piece of code is executed—only the first time.

How does JIT compilation work? Basically, when an object is loaded, the loader attaches a stub to each method. The first time a method is called, the loader passes the stub to the JIT compiler. At that point, the MSIL is converted to native code, and the stub is modified to point to the compiled code. Later calls to the same method will be executed without compilation because the stub will continue to point to the compiled code.

How does this process affect you as a Web developer? Perhaps we should look at how ASP.NET pages are compiled on-the-fly and compare that procedure to how ASP pages are processed today.

ASP.NET Page Execution

In the "classic" ASP model, the ASP processor was implemented as an ISAPI extension (asp.dll). ISAPI is a programming interface that developers can use to extend the functionality of Internet Information Server (IIS). The `asp.dll` simply supports specific interfaces and types to be an Internet Server API (ISAPI) extension. ISAPI extensions are associated in IIS with certain file types. For ASP, the `.asp` file type is associated with the `asp.dll`.

When an HTTP Request is received by IIS, it looks in its Metabase to determine which ISAPI extension is registered to handle this type of file. IIS then routes the HTTP Request to the appropriate ISAPI extension (that is, `asp.dll`).

The `asp.dll` is now responsible for handling the request. ASP loads the file into memory (if it hasn't already been cached), parses it, and based on the language directive at the top of the ASP page, the `asp.dll` loads the appropriate Active Scripting engine. The Active Scripting engine executes the parsed script. The `asp.dll` sends the results of the execution back to the browser in a return string.

The four main problems with the "classic" ASP model are as follows:

- **Performance.** The ASP parser is an incredible piece of software that handles just about everything you can throw at it, whether poorly or well-formed ASP code. But ultimately, even after the code is parsed and cached into memory, it's still just script that relies on an Active Scripting engine to execute. The IIS 5.0 team has optimized this process greatly, but your pages are script, not compiled code.

- **Maintainability.** The ASP pages mixed HTML and server-side script such as VBScript or JScript. The pages also could contain other client-side script, such as VBScript or JavaScript. With all these different code sections intermingled throughout the document, they could get rather unwieldy. As developers wanted to implement more complex business rules in their Web pages, the need for code separation became more evident.

- **State Management.** Some issues must be addressed when you're managing state using the `Application` and `Session` objects:

  - These objects require that the user's Web browser have cookies turned on. A unique identifier stored in a cookie allows the state information to be matched up between the user's request and the cached cookie information.

  - If the user doesn't take action within a set period of time, the cookies expire and the user's data is lost forever.

  - Developers stored object references in the `Application` and `Session` objects, which caused significant memory problems.

  - Session state–using cookies don't work across a Web farm that uses dynamic load balancing because each session was created by a single Web server and wasn't designed to transfer over to multiple servers.

- **Use of COM Components.** Whenever you need to access data, implement security, send mail, or just about anything outside the scope of VBScript or JScript, you must reference a COM component to do it. Although this viable option has proven to be successful, this approach has configuration, deployment and performance problems. In an ideal world, all the services like the ones mentioned here would be built right into ASP, so relying on these services would be more tightly integrated with your application.

The ASP.NET development team sought to create a better way to create Web applications that would improve speed, provide more built-in system services, improve state management, and separate the HTML (interface) from the script (business rules). In a nutshell, they sought to make it easier to build Web-based applications. Also, they wanted to provide additional ways for developers to have access to extensibility points within this new ASP framework that would allow more developers (that is, all developers who weren't C++ developers) to create ISAPI filter-like and extension-like functionality. The culmination of the efforts of several teams at Microsoft lead to the development of ASP.NET.

ASP.NET services include the facility to handle HTTP Requests that come from Internet Information Server. In the Application Services for ASP.NET, you can see that it's further divided into Web Forms and Web Services. Web Forms are similar to "classic" ASP insomuch that they typically have a visual representation in HTML with a programmable element that runs on the Web server. Both adhere to the same ASP.NET application model.

ASP.NET allows you much more flexibility in your Web applications. This includes sophisticated page caching and configurable state management. You will also enjoy better performance. Source code compilation allows for speed enhancements.

ASP.NET is much more extensible than "classic" ASP due to its rich object model. It also allows non-C++ developers to create powerful applications that take advantage of the preprocessing of Web page requests and responses. For example, you can create an HTTP Module that intercepts a request for a Web page and does some validation, such as "Does this user have rights to call this Web page?" or "Should I reroute the use to a different Web page based on what he asked for?" HTTP Modules are the .NET analogy to ISAPI filters. You can also create HTTP Handlers that actually handle different file extensions, so you could create your own type of Web Service with the extension .FOO if you were so inclined. Of course, you would be responsible for writing all the plumbing to handle the requests, invoke objects, and so on. This kind of flexibility is now available, and although you might not imagine why you would ever want it today, over time you will probably come to be thankful such extensibility was built in.

What About SOAP?

What does SOAP have to do with .NET? SOAP—an acronym for Simple Object Access Protocol—is poised to replace DCOM and CORBA as an Internet-based software communication protocol.

SOAP is an XML standards–based way for two .NET services to interact and exchange information across different platforms. By creating a SOAP service, a .NET application provider can provide services to customers in a way that any platform that understands SOAP can use. A SOAP service sends method invocation data streams that travel over TCP/IP in XML format. In .NET, these services are called Web Services because they use port 80, the HTTP port, as their traffic channel.

SOAP is the glue that makes .NET work. It describes the programmatic entry points to a Web site using an XML-based contract language. It has been submitted to the World Wide Web Consortium (W3C, http://www.w3c.org) as a standard and is currently under review.

As I pointed out earlier, when an HTTP Request is made for a particular resource on a Web server—let's say a "classic" Active Server Page—IIS checks its Metabase for the appropriate ISAPI extension to handle the requested file type. In the case of ASP, that ISAPI extension is the asp.dll. In general, ASP parses the code, executes its commands, and returns values to the client. Similarly, when a request is made for an .aspx (Web Forms) file or .asmx (Web Services) file, an ISAPI extension is called, and IIS checks its Metabase and determines that the ASP.NET ISAPI extension, xspisapi.dll, is responsible for handling that request. IIS funnels the request to the xspisapi.dll. The xspisapi.dll is "unmanaged" and, therefore, calls on the xsp.exe, a "managed" parser/handler, to take over.

Note

I'm not suggesting that replacing one ISAPI filter with another increases performance. As you will see later in the chapter, the performance improvements come from several .NET features, the least of which is compiled code.

This process begins a chain of calls that send the HTTP Request through many layers of code (called HTTP Modules) until the Web Services or Web Forms file is executed. HTTP Modules are similar to ISAPI filters.

Figure 2.8 gives you a general idea of the number of layers and the sequence of events in the life of a Web Service's execution.

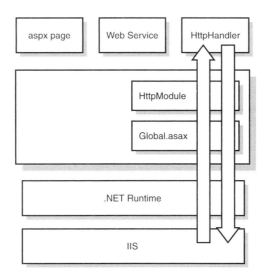

FIGURE 2.8
Events in the life of a Web Service.

The first time your .asmx or .aspx file is called, it must be compiled to run within the ASP.NET runtime as managed code.

After the Web Service or Web Form is compiled, the HTTP Request can then be sent through a "pipeline" and onto the appropriate HTTP Handler for final processing. The pipeline consists of multiple HTTP Modules that perform various functions on the HTTP Requests. Out-of-the-box modules include functionality for logging, authentication, authorization, and session state. You can replace the modules with your own code if necessary, and you can create and add new ones. You also can create your own HTTP Handler.

In the case of Web Services, the WebServiceHandlerFactory (System.Web.Services. Protocols.WebServiceHandlerFactory class) is eventually called. This class performs several functions, not the least of which is that it's responsible for deserializing the SOAP call and then actually invoking your compiled code to perform the logic that you developed in your Web Service. Like most other items in ASP.NET, the Web Services HTTP Handler is configurable as an entry in the config.web. We'll talk about configuration issues at length in Chapter 21, "Deploying the Site."

When your code finishes processing the HTTP Request, it serializes the return values into a SOAP message or HTTP Response and sends it back up the chain of HTTP Modules, then back to IIS, and back to the consumer of the Web Service or Web Form.

Summary

If you are going to build Web-based applications with the .NET Framework, it's helpful to have a general understanding of the Common Language Runtime, managed execution, assemblies, the common type system, cross-language interoperability, and the way ASP.NET page execution works.

This chapter discussed, at a high level, what the .NET Framework is and how it fits into the overall .NET "big picture." It also covered the Common Language Runtime (CLR), metadata and what it is used for, application domains, and the cross-language features available in the .NET Framework.

The next chapter discusses the planning of the B2C site. Specifically, we will discuss the goals, features, page and layout issues, integration considerations, architecture and security planning, and available .NET development tools.

Self Instruction

Throughout the rest of the book, I will include the "Self Instruction" section, which contains a short exercise you can try on your own. This exercise will be related to some piece or pieces of functionality discussed in the chapter and should aid in better understanding of key topics. The first exercise is as follows:

- Use the Intermediate Language Disassembler (ILDASM) to open the manifest for the `System.dll` file. You can find it in the `\WINNT\Microsoft.NET\Framework\v[Version Number]` directory.

Planning MyGolfGear.NET

IN THIS CHAPTER

Objectives

- Define the goals of the site
- Decide on the site's features
- Consider page and layout issues
- Understand the design process
- Look at some integration considerations
- Plan the architecture
- Look at available development tools

As with all software projects, building a robust, scalable e-Commerce site requires planning. This chapter examines, at a high level, what went into planning MyGolfGear.NET and some other considerations that went into our design decisions.

Defining the Goals of MyGolfGear.NET

Before my coauthor and I could start building or even designing our application, we needed to decide the site's goals. On the highest level, we had to decide whether MyGolfGear.NET would migrate an existing site or be a startup. If we had already owned and operated a brick-and-mortar golf shop, we might have wanted to divert some offline sales to the Internet in an attempt to lower administrative costs. Because MyGolfGear.NET was built specifically for this book and wasn't based on an existing site or an existing brick-and-mortar store, approaching the design as though it was a startup was pretty easy.

So, what do I mean when I say we approached the design as though we were creating a site for a startup? Basically, I mean that we didn't have any pre-existing business constraints to consider but also that we didn't have the benefit of a pre-existing database.

At a high level, our goal was to deliver a site with basic e-Commerce functionality as well as some of the advanced features found in many of today's most popular consumer e-Commerce sites. We wanted to implement enough functionality so that our B2C e-Commerce site would be attractive to most online shoppers as well as be easy to use. In doing so, we hoped to provide interesting and worthwhile instruction about how you can develop these features on your own.

As part of our overall design strategy, which I will discuss at length later in this chapter, we decided to create a list of high-level deliverables that we felt were necessary to help manage ourselves throughout the development process. These deliverables included a high-level site-flow map, basic look-and-feel mock-up, a list of desired functionality, design deliverables such as use cases and sequence diagrams, a project plan with estimated delivery dates, and a database model.

Our first task was to decide what kind of business we wanted to create a site for. We decide golf equipment offered some interesting challenges if we intended to offer customization options. This decision was followed quickly by securing the domain name MyGolfGear.NET.

> **CAUTION**
>
> Don't underestimate this step. Domain names can be hard to come by, so after you decide on one, make sure it's available and reserve it immediately. You can find and secure your own domain name at `http://www.NetworkSolutions.com`.

Deciding on Features

When we knew what sort of product we would be offering online, we first wanted to list the features we thought would be beneficial to implement on MyGolfGear.NET. We tried to consider functionality that added value to our theoretical customers, as well as features that would lend to teaching you key aspects of the .NET Framework. Aside from the basic storefront functionality, such as a browsable catalog with configurable products and a shopping cart, we decided on the following list of advanced features:

- Product specials and featured items
- Product feedback and ratings
- Gift registries and wish lists
- Electronic content
- Automated e-mailing of product information
- Cross selling and up selling

> **CAUTION**
>
> Don't get caught in the trap of trying to offer too many features for your first release. Too many software projects never make it because of an overambitious set of requirements.

Product Specials and Featured Items

We thought that featuring a different item on the home page every day would expose products that customers, who came to the site for a specific item, might not otherwise see. We also thought that offering product specials in a similar fashion would have the added allure of a discounted price or other promotion.

> **NOTE**
>
> Other sites rotate featured items on a per-page-view basis. We decided to drive the product rotation based on the date. This way, we are better able to take advantage of some of the built-in caching features available in ASP.NET.

Product Feedback and Ratings

By giving MyGolfGear.NET customers a way to share feedback about products they've purchased, we can provide a value-added service that will perhaps minimize buyer's remorse. To accomplish this task, we decided to implement a rating system for each product and discussion forum–like functionality so that shoppers can comment on and rate products they have bought, as well as see other shoppers' opinions. Amazon.com and other large retail sites offer similar functionality.

> **NOTE**
>
> When a shopper selects items to purchase, begins the checkout process, then abandons their purchase, they are said to be experiencing *buyers remorse*.

Gift Registries or Wish Lists

Offering a gift registry or wish list feature confers many benefits. One main reason we decided to incorporate this functionality into MyGolfGear.NET was to encourage people to share the URL with others. By giving shoppers the functionality to earmark certain products and share these "wishes" with people they know, we hope to reach customers who might not have heard of us otherwise.

Express Purchases

Express purchase options are another excellent way to minimize buyer's remorse. These options might seem like trickery, but by not giving shoppers the opportunity to second-guess their purchase decisions, B2C e-Commerce site operators can capitalize on a larger number of actual sales.

Automated E-mailing of Product Information

One feature I've been asked to implement for various e-Commerce sites is the capability to e-mail a link to a particular product's information. For instance, in one implementation, we were asked to provide a button that users could click to pop up a form requiring to and from names and e-mail addresses. When the user submits this form, a link to the product page the user was on when he submitted the form is e-mailed to the recipient. The motivation for this type of functionality is along the same lines as that of the wish-list functionality. Sites that automate the e-mailing of either a link or an HTML page with product information on it have a good chance of additional shoppers visiting and potentially buying from them.

Cross Selling and Up Selling

Two of the most challenging and yet potentially beneficial features to implement are *cross selling* (suggesting complementary items at checkout time based on what's currently in the shopper's basket) and *up selling* (suggesting additional, more expensive items at checkout time based on what's in the shopper's basket). By appealing to the shoppers' impulse-buying tendencies, sites that implement these two pieces of functionality hope to increase the average dollar amount of each transaction.

Designing MyGolfGear.NET

The purpose of this book is not to teach you about application design methodology, but it is important to outline—at least at a high level—the steps we took in designing MyGolfGear.NET. James and I have worked together, in varying roles, for almost two years now. In that time, we've adopted and successfully used a hybrid approach to object-oriented analysis and design. It was in the spirit of this hybrid methodology that we worked out the details of the MyGolfGear.NET design.

Page and Layout Considerations

After determining the high-level goals, we had to consider how to physically fit these features into the site and how the site should look. This was essentially the starting point for a top-down approach to the technical design of the site.

The home page seemed like the most logical place to begin, so we began our design by making rough drawings of the overall navigation, the initial version, and the finished, full-featured home page. After I sketched out how I envisioned the site, James made a block diagram of each sketch with Visio. (We chose Visio because it is powerful, easy to use, and relatively inexpensive.)

We began laying out the navigation by thinking in terms of both standard navigation practices and achieving the desired functionality. We also wanted to keep the eventual implementation options as flexible as possible. After we agreed on a rough idea of how MyGolfGear.NET would look, we decided to enlist the help of our friend and graphic artist, Kyle Martin. Kyle has several years of experience creating conceptual designs for e-Commerce and other Web-based applications. We gave Kyle our sketches and shared our vision with him. Figure 3.1 shows Kyle's first, nonfunctional mock-up.

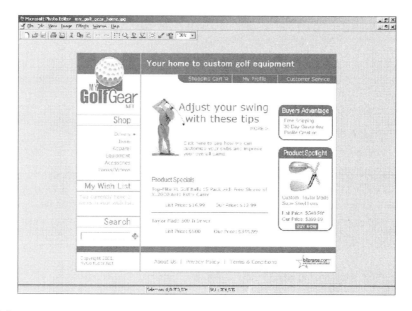

FIGURE 3.1

The first, nonfunctional mock-up of MyGolfGear.NET.

For each high-level piece of functionality, we provided Kyle with either Visio block diagrams of our vision for the layout or a written description from which to work. In the end, he produced "smoke-and-mirror" mock-ups for the basic site layout, including navigation of the basic catalog and basic commerce functionality. He also provided us with screen shots of each additional piece of functionality.

This important step is often overlooked. You can save days of development if you get your user interface design "signed off" by your business users. Changing static screen shots takes far less time than having developers change code.

Site Flow

I have often found it useful, when collaborating on Web-based applications, to develop a *site-flow diagram* to illustrate all possible navigation options based on desired functionality (basically, a site's navigation map). Making such a diagram helps solidify high-level functional requirements and ensures all parties involved agree on the ultimate goal—from a visual perspective, anyway. Figure 3.2 shows a portion of one of our early site-flow diagrams.

We created the site-flow diagrams by using Visio. We looked at each mock-up and documented how users would get to that page as well as how and where users would go from each page. In Visio, we created simple block diagrams using basic flowchart shapes and line connectors to represent each page and navigation decision.

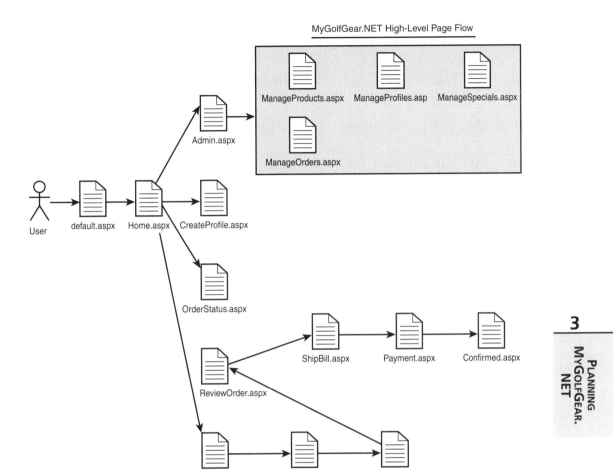

FIGURE 3.2

Site-flow diagram for MyGolfGear.NET.

NOTE

The design methodology James and I used is a hybrid of several others, accented with some of our own experience. Many Object-Oriented Analysis and Design (OOA&D) methodologies shun the practice of UI mock-ups this early in the development cycle. Ultimately, developers need to find the system that works best for them, or come up with their own.

Producing site-flow diagrams did several things for us:

- The diagrams helped us describe the system's overall functionality and acted as the first step in formally documenting what exactly the application is supposed to do.
- They acted as a very simple, pseudo-requirements document.
- Creation of the diagrams led directly to the realization of most of the *use cases*, which define how users and other systems will interact with our system. By looking at a representation of the navigation options available to our users, we could easily flesh out most of the user-oriented, high-level use cases.

Use Cases

After we completed our site-flow diagrams, it was time to create our use cases. Based on the diagrams, we needed to begin the work of fleshing out the high-level objects in the system and their relationship to each other.

Out of this phase of the development cycle came two main deliverables: an essential use case document and a use case diagram document. The intention of spending time creating these two documents was to flesh out the basic objects required by the system.

Figure 3.3 shows a few of the high-level essential use cases derived from the site-flow diagrams and mock-ups. We tried to capture three main things with the high-level use cases:

- We wanted to come up with a descriptive name so that the use case would be easy to refer to.
- We wanted to identify the actors involved. This information would be vital to the creation of sequence diagrams (discussed shortly).
- We needed to capture a clear, concise description.

After we fleshed out all the high-level use cases, it was time to move on to expanded use cases. Basically, we tried to elaborate on any of the high-level uses that represented a collection of smaller, more specific use cases. For instance, the high-level use case Purchase Items could be broken down into purchasing items via the traditional checkout process or via the express checkout. In this case, at lease two separate and more detailed use cases needed to be fleshed out. Figure 3.4 shows a portion of one of our expanded uses cases.

Sequence Diagrams

After documenting every user and outside system interaction we could imagine, we created the sequence diagrams, which capture the interaction of all the different objects in a system. In this step, our goal was to use the high-level class designs from the class design phase to model object interactions and dependencies. Figure 3.5 shows one of the sequence diagrams created for MyGolfGear.NET.

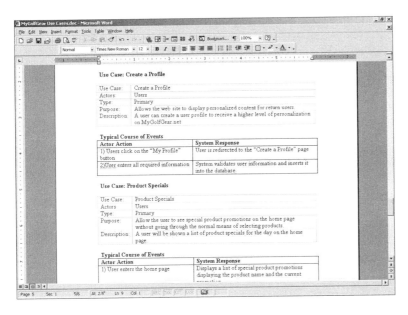

FIGURE 3.3

A few use cases.

Class Design

After we had an idea of the system's high-level objects, who the *actors* were, and what the interactions between all these things would be, we moved on to designing the classes.

> **NOTE**
>
> In software design terms, an *actor* is any person or system that interacts with or uses the system you are designing. In other words, an actor is a user.

In the class design phase, we massaged our high-level objects into specific classes and .aspx pages. It was still a fairly high-level design. In fact, we decided only on class names, their responsibilities, and class dependencies. Figure 3.6 illustrates the kind of information we tried to capture in the class design phase.

Database Design

After we decided what our site was supposed to do and what high-level objects to involve, it was time to design a database schema that would support all the functionality. Our approach was to build the data model first around the basic catalog and shopping cart requirements and then incorporate changes and additions necessary to implement each advanced feature.

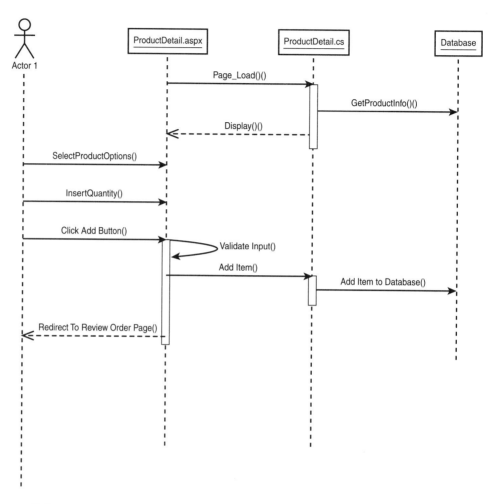

FIGURE 3.4

An expanded use case for MyGolfGear.NET.

The challenge with the basic functionality was creating a data model that would allow us to offer customizable products. One requirement was to allow the customization of any product with any number of options.

NOTE

We will cover the database design in much more detail in Chapter 4, "Building MyGolfGear.NET's Product Catalog with SQL Server 2000."

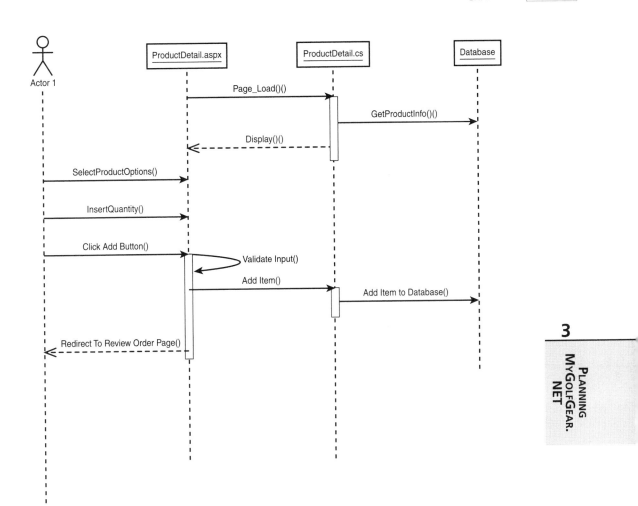

FIGURE 3.5
A sequence diagram for MyGolfGear.NET.

ProductManager
+GetCategoryList()
+GetSubCategories()
+GetProducts()
+GetProductDetails()
+GetCrossSellProducts()
+GetUpSellProducts()

FIGURE 3.6
A MyGolfGear.NET class design.

Integration Considerations

MyGolfGear.NET is fictional, so it has no existing brick-and-mortar or online business with which to integrate. However, companies that do have a real storefront business to integrate with will do much of the e-Commerce site building that likely will take place in the next few years.

As part of the planning phase, it's important to consider opportunities to integrate with existing data or other systems. For instance, if we owned a real-world golf equipment shop and had existing inventory control systems or user databases, we wouldn't want to duplicate any previous effort unless absolutely necessary. When integrating an e-Commerce site with an existing business, three main areas need special consideration: integrating with existing data, integrating with existing transaction services, and determining data conversion requirements with either of the preceding two.

Integrating with Existing Data

Existing data is perhaps the most important aspect of integrating with an existing business. A database administrator who has been in the business for many years once told me, "Most of the applications we write today won't be around in 5 or even 3 years. However, the data we collect and use will be." Because I am an applications developer, that statement was hard to swallow, but I eventually came to realize he was absolutely correct. I've worked for companies that have more than 20 years of company and customer data. Wouldn't it be a shame if I didn't take advantage of that?

> **TIP**
>
> When you're considering integrating with existing data stores, concentrate on catalog, inventory, and customer data.

Integrating with Existing Transaction Services

Next to existing data, the most valuable asset a company has to offer an e-Commerce applications developer is its existing transaction services. Companies for which you build e-Commerce sites may already have in place mechanisms for taking payments electronically, checking and reserving inventory, calculating shipping charges, or even placing orders with an outside order fulfillment house.

Determining Data Conversion Requirements

If you can take advantage of any of the integration scenarios listed in the preceding sections, you will necessarily need to consider the possibility of data conversion. Depending on the nature of a particular company's business, where it has a physical presence, and with what types of legacy systems it currently depends on, be prepared to deal with different monetary systems and different primitive type sizes.

For instance, I have built applications for companies that have branches all over the world and have a wealth of VMS-based data and systems. Creating an e-Commerce site for such a company would require flexible currency exchange and data conversion capabilities.

Architecture Planning

When planning and designing MyGolfGear.NET, we wanted to keep in mind several architectural issues. On a high level, these issues can be broken down into two main areas: logical design and physical design.

Logical Design

A system's *logical design* refers to how the code and other system elements are situated programmatically, not where they reside physically. We wanted MyGolfGear.NET's logical design to follow a couple of basic, good programming practices:

- We wanted to separate our code logically into user services, business services, and data services. By doing so, we hoped to achieve greater reusability, flexibility, and ease of maintenance.
- Wherever possible, we tried to achieve *location transparency*. This simply means the physical location of any particular piece of code doesn't have to be known.

For instance, think about the COM+ world. If we created a data access component in COM+, we would instantiate it from an ASP page the same way syntactically, whether that component was installed locally or on a remote application server.

Physical Design

As the preceding section suggests, a system's physical design dictates, at a higher level, where each piece of the system will reside. In other words, this part of the design says, "We will put all .aspx files on two Web servers and the database and stored procedures on a separate machine." This is also the point in the design phase where we try to determine whether we will use separate application servers for our logical business services layer.

CAUTION

Don't fall into the trap of thinking you have to install your business services tier on a separate physical server. Depending on the site's complexity and amount of traffic, introducing another physical layer into the design may serve only to increase overall network traffic.

When planning for the physical design of the application, we were mindful of two important issues. We knew our application would have to be scalable and highly available.

NOTE

Scalability refers to an application's capability to serve an increasing number of customers. An Internet application's capacity is directly related to its scalability.

On the other hand, an Internet application's availability is directly related to redundancy. If a site has sufficient redundancy, it simply means there is no single point of failure. For instance, if MyGolfGear.NET were deployed to a single Web server and a single database server, it would have at least two separate single points of failure. In other words, if either the Web server or database server crashed, the site wouldn't work. So, to safeguard against such a catastrophe, we planned to deploy MyGolfGear.NET to at least two load-balanced Web servers and an active/active clustered database that is backed up nightly.

NOTE

For more information about deploying Web-based applications, see Barry Bloom's book *Deploying Microsoft.NET Web Farms* (ISBN 0-672-32057-6) from Sams Publishing.

Security Planning

Because most Web-based applications need to restrict access to certain parts of their sites, it's important when developing Internet applications to set aside time during initial planning to consider how security measures will be implemented. Chapter 20, "Securing the Site," will more fully cover security, but it's appropriate at this point to discuss some of the decisions made regarding security while designing MyGolfGear.NET.

Because we developed MyGolfGear.NET using ASP.NET, we needed to plan for three basic functions. Authentication, authorization, and impersonation are provided for in ASP.NET by the .NET Framework and IIS 5.0. *Authentication* means confirming whether a user truly is who she claims to be; *authorization* means determining whether a user has permission to perform a given action; and *impersonation* allows ASP.NET applications to use a given identity to access files and other resources and have that access granted or denied based on the assumed identity's authentication.

> **NOTE**
>
> Authorization can be performed only after authentication.

Certain parts of the site are open to the public, whereas other parts, such as the administrative sections, are available only to those people with the appropriate authorization. The .NET Framework supports two basic ways to authorize access to resources: file authorization and URL authorization.

One of the first steps was deciding which portions of the site would be accessible to the public and which sections needed to be made available only to administrators. Actually, making that decision was just common sense. Basically, any portion of the site that could be used to add, delete, or update products, users, or any other feature of the site would be accessible by administrators only.

The next decision was how to limit access to the site's administrative portions. We decided to rely on a combination of the .NET Framework's URLAuthorizationModule to implement role-based security for MyGolfGear.NET. Chapter 16, "Using .NET Authentication, Authorization, for Personalization," will cover the specific implementation used.

Available Development Tools

When James and I set out to develop MyGolfGear.NET, we had to decide which tools to use. Specifically, we had to decide which editor or integrated development environment (IDE) to use, which language or languages to program in, and which database server to use.

Deciding on an IDE

VisualStudio.NET provides many new features, some of which are simply improvements over the previous version. Some features include a single integrated development environment for developing .NET applications in multiple languages, enhanced visual development of Web form–based applications, simplified development of Web services, and the capability to quickly build middle-tier business components. VisualStudio.NET also simplifies the development of Windows-based applications with the introduction of the new Windows Forms project template.

As great as all these features sound, the stability of the available version of VisualStudio.NET, at the time of this writing, leaves a little to be desired. So, we decided to use basic text editors and the .NET Framework directly. We also didn't want to give the impression that the only way to develop robust, scalable, secure applications was to use any one tool. The real power of .NET lies in the rich framework and overall infrastructure.

Deciding on a Language

Deciding on a language was a little tougher. James's background is mostly VB and ASP, whereas mine is a mixed bag. Therefore, the natural tendency was for James to want to use VB.NET, whereas I was drawn to C#. In the end, we decided to do the bulk of the site development with C#.

Deciding on a Database Server

Deciding on the database server was perhaps the easiest decision to make. First, for both of us, our experience with database servers has been almost exclusively Microsoft SQL Server. So, the question was really whether we should use version 7.0 or 2000.

We decided to go with SQL Server 2000 for several reasons. One reason is its outstanding performance, rich support for XML, and powerful analysis and management tools. With SQL Server 2000, we can take advantage of its full-text search capability, an integrated Transact-SQL (T-SQL) debugger, and Web access to data using flexible online analytical processing (OLAP) cubes.

Admittedly, MyGolfGear.NET doesn't take full advantage of all of SQL Server 2000's great new features, but we felt it was a good idea to start with the best database we could afford. By doing so, we have more flexibility for future site enhancements.

Finally, it made sense for us to go with SQL Server 2000 over version 7.0 because SQL Server 2000 is one of the many .NET Enterprise servers leading the way in Microsoft's .NET initiative.

NOTE

According to the Transaction Processing Performance Council (TPC) results posted April 6, 2001, Microsoft SQL Server 2000 is the first and only database to break the half-million tpmC (measures throughput in business transactions per minute) threshold.

Summary

This chapter discussed, at a high level, the steps involved in planning for and designing MyGolfGear.NET. Specifically, it covered how we defined our goals for the site, what features to include, the specifics of our page and layout decisions, the design process, integration considerations, architectural and security planning, as well as the tools used to develop the site.

The next chapter will begin discussing how we implemented MyGolfGear.NET. It covers building the product catalog with Microsoft SQL Server 2000. It starts with a discussion of the data model before going into the specifics of the stored procedures for the basic catalog functionality.

Self Instruction

Download the project plan from `http://www.MyGolfGear.NET/projectplan` to see a detailed account of what went into the planning and design.

3

PLANNING
MYGOLFGEAR.
NET

Building the B2C Storefront

IN THIS PART

Building MyGolfGear.NET's Product Catalog with SQL Server 2000

IN THIS CHAPTER

Objectives

- Understand the basic MyGolfGear.NET data model

- Learn about the stored procedures used for managing the product catalog.

- Understand how SQL Server database security works.

The first step in the development phase for MyGolfGear.NET was creating the product catalog with SQL Server 2000. This chapter will cover development of the data model, including support for categories, parts, and part options. This chapter also will cover the creation of stored procedures responsible for retrieving categories, parts, part details, and part options, as well as adding, updating, and deleting categories and parts.

NOTE

Parts and products are often used interchangeably when modeling catalog-like relationships. A part can be a golf club, but it might also be a shaft or a grip. A part is anything that can be sold as a unit.

Figure 4.1 shows the data model for the basic catalog in MyGolfGear.NET.

NOTE

The term *basic* is used to emphasize that additional functionality will be added in subsequent chapters.

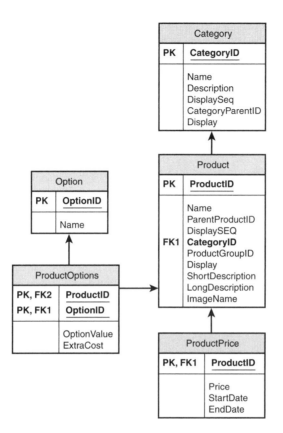

FIGURE 4.1
The basic product catalog for MyGolfGear.NET.

Developing the Data Model

To store data for product categories, products, and product options, we first need to create the MyGolfGear database. As discussed in Chapter 3, "Planning MyGolfGear.NET," James and I chose to use Microsoft SQL Server 2000 for our product catalog. Figure 4.2 shows creating a new database.

FIGURE 4.2
Creating a new database in SQL Server 2000.

You can take the following steps to create your database:

1. Right-click the Databases directory under the SQL Server root and select New Database.

2. Type the name of the database.

The outcome of all these steps is shown in Figure 4.3.

After the database was created, we added the tables to store the product catalog data. The three basic types of tables needed to support a basic catalog that would allow configurable products are category, product, and product option tables.

Categories

At the highest level of the product catalog are Categories. As you will see, the schema for MyGolfGear.NET supports a parent-child relationship between categories. For instance, at the highest level, we have the category Club, which is the parent to the categories Metal Woods, Irons, Wedges, and Putters. Similarly, we have the high-level category Apparel, under which resides the categories Shirts, Pants, Gloves, and Hats. Figure 4.4 shows a diagram of this relationship.

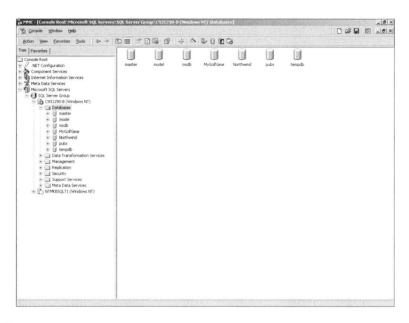

FIGURE 4.3
The newly created database.

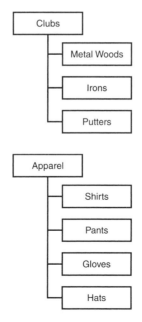

FIGURE 4.4
The newly created database.

To store these categories, we created a new table called Categories. The steps necessary to create a new table in SQL Server 2000 are as follows:

1. Expand the database.
2. Right-click the Tables icon and select New Table.
3. Fill in the field name and data type of each field.

Figure 4.5 shows creating a new table in SQL Server 2000.

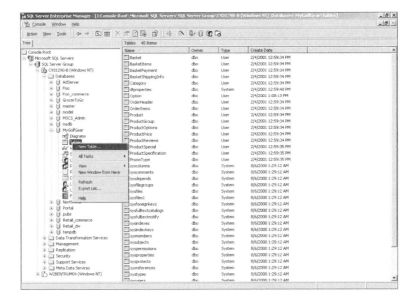

FIGURE 4.5

The new table option in SQL Server 2000.

To house the category data necessary for MyGolfGear.NET, only one table is needed. The Category table contains the fields and data types listed in Table 4.1.

TABLE 4.1 The Category Table

Field Name	Data Type	Length	Description
CategoryID	int	4	A unique ID for each category
Name	varchar	25	
Description	varchar	100	
DisplaySeq	smallint	2	
CategoryParentID	int	4	

Products

The next level down in the database schema for MyGolfGear.NET is products. Like categories, products support a parent-child relationship. The Product table houses the bulk of the product data. Table 4.2 shows the fields, their data types, field lengths, and a short description of the purpose for each column in the Product table.

TABLE 4.2 The Product Table

Field	Data Type	Length	Description
ProductID	int	4	Specifies a unique ID for each product
Name	varchar	25	Indicates the product's name
DisplaySeq	smallint	2	Allows ordering of parts for display purposes
ParentProductID	int	4	Specifies the top-level part in a product group
CategoryID	int	4	Specifies the category this part belongs to
ProductGroupID	int	4	Allows grouping of parts
Display	smallint	2	Allows products to not show up on the page
ShortDescription	varchar	50	Provides a short description of the product
LongDescription	varchar	500	Provides a long description of the product
ImageName	varchar	50	Provides the name of the image associated with the product

Unlike the category support, in the schema implemented for MyGolfGear.NET, more than one table is required to support products. In addition to the Product table, we chose to implement a ProductPrice table so that products could benefit from a date-driven pricing structure. Table 4.3 shows the fields, their data types, field lengths, and a short description of the purpose for each column in the ProductPrice table.

A single product can have multiple entries. Thus, products can be offered at different prices during different time periods.

TABLE 4.3   The ProductPrice Table

Field	Data Type	Length	Description
ProductID	int	4	A unique ID for each product
Price	decimal	9	The part's cost
StartDate	datetime	8	The date and time the specified part should begin being offered at the specified price
EndDate	datetime	8	The date and time the specified part should stop being offered at the specified price

Product Category Mapping

Because we need to house the same products in multiple categories, we created a ProductCategoryMap table. This way, for instance, a pair of men's shoes can be associated with both the Shoes and Men's Apparel categories.

> **NOTE**
>
> Category-product relationships are completely data driven. This way, the site adminis-trator subdivide categories as they see fit. For instance, a category like Apparel can be subdivided into Men's Apparel and Women's Apparel as the product line grows.

Table 4.4 shows the fields, their data types, field lengths, and a short description of the purpose for each column in the ProductCategoryMap table.

TABLE 4.4   The ProductCategoryMap Table

Field	Data Type	Length	Description
ProductID	int	4	A unique ID for each product
CategoryID	int	4	A unique ID for each category

Product Options

One of the more interesting features of the MyGolfGear.NET data model is its capability to support product options. The product options data is housed in two tables: Option and ProductOption.

The Option table simply holds the name of each possible product option, such as Loft or Face Angle. Table 4.5 shows the fields, their data types, field lengths, and a short description of the purpose for each column in the Option table.

TABLE 4.5   The Option Table

Field	Data Type	Length	Description
OptionID	int	4	A unique ID for each option
Name	varchar	100	The option's name

Many products can have these same attributes, so we mapped options to products via the ProductOption table.

TABLE 4.6   The ProductOptions Table

Field	Data Type	Length	Description
UniqueID	int	4	Unique ID for each entry
OptionID	int	4	ID for each option
ProductID	int	4	ID of the product this option value applies to
OptionValue	varchar	100	Actual value of the option
ExtraCost	money	8	Optional value for options that aren't free

In each of the tables mentioned thus far, the primary key is the first field listed. Notice that this is usually the field who's description says, "Unique ID for…".

Developing the Stored Procedures

After we built a structure to house the product data, we needed to create the stored procedures for selecting, adding, updating, and deleting product categories, parts, and part options.

Retrieving Category Information

The stored procedure spGetCategories was created to retrieve all top-level categories. Listing 4.1 shows this stored procedure.

Listing 4.1 *spGetCategories* Code

```
CREATE PROCEDURE spGetCategories AS
SELECT CategoryID, Name
FROM    Category
WHERE   Display <> 0
AND     ParentCategoryId Is Null
ORDER BY DisplaySeq
```

This query is pretty straightforward, but I want to mention a couple of interesting points. The AND line checks that the ParentCategoryID field is null because only child categories have a ParentCategoryID value.

The primary use for this stored procedure is for creating the top-level navigation. The ORDER BY line orders the resultset by the DisplaySeq. When you include a display sequence field, you can change the order in which the categories appear on the home page by making just a simple data change.

The spGetSubCatgories stored procedure was created to retrieve all the categories associated with a particular parent category. For instance, the category Clubs has the child categories Metal Woods, Irons, Wedges, and Putters. Listing 4.2 shows this stored procedure.

Listing 4.2 *spGetSubCategories* Code

```
CREATE PROCEDURE spGetSubCategories @ParentCategoryID int AS
SELECT CategoryID, Name
FROM    Category
WHERE   Display <> 0
AND     ParentCategoryId = @ParentCategoryID
ORDER BY DisplaySeq
```

When you specify a parent category, retrieved by using the spGetCategories stored procedure, subcategories can be retrieved.

Retrieving Product Information

To get a list of products from the MyGolfGear database, we can use the spGetProducts stored procedure. Specifying a category ID returns only products in that category. Listing 4.3 shows the spGetProducts stored procedure.

Listing 4.3 *spGetProducts* Code

```
CREATE PROCEDURE spGetProducts @CategoryID int AS
SELECT ProductID, Name, ShortDescription, ImageName
```

LISTING 4.3 Continued

```
FROM     Product
WHERE    CategoryID = @CategoryID
AND      Display <> 0
ORDER BY DisplaySeq
```

Again, the AND line checks whether it's okay to display this category. The Display field quickly turns the display of the specified product on or off.

The MyGolfGear database supports products with a parent-child relationship. This type of relationship is especially useful for products such as metal woods, for which we want to offer a choice among a 3, 5, or 7 wood, and all the product and display information is the same.

Listing 4.4 shows the code for spGetChildProducts. This stored procedure returns a list of all subparts given a product ID.

LISTING 4.4 *spGetChildProducts* Code

```
CREATE PROCEDURE spGetChildProducts @ParentProductID int AS
SELECT ProductID, Name, ShortDescription, ImageName
FROM     Product
WHERE    ParentProductId = @ParentProductID
ORDER    By DisplaySeq
```

To get details about a specific product, we created another stored procedure: spGetProductDetails. Listing 4.5 shows the code.

LISTING 4.5 *spGetProductDetails* Code

```
CREATE PROCEDURE spGetProductDetails @ProductID int AS
SELECT P.ProductID, P.Name, P.ShortDescription,
       P.LongDescription, P.ImageName, PP.Price
FROM     Product P, ProductPrice PP
WHERE    P.ProductID = @ProductID
AND      P.ProductID = PP.ProductID
AND      ((PP.StartDate IS NULL and PP.EndDate IS NULL)
OR       (PP.StartDate<= GetDate() and PP.EndDate >= GetDate())))
```

This stored procedure simply returns all information needed to display a product on the product details page. This information includes everything from a product's ID and name to its pricing information.

This stored procedure also limits the resultset to those products that either have no date information or haven't expired. The AND line checks that the specified product has any date information. The OR line checks to ensure that any supplied dates are valid. In other words, the OR checks to make sure the specified dates don't take place in the past or haven't yet come.

Retrieving Product Option Data

To offer custom golf equipment, we need a mechanism for individualizing each product. The Option and ProductOptions tables house the data, and the spGetProductOptions and spGetProductOptionValues stored procedures retrieve the data.

Listing 4.6 shows the code for spGetProductOptions.

LISTING 4.6   *spGetProductOptions* Code

```
CREATE PROCEDURE spGetProductOptions @ProductID int AS
SELECT     OptionID
FROM       ProductOptions
WHERE      ProductID =@ProductID
GROUP BY OptionID
```

This stored procedure simply returns the option IDs associated with a particular product. The GROUP BY statement groups the resultset by option ID so that only unique values are returned.

We also need to list all possible values a given product option can have. To store this list, we created the stored procedure spGetProductOptionValues. Listing 4.7 shows the code for spGetProductOptionValues.

LISTING 4.7   *spGetProductOptionValues* Code

```
CREATE PROCEDURE spGetProductOptionValues @ProductID int AS
SELECT OptionID, OptionValue,    ExtraCost
FROM    ProductOptions
WHERE   ProductID =@ProductID
```

This procedure is as straightforward as they come. Given a product ID, a resultset containing all the option IDs, values for that option, and any extra cost associated with that option are returned.

Securing the Product Catalog

This section isn't meant to be an exhaustive look at database security, but I do think it's important to discuss how we decided to handle database security for MyGolfGear.NET and give a brief overview of the options available in SQL Server 2000.

Chapter 16, "Using .NET Authentication and Authorization for Personalization," shows some of the security features used to create a more personalized experience. Chapter 20, "Securing the Site," takes a more in depth look at the security features available when using the .NET Framework.

Authentication Modes

SQL Server 2000 comes with two authentication modes. Users can connect to a SQL Server database through a Windows NT 4.0 or Windows 2000 user account with Windows authentication mode. SQL Server authentication allows administrators to add username and password pairs for groups of users at the SQL Server level (outside the Windows security model).

Windows Authentication

When users connect to SQL Server via Windows authentication, SQL Server uses domain-level security to validate username and password information.

SQL Server relies on a user's network security attributes, established at login and validated by a Windows domain controller, for Windows authentication. So, SQL Server can permit or deny access based on a network username without requiring a separate username and password.

Using Windows authentication instead of SQL Server authentication provides a few benefits. Windows 4.0 and Windows 2000 security provide encryption of passwords, expiration of passwords, account lockout after multiple attempts, and enforcement of minimum password lengths.

A few disadvantages are associated with using Windows authentication, however:

- Resources must be available to administer security at the domain level.
- If the instance of SQL Server is running on anything other than Windows NT 4.0 or Windows 2000 (Windows 98 or Windows ME), Windows authentication won't work, and developers must rely on SQL Server authentication.

SQL Server Authentication

SQL Server can perform the authentication itself. Login accounts with usernames and passwords must be set up within SQL Server, and users must explicitly specify their usernames and passwords at connection time for SQL Server to check that the username/password pairs match previously entered pairs. Otherwise, SQL Server will reject the login attempt, and an error will be raised.

One advantage of using SQL Server authentication is that developers and administrators who've used previous versions of SQL Server will be familiar with the username and password model. Besides, SQL Server authentication is the only available authentication for non–Windows NT 4.0/2000 users.

Mixed Mode

Mixed mode is useful when SQL Server is run in an environment where clients may be connecting from a mixture of operating systems, including Windows 98, Windows NT, and Windows 2000.

In this scenario, four basic steps are required to secure individual database objects using SQL Server authentication: adding logins, adding roles, adding users, and managing permissions at the object level.

Adding Logins

The first step in securing the MyGolfGear database was creating two new logins. We created a login for administrators called MGGAdmin and a login for the application called MGGApp.

To add a new login to SQL Server, follow these steps:

1. Expand the security folder under the server node in Enterprise Manager.
2. Right-click the Logins icon and then select New Login.
3. Specify the new login name.
4. Choose either SQL Server or Windows authentication (I used SQL Server authentication).
5. Enter a password for the new login if you are using SQL Server authentication.
6. Specify the default database.
7. On the Database Access tab, specify which database(s) should be granted access by this login and click the OK button.

Figure 4.6 shows the SQL Server Login Properties sheet.

FIGURE 4.6

The SQL Server Login Properties sheet.

Adding Roles

We decided it was best to keep the security schema simple, so we created only two new roles for the MyGolfGear database: an administrator role called MGGAdmin and an application role called MGGApp. Figure 4.7 shows SQL Server's Database Role Properties sheet.

FIGURE 4.7
The Database Role Properties sheet.

To add a new role to SQL Server, follow these steps:

1. Expand the MyGolfGear database folder under the server node in Enterprise Manager.
2. Right-click the Roles icon and then select New Database Role.
3. Enter a name for the role in the Name text box on the Database Role Properties sheet.
4. Click OK.

Adding Users

The next step was specifying users to go along with our roles. We decided to create users that matched the existing two roles. Figure 4.8 shows SQL Server's Database User Properties sheet.

To add a new user in SQL Server, follow these steps:

1. Expand the MyGolfGear database folder under the server node in Enterprise Manager.
2. Highlight the Roles icon
3. Double click the name of the role you wish to add a user to.
4. Click the Add button under the user list box.
5. Select the user(s) to add to the role and click OK on the Add Role Members dialog and then OK on the Database Role Properties window.

FIGURE 4.8

The Database User Properties sheet.

MyGolfGear.NET has two database users. James and I created the MGGAdmin user to administer and debug the application. We created the MGGApp user for the sole purpose of allowing data access components and other application elements to access data in a secure manner.

Managing Permissions

After the new logins, roles, and users were created, we needed to specify permissions for the individual database objects. This meant that every table and stored procedure had to have permissions set for each user.

To grant access to database objects for a particular user, follow these steps:

1. Click the Users icon under the MyGolfGear database.
2. Double-click the User icon of the user you want to permit access to.
3. Select SELECT, INSERT, UPDATE, DELETE, or EXEC for each database object the user needs access to.

Figure 4.9 shows what this looks like.

For MyGolfGear.NET, the MGGApp user was given EXEC permissions on all stored procedures and was restricted access from all database tables. It's common practice to limit the access of data, by applications, to stored procedures only.

The MGGAdmin user was given execute permission on all stored procedures as well as SELECT, INSERT, and UPDATE permissions for all tables. We decided that not even an administrative login should have the ability to delete data directly.

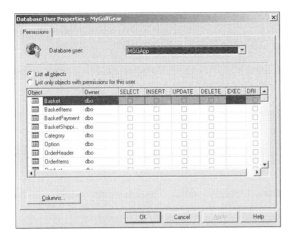

FIGURE 4.9

Managing User Permissions.

> **NOTE**
>
> A SQL script for creating all of the MyGolfGear database tables and stored procedures is available online.

Summary

This chapter discussed building the data model for the basic product catalog of MyGolfGear. NET. It also covered the creation of the stored procedures responsible for retrieving, updating, adding, and deleting categories, parts, and part options. Finally, it covered securing each of these database objects.

The next chapter will cover using ASP.NET to administer the product catalog. Specifically, it will cover creating the components and page elements necessary to add, remove, and update category, and part data.

Self Instruction

Based on what you've read in this chapter, create a database of your own for MyGolfGear.NET and add the following pieces of functionality:

- Implement SQL Server Authentication for the newly created database.
- Write your own update and insert stored procedures for the catalog.

4

**MyGolfGear.
NET's Product
Catalog**

Using ASP.NET to Administer the Product Catalog

IN THIS CHAPTER

Objectives

- Understand how the catalog administration functionality for MyGolfGear.NET was implemented

- Explore the CatalogDS class.

- Learn about the user interface elements created to support the catalog administration features

After we developed the data model and select stored procedures for the MyGolfGear.NET product catalog, we needed to build an administrative application. This chapter covers the use of ASP.NET in MyGolfGear.NET, to implement these administrative features. It will discuss the creation of the `CatalogDS.xsd` file, the generation of the `CatalogDS` class from the `.xsd` file using the XML Schema Definition Tool, as well as `Admin.aspx`.

From looking at the catalog database, you can see that we need some way to update, delete, and add categories, products, and options as well as a way to associate options with products and products with categories.

The administrative features for MyGolfGear.NET can be broken down into six main areas: the database, a strongly typed dataset, a data provider component to interact with the dataset, a code behind to separate business logic from the user interface, several `.ascx` user controls, and an administrative aspx for each to contain all the user controls. Figure 5.1 illustrates MyGolfGear.NET's conceptual architecture.

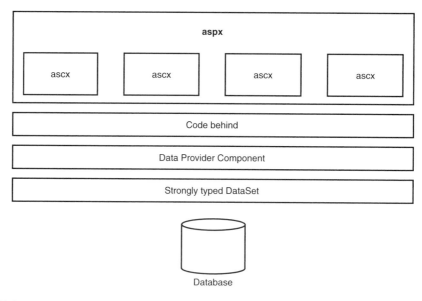

FIGURE 5.1

High-level architecture.

The files needed to create the administrative functionality for MyGolfGear.NET are `Admin.aspx`, `Admin.aspx.cs`, `CategoryAdmin.aspx`, `CategoryAdmin.aspx.cs`, `ProductAdmin.aspx`, `ProductAdmin.aspx.cs`, `CatalogDS.xsd`, `CatalogDS.cs`, and `MyGolfGearDP.cs`. I will discuss most file in this chapter. `MyGolfGearDP`, `CatalogDS.cs`, and `CatalogDS.xsd` will be discussed throughout the rest of the book.

Component Development

Chapter 4, "Building MyGolfGear.NET's Product Catalog with SQL Server 2000," discussed the database design for the simple catalog requirements. Now we need a programmatic way to interact with the database objects. The functionality needed to add, update, and delete items from the product catalog has been encapsulated in a component layer, as illustrated in Figure 5.1.

The Catalog Dataset

With previous versions of ADO, you had access to Recordset variables via late-bound, weakly typed variables. ADO.NET provides strongly typed, early-bound access to data members via *strongly typed datasets*.

> **NOTE**
>
> *Strongly typed datasets* are classes derived from `System.Data.DataSet`. So, a strongly typed dataset inherits properties and methods from the `DataSet` class, but also provides access to tables and columns by name instead of the traditional collection-based means.

You can go about using strongly typed datasets with .NET in two ways. You could create your own class and derive it from `System.Data.DataSet` and then manually create and implement properties that map to all the tables that will be present in your dataset. Additionally, you might choose to implement custom events for detecting when rows in your dataset changed as well as other methods that would allow for adding rows, searching for specific rows, and so on.

Fortunately, the .NET Framework provides a tool that greatly simplifies the creation of such classes. Using the XML Schema Definition Tool (`xsd.exe`), you can generate strongly typed dataset classes with robust properties, methods, and events by simply specifying the schema the dataset should adhere to. The XML schema definitions used by `xsd.exe` must adhere to the proposed World Wide Web Consortium (W3C) format.

For MyGolfGear.NET, we created the `CatalogDS.cs` class by using `CatalogDS.xsd` and `xsd.exe`. The following sections cover each of these files.

CatalogDS.xsd

The CatalogDS schema file is simply an XML document that specifies what the fields and types of each DataSet element should be. My coauthor, James, used VisualStudio.NET to generate the Catalog.xsd file used for MyGolfGear.NET, but it could have been created manually without too much trouble.

A complete discussion of XML Schema Definitions is beyond the scope of this book. However, there are a few things worth mentioning before we proceed with the discussion of the CatalogDS schema.

An *XML schema* is an XML-based way of defining how an XML document should be marked up. Basically, a schema defines a set, or class, of XML documents. You can think of an XML document that adheres to a specific schema as being an "instance" of that schema.

Each element in the schema is prefixed with xsd:, which simply associates the XML namespace used. The second line in the document specifies the namespaces used throughout the document:

```
<xsd:schema id="CatalogDS" targetNamespace="http://tempuri.org/XMLSchema.xsd"
➥xmlns="http://tempuri.org/XMLSchema.xsd" xmlns:xsd=
➥"http://www.w3.org/2000/10/XMLSchema" xmlns:msdata=
➥"urn:schemas-microsoft-com:xml-msdata">.
```

When you're defining an XML schema, note that you can choose from two basic data types: simple and complex. Complex types allow the inclusion of other elements and attributes. Additionally, there is a distinction between *declarations,* which allow elements and attributes with specific names to be used in a document, and *definitions,* which create new types.

Let's talk about CatalogDS.xsd so that you can have some idea what it would take to create a file of your own if you don't have access to VisualStudio.NET. Listing 5.1 shows a portion of the xsd file used to create the CatalogDS.cs file. The actual schema definition is quite lengthy, so I will cover the catalog, product, and option sections separately.

LISTING 5.1 Part of the *CatalodDS.xsd* File

```
1: <xsd:element name="Category">
2:     <xsd:complexType>
3:         <xsd:all>
4:             <xsd:element name="CategoryID" msdata:DataType="System.Guid"
➥type="xsd:string" />
5:             <xsd:element name="Name" minOccurs="0" type="xsd:string" />
6:             <xsd:element name="ParentCategoryID" msdata:DataType="System.Guid"
➥ minOccurs="0" type="xsd:string" />
7:             <xsd:element name="Description" minOccurs="0" type="xsd:string" />
8:             <xsd:element name="DisplaySeq" minOccurs="0" type="xsd:short" />
9:             <xsd:element name="Display" minOccurs="0" type="xsd:short" />
```

LISTING 5.1   Continued

```
10:         </xsd:all>
11:       </xsd:complexType>
12:       <xsd:key name="TableKey1" msdata:PrimaryKey="true">
13:         <xsd:selector xpath="." />
14:         <xsd:field xpath="CategoryID" />
15:       </xsd:key>
16:     </xsd:element>
```

> **NOTE**
>
> You can find the complete `CatalogDS.xsd` schema online.

This discussion will stay fairly high-level and focus primarily on the elements most necessary to create the `CatalogDS.cs` file. Basically, each database element that needs to be represented in the strongly typed dataset needs to be described via XML.

The first line in Listing 5.1 begins the declaration of the `Category`. Notice that it is a complex type, so all its subelements need to be described as well. The real meat is the information between the `<xsd:all>` tags. Every table field name that needs to map to a method or property is described here, along with its type. Adding these field names enables you to create a strongly typed dataset that contains properties corresponding to these names.

After the definition of the complex type `Category`, a new `xsd` element appears on line 12. The `xsd:key` element specifies that the field named CategoryID is the primary key for the data entity named `Category`.

For each table in the MyGolfGear database that needs to be represented by the strongly typed dataset, a corresponding entry in `CatalogDS.xsd` appears similar to that of `Category`, as shown in Listing 5.1.

> **NOTE**
>
> For more information on XML Schema Definitions, visit `http://www.w3.org/XML/Schema`.

xsd.exe

The next step in the process is the creation of the strongly typed dataset. If you are daunted by the thought of having to create your own schema, fear not. The generation of a strongly type dataset is trivial in comparison.

We used `xsd.exe` to create the `CatalogDS.cs` file. It is located in the `Microsoft.NET\` `FrameworkSDK\bin` directory in the folder where you installed the .NET Framework.

To use this file, simply open a command prompt window and navigate to its location. To properly create a strongly typed dataset, you need to use the following command-line arguments:

- The path and name of the xsd file.
- `/d`, which tells the tool to create a `DataSet` sub-classed class. Using `/c` would result in the generation of simple classes for each table represented in the schema.
- `/l:CS`, which tells `xsd.exe` to generate C# code. We could have just as easily used `/l:VB` to generate VB.NET classes.
- `/n`: followed by a namespace tells `xsd.exe` in which namespace to include the newly created class or classes.
- `/o`: followed by a path determines the output directory.

CatalogDS.cs

The `xsd.exe` file generated more than 1,800 lines of code based on `CatalogDS.xsd`. Needless to say, I won't cover every line it generated, but I would like to point out the majority of the functionality it provided.

Perhaps the best way to cover all this information would be to break down the components into functional areas. Listing 5.2 shows the first major portion of `CatalogDS.cs`, which includes the namespace and class declaration.

LISTING 5.2 *CatalogDS.cs*

```
1: namespace MyGolfGear.DataAccess {
2:     using System;
3:     using System.Data;
4:
5:
6:     [System.ComponentModel.DesignerCategoryAttribute("code")]
7:     public class CatalogDS : System.Data.DataSet {
8:
9:         private CategoryDataTable tableCategory;
10:
11:        private CategoryProductMappingDataTable
➥tableCategoryProductMapping;
12:
13:        private ProductDataTable tableProduct;
14:
15:        private ProductOptionsDataTable tableProductOptions;
16:
```

LISTING 5.2 Continued

```
17:          private ProductPriceDataTable tableProductPrice;
18:
19:          private OptionDataTable tableOption;
20:
21:          private DataRelation relationCategoryProductMapping;
22:
23:          private DataRelation relationProductCategoryMapping;
24:
25:          private DataRelation relationProductOptions;
26:
27:          private DataRelation relationOptions;
28:
29:          private DataRelation relationProductPrice;
30:
31:          public CatalogDS() {
32:              this.InitClass();
33:          }
```

This section of `CatalogDS.cs` begins with the declaration of the `MyGolfGear.DataAccess` namespace. Using the `namespace` keyword in this manner simply includes the `CatalogDS` class in the `MyGolfGear.DataAccess` namespace. As the name implies, this namespace is used for all components whose functionality is data access–centric.

The next interesting portion of this code snippet is the attribute declaration on line 6. The `System.ComponentModel.DesignerCategoryAttribute` attribute is inserted by `xsd.exe` so that any visual designer, such as VisualStudio.NET, can tell which category the class belongs to. It actually has no bearing on the functionality of the class at runtime, so I won't spend any more time discussing it.

Throughout the class, several attribute names start with `System.ComponentModel.Designer`. In the interest of time, I won't discuss any of these attributes because they are inserted mostly for integration with VisualStudio.NET (though other visual designers could take advantage of them as well).

Line 7 contains the actual declaration of the `CatalogDS` class. Notice that it inherits from `System.Data.DataSet`, which is the base class for any strongly typed dataset.

Lines 9 through 29 show the declarations for the private fields representing all the tables and their relationships in the dataset. In other words, every table and its relationship to other tables present in the dataset will have a read-only property. These private fields are used by the read-only properties shown in Listing 5.3, but I will come back to this point later.

5

THE PRODUCT CATALOG

The only other important aspect of Listing 5.2 is the declaration of the default constructor on lines 31–33. I will cover the `InitClass()` method it calls later.

As mentioned earlier, the `CatalogDS` strongly typed dataset contains read-only properties corresponding to every table represented in the dataset along with its `DataRelation` objects. Listing 5.3 shows one of these read-only properties. Their basic structure and functionality are the same, so I have included only one.

LISTING 5.3 A *CatalogDS* Read-Only Property

```
public CategoryDataTable Category {
   get {
      return this.tableCategory;
   }
}
```

Listing 5.3 shows the read-only property `Category`, which returns the private instance variable `tableCategory`. This table object, which is defined later in the `CatalogDS.cs` file, inherits from `System.Data.DataTable` and implements the `System.Collection.IEnumerable` interface. The `CategoryDataTable` class will be discussed in greater detail later in this section.

As mentioned earlier, the default constructor for the `CategoryDS` class calls the `InitClass()` method, which is shown in Listing 5.4.

LISTING 5.4 *InitClass* Method

```
private void InitClass() {
  this.DataSetName = "CatalogDS";
  this.Namespace = "http://tempuri.org/XMLSchema.xsd";
  this.tableCategory = new CategoryDataTable();
  this.Tables.Add(this.tableCategory);
  this.tableCategoryProductMapping = new CategoryProductMappingDataTable();
  this.Tables.Add(this.tableCategoryProductMapping);
  this.tableProduct = new ProductDataTable();
  this.Tables.Add(this.tableProduct);
  this.tableProductOptions = new ProductOptionsDataTable();
  this.Tables.Add(this.tableProductOptions);
  this.tableProductPrice = new ProductPriceDataTable();
  this.Tables.Add(this.tableProductPrice);
  this.tableOption = new OptionDataTable();
  this.Tables.Add(this.tableOption);
  this.tableCategoryProductMapping.Constraints.Add
➥(new System.Data.ForeignKeyConstraint("CategoryProductMapping",
➥new DataColumn[] {this.tableCategory.CategoryIDColumn}, new DataColumn[]
➥{this.tableCategoryProductMapping.CategoryIDColumn}));
```

LISTING 5.4   Continued

```
  this.tableCategoryProductMapping.Constraints.Add
➥(new System.Data.ForeignKeyConstraint("ProductCategoryMapping",
➥new DataColumn[] {this.tableProduct.ProductIDColumn}, new DataColumn[]
➥{this.tableCategoryProductMapping.ProductIDColumn}));
  this.tableProductOptions.Constraints.Add
➥ (new System.Data.ForeignKeyConstraint("ProductOptions",
➥new DataColumn[]
➥ {this.tableProduct.ProductIDColumn}, new DataColumn[]
➥{this.tableProductOptions.ProductIDColumn}));
  this.tableProductOptions.Constraints.Add
➥ (new System.Data.ForeignKeyConstraint("Options", new DataColumn[]
➥{this.tableOption.OptionIDColumn}, new DataColumn[]
➥{this.tableProductOptions.OptionIDColumn}));
  this.tableProductPrice.Constraints.Add(new System.Data.ForeignKeyConstraint
➥ ("ProductPrice", new DataColumn[] {this.tableProduct.ProductIDColumn}
➥, new DataColumn[] {this.tableProductPrice.ProductIDColumn}));
  this.relationCategoryProductMapping = new DataRelation(
➥"CategoryProductMapping", new DataColumn[]
➥{this.tableCategory.CategoryIDColumn}, new DataColumn[]
➥ {this.tableCategoryProductMapping.CategoryIDColumn}, false);
  this.Relations.Add(this.relationCategoryProductMapping);
  this.relationProductCategoryMapping = new DataRelation(
➥"ProductCategoryMapping", new DataColumn[]
➥{this.tableProduct.ProductIDColumn}, new DataColumn[]
➥{this.tableCategoryProductMapping.ProductIDColumn}, false);
  this.Relations.Add(this.relationProductCategoryMapping);
  this.relationProductOptions = new DataRelation("ProductOptions",
➥new DataColumn[] {this.tableProduct.ProductIDColumn}, new DataColumn[]
➥{this.tableProductOptions.ProductIDColumn}, false);
  this.Relations.Add(this.relationProductOptions);
  this.relationOptions = new DataRelation("Options", new DataColumn[]
➥{this.tableOption.OptionIDColumn}, new DataColumn[]
➥{this.tableProductOptions.OptionIDColumn}, false);
  this.Relations.Add(this.relationOptions);
  this.relationProductPrice = new DataRelation("ProductPrice",
➥new DataColumn[] {this.tableProduct.ProductIDColumn}, new DataColumn[]
➥{this.tableProductPrice.ProductIDColumn}, false);
  this.Relations.Add(this.relationProductPrice);
}
```

5

As the name implies, `InitClass()` simply initializes the `CatalogDS` class. Basically, it provides default values for all the private member variables discussed in the first part of this section. More specifically, it initializes all the `DataTable` subclasses that represent each `DataTable` object in the strongly typed dataset. So, this means that a `DataTable` subclass corresponds to

THE PRODUCT
CATALOG

the Category, Product, CategoryProductMapping, ProductOptions, ProductPrice, and Options tables.

After creating a new instance of each DataTable object, the InitClass() method adds them to the dataset using the this.Tables.Add notation.

In addition, the InitClass() method adds constraints to the CategoryProductMapping, ProductOptions, and ProductPrice DataTable classes. Doing so enforces the in-memory CatalogDS dataset to adhere to the same foreign key constraints the MyGolfGear database does.

This method also makes additions to the DataRelations collection for the CategoryProductMapping, ProductOptions, Options, and ProductPrice tables. Doing so enforces referential integrity and allows for the traversal of the dataset in-memory without having to use joins or other SQL-based syntax on the database server.

Next, CatalogDS sets up events for row changes in each of the represented DataTable classes. The declaration for the CategoryRowChangeEvent event handler looks like this:

```
public delegate void CategoryRowChangeEventHandler(object sender,
➥ CategoryRowChangeEvent e);
```

Similar event handlers for the CategoryProductMapping, Product, ProductOptions, ProductPrice, and Option tables are created as well.

The rest of CatalogDS is made up of the DataTable definitions I mentioned earlier. Listing 5.5 shows the first part of the CategoryDataTable definition.

LISTING 5.5   *CategoryDataTable* Class

```
 1: public class CategoryDataTable : DataTable, System.Collections.Ienumerable
➥ {
 2:
 3:     private DataColumn columnCategoryID;
 4:
 5:     private DataColumn columnName;
 6:
 7:     private DataColumn columnParentCategoryID;
 8:
 9:     private DataColumn columnDescription;
10:
11:     private DataColumn columnDisplaySeq;
12:
13:     private DataColumn columnDisplay;
```

Notice how similar the CategoryDataTable definition is in structure to the CatalogDS class definition. The first part of the class definition is made up of private fields for properties corresponding to the datatable's DataColumn objects.

NOTE

You can find the complete CatalogDS.cs class online.

MyGolfGearDP.cs

At the next layer of abstraction is MyGolfGearDP.cs. The job of this component is to interact with the strongly typed dataset objects used throughout the site and provide a layer of abstraction between the user interface code and the data access code. MyGolfGearDP.cs is a data provider class whose only job is to fill and update the strongly typed CatalogDS dataset. Listing 5.6 shows the code for the MyGolfGearDP class.

LISTING 5.6 *MyGolfGearDP.cs*

```
1: namespace MyGolfGear{
2:      using System;
3:      using System.Data;
4:      using System.Data.SqlClient;
5:      using System.Xml;
6:      using System.Web;
7:      using System.Web.UI.WebControls;
8:      using MyGolfGear.DataAccess;
9:
10:     public class MyGolfGearDP{
11:
12:       public void FillCatalog(CatalogDS ds){
13:           SqlConnection con = new SqlConnection("server=localhost;uid=sa;
➥pwd=;database=MyGolfGear");
14:           SqlDataAdapter sda = new SqlDataAdapter
➥ ("spGetCompleteCatalog", con);
15:           sda.SelectCommand.CommandType = CommandType.StoredProcedure;
16:
17:           con.Open();
18:
19:           sda.TableMappings.Add("Table", "Category");
20:           sda.TableMappings.Add("Table1", "CategoryProductMapping");
21:           sda.TableMappings.Add("Table2", "Product");
22:
23:           sda.Fill(ds);
24:
25:           con.Close();
26:       }
27:
28:       public void UpdateCatalog(CatalogDS ds){
```

LISTING 5.6   Continued

```
29:          SqlConnection con = new SqlConnection("server=localhost;uid=sa;
➥pwd=;database=MyGolfGear");
30:        SqlDataAdapter sda = new SqlDataAdapter("spGetCompleteCatalog",
➥con);
31:
32:        //Insert-Update-Delete Category Rows
33:        sda.DeleteCommand = new SqlCommand("spDeleteCategory", con);
34:        sda.DeleteCommand.CommandType = CommandType.StoredProcedure;
35:        sda.DeleteCommand.Parameters.Add("@CategoryID",
➥SqlDbType.UniqueIdentifier,4,"CategoryID");
36:        sda.InsertCommand = new SqlCommand("spInsertCategory", con);
37:        sda.InsertCommand.CommandType = CommandType.StoredProcedure;
38:        sda.InsertCommand.Parameters.Add("@CategoryID",
➥SqlDbType.UniqueIdentifier,4,"CategoryID");
39:        sda.InsertCommand.Parameters.Add("@Name",
➥SqlDbType.VarChar, 25,"Name");
40:        sda.InsertCommand.Parameters.Add("@ParentCategoryID",
➥SqlDbType.UniqueIdentifier,4,"ParentCategoryID");
41:        sda.InsertCommand.Parameters.Add("@Description",
➥SqlDbType.VarChar,100,"Description");
42:        sda.InsertCommand.Parameters.Add("@DisplaySeq",
➥SqlDbType.SmallInt,2,"DisplaySeq");
43:        sda.InsertCommand.Parameters.Add("@Display",
➥SqlDbType.SmallInt,2,"Display");
44:        sda.UpdateCommand = new SqlCommand("spUpdateCategory", con);
45:        sda.UpdateCommand.CommandType = CommandType.StoredProcedure;
46:        sda.UpdateCommand.Parameters.Add("@CategoryID",
➥SqlDbType.UniqueIdentifier,4,"CategoryID");
47:        sda.UpdateCommand.Parameters.Add("@Name",
➥SqlDbType.VarChar, 25,"Name");
48:        sda.UpdateCommand.Parameters.Add("@ParentCategoryID",
➥SqlDbType.UniqueIdentifier,4,"ParentCategoryID");
49:        sda.UpdateCommand.Parameters.Add("@Description",
➥SqlDbType.VarChar,100,"Description");
50:        sda.UpdateCommand.Parameters.Add("@DisplaySeq",
➥SqlDbType.SmallInt,2,"DisplaySeq");
51:        sda.UpdateCommand.Parameters.Add("@Display",
➥SqlDbType.SmallInt,2,"Display");
52:
53:        sda.Update(ds, "Category");
54:      }
55:    }
56:}
```

The first method in the `MyGolfGearDP` class is `FillCatalog()`, which is shown in lines 12 through 26. In this method, a `SqlConnection` object is created, and the connection to the MyGolfGear database is opened. Next, a `SqlDataAdapter` object is created, the stored procedure `spGetCompleteCatalog` is specified as the select command text, and the newly opened `SqlConnection` object is passed in.

Before actually filling the dataset (line 23), `TableMappings` are added to the dataset to associate the `Product` and `Category` tables with the `CategoryProductMappings` table.

The instance of `CatalogDS` that is passed into the `FillCatalog()` method is filled, and the connection to the database is closed.

The only other method in the `MyGolfGearDP` class is `UpdateCatalog()`. Like the `FillCatalog()` method, this method accepts only one parameter—a reference to a `CatalogDS` object. The `UpdateCatalog()` method creates and uses `SqlConnection` and `SqlDataAdapter` objects just like the `FillCatalog()` method does.

Perhaps the most interesting aspect of the `UpdateCatalog()` method is the specification of `Delete`, `Insert`, and `Update` command objects in lines 33 through 51. When you specify the stored procedure and a parameter used for each of these actions, the `SqlDataAdapter` object will call the appropriate method based on how the data in the `DataSet` object has changed.

Page Development

The following sections will cover the user interface portion of the administrative section of MyGolfGear.NET. The files associated with the user interface are `Admin.aspx`, `Admin.aspx.cs`, `CategoryAdmin.aspx`, `CategoryAdmin.aspx.cs`, `ProductAdmin.aspx`, and `ProductAdmin.aspx.cs`.

Admin.aspx

`Admin.aspx` is the container or control center for all the administrative features available to the administrators of MyGolfGear.NET. It contains links to the various administrative features of the site. Chapter 18, "Maintaining MyGolfGear.NET's User Information," will discuss administering users and other entities and will cover the `Admin.aspx` page as well. The remainder of this chapter will stick to the catalog administration.

CategoryAdmin.aspx

As its name suggests, the Category Manager is the user interface portion of the category administration feature of MyGolfGear.NET. The Category Manager is made up of the ASP.NET page named `CategoryAdmin.aspx` and the ASP.NET code behind class named `CategoryAdmin.aspx.cs`. Figure 5.2 shows the MyGolfGear.NET Category Manager.

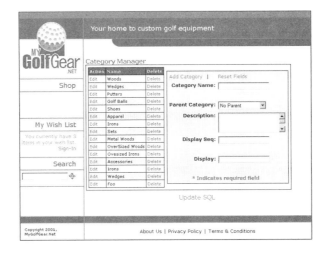

FIGURE 5.2
MyGolfGear.NET Category Manager.

The Category Manager allows for adding, updating, and deleting of categories. It also allows an administrator to assign categories to parent categories. For instance, we could have added the Shoes category to the Apparel category.

The job of the code behind is to separate the display formatting from any business or data access logic. I like to think of the code behind as the goo that ties the user interface to the business objects. The code behind file named `CategoryAdmin.aspx.cs` is shown in Listing 5.7.

LISTING 5.7   `CategoryAdmin.aspx.cs`

```
namespace MyGolfGear
{
    using System;
    using System.Collections;
    using System.ComponentModel;
    using System.Data;
    using System.Data.SqlClient;
    using System.Xml;
    using System.Drawing;
    using System.Web;
    using System.Web.SessionState;
    using System.Web.UI;
    using System.Web.UI.WebControls;
    using System.Web.UI.HtmlControls;
    using System.Runtime.Serialization;
      using DataAccess;
```

LISTING 5.7 Continued

```
public class CategoryAdmin : System.Web.UI.Page
  protected System.Web.UI.WebControls.TextBox txtDisplay;
  protected System.Web.UI.WebControls.Label Label2;
  protected System.Web.UI.HtmlControls.HtmlGenericControl Message;
  protected System.Web.UI.WebControls.TextBox txtDisplaySeq;
  protected System.Web.UI.WebControls.Label Label5;
  protected System.Web.UI.HtmlControls.HtmlTextArea txtDescription;
  protected System.Web.UI.WebControls.Label Label4;
  protected System.Web.UI.WebControls.DropDownList lstParentCategory;
  protected System.Web.UI.WebControls.Label Label3;
  protected System.Web.UI.WebControls.TextBox txtCategoryName;
  protected System.Web.UI.WebControls.Label Label1;
  protected System.Web.UI.WebControls.LinkButton btnUpdateCategory;
  protected System.Web.UI.WebControls.LinkButton LinkButton1;
  protected System.Web.UI.WebControls.LinkButton btnReset;
  protected System.Web.UI.WebControls.DataGrid CategoryDataGrid;
  protected CatalogDS catds;

  public CategoryAdmin(){
    Page.Init += new System.EventHandler(Page_Init);
  }

  protected void Page_Load(object sender, EventArgs e){
    // get the category data from the session state
    catds = (CatalogDS)Session["dsCategoryList"];
    if (catds == null){
      LoadCatalog();
      Session["dsCategoryList"] = catds;
    }
    if (!IsPostBack){
      RebindDataGrid();
      //Sort Category by Display Seq & Add default category
      //catds.Category.AddCategoryRow("No Parent Category",0,"",0,1);
      DataView Source = catds.Category.DefaultView;

      Source.Sort = "DisplaySeq";
      //Populate Category list box
      lstParentCategory.DataSource = Source;
      lstParentCategory.DataTextField = "Name";
      lstParentCategory.DataValueField = "CategoryID";
        lstParentCategory.DataBind();
          lstParentCategory.Items.Add(new
➥System.Web.UI.WebControls.ListItem
➥ ("No Parent",System.Guid.Empty.ToString()));
```

5

THE PRODUCT
CATALOG

LISTING 5.7   Continued

```
            lstParentCategory.SelectedIndex =
➥lstParentCategory.Items.Count - 1;
        }else{
        if (catds.HasChanges()){
          DataView Source = catds.Category.DefaultView;
          Source.Sort = "DisplaySeq";
          //Populate Category list box
          lstParentCategory.DataSource = Source;
          lstParentCategory.DataTextField = "Name";
          lstParentCategory.DataValueField = "CategoryID";
          lstParentCategory.DataBind();
          lstParentCategory.Items.Add
➥(new System.Web.UI.WebControls.ListItem("No Parent",System.Guid.Empty.
➥ToString())));
          lstParentCategory.SelectedIndex = lstParentCategory.Items.Count - 1;
        }
      }
    }

    protected void Page_Init(object sender, EventArgs e){
        InitializeComponent();
    }

    private void InitializeComponent() {
      CategoryDataGrid.CancelCommand += new
➥System.Web.UI.WebControls.DataGridCommandEventHandler (this.Cancel);
      CategoryDataGrid.EditCommand += new
➥System.Web.UI.WebControls.DataGridCommandEventHandler (this.Edit);
      CategoryDataGrid.UpdateCommand += new
➥System.Web.UI.WebControls.DataGridCommandEventHandler (this.Update);
      this.Load += new System.EventHandler (this.Page_Load);
    }

  protected void LoadCatalog(){
    MyGolfGearDP dp = new MyGolfGearDP();
    catds = new CatalogDS();
      dp.FillCatalog(catds);
        }

    protected void UpdateCatalog(object sender, EventArgs e){
        MyGolfGearDP dp = new MyGolfGearDP();
      if( catds.HasChanges() ){
          try{
              dp.UpdateCatalog((CatalogDS)catds.GetChanges());
```

LISTING 5.7   Continued

```
                Message.InnerHtml = "SQL Updated Successfully";
            }catch(System.Exception ex){
                Message.InnerHtml = "ERROR: Could not Update SQL";
                Message.InnerHtml += "<br />" + ex.ToString();
                Message.Style["color"] = "red";
            }
        }else{
            Message.InnerHtml = "SQL is up-to-date";
        }
        catds.AcceptChanges();
        RebindDataGrid();
    }

    protected void RebindDataGrid(){
        CategoryDataGrid.DataSource = catds.Category.DefaultView;
        CategoryDataGrid.DataBind();
        lstParentCategory.DataBind();
    }

    public void btnReset_OnClick(Object sender, EventArgs e){
        this.txtCategoryName.Text = "";
        this.lstParentCategory.SelectedIndex = 0;
        this.txtDescription.Value = "";
        this.txtDisplaySeq.Text = "";
        this.txtDisplay.Text = "";
    }

    public void btnAdd_OnClick(Object sender, EventArgs e){
        if ( IsValid ){
          try{
            System.Guid i;
                //Determine if a parent category was selected
            i = new System.Guid
➥ ((lstParentCategory.Items[lstParentCategory.SelectedIndex].Value));
            //Add new category row
            CatalogDS.CategoryRow CatRow = catds.Category.NewCategoryRow();
            CatRow.CategoryID = System.Guid.NewGuid();
                CatRow.Name = this.txtCategoryName.Text;
            CatRow.ParentCategoryID = i;
            CatRow.Description = this.txtDescription.Value;
            CatRow.DisplaySeq = Convert.ToInt16(this.txtDisplaySeq.Text);
            CatRow.Display = Convert.ToInt16(this.txtDisplay.Text);

            catds.Category.AddCategoryRow(CatRow);
```

5

THE PRODUCT CATALOG

LISTING 5.7 Continued

```
            RebindDataGrid();

            DataView Source = catds.Category.DefaultView;

            Source.Sort = "DisplaySeq";
            //Populate Category list box
            lstParentCategory.DataSource = Source;
            lstParentCategory.DataTextField = "Name";
            lstParentCategory.DataValueField = "CategoryID";
            lstParentCategory.DataBind();
            lstParentCategory.Items.Add(new
➡System.Web.UI.WebControls.ListItem
➡ ("No Parent",System.Guid.Empty.ToString()));
            lstParentCategory.SelectedIndex = lstParentCategory.Items.Count - 1;

            //Display add successful message
            Message.InnerHtml = "<b>" + this.txtCategoryName.Text +
➡" category successfully added.</b>";
            this.txtCategoryName.Text = "";
            this.lstParentCategory.SelectedIndex = 0;
            this.txtDescription.Value = "";
            this.txtDisplaySeq.Text = "";
            this.txtDisplay.Text = "";

        }catch( System.Exception ex ){
            Message.InnerHtml = "ERROR: Could not insert record,
➡please ensure the fields are correctly filled out";
                Message.InnerHtml += "<br>" + ex.ToString();
            Message.Style["color"] = "red";
        }
      }
    }

    public void Edit(Object sender, DataGridCommandEventArgs e){
        System.Guid CategoryId = (System.Guid)
➡CategoryDataGrid.DataKeys[e.Item.ItemIndex];
        DataRow r = catds.Category.FindByCategoryID(CategoryId);

        this.txtCategoryName.Text = r[1].ToString();
        string ParentCatId = r[2].ToString();
        int i = 0;

        foreach (ListItem li in lstParentCategory.Items){
            if (li.Value == ParentCatId){
```

LISTING 5.7   Continued

```
          lstParentCategory.SelectedIndex = i;
          break;
      }
      i++;
    }

    if (r[3].ToString() == "")
      this.txtDescription.Value = "";
    else
      this.txtDescription.Value = r[3].ToString();
    this.txtDisplaySeq.Text = r[4].ToString();
    this.txtDisplay.Text = r[5].ToString();
    CategoryDataGrid.EditItemIndex = e.Item.ItemIndex;
      RebindDataGrid();
  }

  public void Delete(Object sender, DataGridCommandEventArgs e){
    try{
      System.Guid CategoryId = (System.Guid)CategoryDataGrid.DataKeys[e.
➥Item.ItemIndex];
      Trace.Write("MyTrace","CategoryID= " + CategoryId);
      CatalogDS.CategoryRow CatRow = catds.Category.FindByCategoryID
➥ (CategoryId);
      String CatName = CatRow.Name;

      CatRow.Delete();

      RebindDataGrid();

      Message.InnerHtml = "<b>" + CatName + "
➥category successfully deleted.</b>";
    }catch{
        Message.InnerHtml = "ERROR: Could not delete record.";
        Message.Style["color"] = "red";
    }
  }

  public void Cancel(Object sender, DataGridCommandEventArgs e){
    this.txtCategoryName.Text = "";
    this.lstParentCategory.SelectedIndex = 0;
    this.txtDescription.Value = "";
    this.txtDisplaySeq.Text = "";
    this.txtDisplay.Text = "";
    CategoryDataGrid.EditItemIndex = -1;
```

5

THE PRODUCT CATALOG

LISTING 5.7 Continued

```
    RebindDataGrid();
  }

  public void UpdateDataGrid(Object sender, DataGridCommandEventArgs e){
    if ( IsValid ){
      System.Guid CategoryId =
➡ (System.Guid)CategoryDataGrid.DataKeys[e.Item.ItemIndex];
      CatalogDS.CategoryRow CatRow =
➡catds.Category.FindByCategoryID(CategoryId);

      CatRow.Name = this.txtCategoryName.Text;
      int i = lstParentCategory.SelectedIndex;

      CatRow.ParentCategoryID = new
➡System.Guid((lstParentCategory.Items[i].Value));
      CatRow.Description = this.txtDescription.Value;
      CatRow.DisplaySeq = Convert.ToInt16(this.txtDisplaySeq.Text);
      CatRow.Display = Convert.ToInt16(this.txtDisplay.Text);
      //Update SQL
      Trace.Write("MyTrace","Cat Id = " + CatRow.CategoryID);

        RebindDataGrid();

      Message.InnerHtml = "<b>" + CatRow.Name + "
➡category updated successfully.</b>";

      Cancel(sender, e);
    }
  }
 }
}
}
```

The code behind class inherits from System.Web.UI.Page and is, in turn, inherited by the .aspx page.

The LoadCatalog() method creates an instance of the strongly typed dataset named CatalogDS and a MyGolfGearDP object to fill the CatalogDS object. All the catalog data is loaded into the strongly typed dataset here. As you will see later, this dataset is used to bind to ASP.NET Web controls.

This same dataset is used throughout the rest of the class to update, delete, and add categories. It is also used to assign parent-child relationships to categories.

If changes have been made to CatalogDS, the UpdateCatalog() method passes the dataset to the MyGolfGearDP object, which handles the update. This method is shown on lines 97–113.

The Delete() method removes rows from CatalogDS by passing it to an instance of the MyGolfGear class.

The next method shown, UpdateDatagrid(), updates the DataGrid control shown in the next section. It uses the category ID to retrieve the specific data row that needs to be updated.

The CategoryAdmin.aspx ASP.NET page gathers all the data elements used in CategoryAdmin.aspx.cs. The code for this page is shown in Listing 5.8.

LISTING 5.8   *CategoryAdmin.aspx*

```
<%@ Page language="c#" Codebehind="CategoryAdmin.aspx.cs" Trace="true"
➥Debug="true" AutoEventWireup="false"
➥Inherits="MyGolfGear.CategoryAdmin" %>
<%@ Register TagPrefix="MyGolfGear" TagName="LeftNav"
➥Src="../UserControls/LeftNav.ascx" %>
<%@ Register TagPrefix="MyGolfGear" TagName="Header"
➥Src="../UserControls/Header.ascx" %>
<%@ Register TagPrefix="MyGolfGear" TagName="Footer"
➥Src="../UserControls/Footer.ascx" %>
<%@ Register TagPrefix="MyGolfGear" TagName="SpecialsContent"
➥Src="../UserControls/SpecialsContent.ascx" %>
<html>
<head>
<title>
MyGolfGear.net -- Manage Product Categories
</title>
<link REL="stylesheet" TYPE="text/css" HREF="../css_mygolfgear.css">
</head>
<body bgcolor="#FFFFFF" link="#336699" text="#000000" alink="#336699">
<!--START MAIN TABLE-->
<div align="center">
<center>
<table border="0" width="790" cellspacing="0" cellpadding="0">
<tr>
<td width="2" bgcolor="#808080">
<img border="0" src="../images/spacer_clear.gif" width="2" height="2">
</td>
<td width="786" bgcolor="#808080">
<img border="0" src="../images/spacer_clear.gif" width="786" height="2">
</td>
<td width="2" bgcolor="#808080">
```

LISTING 5.8   Continued

```
<img border="0" src="../images/spacer_clear.gif" width="2" height="2">
</td>
</tr>
<tr>
<td width="2" bgcolor="#808080" valign="top">
</td>
<td width="786" valign="top">
<table border="0" width="786" cellspacing="0" cellpadding="0">
<tr>
<td width="172" valign="top">
<!--START LEFT COLUMN CONTENT MASTR TABLE-->
<MyGolfGear:LeftNav id=LeftNav runat="server" NAME="LeftNav" />
<!--END LEFT COLUMN CONTENT-->
<!--</center>
-->
</td>
<td width="2" valign="top" bgcolor="#808080">
</td>
<td width="616" valign="top" align=left>
<!-- Insert Top Nav -->
<MyGolfGear:Header id=Header runat="server" />
</MyGolfGear:Header>
<!--START MAIN CONTENT-->
<table border="0" width="100%" cellspacing="0" cellpadding="5">
<tr>
<td width="100%" valign="top">
<form method="post" runat="server" ID="Form1">
<font color="#336699"><B>Category Manager</B></font>
<BR>
<table style="background-color:white; font: 10pt verdana;border-width:1;
➥border-style:solid;border-color:black;" cellspacing=5>
<tr>
<td valign=top>
<asp:DataGrid id=CategoryDataGrid BorderColor="black" BorderWidth="1"
➥CellPadding="3" Font-Name="Verdana" Font-Size="8pt"
➥OnEditCommand="Edit" OnDeleteCommand="Delete" OnCancelCommand="Cancel"
➥ datakeyfield="CategoryID" AutoGenerateColumns="false" runat="server"
➥AlternatingItemStyle-BackColor="Beige" FooterStyle-BackColor="Silver"
➥FooterStyle-ForeColor="White" ItemStyle-BackColor="White"
➥EditItemStyle-BackColor="yellow" HeaderStyle-BackColor="DarkGreen"
➥HeaderStyle-Font-Bold="True" HeaderStyle-ForeColor="Beige">
<Columns>
<ASP:EditCommandColumn HeaderText="Action" EditText="Edit" CancelText="Cancel"
➥ UpdateText="Update" ItemStyle-Wrap="false" HeaderStyle-Wrap="false" />
```

LISTING 5.8   Continued

```
<ASP:TemplateColumn HeaderText="Name">
    <ItemTemplate>
        <%# DataBinder.Eval(Container.DataItem, "Name") %>
    </ItemTemplate>
</ASP:TemplateColumn>
<asp:ButtonColumn HeaderText="Delete" Text="Delete" CommandName="Delete" />
</Columns>
</asp:DataGrid>
</td>
</td>
<td>
<span id="Message" EnableViewState="false" style="font: arial 11pt;"
➡runat="server" />
<p>
<table style="background-color:beige; font: 10pt verdana;border-width:1;border
➡-style:solid;border-color:black;" cellspacing=5>
<tr>
<td>
<ASP:LINKBUTTON id=LinkButton1 onclick=btnAdd_OnClick runat="server" Text="Add
➡ Category" NAME="LinkButton1" />
 |
</td>
<td align=left>
<ASP:LINKBUTTON id=btnReset onclick=btnReset_OnClick runat="server"
➡Text="Reset Fields" />
</td>
</tr>
<tr>
<td align=right valign=top>
<b>
<asp:label id=Label1 runat="server">
Category Name:
</asp:label>
</b>
</td>
<td valign=top>
<asp:textbox id=txtCategoryName runat="server" NAME="txtCategoryName" />
</td>
</tr>
<tr>
<td colspan=2>
<asp:RequiredFieldValidator id="RequiredFieldValidator1" ControlToValidate=
➡"txtCategoryName" Display="Static" Width="100%" runat="server"
➡NAME="RequiredFieldValidator1">
```

5

THE PRODUCT
CATALOG

LISTING 5.8   Continued

```
<font color="red">* Category Name</font>
</asp:RequiredFieldValidator>
</td>
</tr>
<tr>
<td align=right valign=top>
<b>
<asp:label id=Label3 runat="server">
Parent Category:
</asp:label>
</b>
</td>
<td valign=top colspan=2>
<asp:dropdownlist id=lstParentCategory runat="server"
➥NAME="lstParentCategory">
</asp:dropdownlist>
</td>
</tr>
<tr>
<td align=right valign=top>
<b>
<asp:label id=Label4 runat="server">
Description:
</asp:label>
</b>
</td>
<td valign=top colspan=2>
<textarea id="txtDescription" cols=20 rows=3 runat="server"
➥NAME="txtDescription">
</textarea>
</td>
</tr>
<tr>
<td align=right valign=top>
<b>
<asp:label id=Label5 runat="server">
Display Seq:
</asp:label>
</b>
</td>
<td valign=top>
<asp:textbox id="txtDisplaySeq" runat="server" NAME="txtDisplaySeq">
</asp:textbox>
</td>
</tr>
```

LISTING 5.8   Continued

```
<tr>
<td colspan=2>
<asp:CompareValidator id="CompareValidator1" runat="server"
➥ControlToValidate="txtDisplaySeq" ValueToCompare="0"
➥Type="Double" Operator="GreaterThan" ErrorMessage
➥="Must be greater than zero." ForeColor="Red" NAME=
➥"CompareValidator1" />
</td>
</tr>
<tr>
<td align=right valign=top>
<b>
<asp:label id=Label2 runat="server">
Display:
</asp:label>
</b>
</td>
<td valign=top>
<asp:textbox id=txtDisplay runat="server">
</asp:textbox>
</td>
</tr>
<tr>
<td colspan=2>
<asp:RangeValidator id="rangeVal" Type="Integer" ControlToValidate=
➥"txtDisplay" MinimumValue="0" MaximumValue="1" runat="server"
➥ErrorMessage="(1) to show
category and (0) to hide." />
</td>
</tr>
<tr>
<td colspan=2 align=center>
<font color=red><b>* Indicates required field</b></font>
</td>
</tr>
</table>
</td>
</tr>
</table>
<!-- END OF MAIN CONTENT -->
</td>
</tr>
<tr align = center>
<td>
```

LISTING 5.8 Continued

```
<asp:LinkButton Text="Update SQL" OnClick=UpdateCatalog Runat=server
➡ID="Linkbutton2" NAME="Linkbutton2" />
</td>
</tr>
</form>
</table>
<!--END MAIN CONTENT-->
<p>
 
</td>
</tr>
<!-- Insert Footer -->
<MyGolfGear:Footer id=Footer runat="server" />
</MyGolfGear:Footer>
</table>
</div>
<!--END MASTER TABLE-->
<p />
</body>
</html>
```

The CategoryAdmin.aspx page uses ASP server controls and .ascx user controls to create the physical layout of the page. Four .ascx user controls are used throughout the MyGolfGear.NET site: LeftNav.ascx, Header.ascx, Footer.ascx, and SpecialContent.ascx. When I discuss building the home page in Chapter 6, "Using ASP.NET to Display the Simple Catalog," I will cover the creation of these ASP.NET files.

This listing shows the creation of the CategoryAdmin data grid, which uses ADO.NET data binding to display the category names as well as provide links for editing and deleting each category.

To add new or edit existing category information, the CategoryAdmin.aspx file uses a simple form with ASP.NET Label and RequiredFieldValidator server controls. It also uses LinkButton, DropDownList, TextArea, and TextBox controls. This is shown in the code following the CategoryAdmin data grid.

ProductAdmin.aspx

The Product Manager allows for adding, updating, and deleting of products. It also allows an administrator to assign products to categories. For instance, an administrator could assign a particular golf shoe to the Shoes category. Figure 5.3 shows the MyGolfGear.NET Product Manager.

FIGURE 5.3

MyGolfGear.NET Product Manager.

Like the Category Manager, the Product Manager is made up of an ASP.NET page with a code behind class that uses the `MyGolfGearDP` and `CatalogDS` classes to manipulate the data. The code behind file named `ProductAdmin.aspx.cs` is shown in Listing 5.9.

LISTING 5.9   *ProductAdmin.aspx.cs*

```
namespace MyGolfGear
{
    using System;
    using System.Collections;
    using System.ComponentModel;
    using System.Data;
    using System.Drawing;
    using System.Web;
    using System.Web.SessionState;
    using System.Web.UI;
    using System.Web.UI.WebControls;
    using System.Web.UI.HtmlControls;
    using MyGolfGear.DataAccess;

    public class ProductAdmin : System.Web.UI.Page
    {
        protected System.Web.UI.WebControls.DropDownList lstProduct;
        protected System.Web.UI.WebControls.DropDownList lstProductParent;
        protected System.Web.UI.WebControls.Label lblTemp;
        protected System.Web.UI.WebControls.TextBox ProductNum;
        protected System.Web.UI.WebControls.TextBox ProductName;
```

5

THE PRODUCT
CATALOG

LISTING 5.9   Continued

```
protected System.Web.UI.WebControls.TextBox ShortDesc;
protected System.Web.UI.WebControls.TextBox LongDesc;
protected System.Web.UI.WebControls.TextBox DisplaySeq;
protected System.Web.UI.WebControls.CheckBox Display;
protected System.Web.UI.WebControls.TextBox ImageName;
protected CatalogDS catds;

public ProductAdmin()
{
    Page.Init += new System.EventHandler(Page_Init);
}

protected void Page_Load(object sender, System.EventArgs e)
{
    catds = (CatalogDS)Session["dsCategoryList"];
    if (catds == null)
    {
        LoadCatalog();
        Session["dsProductList"] = catds;
    }

    if( !IsPostBack ){
        ReBind();
    }else{
        if( catds.HasChanges() ){
            ReBind();
        }
    }
}

protected void ReBind(){
    DataView Source = catds.Product.DefaultView;
    Source.Sort = "DisplaySeq";
    lstProduct.DataSource = Source;
    lstProduct.DataTextField = "Name";
    lstProduct.DataValueField = "ProductID";
    lstProduct.DataBind();

    lstProductParent.DataSource = Source;
    lstProductParent.DataTextField = "Name";
    lstProductParent.DataValueField = "ProductID";
    lstProductParent.DataBind();

    lstProductParent.Items.Add(new ListItem("No Parent Product" ,
➥System.Guid.Empty.ToString()));
```

LISTING 5.9 Continued

```
            ViewItem();
        }

        protected void LoadCatalog(){
            MyGolfGearDP dp = new MyGolfGearDP();
            catds = new CatalogDS();
            dp.FillCatalog(catds);
        }

        protected void Page_Init(object sender, EventArgs e){
            InitializeComponent();
        }

        public void lstProduct_OnSelectedIndexChanged
➥ ( object sender, EventArgs e ){
            ViewItem();
        }

        public void btnAdd_OnClick( object sender, EventArgs e ){
        }

        public void btnUpdate_OnClick( object sender, EventArgs e ){
        }

        public void btnDelete_OnClick( object sender, EventArgs e ){
CatalogDS.ProductRow r = catds.Product.FindByProductID(new
System.Guid(lstProduct.Items[lstProduct.SelectedIndex].Value));
            r.Delete();
            ReBind();
        }

        public void btnUpdateSQL_OnClick( object sender, EventArgs e ){
        }

        public void ViewItem(){
            int i = 0;

            DataRow r = catds.Product.FindByProductID(new
System.Guid(lstProduct.Items[lstProduct.SelectedIndex].Value));
            if( r["ParentProductID"].ToString() !=
➥System.Guid.Empty.ToString() ){
                foreach (ListItem li in lstProductParent.Items){
                    if (li.Value == r["ParentProductID"].ToString()){
                        lstProductParent.SelectedIndex = i;
```

5

LISTING 5.9 Continued

```
                        break;
                    }
                    i++;
                }
            }
            else{
                foreach (ListItem li in lstProductParent.Items){
                    if (li.Text == "No Parent Product"){
                        lstProductParent.SelectedIndex = i;
                        break;
                    }
                    i++;
                }
            }
            ProductNum.Text = r["ProductNum"].ToString();
            ProductName.Text = r["Name"].ToString();
            ShortDesc.Text = r["ShortDescription"].ToString();
            LongDesc.Text = r["LongDescription"].ToString();
            DisplaySeq.Text = r["DisplaySeq"].ToString();
            Display.Checked = (r["Display"].ToString() == "1") ? true : false;
            ImageName.Text = r["ImageName"].ToString();
        }

    private void InitializeComponent(){
      this.Load += new System.EventHandler(this.Page_Load);
    }
    }
}
```

The `ProductAdmin.aspx.cs` class is built in much the same way as the `CategoryAdmin.aspx.cs` class is. It contains a function for deleting rows from `CatalogDS`, a function for updating a given `CatalogDS` row, a function for adding a new row to `CatalogDS` on lines, and an `UpdateSql` function that actually persists changes made to `CatalogDS` to the database.

The display and editing of the product administration data is handled via the ASP.NET page named `ProductAdmin.aspx`. This page is shown in Listing 5.10.

LISTING 5.10 *ProductAdmin.aspx*

```
<%@ Page language="c#" Src="ProductAdmin.aspx.cs" Trace="true" Debug="true"
➥AutoEventWireup="false" Inherits="MyGolfGear.ProductAdmin"  %>
<%@ Register TagPrefix="MyGolfGear" TagName="LeftNav"
➥Src="../UserControls/LeftNav.ascx" %>
```

LISTING 5.10 Continued

```
<%@ Register TagPrefix="MyGolfGear" TagName="Header"
➥Src="../UserControls/Header.ascx" %>
<%@ Register TagPrefix="MyGolfGear" TagName="Footer"
➥Src="../UserControls/Footer.ascx" %>
<%@ Register TagPrefix="MyGolfGear" TagName="SpecialsContent"
➥Src="../UserControls/SpecialsContent.ascx" %>
<html>
<head>
<title>
MyGolfGear.net -- Manage Products
</title>
<link REL="stylesheet" TYPE="text/css" HREF="../css_mygolfgear.css">
</head>
<body bgcolor="#FFFFFF" link="#336699" text="#000000" alink="#336699">
<!--START MAIN TABLE-->
<div align="center">
<center>
<table border="0" width="790" cellspacing="0" cellpadding="0">
<tr>
<td width="2" bgcolor="#808080">
<img border="0" src="../images/spacer_clear.gif" width="2" height="2">
</td>
<td width="786" bgcolor="#808080">
<img border="0" src="../images/spacer_clear.gif" width="786" height="2">
</td>
<td width="2" bgcolor="#808080">
<img border="0" src="../images/spacer_clear.gif" width="2" height="2">
</td>
</tr>
<tr>
<td width="2" bgcolor="#808080" valign="top">
</td>
<td width="786" valign="top">
<table border="0" width="786" cellspacing="0" cellpadding="0">
<tr>
<td width="172" valign="top">
<!--START LEFT COLUMN CONTENT MASTR TABLE-->
<MyGolfGear:LeftNav id=LeftNav runat="server" NAME="LeftNav" />
<!--END LEFT COLUMN CONTENT-->
<!--</center>
-->
</td>
<td width="2" valign="top" bgcolor="#808080">
</td>
```

LISTING 5.10   Continued

```
<td width="616" valign="top" align=left>
<!-- Insert Top Nav -->
<MyGolfGear:Header id=Header runat="server" />
</MyGolfGear:Header>
<!--START MAIN CONTENT-->
<table border="0" width="100%" cellspacing="0" cellpadding="5">
<tr>
<td width="100%" valign="top">
<form method="post" runat="server" ID="Form1">
<font color="#336699"><B>Product Manager</B></font>
<BR>
<table style="background-color:white; font: 10pt verdana;border-width:1;
➥border-style:solid;border-color:black;" cellspacing=5>
<tr>
<td valign=top>
<asp:Label ID=lblTemp Runat=server />
<table border=0>
<tr>
<td>
  Product:
</td>
<td colspan=3>
  <asp:DropDownList Width=100% AutoPostBack=True ID=lstProduct
OnSelectedIndexChanged=lstProduct_OnSelectedIndexChanged runat=server />
</td>
</tr>
<tr>
<td>
  Parent Product:
</td>
<td colspan=3>
  <asp:DropDownList Width=100% ID=lstProductParent Runat=server />
</td>
</tr>
<tr>
<td>
  Number:
</td>
<td>
  <asp:TextBox ID=ProductNum Runat=server />
</td>
<td>
  Name:
</td>
```

LISTING 5.10   Continued

```
<td>
  <asp:TextBox ID=ProductName Runat=server />
</td>
</tr>
<tr>
<td>
  Short Description:
</td>
<td colspan=3>
  <asp:TextBox ID=ShortDesc Runat=server Width=100% />
</td>
</tr>
<tr>
<td>
  Long Description:
</td>
<td colspan=3>
  <asp:TextBox TextMode=MultiLine Rows=6 ID=LongDesc Runat=server Width=100% />
</td>
</tr>
<tr>
<td>
  Image Name:
</td>
<td colspan=3>
  <asp:TextBox ID=ImageName Runat=server Width=100% />
</td>
</tr>
<tr>
<td>
  Display Seq:
</td>
<td>
  <asp:TextBox ID=DisplaySeq Runat=server />
</td>
<td>
  Display:
</td>
<td>
  <asp:CheckBox ID=Display Runat=server />
</td>
</tr>
<tr>
<td colspan=3>
```

LISTING 5.10 Continued

```
  <asp:LinkButton Text="Add" OnClick=btnAdd_OnClick ID=btnAdd Runat=server />
  |
  <asp:LinkButton Text="Update" OnClick=btnUpdate_OnClick ID=btnUpdate
➥Runat=server />
  |
  <asp:LinkButton Text="Delete" OnClick=btnDelete_OnClick ID=btnDelete
➥Runat=server />
</td>
<td>
  <asp:LinkButton Text="Update SQL" OnClick=btnUpdateSQL_OnClick
➥ID=btnUpdateSQL
➥Runat=server />
</td>
</tr>
</table>
</td>
</td>
<td>
<span id="Message" EnableViewState="false" style="font: arial 11pt;"
➥runat="server" />
<p>
</td>
</tr>
</table>
<!-- END OF MAIN CONTENT -->
</td>
</tr>
</form>
</table>
<!--END MAIN CONTENT-->
<p>
 
</td>
</tr>
<!-- Insert Footer -->
<MyGolfGear:Footer id=Footer runat="server" />
</table>
</div>
<!--END MASTER TABLE-->
<p />
</body>
</html>
```

The result of all this code is similar to the page shown in Figure 5.4.

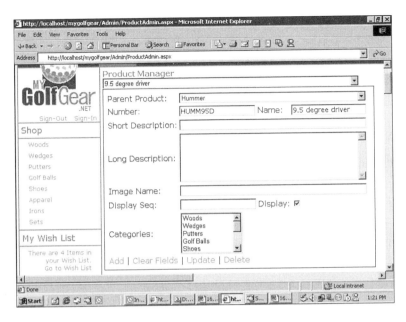

FIGURE 5.4
The Product Administration page.

ADO.NET data binding is used to bind product names to two drop-down list controls, four text boxes, one text area, one check box control, and two multi-selectable list box controls.

LinkButton server controls are used to fire the add, update, delete, and update SQL functionality discussed in the section on ProductAdmin.aspx.cs.

Options Manager

The Options Manager allows administrators to add, update, or delete product options. This functionality is useful in situations in which the same product comes in multiple configurations. For instance, a golf club might be available in a left-handed model or with different size heads.

The functionality of the Options Manager is similar to that of the Category and Product Managers. Although the database and components will support an Options Manager, we chose not to implement one with this version of MyGolfGear.NET.

Summary

This chapter discussed administering the product catalog using ASP.NET. Specifically, it covered the creation of the CatalogDS.xsd file, the generation of the CatalogDS class from the

5

THE PRODUCT
CATALOG

xsd using the XML Schema Definition Tool, as well as the `Admin.aspx`, `Category.aspx`, `Product.aspx`, `Option.aspx`, and other `.ascx` files.

The next chapter will cover using ASP.NET to display the product catalog. Specifically, it will cover creating the components and page elements necessary to view and navigate MyGolfGear.NET's product catalog.

Self Instruction

Based on what you've read in this chapter, try the following:

- Create your own `Catalog.xsd` file. Be sure to include the following lines at the beginning of the file:

```
<?xml version="1.0" encoding="utf-8" ?>
<xsd:schema id="CatalogDS" targetNamespace="http://tempuri.org/XMLSchema.xsd"
xmlns="http://tempuri.org/XMLSchema.xsd"
xmlns:xsd="http://www.w3.org/2000/10/XMLSchema"
xmlns:msdata="urn:schemas-microsoft-com:xml-msdata">
```

- Create an Options Manager console using the techniques discussed in this chapter. Follow the category and product administration implementation as a guide.

Using ASP.NET to Display the Simple Catalog

IN THIS CHAPTER

Objectives

- Learn how the MyGolfGear.NET product catalog is displayed

- Understand the role the CatalogDS class plays

- Discover how categories of products and product details are displayed on MyGolfGear.NET

The ability to browse an e-Commerce site's goods and services is one of the most basic requirements for today's business-to-consumer (B2C) Web sites. In this chapter, I will show how we used ADO.NET and ASP.NET to develop the bare bones of the online store for MyGolfGear.NET. In subsequent chapters, we will describe some more advanced features that are common in some of the better B2C e-Commerce sites.

Although most of the functionality we are implementing in this chapter is pretty basic, we will be taking advantage of some of the advanced ASP.NET data binding features, such as templates and repeater controls. This chapter will show how we used these features to create the category list menu, create the product list for each category, create a product detail page, and create the simple home page.

Creating the Category List

The most logical way to navigate a product catalog is to start with categories and drill down into product lists and then into product details. For MyGolfGear.NET, we use a category list as the highest level of navigation. This list of categories creates a menu with which users can browse through the categories. Figure 6.1 shows the home page. Notice the menu with the category list on the left side of the page.

The creation of the category list is made possible by three major elements:

- `CatalogDS.cs`—The strongly typed dataset that was covered in the preceding chapter
- `LeftNav.ascx.cs`—The code behind class for the `LeftNav` user control
- `LeftNav.ascx`—The user control that handles the layout and display of the category menu

Using the `CatalogDS` Class to Display the Simple Catalog

The strongly typed dataset named `CatalogDS`, which we covered in Chapter 5, "Using ASP.NET to Administer the Product Catalog," is the most important part of creating the category menu. I will, however, cover the portions of the `CatalogDS` dataset that are significant to the creation of the category menu.

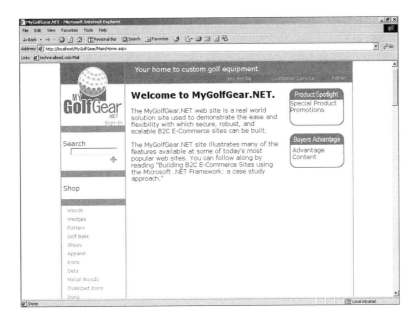

FIGURE 6.1

The category menu list.

A dataset contains one or more `DataTable` objects that hold a recordset-like in-memory view of data. The data that is important for creating the category menu is part of the strongly typed dataset and can be referenced from `CatalogDS` via the `Category` property like this:

```
DataTable categories = myCatalogDS.Category;
```

This technique is significant because it allows us to bind the category information to a data list, which will be covered in the section titled "`LeftNav.ascx`."

So, the real question is, how does the `Category` datatable get created within `CatalogDS`? To answer this question, we can take another look at the code created for `CatalogDS`. Before we do that, however, I think it's important to discuss, at a high level, how the `Category` datatable code fits into `CatalogDS`.

`CatalogDS` contains a `Category` property that returns a reference to an object of type `CategoryDataTable` that is defined within the `CatalogDS` definition. The `CategoryDataTable` class inherits from the base class named `DataTable` and the interface `IEnumerable`. This means that the object reference returned by the `CatalogDS` `Category` property has all the same methods and properties as a datatable, it implements all necessary methods and properties to satisfy the requirements to be an `IEnumerable` type, and it implements some of its own properties and methods.

Because we created `CatalogDS` by using a wizard, going through every line of code would have limited value at best. I have included it here for completeness, however. Listing 6.1 shows the definition of the `CategoryDataTable` class.

Using `xsd.exe`

Although we have used `xsd.exe` to generate `DataSet` classes from an XSD schema file, xsd.exe performs other operations as well.

The XML Schema Definition tool (`xsd.exe`) creates strongly typed dataset classes, as well as other XML schema or CLR classes. It uses XDR, XML, XSD, or other classes in a runtime assembly to do so.

`xsd.exe` can generate an XML schema from an XML Data-Reduced (XDR) schema file. The XDR is an older XML-based schema format. `xsd.exe` can also generate XSD files from an XML file.

Besides creating `DataSet` classes, xsd.exe can also generate CLR classes from an XSD file. These classes can be used with the `XMLSerializer` class to read and write XML that follows the same schema.

Additionally, `xsd.exe` can be used to generate XSD files from a class, struct, or other type.

The XML schemas that can be manipulated by `xsd.exe` must adhere to the W3C XML Schema Definition (XSD) proposal, which you can find at `http://w3c.org`.

LISTING 6.1   The `CategoryDataTable` Class

```csharp
public class CategoryDataTable : DataTable, System.Collections.IEnumerable {

        private DataColumn columnCategoryID;
        private DataColumn columnName;
        private DataColumn columnParentCategoryID;
        private DataColumn columnDescription;
        private DataColumn columnDisplaySeq;
        private DataColumn columnDisplay;

        internal CategoryDataTable() :
                base("Category") {
            this.InitClass();
        }

        [System.ComponentModel.Browsable(false)]
        public int Count {
            get {
```

Using ASP.NET to Display the Simple Catalog

CHAPTER 6

117

6

USING ASP.NET
TO DISPLAY THE
SIMPLE CATALOG

LISTING 6.1 Continued

```
            return this.Rows.Count;
        }
    }

    internal DataColumn CategoryIDColumn {
        get {
            return this.columnCategoryID;
        }
    }

    internal DataColumn NameColumn {
        get {
            return this.columnName;
        }
    }

    internal DataColumn ParentCategoryIDColumn {
        get {
            return this.columnParentCategoryID;
        }
    }

    internal DataColumn DescriptionColumn {
        get {
            return this.columnDescription;
        }
    }

    internal DataColumn DisplaySeqColumn {
        get {
            return this.columnDisplaySeq;
        }
    }

    internal DataColumn DisplayColumn {
        get {
            return this.columnDisplay;
        }
    }

    public CategoryRow this[int index] {
        get {
            return ((CategoryRow)(this.Rows[index]));
        }
    }
```

LISTING 6.1   Continued

```
        public event CategoryRowChangeEventHandler CategoryRowChanged;

        public event CategoryRowChangeEventHandler CategoryRowChanging;

        public event CategoryRowChangeEventHandler CategoryRowDeleted;

        public event CategoryRowChangeEventHandler CategoryRowDeleting;

        public void AddCategoryRow(CategoryRow row) {
            this.Rows.Add(row);
        }

        public CategoryRow AddCategoryRow(System.Guid CategoryID,
➼string Name, System.Guid ParentCategoryID, string Description, short
➼DisplaySeq, short Display) {
            CategoryRow rowCategoryRow = ((CategoryRow)(this.NewRow()));
            rowCategoryRow.ItemArray = new Object[] {CategoryID,
                Name,
                ParentCategoryID,
                Description,
                DisplaySeq,
                Display};
            this.Rows.Add(rowCategoryRow);
            return rowCategoryRow;
        }

        public CategoryRow FindByCategoryID(System.Guid CategoryID) {
            return ((CategoryRow)(this.Rows.Find(new Object[]
➼{CategoryID})));
        }

        public System.Collections.IEnumerator GetEnumerator() {
            return this.Rows.GetEnumerator();
        }

        private void InitClass() {
            this.columnCategoryID = new DataColumn("CategoryID",
➼typeof(System.Guid), "", System.Data.MappingType.Element);
            this.columnCategoryID.AllowDBNull = false;
            this.columnCategoryID.Unique = true;
            this.Columns.Add(this.columnCategoryID);
            this.columnName = new DataColumn("Name", typeof(string), "",
➼System.Data.MappingType.Element);
```

LISTING 6.1   Continued

```
            this.Columns.Add(this.columnName);
            this.columnParentCategoryID = new DataColumn(
➥"ParentCategoryID", typeof(System.Guid), "",
➥System.Data.MappingType.Element);
            this.Columns.Add(this.columnParentCategoryID);
            this.columnDescription = new DataColumn("Description",
➥typeof(string), "", System.Data.MappingType.Element);
            this.Columns.Add(this.columnDescription);
            this.columnDisplaySeq = new DataColumn("DisplaySeq",
➥typeof(short), "", System.Data.MappingType.Element);
            this.Columns.Add(this.columnDisplaySeq);
            this.columnDisplay = new DataColumn("Display", typeof(short),
➥"", System.Data.MappingType.Element);
            this.Columns.Add(this.columnDisplay);
            this.PrimaryKey = new DataColumn[] {this.columnCategoryID};
        }

        public CategoryRow NewCategoryRow() {
            return ((CategoryRow)(this.NewRow()));
        }

        protected override DataRow NewRowFromBuilder
➥ (DataRowBuilder builder) {
            // We need to ensure that all Rows in the tables
➥are typed rows.
            // Table calls newRow whenever it needs to create a row.
            // So the following conditions are covered by Row newRow(
➥Record record)
            // * Cursor calls table.addRecord(record)
            // * table.addRow(object[] values) calls newRow(record)
            return new CategoryRow(builder);
        }

        protected override System.Type GetRowType() {
            return typeof(CategoryRow);
        }

        protected override void OnRowChanged(DataRowChangeEventArgs e) {
            base.OnRowChanged(e);
            if ((this.CategoryRowChanged != null)) {
                this.CategoryRowChanged(this, new CategoryRowChangeEvent
➥ (((CategoryRow)(e.Row)), e.Action));
            }
        }
```

LISTING 6.1   Continued

```
            protected override void OnRowChanging(DataRowChangeEventArgs e) {
                base.OnRowChanging(e);
                if ((this.CategoryRowChanging != null)) {
                    this.CategoryRowChanging(this, new CategoryRowChangeEvent
➡ (((CategoryRow)(e.Row)), e.Action));
                }
            }

            protected override void OnRowDeleted(DataRowChangeEventArgs e) {
                base.OnRowDeleted(e);
                if ((this.CategoryRowDeleted != null)) {
                    this.CategoryRowDeleted(this, new CategoryRowChangeEvent
➡ (((CategoryRow)(e.Row)), e.Action));
                }
            }

            protected override void OnRowDeleting(DataRowChangeEventArgs e) {
                base.OnRowDeleting(e);
                if ((this.CategoryRowDeleting != null)) {
                    this.CategoryRowDeleting(this, new CategoryRowChangeEvent
➡ (((CategoryRow)(e.Row)), e.Action));
                }
            }

            public void RemoveCategoryRow(CategoryRow row) {
                this.Rows.Remove(row);
            }
        }

        public class CategoryRow : DataRow {

            private CategoryDataTable tableCategory;

            internal CategoryRow(DataRowBuilder rb) :
                    base(rb) {
                this.tableCategory = ((CategoryDataTable)(this.Table));
            }

            public System.Guid CategoryID {
                get {
                    return ((System.Guid)(this[this.tableCategory.
➡CategoryIDColumn]));
                }
```

LISTING 6.1   Continued

```
                set {
                    this[this.tableCategory.CategoryIDColumn] = value;
                }
            }

        public string Name {
            get {
                try {
                    return ((string)(
➥this[this.tableCategory.NameColumn]));
                }
                catch (InvalidCastException e) {
                    throw new StrongTypingException(
➥"Cannot get value because it is DBNull.", e);
                }
            }
            set {
                this[this.tableCategory.NameColumn] = value;
            }
        }

        public System.Guid ParentCategoryID {
            get {
                try {
                    return ((System.Guid)(this[this.tableCategory.
➥ParentCategoryIDColumn]));
                }
                catch (InvalidCastException e) {
                    throw new StrongTypingException(
➥"Cannot get value because it is DBNull.", e);
                }
            }
            set {
                this[this.tableCategory.ParentCategoryIDColumn] = value;
            }
        }

        public string Description {
            get {
                try {
                    return ((string)(
➥this[this.tableCategory.DescriptionColumn]));
                }
```

LISTING 6.1   Continued

```
                    catch (InvalidCastException e) {
                        throw new StrongTypingException(
➥"Cannot get value because it is DBNull.", e);
                    }
                }
                set {
                    this[this.tableCategory.DescriptionColumn] = value;
                }
            }

            public short DisplaySeq {
                get {
                    try {
                        return ((short)(this[this.tableCategory.
➥DisplaySeqColumn]));
                    }
                    catch (InvalidCastException e) {
                        throw new StrongTypingException("Cannot get value
➥because it is DBNull.", e);
                    }
                }
                set {
                    this[this.tableCategory.DisplaySeqColumn] = value;
                }
            }

            public short Display {
                get {
                    try {
                        return ((short)(
➥this[this.tableCategory.DisplayColumn]));
                    }
                    catch (InvalidCastException e) {
                        throw new StrongTypingException(
➥"Cannot get value because it is DBNull.", e);
                    }
                }
                set {
                    this[this.tableCategory.DisplayColumn] = value;
                }
            }

            public bool IsNameNull() {
                return this.IsNull(this.tableCategory.NameColumn);
            }
```

LISTING 6.1   Continued

```
        public void SetNameNull() {
            this[this.tableCategory.NameColumn] = System.Convert.DBNull;
        }

        public bool IsParentCategoryIDNull() {
            return this.IsNull(this.tableCategory.ParentCategoryIDColumn);
        }

        public void SetParentCategoryIDNull() {
            this[this.tableCategory.ParentCategoryIDColumn] =
➥System.Convert.DBNull;
        }

        public bool IsDescriptionNull() {
            return this.IsNull(this.tableCategory.DescriptionColumn);
        }

        public void SetDescriptionNull() {
            this[this.tableCategory.DescriptionColumn] =
➥System.Convert.DBNull;
        }

        public bool IsDisplaySeqNull() {
            return this.IsNull(this.tableCategory.DisplaySeqColumn);
        }

        public void SetDisplaySeqNull() {
            this[this.tableCategory.DisplaySeqColumn] =
➥System.Convert.DBNull;
        }

        public bool IsDisplayNull() {
            return this.IsNull(this.tableCategory.DisplayColumn);
        }

        public void SetDisplayNull() {
            this[this.tableCategory.DisplayColumn] =
➥System.Convert.DBNull;
        }

        public CategoryProductMappingRow[]
➥GetCategoryProductMappingRows() {
            return ((CategoryProductMappingRow[])(this.GetChildRows(
➥this.Table.ChildRelations["CategoryProductMapping"]))));
        }
    }
```

This class encapsulates all the Category table attributes. This includes the `CategoryID`, `Name`, `ParentCategoryID`, `Description`, `DisplaySequence`, and `Display` flags. All these attributes are accessible via instances of `DataColumn` classes that are contained within the `Category` `DataTable` class. Notice that this class also contains custom event handlers for row change events.

The important point to take away from this discussion is how to use `CatalogDS` and the `CategoryDataTable` object, which will be covered in the next section.

LeftNav.ascx.cs

`CategoryList.ascs.cs` is the code behind for the `LeftNav` user control that displays the category menu. The primary responsibility of the code behind is to tie the data provider, `CatalogDS`, to the user interface elements (in this case, as you will see in the next section, a data grid). The code behind is basically a new class that inherits from `System.Web.UI.UserControl`. The user control `LeftNav` will, in turn, inherit from this code behind class.

The important part of this class is the `Page_Load` event handler. In this method, the user interface elements are tied to the data provider. Listing 6.2 shows what this looks like.

LISTING 6.2 The *Page_Load* Event Handler

```
protected void Page_Load(object sender, System.EventArgs e)
        {
            DataView dv;
            CatalogDS catalogds = (CatalogDS)HttpRuntime.Cache.Get("Catalog");
            if (catalogds == null)
            {
                // Re-insert catalog into the cache
                MyGolfGearDP dp = new MyGolfGearDP();
                catalogds = new CatalogDS();
                dp.FillCatalog(catalogds);
                HttpRuntime.Cache.Insert("Catalog",catalogds,null,System.
                ➥DateTime.
➥MaxValue,System.TimeSpan.FromHours(24),CacheItemPriority.High,
➥CacheItemPriorityDecay.Never,null);
                dv = catalogds.Category.DefaultView;
            }
            else
            {
                dv = catalogds.Category.DefaultView;
            }
```

LISTING 6.2 Continued

```
        Trace.Write(System.Guid.Empty.ToString());
        dv.Sort = "DisplaySeq";
        dv.RowFilter = "Display = '1'";
        CategoryList.DataSource = dv;
        CategoryList.DataBind();
    }
```

The Page_Load method does a great deal of work, but it is not as complicated as it seems. It tries to find the catalog dataset in the runtime cache. If it does not find an existing catalog, it creates a new instance of the CatalogDS class, uses the data provider named MyGolfGearDP to fill it, and then inserts it into the cache. Using this method is great for increasing the overall throughput of an application because it reduces the number of network round trips.

Next, this method assigns the DefaultView from the CategoryDataTable object to the local DataView object variable named dv. The DataView object filters and sorts the data in the datatable.

Finally, the Page_Load method assigns the dv DataView object to the CategoryList data list's DataSource property and calls DataBind(). When you assign a data source and ask the data list to bind to it, the control takes care of displaying the data contained in the DataSource property. As you will see in the next section, the layout, look, and feel of the data grid are controlled in the user interface portion.

LeftNav.ascx

All the user interface elements are coded into the LeftNav.ascx user control file. This file is actually responsible for laying out the left column of all the pages within MyGolfGear.NET. They include the logo/home link at the top-left corner of the page; the category navigation (what we are interested in for this chapter); the wish list feature discussed in Chapter 9, "Using ASP.NET to Implement Wish Lists"; and the search feature. The code necessary to create the category list portion of the LeftNav user control is shown in Listing 6.3.

LISTING 6.3 The *CategoryList* User Control

```
<table border="0" width="172" cellspacing="0" cellpadding="0">
    <tr>
        <td width="152">
            <p align="left">
                 <font color="#336699" size="4">Shop</font></p>
        </td>
        <td width="20">
        </td>
```

LISTING 6.3   Continued

```
        </tr>
        <tr>
            <td width="172" colspan="2">
                <img border="0" src="../images/spacer_clear.gif" width="1"
➥height="5">
            </td>
        </tr>
        <tr>
            <td width="172" colspan="2" bgcolor="#808080">
                <img border="0" src="../images/spacer_clear.gif" width="1"
➥height="2">
            </td>
        </tr>
        <tr>
            <td width="152" align="right">
                <asp:DataList ItemStyle-CssClass="clsMenu" datakeyfield=
➥"CategoryID" id="CategoryList" runat="server" cellpadding="3"
➥cellspacing="0" width="145" SelectedItemStyle-Font-Size=4
➥SelectedItemStyle-BackColor="black" EnableViewState=True>
                    <ItemTemplate>  <asp:HyperLink itemstyle-cssclass=
➥"clsMenu" id=HyperLink1 Text='<%# DataBinder.Eval
➥ (Container.DataItem, "Name") %>' NavigateUrl='
➥<%# "../Main/productselection.aspx?CatID=" +
➥DataBinder.Eval(Container.DataItem, "CategoryID") +
➥"&selection=" + Container.ItemIndex %>' runat="server" />
                    </ItemTemplate>
                    <SelectedItemTemplate>  <asp:HyperLink
➥itemstyle-cssclass="clsMenu" id=HyperLink2 Text='
➥<%# DataBinder.Eval(Container.DataItem, "Name") %>'
➥NavigateUrl='<%# "../Main/productselection.aspx?CatID=" +
➥DataBinder.Eval(Container.DataItem, "CategoryID") + "&selection=" +
➥Container.ItemIndex %>' runat="server" /></SelectedItemTemplate>
                </asp:DataList>
            </td>
        </tr>
</table>
```

The code that creates the category list is contained within a simple HTML table. The top portion of the table doesn't do anything special. It just lays out the "Shop" header and uses some clear .GIF images to insert whitespace. The interesting stuff is in the lower half of the table.

The lower half of the table contains the declarative portion of the DataList user control that is used to format the actual category menu. The data list allows for the specification of more than 60 properties. The following properties were used to implement the category menu:

Using ASP.NET to Display the Simple Catalog

CHAPTER 6

127

6

USING ASP.NET
TO DISPLAY THE
SIMPLE CATALOG

- `ItemStyle-CssClass`—Specifies the name of the Cascading Style Sheet (CSS) to use for HTML elements created by the control
- `DataKeyField`—Gets and sets the primary key field in the `DataSource`
- `SelectedItemStyle-Font-Size`—Specifies the font size of a data list item that has been selected
- `SelectedItemStyle-BackColor`—Gets and sets the background color of the selected item
- `EnableViewState`—Tells the control it should maintain its view state

The typical `ID` and `RunAt` attributes as well as the table properties `CellPadding`, `CellSpacing`, and `Width` were also used.

Within the `DataList` tags, `ItemTemplate` and `SelectedItemTemplate` tags are used to define the look and feel as well as the location of the needed fields from the `DataSource` property.

The `ItemTemplate` tag tells the data list where to get each piece of data needed to display. For this `ItemTemplate`, the most important properties are `Text` and `NavigateUrl`. When you use the `DataBinder` object, the name of each category is displayed and hyperlinked to the product selection page. The category ID is passed to the `ProductSelection.aspx` page to display all the products associated with a particular category.

DataBinder.Eval

The `DataBinder.Eval` method uses reflection to evaluate data binding information at runtime. It is used from `.aspx` pages to declaratively cast text for display in a Web browser and must be enclosed in `<%#` and `%>` tags.

The first parameter is a reference to the object the expression is evaluated against. The second parameter is a string that represents the name of the property that should be used to bind to.

The `DataBinder.Eval` method returns an `Object`. It is, in most cases, a `String` or other data object that can be displayed on a page.

After we developed the ability to display the category menu, we needed a place to put it. The `.ascx` file that was used to create the menu is included in virtually every page within the site, starting with the home page.

Developing the Simple Home Page

The MyGolfGear.NET home page is made up of the following five main functional units:

- `LeftNav`—Consists of the category menu, search feature, wish list, and logo/home button.
- Main content area—Contains any additional content or functionality. For instance, this section may contain a product's description and image or a shopper's basket contents.

- Header—Contains links to the shopping cart, the current customer's profile page, customer service information, and an administrator's link that shows up only when an appropriately authorized user logs on to the site.

- SpecialsContent—Consists of the product spotlight and Buyer's Advantage areas.

- Footer—Contains copyright information, and links to the About Us page, Privacy Policy, and Terms and Conditions page.

> **NOTE**
>
> The home page layout serves as the basic framework from which all other content pages were created. In reality, the home page could have been reused for all the category, product detail, and basket pages. We decided to separate those pages for simplicity and ease of explanation.

Figure 6.2 shows what these elements look like together on the home page.

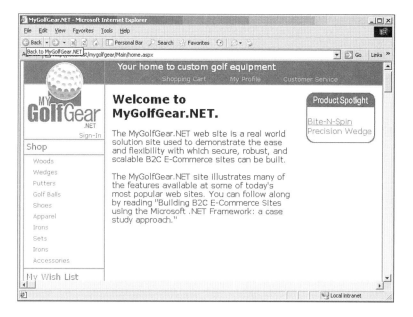

FIGURE 6.2

The home page.

The home page is made up of several other code elements and user controls. Specials
Content.ascx, Footer.ascx, Header.ascx, and LeftNav.ascx are all used by the home.aspx
page to create the look of the home page. Listing 6.4 shows the code for the home page.

LISTING 6.4   *Home.aspx*

```
<%@ Register TagPrefix="MyGolfGear" TagName="SpecialsContent"
➥Src="../UserControls/SpecialsContent.ascx" %>
<%@ Register TagPrefix="MyGolfGear" TagName="Footer"
➥Src="../UserControls/Footer.ascx" %>
<%@ Register TagPrefix="MyGolfGear" TagName="Header"
➥Src="../UserControls/Header.ascx" %>
<%@ Register TagPrefix="MyGolfGear" TagName="LeftNav"
➥Src="../UserControls/LeftNav.ascx" %>

<%@ Page language="c#" trace="true" src="Home.aspx.cs"
➥AutoEventWireup="false" Inherits="MyGolfGear.Main.Home"
➥CodeBehind="Home.aspx.cs" %>
<html>
   <head>
      <title>
         MyGolfGear.NET
      </title>
      <LINK REL="stylesheet" TYPE="text/css" HREF="../css_mygolfgear.css">
   </head>
   <body bgcolor="#FFFFFF" link="#336699" text="#000000" alink="#336699">
      <!--START MAIN TABLE-->
      <div align="center">
         <form method="post" runat=server>
            <center>
               <table border="0" width="790" cellspacing="0" cellpadding="0">
                  <tr>
                     <td width="2" bgcolor="#808080">
                        <img border="0" src="images/spacer_clear.gif"
➥width="2" height="1">
                     </td>
                     <td width="786" bgcolor="#808080">
                        <img border="0" src="images/spacer_clear.gif"
➥width="786" height="1">
                     </td>
                     <td width="2" bgcolor="#808080">
                        <img border="0" src="images/spacer_clear.gif"
➥width="2" height="1">
                     </td>
                  </tr>
```

LISTING 6.4 Continued

```
                        <tr>
                           <td width="2" bgcolor="#808080" valign="top">
                           </td>
                           <td width="786" valign="top">
                              <table border="0" width="786" cellspacing="0"
➥cellpadding="0">
                                 <tr>
                                    <td width="172" valign="top">
                                       <!--START LEFT COLUMN CONTENT MASTER TABLE-->
                                       <MyGolfGear:LeftNav id=LeftNav runat="server"
➥NAME="LeftNav" />

                                       <!--END LEFT COLUMN CONTENT-->
                                    </td>
                                    <td width="2" valign="top" bgcolor="#808080">
                                    </td>
                                    <td width="616" valign="top" align=left>
                                       <!-- Insert Top Nav -->
                                       <MyGolfGear:Header id=Header runat="server" />
                                       <!--START MAIN CONTENT-->
                                       <table border="0" width="100%" cellspacing="0"
➥cellpadding="15">
                                          <tr>
                                             <td width="70%" valign="top">
                                                <h2> Welcome to MyGolfGear.NET.</h2>
➥The MyGolfGear.NET web site is a real world solution site used to
➥demonstrate the ease and flexibility with which secure, robust,
➥and scalable B2C E-Commerce sites can be built. </br></br>The
➥MyGolfGear.NET site illustrates many of the features available at some
➥ of today's most popular web sites. You can follow along by reading
➥"Building B2C E-Commerce Sites using the Microsoft .NET Framework:
➥a case study approach."</td>
                                             <td width="176" valign="top">
                                                <!--START SPECIALS CONTENT-->
                                                <MyGolfGear:SpecialsContent
➥id=SpecialsContent runat="server" NAME="SpecialsContent" />
                                                <!--END SPECIALS CONTENT-->
                                             </td>
                                          </tr>
                                       </table>
                                       <!--END MAIN CONTENT-->
                                       <p>
                                        
                                    </td>
                                 </tr>
                                 <!-- Insert Footer -->
```

Using ASP.NET to Display the Simple Catalog

CHAPTER 6

131

6

USING ASP.NET
TO DISPLAY THE
SIMPLE CATALOG

LISTING 6.4 Continued

```
                    <MyGolfGear:Footer id=Footer runat="server" />
                </table>
    </div>
    </form>
    <!--END MASTER TABLE-->
    <p>
         
    </p>
    </body>
</html>
```

The code for the home page is fairly self-explanatory if you are familiar with basic HTML. I will point out a couple of interesting aspects, however. First, note the `<%@ Register %>` tags at the top of Listing 6.4. These `@Register` tags associate aliases with class names and namespaces. This allows for a more concise notation when specifying custom controls.

The tag notation is made up of a minimum of three parts: the tag prefix, which is used to alias a namespace; the tag name, which is used to alias the class; and a Source property, which is used to specify the location of the user control. Optionally, you can specify a namespace and assembly to further narrow down the control's location.

The only other thing to point out about this page is the actual custom user control tags. The home page uses the `LeftNav`, `Header`, `SpecialsContent`, and `Footer` customer user controls. Using the tag prefix and tag name attributes separated by a colon specifies these user controls—for instance, `MyGolfGear:Footer`. Notice also that these tags also require the ID and `Runat` attributes to be specified as well.

Developing the Product Selection Page

When a user clicks a category name on the category menu, she is taken to the product selection page. This page lists all products in the specified category. The product selection page is constructed similarly to the category menu user control. That is, it is made up of a user interface piece, a code behind class, and the strongly typed dataset named `CatalogDS.cs`.

To better understand how this functionality was achieved, we'll start with `CatalogDS`. After we describe the `CatalogDS` functionality, we can discuss the code behind and user interface.

CatalogDS

The main functionality, for product selection, provided by `CatalogDS` is the `FindByCategoryID` method. This method takes a category ID as a parameter and returns the corresponding `DataRow` object if one is found. Listing 6.5 shows this code.

LISTING 6.5   The *FindByCategoryID* Method

```
public CategoryRow FindByCategoryID(System.Guid CategoryID) {
    return ((CategoryRow)(this.Rows.Find(new Object[] {CategoryID})));
}
```

The `FindByCategoryID` method uses the `DataRowCollection.Find()` method to locate any row whose primary key matches the value passed in. Notice that the return value is coerced to the `CategoryRow` type.

ProductSelection.aspx.cs

The product selection code behind page named `ProductSelection.aspx.cs` uses the `CategoryRow` object retrieved from the `FindByCategoryID` method to create a temporary `DataTable` object to bind to the product selection page. Listing 6.6 shows what this looks like.

LISTING 6.6   The *FillProductList* Method

```
protected void FillProductList()
{

    //Find the Category row Selected
    System.Guid CategoryID = new System.Guid(Request.Params["CatId"]);
    CatalogDS.CategoryRow CatRow = catalogds.Category.FindByCategoryID
➥ (CategoryID);
    CatName.Text = CatRow["Name"].ToString();

    //Create temp datatable with associated products for the selected category
    CatalogDS.CategoryProductMappingRow[] cpmr =
➥CatRow.GetCategoryProductMappingRows();
    //Create datatable to insert the cat/product mapping rows in to
➥populate the grid
    DataTable dt = new DataTable("Products");
    dt.Columns.Add("ProductID");
    dt.Columns.Add("Name");
    dt.Columns.Add("ImageName");
    dt.Columns.Add("Price");
    dt.Columns.Add("Promo");
    dt.Columns.Add("PromoPart");

    //Iterate through the cat/mapping table adding the product rows to
➥this new datatable
    foreach(CatalogDS.CategoryProductMappingRow mr in cpmr)
    {
```

LISTING 6.6   Continued

```
        DataRow tempRow = dt.NewRow();
        tempRow["ProductID"] = mr.ProductID;
        tempRow["Name"] = mr.ProductRow.Name;
        if (mr.ProductRow.IsImageNameNull())
        {
            tempRow["ImageName"] = "";
        }
        else
        {
            tempRow["ImageName"] = mr.ProductRow.ImageName.ToString();
        }
        //Determine the price of the product
        CatalogDS.ProductPriceRow[] ppr = mr.ProductRow.GetProductPriceRows();
        foreach(CatalogDS.ProductPriceRow r in ppr)
        {
            if (r.IsStartDateNull() && r.IsEndDateNull())
            {
                tempRow["Price"] = String.Format("{0:c}", r.Price);
            }
            else if ((r.StartDate < System.DateTime.Today) && (r.EndDate >
➥System.DateTime.Today))
            {
                tempRow["Price"] = String.Format("{0:c}", r.Price);
            }
            price = r.Price;
        }

        dt.Rows.Add(tempRow);
    }
    //Populate DataGrid
    if (dt.Rows.Count == 0)
    {
        lblNoProduct.Text = "Currently there are no products available.";
        lblNoProduct.Visible = true;
    }
    ProductList.DataSource = dt.DefaultView;
    ProductList.DataKeyField = "ProductID";
    ProductList.DataBind();
}
```

The FillProductList method shown in Listing 6.6 appears to have quite a bit going on, but it is actually quite simple. This method takes the CategoryDataRow returned from the FindByCategoryID method and uses the category product-mapping table to iterate through and create a temporary datatable of all the products in the given category. After the temporary datatable is constructed and populated, it is used to bind to the ProductList data list.

ProductSelection.aspx

Displaying the products of a given category is relatively easy with the help of a data list.
ProductSelection.aspx displays the products in a given category for MyGolfGear.NET. The
code necessary to display the products in a category is similar to the code used to display the
category names in the category menu. Listing 6.7 shows the user interface code used to display
a category's products.

LISTING 6.7   The *ProductList* Data List

```
<asp:DataList id="ProductList" ItemStyle-CssClass="clsMenu"
➡runat="server" RepeatColumns="2">
   <ItemTemplate>
      <table CellPadding=3 cellspacing=4 border=0 width="275">
         <tr valign=top>
            <td valign=top width="125" align=left>
               <a href='ProductDetails.aspx?productID=<%#
➡DataBinder.Eval(Container.DataItem,"ProductID") %>'>
                  <img src='../Images/ProductImages/thumbnails/
➡<%# DataBinder.Eval(Container.DataItem, "ImageName") %>
➡' width="100" height="75" border="0">
               </a>
               <br>
               <a href='AddProductsToOrder.aspx?productID=<%#
➡DataBinder.Eval(Container.DataItem, "ProductID") %>'>
➡<font color="green" size="2"><b>Add To Cart</b></font></a></td>
            <td valign=top width="150" align=left>
               <font size=2><a href='ProductDetails.aspx?productID=
➡<%# DataBinder.Eval(Container.DataItem, "ProductID") %>'>
<%# DataBinder.Eval(Container.DataItem, "Name") %></a>
               <br>
               Price: <%# DataBinder.Eval(Container.DataItem, "Price") %>
               <BR>
               <font size=2 color=red><%# DataBinder.Eval(
➡Container.DataItem, "Promo") %>
                  <%# DataBinder.Eval(Container.DataItem, "PromoPart") %>
               </font></td>
         </tr>
      </table>
   </ItemTemplate>
</asp:DataList>
```

Listing 6.7 shows the DataList code used to bind product data. With every item, an
ItemTemplate is used to format a link to the product detail page, the product image, the

Using ASP.NET to Display the Simple Catalog

CHAPTER 6

135

6

USING ASP.NET
TO DISPLAY THE
SIMPLE CATALOG

product's name, and its price. In addition, this listing also includes the ability to add the current product to the user's basket by linking to the AddProductsToOrder.aspx page.

Developing the Product Detail Page

When a user clicks either a product image or product name on the product selection page, he is taken to the product detail page. This page does exactly what its name implies; that is, it displays detailed information about a given product.

Like the product selection page, the product detail page functionality is made up of a data access component, a code behind class, and an .aspx page for the user interface portion.

> **NOTE**
>
> The strongly typed dataset named CatalogDS can be used to retrieve product detail information.

ProductDetail.aspx.cs

The product detail code -behind class named ProductDetail.aspx.cs uses CatalogDS in much the same way as the product selection code behind does. It uses the protected method named PopulateDetails(). Listing 6.8 shows the code for this method.

LISTING 6.8   The *PopulateDetails* Method

```
protected void PopulateDetails()
{
    System.Guid ProductID = new System.Guid(Request.Params["ProductID"]);

    GetCatalog();
    //Find the Product row Selected
    CatalogDS.ProductRow ProductRow = catalogds.Product.
➥FindByProductID(ProductID);
    ProductName.Text = ProductRow.Name.ToString();
    if (!ProductRow.IsLongDescriptionNull())
➥{Description.Text = ProductRow.LongDescription.ToString();}
    AddToCart.NavigateUrl = "AddProductsToOrder.aspx?productID=" +
➥ProductID.ToString();
    AddToCart.Text = "Add To Basket";
    if (ProductRow.IsImageNameNull())
    {
        ProdImage.Visible = false;
        lblNoImage.Visible = true;              }
```

LISTING 6.8   Continued

```
    else
    {
        lblNoImage.Visible = false;
        ProdImage.ImageUrl = "../images/ProductImages/" +
➥ProductRow.ImageName.ToString();
    }
    //Locate the price for this product.
    CatalogDS.ProductPriceRow PriceRow = catalogds.ProductPrice.
➥FindByProductID(ProductID);
    lblPrice.Text =  String.Format("{0:c}", PriceRow.Price);


}
```

When the Page_Load event is fired, the PopulateDetails() method is called. This method first gets the latest version of CatalogDS by calling the GetCatalog() method. Then it uses CatalogDS to call the Product.FindByProductID method. This method is similar to FindByCategoryID, which was discussed previously. After the ProductRow object is retrieved, it can be used to populate the ASP.NET Web controls used to display the product information.

ProductDetail.aspx

The product detail page named ProductDetail.aspx is responsible for the user interface portion that displays a given product's detail information. For this instance, data binding was not used. Instead, simple Web controls were used.

Three types of Web controls are used to display the product information. Label objects are used for the product name, price, and description. An Image object is used to specify the product image, and a HyperLink object is used to create a link to the shopping cart functionality. Listing 6.9 shows the relevant ASP.NET code for displaying the product details.

LISTING 6.9   *ProductDetail* Web Controls

```
<b>Product:<asp:Label ID="ProductName" ForeColor="#336699" Runat=server>
    </asp:Label>
</b>
<br>
<br>
<asp:Label Visible=False ID="lblNoProduct" Runat=server>
</asp:Label>
<table height="100%" valign="top" align="left" cellspacing=3 cellpadding=0
➥width="100%" border=0>
    <TBODY>
```

Using ASP.NET to Display the Simple Catalog

CHAPTER 6

137

6

USING ASP.NET
TO DISPLAY THE
SIMPLE CATALOG

LISTING 6.9   Continued

```
        <tr height="100%" valign="top">
            <td nowrap>
                <table CellPadding=3 cellspacing=4 border=0 width="500">
                    <TBODY>
                        <tr valign=top>
                            <td valign=top width="250" align=left>
                                <asp:Label id="Description" runat="server">
                                </asp:Label>
                            </td>
                            <td valign=top width="250" align=middle border=0>
                                <asp:image id="ProdImage" border=0 runat="server">
                                </asp:image>
                                <asp:Label id="lblNoImage" ForeColor="red" Text=
➥"No image available" runat="server" visible="false">
                                </asp:Label>
                                <br>
                                <BR>
                                <BR>
                                <table border=0>
                                    <TBODY>
                                        <tr>
                                            <td bgcolor=beige>
                                                <asp:Label ID="label1" Text="Your Price:"
➥align=right runat="server">
                                                </asp:Label>
                                            </td>
                                            <td width=50>
                                                <asp:Label ID="lblPrice" Runat=server>
                                                </asp:Label>
                                            </td>
                                        </tr>
                                        <tr>
                                            <td width=50>
                                                <font color=red>
                                                    <asp:Label ID="lblPromoPrice"
➥Runat=server>
                                                    </asp:Label>
                                                </font></td>
                                        </tr>
                                        <tr>
                                            <td colspan=2>
                                                <font color=red>
                                                    <asp:Label ID="lblPromoPart"
➥Runat=server>
                                                    </asp:Label>
```

LISTING 6.9 Continued

```
                                    </font></td>
                        </tr>
                      </TBODY>
                    </table>
                    <BR>
                    <asp:HyperLink id="AddToCart" runat="server" fontsize=2
➥ forecolor=green></asp:HyperLink></td>
                  </tr>
                </TBODY>
              </table>
            </td>
          </tr>
        </TBODY>
</table>
```

As Listing 6.9 shows, product detail information is displayed by using ASP.NET Label Web
Server controls.

> **TIP**
>
> Label Web Server controls can be used to display static text, but they also allow you
> to manipulate their text programmatically.

Developing the Product Search Functionality

The product search functionality is made up of four main parts: a stored procedure, an additional method in the MyGolfGearDP class, the SearchResult code behind class, and the
SearchResult.aspx file.

spFindProducts

The easiest way to search for a product is to search by name and/or description. The
MyGolfGear.NET database has a single stored procedure called spFindProduct that serves
this purpose. Listing 6.10 shows the code for this stored procedure.

LISTING 6.10 The *spFindProduct* Stored Procedure

```
CREATE PROCEDURE spFindProducts
(
@SearchText varchar(50)
)
 AS
SELECT ProductID, [Name], ShortDescription, LongDescription  FROM Product
```

LISTING 6.10   Continued

```
WHERE
    Name LIKE '%' +  @SearchText + '%' OR
    ShortDescription LIKE '%' +  @SearchText + '%' OR
    LongDescription LIKE '%' +  @SearchText + '%'
```

spFindProduct is a simple stored procedure. It accepts a string of 50 or fewer characters and compares it to the Name, ShortDescription, and LongDescription fields in the Product table. Any product that contains the @SearchText value in its name or description will be returned.

MyGolfGearDP.FindProduct

The FindProduct method was added to the MyGolfGearDP class to retrieve the results of the spFindProduct stored procedure. This new method uses ADO.NET to call the stored procedure, passing in the needed parameter. Listing 6.11 shows this method.

LISTING 6.11   The *FindProduct* Method

```
public DataSet FindProduct(String searchText)
{
    NameValueCollection configInfo =
➡ (NameValueCollection)HttpContext.Current.GetConfig("appSettings");
    SqlConnection conn = new SqlConnection(
➡ (String)configInfo["ConnectString"]);
    conn.Open();

    SqlDataAdapter myCommand = new SqlDataAdapter();

    myCommand.SelectCommand = new SqlCommand("spFindProduct", conn);

    SqlParameter parameterSearchText = new SqlParameter("@SearchText",
➡SqlDbType.VarChar , 50);
    parameterSearchText.Value = searchText;
    myCommand.SelectCommand.Parameters.Add(parameterSearchText);

    DataSet ds = new DataSet();

    myCommand.Fill(ds);

    return ds;
}
```

The FindProduct method uses a SqlDataAdapter to fill a DataSet object that can then be bound to a repeating control.

SearchResult.aspx.cs

The SearchResult.aspx.cs class uses the FindProduct method of the MyGolfGearDP class to retrieve a DataSet that can then be bound to a DataList object. Listing 6.12 shows the creation and use of this class.

LISTING 6.12   The *SearchResult.aspx.cs* Class' *Page_Load Method*

```
private void Page_Load(object sender, System.EventArgs e)
{
    String searchText = Request.Form["SearchText"];

    MyGolfGearDP dp = new MyGolfGearDP();

    SearchResultList.DataSource =
➥dp.FindProduct(searchText).Tables[0].DefaultView;
    SearchResultList.DataBind();
}
```

NOTE

The code for Home.aspx, Home.aspx.cs, ProductSelection.aspx, ProductSelection. aspx.cs, ProductDetails.aspx, and ProductDetails.aspx.cs is available online.

Summary

This chapter discussed the implementation of MyGolfGear.NET's simple catalog using ASP. NET and ADO.NET. Specifically, it covered the creation of the category navigation, the product list for each category, the product detail page, and the simple home page.

The next chapter begins section III on creating advanced features for MyGolfGear.NET. Chapter 7, "Using ASP.NET to Implement Product Spotlights," discusses how featured items and specials are implemented for MyGolfGear.NET. It will cover the necessary additions to the data model and stored procedures, the enhancements to the component layer, the creation of the user controls, and the modifications to the home page.

Self Instruction

The SearchResult.aspx file uses the same template as the home, product detail, and category pages do. In fact, it is similar in functionality to the product detail page. Implement your own SearchResult.aspx page based on the code shown for the SearchResult.aspx.cs class.

Building Advanced Features

IN THIS PART

Using ASP.NET to Implement Product Spotlights

IN THIS CHAPTER

Objectives

- Understand what a product spotlight is.

- Learn about the database objects created to support product spotlights in MyGolfGear.NET.

- Understand how the code behind class for the product spotlight feature was implemented.

- Learn how the featured item page was created and how it is used by MyGolfGear.NET to support the product spotlight feature.

Many of today's most popular Web sites (such as Chipshot.com) spotlight different items on their home page in an attempt to increase sales. By strategically pointing out items that either are not selling well on their own or that have higher margins associated with them, retailers can improve their bottom line. When a Web site does this, the products it is drawing attention to are called either *featured items* or *product spotlights*.

MyGolfGear.NET implements a product spotlight feature by utilizing some common yet powerful ASP.NET functionality, such as custom user controls, data grids, and use of the `Web.Config` file. This chapter covers the implementation of the MyGolfGear.NET product spotlight feature. Specifically, it covers the new database elements, new data access layer, and new presentation layer. Additionally, it discusses the steps necessary to integrate this feature into the existing MyGolfGear.NET framework.

Product Spotlight Database Object

To implement the MyGolfGear.NET product spotlight feature, we added three new database objects. Specifically, we added a new table called `FeaturedItems`. Additionally, we added the two new stored procedures `spInsertFeaturedItem` and `spGetFeaturedItems`.

The `FeaturedItems` Table

The new MyGolfGear table named `FeaturedItems` was added. This simple table has only four columns: `FeatureID`, `ProductID`, `StartDate`, and `EndDate`. Table 7.1 describes the fields and types used in this table.

NOTE

Some sites rotate their spotlight features based on page views. We chose to rotate the MyGolfGear.NET product spotlights based on the date.

TABLE 7.1 The *FeaturedItems* Table

Field Name	Data Type	Description
FeatureID	int	An identity for each featured item
ProductID	uniqueidentifier	The product ID of the item being spotlighted
StartDate	datetime	The date and time this item begins being spotlighted
EndDate	datetime	The date and time this item is no longer spotlighted

As mentioned earlier, two new stored procedures were also created to support the product spotlight feature. One was created to insert new featured items, and the other was created for selecting the current featured items.

The `spInsertFeaturedItem` Stored Procedure

We created the insert-stored procedure named `spInsertFeaturedItem` so that an administrative feature could be added to the site as necessary. This stored procedure, shown in Listing 7.1, takes a product ID, a start date, and an end date as parameters and inserts the data into the `FeaturedItems` table.

LISTING 7.1 The *spInsertFeatureItem* Stored Procedure

```
CREATE PROCEDURE spInsertFeaturedItem
        (
        @ProductID uniqueidentifier,
        @StartDate datetime,
        @EndDate datetime
        )
AS
INSERT INTO FeaturedItems
                        (
        ProductID,
        StartDate,
        EndDate
        )
VALUES
        (
        @ProductID,
        @StartDate,
        @EndDate
        )
```

This stored procedure accepts a product ID and two dates representing the date the product should begin being spotlighted on the site and the date the product should no longer be featured as a spotlight product. It then inserts these values directly into the FeaturedItems table.

> **NOTE**
>
> No value is inserted into the FeatureID column because the FeatureID field is an identity field and is automatically incremented by the SQL Server database any time a row is added.

The spGetFeaturedItems Stored Procedure

The other stored procedure added to the MyGolfGear database to support the product spotlight feature was a select stored procedure. As you might guess, this stored procedure, named spGetFeaturedItems, returns a list of product information corresponding to all the currently eligible featured items. Listing 7.2 shows what this stored procedure looks like.

LISTING 7.2   The *spGetFeaturedItems* Stored Procedure

```
CREATE    PROCEDURE spGetFeaturedItems
(
    @OrderDate datetime = NULL
)
AS

IF @OrderDate IS NULL
BEGIN
    SELECT @OrderDate = CONVERT(datetime, GETDATE())
END

SELECT FeaturedItems.ProductID, Product.Name, Product.ImageName
FROM FeaturedItems
JOIN Product
ON FeaturedItems.ProductID=Product.ProductID
AND FeaturedItems.StartDate <= @OrderDate
AND FeaturedItems.EndDate >=@OrderDate
GO
```

The spGetFeaturedItems stored procedure accepts one parameter: datetime, which corresponds to the date and time the order is to be created.

> **NOTE**
>
> The SQL Server getDate function could have been used in lieu of passing a datetime parameter into the stored procedure. However, if you allow a client to pass in a date, an historical list of featured items can be retrieved.

After a value for the @OrderDate parameter has been either verified or assigned, the product spotlight data can be retrieved. The product ID from the FeaturedItems table is joined with the product ID of the Product table to create a resultset containing the product IDs, product names, and product image names of the products that are in the FeaturedItems table and whose start and end dates are valid for the value either passed in or defaulted.

The `FeaturedItems.ascx.cs` Code Behind Class

We needed to add code to get the list of featured items out of the database and display it on the Web site. This functionality was easily added to the FeaturedItems.ascx.cs code behind class.

The easiest and most logical place to add the data access code was the Page_Load method. Listing 7.3 shows the implementation of this method.

LISTING 7.3   The *FeaturedItems.ascx.cs* Code Behind Class' *Page_Load* Method

```
private void Page_Load(object sender, System.EventArgs e)
{

    SqlConnection conn = new SqlConnection(ConnectionString);
    SqlCommand myCommand = new SqlCommand("spGetFeaturedItems", conn);

    // set the command type as a SP
    myCommand.CommandType = CommandType.StoredProcedure;

    // Add Parameters
    SqlParameter parameterOrderDate = new SqlParameter("@OrderDate",
➥SqlDbType.DateTime ,8);
    parameterOrderDate.Value = OrderDate;
    myCommand.Parameters.Add(parameterOrderDate);

    // Populate the data reader
    conn.Open();
    SqlDataReader myReader;
    myReader = myCommand.ExecuteReader();
```

7

PRODUCT
SPOTLIGHTS

LISTING 7.3   Continued

```
FeaturedItemsDataGrid.DataSource = myReader;
FeaturedItemsDataGrid.DataBind();

}
```

> **NOTE**
>
> You can find the complete source code for the `FeaturedItems.ascx.cs` code behind class online.

The `Page_Load` method uses the following four `System.Data.SqlClient` classes:

- `SqlConnection`
- `SqlCommand`
- `SqlParameter`
- `SqlDataReader`

`SqlConnection` is opened using the protected member variable `ConnectionString`, which is populated in the class' constructor. The value for the connection string is kept in the application's `Web.Config` file. Listing 7.4 shows how this value is accessed.

LISTING 7.4   The *FeaturedItems* Constructor

```
public FeaturedItems()
{
    this.Init += new System.EventHandler(Page_Init);
    OrderDate = DateTime.Now;
    NameValueCollection configInfo =
➥(NameValueCollection)HttpContext.Current.GetConfig("appSettings");
    ConnectionString = (String)configInfo["ConnectString"];
}
```

The value stored in the `ConnectionString` variable is stored within the `appSetting` element of the `Web.Config` file. Listing 7.5 shows what the content of this element looks like.

LISTING 7.5 The *appSettings* Element

```
<appSettings>
    <add key="ConnectString" value="Data Source=localhost; User ID=sa;
➥Password=; Initial Catalog=MyGolfGear" />
</appSettings>
```

After the connection is created and opened, a `SqlCommand` object is created using the name of the select stored procedure discussed previously. The `CommandType.StoreProcedure` is then specified.

A `SqlParameter` object is then created, populated, and added to the `SqlCommand`'s `Parameters` collection.

Finally, a `SqlDataReader` is created and populated. The `SqlCommand` method named `ExecuteReader` is used to do so.

In addition to the `SqlClient` objects discussed earlier, this method also uses the data grid used in the `.aspx` page corresponding to this class. The `SqlDataReader` named `myReader` is used to specify the `DataSource` property of the `FeaturedItemsDataGrid`. The only thing left to do is to call the data grid's `DataBind` method, which actually causes the data binding to occur on the invoked Web server control.

The `FeaturedItems.ascx` User Control File

The `FeaturedItems.ascx` Web server control was created to display the list of featured items. As mentioned in the previous section, a data grid was used for this purpose. Listing 7.6 shows this code.

LISTING 7.6 The *FeaturedItems.ascx* Web Server Control

```
<%@ Control Language="c#" AutoEventWireup="false" src="FeaturedItems.ascx.cs"
➥Codebehind="FeaturedItems.ascx.cs" Inherits="MyGolfGear.UserControls.
➥FeaturedItems"%>
<table border="0" width="146" cellspacing="0" cellpadding="0">
    <tr>
        <td BGCOLOR="#336633" valign=bottom ALIGN=CENTER width="100%"
➥colspan="3">
            <img border="0" align=absbottom
➥src="../images/win_hdr_productspotlight.gif" width="146" height="30">
        </td>
    </tr>
```

LISTING 7.6   Continued

```
   <tr>
      <td valign=top width="2" bgcolor="#336633">
         <img border="0" src="../images/spacer_clear.gif" width="2"
➡height="1">
      </td>
      <td valign=top width="142">
         <!--SPOTLIGHT-->
         <table border="0" width="100%" cellspacing="0" cellpadding="0">
            <tr>
               <td>
                  <asp:DataGrid DataKeyField="ProductID" AutoGenerateColumns=
➡"false" id=FeaturedItemsDataGrid runat="server" gridlines=None NAME=
➡"FeaturedItemsDataGrid">
                  <Columns>
                     <asp:HyperLinkColumn itemstyle-horizontalalign="left" itemstyle
➡-cssclass="clsFeaturedItems" DataTextFormatString="{0}" DataTextField=
➡"Name" DataNavigateUrlField="ProductID" DataNavigateUrlFormatString=
➡"../Main/ProductDetails.aspx?ProductID={0}" Target
➡="_self" />
                  </Columns>
               </asp:DataGrid>
               </td>
            </tr>
         </table>
         <!--END SPOTLIGHT-->
      </td>
      <td valign=top width="2" bgcolor="#336633">
         <img border="0" src="../images/spacer_clear.gif" width="2"
➡height="1">
      </td>
   </tr>
   <tr>
      <td width="100%" colspan="3">
         <img border="0" src="../images/win_footer.gif" width="146"
➡height="15">
      </td>
   </tr>
   <tr>
      <td width="100%" colspan="3">
         <img border="0" src="../images/spacer_clear.gif" width="1"
➡height="15">
      </td>
   </tr>
</table>
```

NOTE

You can find the complete source code for the `FeaturedItems.ascx` Web server control online.

Most of Listing 7.6 is related to the overall formatting and layout of the control. The important part falls within the `asp:DataGrid` tags. Here, the link to the product detail page is constructed from the featured items data.

Within the `asp:DataGrid` tags is a set of `Columns` tags. These tags are for formatting each data item that is to be represented in the data grid. It is within these tags that `HyperLinkColumn` is created.

NOTE

Besides `HyperLinkColumn`, a data grid's columns can contain instances of `BoundColumn`, `ButtonColumn`, `EditColumn`, and `TemplateColumn`.

As its name suggests, `HyperLinkColumn` tells the data grid to display each item in the column as a hyperlink. The contents of this column can be bound either to a field in the data grid's data source or static text.

In the `FeaturedItems.ascx` Web server control, `HyperLinkColumn` is bound to the `ProductID` field, and the `Name` field is used as the text for the link.

Adding Web Server Controls to the Home.aspx Page

Web server controls cannot be displayed by themselves. Therefore, they must be used in conjunction with a container. The `FeaturedItems.ascx` Web server control is contained within the `Home.aspx` page.

The featured items list is displayed prominently on the upper-right quadrant of the home page. Figure 7.1 shows what the home page looks like containing the `FeaturedItems.ascx` Web control.

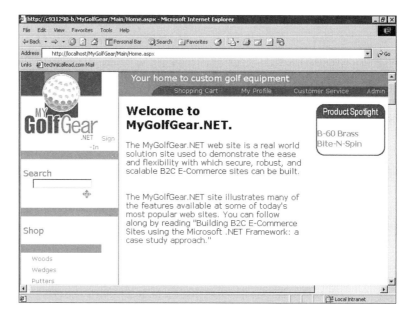

FIGURE 7.1
The home page displaying the FeaturedItems *control.*

To display the Web control, you must first register it. You use the Register page directive to do so. The entire line of code looks like this:

```
<%@ Register TagPrefix="MyGolfGear" TagName="FeaturedItems"
➥Src="../UserControls/FeaturedItems.ascx" %>
```

The Register tag associates aliases with namespaces and class names. This capability is useful for more concise notation. The Register tag also specifies the location of the Web control source code so that it can be just-in-time (JIT) compiled.

To use the control within the page, you combine the tag prefix with the class name like this: Tag:Control. In the Home.aspx page, the control looks like this:

```
<MyGolfGear:FeaturedItems id=FeaturedItems runat="server"
➥NAME="FeaturedItems" />
```

NOTE

You can find the complete source code for the Home.aspx page online.

Summary

This chapter discussed the implementation of MyGolfGear.NET's product spotlight feature. It covered the new database table and stored procedures that were created. It also discussed the implementation of the new `FeaturedItems.ascx` Web Server control that was created as well as the `FeaturedItems.ascx.cs` code behind class. Additionally, it showed how this new featured was added to the existing home page.

The next chapter covers how MyGolfGear.NET implements discount specials. It covers the changes made to the data model, as well as the new stored procedures and business components created to support this functionality.

Self Instruction

Most often, data access and business logic are encapsulated in their own class—separate from the code behind class. Using what you've learned in this chapter, implement a suitable business component to house the data access functionality that currently resides in the `FeaturedItems.ascx.cs` code behind class.

Using ASP.NET to Implement Discount Specials

IN THIS CHAPTER

Objectives

- **Learn about the necessary changes to the data model and additional stored procedures to support product discounts**

- **Understand the new** `OrderManager` **class' role in supporting product discounts.**

- **Understand the additions made to the strongly typed dataset** `CatalogDS`

- **See how displaying discounted products fits into the existing MyGolfGear.NET user interface layer**

Many online businesses offer special pricing on select products depending on other items being purchased. This feature gives online retailers another mechanism for moving over stocked inventory and creating additional incentives for shoppers to visit their sites. MyGolfGear.NET supports discount specials by allowing administrators to offer any products, for a given period of time, at a reduced rate. They can do so either by offering a percentage off the regular price or a fixed amount off the regular price.

This chapter will cover the changes made to MyGolfGear.NET that enabled the support of product discounts. Specifically, it will cover the changes to the data model, additional stored procedures, business components, and user interface elements that enable the support of discount specials.

Changes to the Database to Support Discount Specials

The most logical place to start, when explaining how this functionality was implemented, is with the changes to the database. At a very high level, some additional data needs to be stored, and some means of accessing this new data needs to be developed. For MyGolfGear.NET, this meant the addition of the `ProductSpecial` and `PromoType` tables. It also meant updating the `spGetCompleteCatalog` stored procedure, which is used in conjunction with the `CatalogDS` class.

The `ProductSpecial` and `PromoType` Tables

To support the notion of discounted items, we needed a new place to store this information. We therefore added the `ProductSpecial` and `PromoType` tables to the MyGolfGear database for this purpose.

The `PromoType` table stores the metadata necessary to describe the types of promotions MyGolfGear.NET is capable of supporting. The current implementation supports percentage-based discounts, fixed-price discounts, and product bonuses. Table 8.1 shows the table's fields and types.

TABLE 8.1   The *PromoType* Table

Field	Data Type	Length	Description
PromoTypeID	int	4	Unique ID for each promo type
PromoType	varchar	50	Descriptive name of the promotion type

The ProductSpecial table houses the details of all the promotions that are possible. The current implementation allows for the specification of discount percentages and flat discounts. Table 8.2 shows this table's fields.

TABLE 8.2   The *ProductSpecial* Table

Field	Data Type	Description
ProductSpecialID	int	Unique ID for each promotion
ProductID	uniqueidentifier	ID of the product the given promotion is to apply to
StartDate	datetime	Date the given promotion starts
EndDate	datetime	Date the given promotion ends
PromoTypeID	int	Type of promotion
PromoDiscount	decimal	Percentage or flat discount for the current promotion

8

DISCOUNT SPECIALS

> **NOTE**
>
> This model is not as normalized as it could be. We chose to model the product special support this way for ease of implementation, but also for ease of explanation.

Changes to the `spGetCompleteCatalog` Stored Procedure

After we created a place to store the promotional data, we needed a way to retrieve the data. Because we decided that the primary mechanism for handling the promotions would be via the CatalogDS class, the only change necessary was to the spGetCompleteCatalog stored procedure. Listing 8.1 shows the code for this stored procedure.

LISTING 8.1   The *spGetCompleteCatalog* Stored Procedure

```
CREATE PROCEDURE spGetCompleteCatalog
AS
SELECT   *
FROM     Category

SELECT   *
FROM     Product

SELECT   *
FROM     CategoryProductMapping

SELECT   *
FROM     ProductPrice

SELECT   *
FROM     ProductOptions

SELECT *
FROM ProductSpecial
```

This simple stored procedure returns resultsets containing the data stored in each of the MyGolfGear product tables. The support for the new product special functionality is italicized in Listing 8.1. Notice that this addition simply returns all the data in the ProductSpecial table.

Implementing the `ProductSpecialDataTable` Class

The CatalogDS class is a strongly typed dataset that allows access to tables and columns within the dataset with user-friendly names. This class is derived from DataSet, which means it inherits all the DataSet methods, properties, and events. It also allows for the creation of custom strongly typed methods, properties, and events. So, instead of collection-based access, programmers can access the data in CatalogDS via their names. This also means that data being retrieved via the strongly typed dataset will always be of the correct type because the compiler catches type-mismatch errors instead of waiting for runtime errors to occur.

So, what does all this information have to do with the ProductSpecialDataTable class? This class is one of the strongly typed members created from the schema of the ProductSpecial table. This, in turn, allows for strongly typed access to the information within this table. Listing 8.2 shows the ProductSpecialDataTable class that is part of the CatalogDS class.

LISTING 8.2 The *ProductSpecialDataTable* Class

```
public class ProductSpecialDataTable : DataTable, System.Collections.
➥IEnumerable {

    private DataColumn columnProductSpecialID;

    private DataColumn columnProductID;

    private DataColumn columnStartDate;

    private DataColumn columnEndDate;

    private DataColumn columnPromoTypeID;

    private DataColumn columnPromoValue;

    private DataColumn columnPromoDiscount;

    private DataColumn columnPromoPartID;

    internal ProductSpecialDataTable() :
            base("ProductSpecial") {
        this.InitClass();
    }

    [System.ComponentModel.Browsable(false)]
    public int Count {
        get {
            return this.Rows.Count;
        }
    }

    internal DataColumn ProductSpecialIDColumn {
        get {
            return this.columnProductSpecialID;
        }
    }

    internal DataColumn ProductIDColumn {
        get {
            return this.columnProductID;
        }
    }
```

8

DISCOUNT
SPECIALS

LISTING 8.2   Continued

```
internal DataColumn StartDateColumn {
    get {
        return this.columnStartDate;
    }
}

internal DataColumn EndDateColumn {
    get {
        return this.columnEndDate;
    }
}

internal DataColumn PromoTypeIDColumn {
    get {
        return this.columnPromoTypeID;
    }
}

internal DataColumn PromoValueColumn {
    get {
        return this.columnPromoValue;
    }
}

internal DataColumn PromoDiscountColumn {
    get {
        return this.columnPromoDiscount;
    }
}

internal DataColumn PromoPartIDColumn {
    get {
        return this.columnPromoPartID;
    }
}

public ProductSpecialRow this[int index] {
    get {
        return ((ProductSpecialRow)(this.Rows[index]));
    }
}

public event ProductSpecialRowChangeEventHandler ProductSpecialRowChanged;
public event ProductSpecialRowChangeEventHandler ProductSpecialRowChanging;
```

LISTING 8.2   Continued

```
    public event ProductSpecialRowChangeEventHandler ProductSpecialRowDeleted;
    public event ProductSpecialRowChangeEventHandler ProductSpecialRowDeleting;
    public void AddProductSpecialRow(ProductSpecialRow row) {
            this.Rows.Add(row);
    }

    public ProductSpecialRow AddProductSpecialRow(ProductRow
➥parentProductRowByProductSpecial, System.DateTime StartDate,
➥System.DateTime EndDate, int PromoTypeID, string PromoValue,
➥System.Decimal PromoDiscount, System.Guid PromoPartID) {
            ProductSpecialRow rowProductSpecialRow = ((ProductSpecialRow)
➥(this.NewRow()));
            rowProductSpecialRow.ItemArray = new Object[] {null,
                    parentProductRowByProductSpecial[0],
                    StartDate,
                    EndDate,
                    PromoTypeID,
                    PromoValue,
                    PromoDiscount,
                    PromoPartID};
            this.Rows.Add(rowProductSpecialRow);
            return rowProductSpecialRow;
    }

    public ProductSpecialRow FindByProductSpecialID(int ProductSpecialID) {
            return ((ProductSpecialRow)(this.Rows.Find(new Object[]
➥{ProductSpecialID})));
    }

    public System.Collections.IEnumerator GetEnumerator() {
            return this.Rows.GetEnumerator();
    }

    private void InitClass() {
            this.columnProductSpecialID = new DataColumn("ProductSpecialID",
➥typeof(int), "", System.Data.MappingType.Element);
            this.columnProductSpecialID.AutoIncrement = true;
            this.columnProductSpecialID.AllowDBNull = false;
            this.columnProductSpecialID.ReadOnly = true;
            this.columnProductSpecialID.Unique = true;
            this.Columns.Add(this.columnProductSpecialID);
            this.columnProductID = new DataColumn("ProductID",
➥typeof(System.Guid), "", System.Data.MappingType.Element);
            this.Columns.Add(this.columnProductID);
```

8

DISCOUNT SPECIALS

LISTING 8.2   Continued

```
        this.columnStartDate = new DataColumn("StartDate",
➡typeof(System.DateTime), "", System.Data.MappingType.Element);
        this.Columns.Add(this.columnStartDate);
        this.columnEndDate = new DataColumn("EndDate",
➡typeof(System.DateTime), "", System.Data.MappingType.Element);
        this.Columns.Add(this.columnEndDate);
        this.columnPromoTypeID = new DataColumn("PromoTypeID", typeof(int),
➡"", System.Data.MappingType.Element);
        this.Columns.Add(this.columnPromoTypeID);
        this.columnPromoValue = new DataColumn("PromoValue", typeof(string),
➡"", System.Data.MappingType.Element);
        this.Columns.Add(this.columnPromoValue);
        this.columnPromoDiscount = new DataColumn("PromoDiscount",
➡typeof(System.Decimal), "", System.Data.MappingType.Element);
        this.Columns.Add(this.columnPromoDiscount);
        this.columnPromoPartID = new DataColumn("PromoPartID",
➡typeof(System.Guid), "", System.Data.MappingType.Element);
        this.Columns.Add(this.columnPromoPartID);
        this.PrimaryKey = new DataColumn[] {this.columnProductSpecialID};
    }

    public ProductSpecialRow NewProductSpecialRow() {
        return ((ProductSpecialRow)(this.NewRow()));
    }

    protected override DataRow NewRowFromBuilder(DataRowBuilder builder) {
        // We need to ensure that all Rows in the tables are typed rows.
        // Table calls newRow whenever it needs to create a row.
        // So the following conditions are covered by Row newRow(Record record)
        // * Cursor calls table.addRecord(record)
        // * table.addRow(object[] values) calls newRow(record)
        return new ProductSpecialRow(builder);
    }

    protected override System.Type GetRowType() {
        return typeof(ProductSpecialRow);
    }

    protected override void OnRowChanged(DataRowChangeEventArgs e) {
        base.OnRowChanged(e);
        if ((this.ProductSpecialRowChanged != null)) {
            this.ProductSpecialRowChanged(this, new
➡ProductSpecialRowChangeEvent(((ProductSpecialRow)(e.Row)), e.Action));
        }
```

LISTING 8.2   Continued

```
    }

  protected override void OnRowChanging(DataRowChangeEventArgs e) {
        base.OnRowChanging(e);
        if ((this.ProductSpecialRowChanging != null)) {
            this.ProductSpecialRowChanging(this, new
➥ProductSpecialRowChangeEvent(((ProductSpecialRow)(e.Row)), e.Action));
        }
    }

  protected override void OnRowDeleted(DataRowChangeEventArgs e) {
        base.OnRowDeleted(e);
        if ((this.ProductSpecialRowDeleted != null)) {
            this.ProductSpecialRowDeleted(this, new
➥ProductSpecialRowChangeEvent(((ProductSpecialRow)(e.Row)), e.Action));
        }
    }

  protected override void OnRowDeleting(DataRowChangeEventArgs e) {
        base.OnRowDeleting(e);
        if ((this.ProductSpecialRowDeleting != null)) {
            this.ProductSpecialRowDeleting(this, new
➥ProductSpecialRowChangeEvent(((ProductSpecialRow)(e.Row)), e.Action));
        }
    }

  public void RemoveProductSpecialRow(ProductSpecialRow row) {
        this.Rows.Remove(row);
    }
}
```

The class in Listing 8.2 is the most significant addition to the CatalogDS strongly typed dataset. After the schema for the ProductSpecial table is added to CatalogDS.xsd, the XSD.EXE utility can be used to generate the CatalogDS class again.

The ProductSpecialDataTable class inherits from the DataTable class, so it has the same functionality as the DataTable class. Additionally, it has functionality specific to the ProductSpecial table.

8

DISCOUNT SPECIALS

NOTE

You can find the code for the entire CatalogDS class online.

Using the `OrderManager` Class to Implement Discount Specials

The `OrderManager` class is instrumental in implementing the product special features in MyGolfGear.NET. This class is responsible for basic order manipulation, such as basic basket manipulation and order processing (including shipping and tax calculations as well as credit card authorization).

The `OrderManager` class is responsible for using the `CatalogDS` and `ProductSpecialDataTable` classes to determine a product's promotional price. The `GetPromoPrice` method, shown in Listing 8.3, does this.

LISTING 8.3   The *GetPromoPrice* Method

```
public decimal GetPromoPrice(System.Guid productid, decimal price)
{
    decimal promoprice = 0;
    CatalogDS catalogds = (CatalogDS)HttpRuntime.Cache.Get("CatalogDS");
    if (catalogds == null)
    {
        // Re-insert catalog into the cache
        MyGolfGearDP dp = new MyGolfGearDP();
        catalogds = new CatalogDS();
        dp.FillCatalog(catalogds);
        HttpRuntime.Cache.Insert("Catalog",catalogds,null,System.DateTime.
➥MaxValue, System.TimeSpan.FromHours(24),CacheItemPriority.High,
➥CacheItemPriorityDecay.Never,null);
    }
    CatalogDS.ProductRow productrow = catalogds.Product.FindByProductID
➥ (productid);

    //Determine if there is a current special for this product
    CatalogDS.ProductSpecialRow[] psr = productrow.GetProductSpecialRows();
    foreach(CatalogDS.ProductSpecialRow r in psr)
    {
        if ((r.IsStartDateNull() && r.IsEndDateNull()) || ((r.StartDate <
➥System.DateTime.Today) && (r.EndDate > System.DateTime.Today)) )
        {
            switch (r.PromoTypeID)
            {
                case 1:  //Percent Discount
                            if (! r.IsPromoDiscountNull()) {promoprice =
```

LISTING 8.3   Continued

```
➥price * r.PromoDiscount;}
                break;
            case 2:  //Price Discount
                if (! r.IsPromoDiscountNull()) {promoprice =
➥r.PromoDiscount;}
                break;
            }
        }
    }
return promoprice;
}
```

The `GetPromoPrice` method first gets and fills an instance of `CatalogDS` and inserts it into the runtime cache. Next, it gets `ProductRow` by using the `FindByProductID` method. Next, it fills an array of `ProductSpecialRow` objects and iterates through them, applying either a percentage-based discount or a flat-price discount depending on the `PromoTypeID`. Finally, it returns a double value representing the promotional price of the product.

> **NOTE**
>
> The `OrderManager` class will be covered in more detail in Chapter 14, "Using ASP.NET to Build the Shopping Cart." You can find the code for this entire class online.

Modifying the Product Selection Page to Display Discount Information

We needed to make some modifications to a few pages to convey to users a product's special price or discount. The first page we modified was the Product Selection page. As with most of the ASP.NET code in the MyGolfGear.NET application, we had to make changes to a code behind class as well as an .aspx file.

ProductSelection.aspx.cs

When the `Page_Load` method is called, it in turn calls the `FillProductList` method. The `FillProductList` method, shown in Listing 8.4, is responsible for filling in the `DataList` object used on the `ProductSelection.aspx` page.

LISTING 8.4   The *FillProductList* Method

```
protected void FillProductList()
{
    OrderManager ordermanager = new OrderManager();
    decimal promoprice;
    decimal price = 0;

    //Find the Category row Selected
    System.Guid CategoryID = new System.Guid(Request.Params["CatId"]);
    CatalogDS.CategoryRow CatRow = catalogds.Category.FindByCategoryID
➥ (CategoryID);
    CatName.Text = CatRow["Name"].ToString();

    //Create temp datatable with associated products for the selected category
    CatalogDS.CategoryProductMappingRow[] cpmr = CatRow.
➥GetCategoryProductMappingRows();
    //Create datatable to insert the cat/product mapping rows in to
➥populate the grid
    DataTable dt = new DataTable("Products");
    dt.Columns.Add("ProductID");
    dt.Columns.Add("Name");
    dt.Columns.Add("ImageName");
    dt.Columns.Add("Price");
    dt.Columns.Add("Promo");
    dt.Columns.Add("PromoPart");

    //Iterate through the cat/mapping table adding the product rows to
➥this new datatable
    foreach(CatalogDS.CategoryProductMappingRow mr in cpmr)
    {
        DataRow tempRow = dt.NewRow();
        tempRow["ProductID"] = mr.ProductID;
        tempRow["Name"] = mr.ProductRow.Name;
        if (mr.ProductRow.IsImageNameNull())
        {
            tempRow["ImageName"] = "";
        }
        else
        {
            tempRow["ImageName"] = mr.ProductRow.ImageName.ToString();
        }
        //Determine the price of the product
        CatalogDS.ProductPriceRow[] ppr = mr.ProductRow.GetProductPriceRows();
        foreach(CatalogDS.ProductPriceRow r in ppr)
        {
            if (r.IsStartDateNull() && r.IsEndDateNull())
```

LISTING 8.4   Continued

```
            {
                tempRow["Price"] = String.Format("{0:c}", r.Price);
            }
            else if ((r.StartDate < System.DateTime.Today) &&
(r.EndDate > System.DateTime.Today))
            {
                tempRow["Price"] = String.Format("{0:c}", r.Price);
            }
            price = r.Price;
        }
        //Determine if there is a current special for this product
        promoprice = ordermanager.GetPromoPrice(mr.ProductID,price);
        if (promoprice != 0) {tempRow["Promo"] = String.Format
("SALE: {0:c}", promoprice);}


        dt.Rows.Add(tempRow);
    }
    //Populate DataList
    if (dt.Rows.Count == 0)
    {
        lblNoProduct.Text = "Currently there are no products available.";
        lblNoProduct.Visible = true;
    }
    ProductList.DataSource = dt.DefaultView;
    ProductList.DataKeyField = "ProductID";
    ProductList.DataBind();
}
```

The significant changes are italicized in the Listing 8.4. The OrderManager object's
GetPromoPrice method returns the promotional price of any part in the ProductSpecial table.
If a promotional price is found for a given product, a new row is added to the Products
DataTable. From there, the default DataView can be bound to the ProductList DataList that
displays the product information.

ProductSelection.aspx

The ProductSelection.aspx page is responsible for displaying the product special information, along with the basic product information for a given category. Figure 8.1 shows what this
page looks like.

Only slight additions were needed to support the product special functionality. Listing 8.5
shows the relevant code for this functionality.

FIGURE 8.1

The Product Selection page.

LISTING 8.5 The *ProductSelection* *ProductList* *DataList*

```
<asp:DataList id="ProductList" ItemStyle-CssClass="clsMenu" runat="server"
➥RepeatColumns="2">
    <ItemTemplate>
        <table CellPadding=3 cellspacing=4 border=0 width="275">
            <tr valign=top>
                <td valign=top width="125" align=left>
                    <a href='ProductDetails.aspx?productID
➥ =<%# DataBinder.Eval(Container.DataItem,"ProductID") %>'>
                        <img src='../Images/ProductImages
/thumbnails/<%# DataBinder.Eval(Container.DataItem, "ImageName") %>'
➥width="100" height="75" border="0">
                    </a>
                    <br>
                    <a href='AddProductsToOrder.aspx?
➥productID=<%# DataBinder.Eval(Container.DataItem, "ProductID")
➥%>'><font color=
➥"green" size="2"><b>Add To Cart</b></font></a> | 
                    <a href='AddToWishList.aspx?productID=
➥<%# DataBinder.Eval(Container.DataItem, "ProductID")  %>'>
➥<font color="green" size="2"><b>Add To Wish List</b></font></a>
```

LISTING 8.5   Continued

```
                </td>
                <td valign=top width="150" align=left>
                    <font size=2><a href='ProductDetails.aspx?
➥productID=<%# DataBinder.Eval(Container.DataItem, "ProductID")
➥ %>'><%# DataBinder.Eval(Container.DataItem, "Name") %></a>
                        <br>
                            Price: <%# DataBinder.
➥Eval(Container.DataItem, "Price") %>
                        <BR>
                        <font size=2 color=red>
                        <%# DataBinder.Eval
➥ (Container.DataItem, "Promo") %>
                        </font>
                </td>
            </tr>
        </table>
    </ItemTemplate>
</asp:DataList>
```

The only significant changes to the `ProductSelection.aspx` page are italicized in Listing 8.5. Adding a reference to and formatting the new `"Promo"` `DataRow` were the only changes we needed to make.

Adding Discount Information to the Product Details Page

The same discount information needs to be displayed on the product details page as well. Adding this information involved making changes to the `ProductDetails` code behind class and the `.aspx` page as well.

ProductDetails.aspx.cs

The `ProductDetails` code behind class needed only slight modifications to support the product special functionality. As with the product selection class, the special price or discount of any product that qualifies must be displayed. Listing 8.6 shows the method in which this functionality was implemented.

LISTING 8.6   The *PopulateDetails* Method

```
protected void PopulateDetails()
{
    OrderManager ordermanager = new OrderManager();
```

LISTING 8.6 Continued

```
    decimal promoprice;
    // Put user code to initialize the page here
    System.Guid ProductID = new System.Guid(Request.Params["ProductID"]);

    GetCatalog();
    //Find the Product row Selected
    CatalogDS.ProductRow ProductRow = catalogds.Product.FindByProductID
➡ (ProductID);
    ProductName.Text = ProductRow.Name.ToString();
    if (!ProductRow.IsLongDescriptionNull()) {Description.Text =
➡ProductRow.LongDescription.ToString();}
    AddToCart.NavigateUrl = "AddProductsToOrder.aspx?productID=" +
➡ProductID.ToString();
    AddToCart.Text = "Add To Basket";
    if (ProductRow.IsImageNameNull())
    {
        ProdImage.Visible = false;
        lblNoImage.Visible = true;              }
    else
    {
        lblNoImage.Visible = false;
        ProdImage.ImageUrl = "../images/ProductImages/" +
➡ProductRow.ImageName.ToString();
    }
    //Locate the price for this product.
    CatalogDS.ProductPriceRow PriceRow = catalogds.ProductPrice.
➡FindByProductID(ProductID);
    lblPrice.Text =  String.Format("{0:c}", PriceRow.Price);
    //Determine if this product is on sale
    promoprice = ordermanager.GetPromoPrice
➡ (ProductRow.ProductID,PriceRow.Price);
    if (promoprice != 0)
    {
        label2.Visible = true;
        lblPromoPrice.Text = String.Format("{0:c}", promoprice);
    }
    else
    {
        label2.Visible = false;
    }
}
```

The italicized portion of Listing 8.6 represents the only additional code in the code behind class that we added to support product special discounts on MyGolfGear.NET. As with the product selection code behind class, the promotional price was retrieved using the `OrderManager` class' `GetPromoPrice` method. The only real difference is that this information is not bound using data binding. Instead, the `Label` class' `Text` property is used to display the new information.

ProductDetails.aspx

The `ProductDetails.aspx` page is responsible for displaying the new promotional price if a product has one. As with the product selection page, making these changes took very little work. Listing 8.7 shows the relevant part of the `ProductDetails.aspx` page.

LISTING 8.7   The *ProductDetails.aspx* Page

```
<table border="0" width="100%" cellspacing="0" cellpadding="15">
<tr>
<td width="100%" valign="top">
<b>Product:
<asp:Label ID="ProductName" ForeColor="#336699" Runat=server />
</b>
<br>
<br>
<asp:Label Visible=False ID="lblNoProduct" Runat=server />
<table height="100%" valign="top" align="left" cellspacing=3 cellpadding=0
➥width="100%" border=0>
<tr height="100%" valign="top">
<td nowrap>
<table CellPadding=3 cellspacing=4 border=0 width="500">
<tr valign=top>
<td valign=top width="250" align=left>
<asp:Label id="Description" runat="server" />
</td>
<td valign=top width="250" align=center border=0>
<asp:image id="ProdImage" border=0 runat="server"/>
<asp:Label id="lblNoImage" ForeColor="red" Text="No image available"
➥runat="server" visible="false"/>
<br>
<BR>
<BR>
<table border=0>
<tr >
<td bgcolor=beige>
    <asp:Label ID="label1" Text="Your Price:" align=right runat=server/>
</td>
<td width=50>
    <asp:Label ID="lblPrice" Runat=server />
```

LISTING 8.7   Continued

```
</td>
</tr>
<tr >
<td bgcolor=beige>
    <font color=red><asp:Label ID="label2" Text="Sale Price:" align=right
➥runat=server/></font>
</td>
<td width=50>
    <font color=red>
    <asp:Label ID="lblPromoPrice" Runat=server />
    </font>
</td>
</tr>
</table>
<BR>
<asp:HyperLink id="AddToCart" runat="server" fontsize=2 forecolor=green/>
</td>
</tr>
</table>
</td>
</tr>
</table>
```

The italicized portion of Listing 8.7 shows the only additions needed to display the promotional price information. We used a simple Web Server Label control to bind the new information to.

Summary

This chapter covered the modifications necessary to support product specials on the MyGolfGear.NET site. It discussed how ASP.NET was used to implement flat rate discounts and percentage-based discounts so that product specials could be supported. Specifically, it covered the necessary modifications to the data model, the modifications to the spGetCompleteCatalog stored procedure, the updates to the CatalogDS component, and the modifications made to the product selection and product details page.

The next chapter, "Using ASP.NET to Implement Wish Lists," describes the necessary changes made to MyGolfGear.NET to support wish list functionality. Specifically, it covers the data model and stored procedure additions, as well as the addition of a new component and new user interface elements.

Self Instruction

Based on what you've learned about the MyGolfGear.NET discount special implementation in this chapter, implement a third type (MyGolfGear.NET supports flat discounts and percentage-based discounts) of promotion that allows for the awarding of bonus items when certain products are purchased. An example might be a free sleeve of golf balls that is awarded when a shopper buys a particular type of driver.

Using ASP.NET to Implement Wish Lists

IN THIS CHAPTER

Objectives

- Discover the necessary data model modifications for MyGolfGear.NET to implement wish lists

- Learn the details of the three new stored procedures used to implement wish lists in MyGolfGear.NET

- Discover the details of the data access component used in creating the MyGolfGear.NET wish list functionality

- Understand the additional user interface elements needed to implement wish lists in MyGolfGear.NET

A business-to-consumer (B2C) e-Commerce site feature that is becoming more common is *wish lists*. MyGolfGear.NET supports a wish list.

To achieve the desired functionality, we needed to make an addition to the data model and add three stored procedures, a new data access component, and three new user interface elements. This chapter covers the modifications to MyGolfGear.NET to enable the use of wish lists.

Additions to the Data Model

The data model modifications necessary to create the wish list functionality for MyGolfGear.NET were minimal. We created a single table to house the relationship between users and the products they wish to purchase. The WishList table contains the fields and data types described in Table 9.1.

TABLE 9.1   The *WishList* Table

Column Name	Data Type	Length	Description
UserID	int	4	A unique ID for each user
ProductID	uniqueidentifier	16	The product ID of the item a user wishes to buy

As you can see from Table 9.1, the implementation of wish lists is simple. Users are issued a unique ID that can be used for wish lists and other targeted content. As noted earlier, the details of this mechanism are discussed in Chapter 16.

The New Stored Procedures

After we created a schema to tie users to the products they wished to buy (or have bought for them), we needed a way to add, delete, and list the data. Three new stored procedures were added to achieve this functionality: spAddToWishList, spDeleteFromWishList, and spGetWishList.

The `spAddToWishList` Stored Procedure

As its name implies, the spAddToWishList stored procedure was created to allow for the addition of products to a particular user's wish list. Listing 9.1 shows the code for this stored procedure.

LISTING 9.1 *spAddToWishList*

```
CREATE PROCEDURE dbo.spAddToWishList
(
    @userid int,
    @productid uniqueidentifier
)
AS
if not exists (
select * from WishList where userid = @Userid and productid = @productID
)
BEGIN
insert into wishlist values( @Userid, @productid)
END
GO
```

The spAddToWishList stored procedure accepts two parameters. The first one is an integer representing the current user's ID. The second one, which is of type uniqueidentifier, represents the product being added to the wish list.

This stored procedure first checks to see whether the relationship already exists. If it does not, a new row is inserted into the WishList table using the @UserID and @ProductID parameters.

The `spDeleteFromWishList` Stored Procedure

The spDeleteFromWishList stored procedure makes it possible to delete items from a user's wish list. Listing 9.2 shows this stored procedure.

LISTING 9.2 *spDeleteFromWishList*

```
CREATE PROCEDURE dbo.spDeleteFromWishList
(
    @userid int,
    @productid uniqueidentifier
)
AS
DELETE FROM wishlist WHERE userid = @userid AND productid = @productid
```

The spDeleteFromWishList stored procedure accepts the same two parameters as the spAddToWishList stored procedure. These two parameters are used to remove any record that matches the user ID *and* the product ID.

The spGetWishList Stored Procedure

To get a list of the items in a user's wish list, you use the spGetWishList stored procedure. Listing 9.3 shows this stored procedure.

LISTING 9.3 *spGetWishList*

```
CREATE     PROCEDURE dbo.spGetWishList
(
    @userid int
)
AS

SELECT
wishlist.ProductID,
b.name as ParentName,
a.name as ProductName
FROM WishList JOIN product a ON wishlist.productid = a.productid
LEFT JOIN product b ON a.parentproductid = b.productid
WHERE
wishlist.userid = @Userid
```

The spGetWishList stored procedure accepts a single parameter of type int. This parameter represents the ID of the current user.

The product ID in the WishList table is joined with the product ID in the product table where the product ID matches the parent product ID and the wish list's user ID matches the one passed in.

The New Data Access Component

On top of the database layer, we needed a component that could use the stored procedures for adding, deleting, and getting a list of wish lists. For MyGolfGear.NET, the new component `WishList.cs` was created. This component is made up of the two private fields named `userid` and `connectionstring` as well as three public methods called `GetWishList`, `AddToWishList`, and `DeleteFromWishList`. It also implements the `Wishlist` constructor.

The `Wishlist` Constructor

The two private fields `userid` and `connectionstring` have their values assigned only in the constructor. Listing 9.4 shows the namespace and class declarations as well as private fields and the constructor.

LISTING 9.4   *Wishlist.cs*

```
namespace MyGolfGear {
    using System;
    using System.Data.SqlClient;

    public class Wishlist {
        private int userid;
        private string connectionstring;

        public Wishlist(int u) {
            userid = u;
            NameValueCollection configInfo = (NameValueCollection)HttpContext.
➥Current.GetConfig("appSettings");
            connectionstring = (String)configInfo["ConnectString"];
        }
    }
}
```

Listing 9.4 begins with the namespace declaration, which includes the `Wishlist` class in the `MyGolfGear` namespace. It is followed by the typical `using System` and `using System.Data.SqlClient` statements. Next, the declarations of the `Wishlist` class and private fields are made, followed by the `Wishlist` constructor.

The `Wishlist` constructor takes one parameter: an integer corresponding to the current user's ID. The `connectionstring` variable is then assigned the value found in the `HttpContext` configuration information.

The `GetWishList` Method

The next part of the `Wishlist` class is the definition of the public method named `GetWishList`. This method is shown in Listing 9.5.

> **NOTE**
>
> We intentionally left exception handling out of the listings in this chapter to simplify the explanations.

LISTING 9.5   *GetWishList*

```
public SqlDataReader GetWishList(){
    SqlConnection conn = new SqlConnection(connectionstring);
    SqlCommand myCommand = new SqlCommand("spGetWishList", conn);

    // set the command type as a SP
    myCommand.CommandType = CommandType.StoredProcedure;

    // Add Parameters
    SqlParameter parameterUserID = new SqlParameter(
➥"@Userid", SqlDbType.Int,4);
    parameterUserID.Value = userid;
    myCommand.Parameters.Add(parameterUserID);

    // Populate the data reader
    conn.Open();
    SqlDataReader myReader = myCommand.ExecuteReader();
    conn.Close();

    // return the data reader
    return myReader;
}
```

The `GetWishList` method first creates and opens a connection to the MyGolfGear database. After a connection object is created, it can be used to create a `SqlCommand` object by passing in the name of the stored procedure that needs to be run, along with a reference to the newly created `SqlConnection` object.

Because `SqlCommand` objects can be created by passing in raw SQL text as the first parameter of the constructor, you then need to specify that the `CommandType` is a `StoredProcedure`.

At this point, a single parameter for the user ID is created and added to the `SqlCommand` object's `Parameters` collection.

Finally, a new `SqlDataReader` is created and assigned the value returned from calling the `SqlCommand` object's `ExecuteReader()` method. This method sends the command text to the connection object; then it builds and returns the `SqlDataReader` object.

> **CAUTION**
>
> When you use the `SqlDataReader`, don't forget to explicitly close the connection object. The `SqlDataReader` object is *not* disconnected like the `DataSet` object is, and failing to close a database connection after each use can degrade performance.

The `AddToWishList` Method

To associate users with a list of products, we needed a way to add products to the users' wish lists. To do so, we created the public method `AddToWishList`. This method takes a GUID representing a product ID as its only parameter and adds it to the current user's wish list. Listing 9.6 shows this method.

LISTING 9.6 The *AddToWishList* Method

```
public void AddToWishList(Guid p){
    SqlConnection conn = new SqlConnection(connectionstring);
    SqlCommand myCommand = new SqlCommand("spAddToWishList", conn);

    myCommand.CommandType = CommandType.StoredProcedure;

    SqlParameter parameterUserID = new SqlParameter("@Userid",
➥SqlDbType.Int,4);
    parameterUserID.Value = userid;
    myCommand.Parameters.Add(parameterUserID);

    SqlParameter parameterProductID = new SqlParameter("@ProductID",
➥SqlDbType.UniqueIdentifier, 16);
    parameterProductID.Value = p;
    myCommand.Parameters.Add(parameterProductID);

    conn.Open();
    myCommand.ExecuteNonQuery();
}
```

First, a `SqlConnection` object is created using the protected field `connectionstring` as the only parameter. Then a `SqlCommand` object is created using the string `"spAddToWishList"` and the `SqlConnection` just created as the constructor parameters.

9

USING ASP.NET
TO IMPLEMENT
WISH LISTS

Next, two `SqlParameter` objects are created. The first one is for passing the current user's ID to the `spAddToWishList` stored procedure. The second one is for passing in the product ID.

Finally, the connection is opened and the command is executed using the `ExecuteNonQuery` method. This method executes a statement that does not return any rows; it does, however, return an integer representing the number of rows affected.

The `DeleteFromWishList` Method

For a user to remove items from his wish list, we needed a method to remove the association between that user and a specified product. For that reason, we added the `DeleteFromWishList` method to the `Wishlist` class. Listing 9.7 shows this method.

LISTING 9.7 The *DeleteFromWishList* Method

```
public void DeleteFromWishList(Guid p){
    SqlConnection conn = new SqlConnection(connectionstring);
    SqlCommand myCommand = new SqlCommand("spDeleteFromaWishList", conn);

    myCommand.CommandType = CommandType.StoredProcedure;

    SqlParameter parameterUserID = new SqlParameter("@Userid",
➥SqlDbType.Int,4);
    parameterUserID.Value = userid;
    myCommand.Parameters.Add(parameterUserID);

    SqlParameter parameterProductID = new SqlParameter("@ProductID",
➥SqlDbType.UniqueIdentifier, 16);
    parameterProductID.Value = p;
    myCommand.Parameters.Add(parameterProductID);

    conn.Open();
    myCommand.ExecuteNonQuery();
}
```

The `DeleteFromWishList` method is implemented almost exactly the same as the `AddToWishList` method. The only difference between the two methods is the name of the stored procedure passed into the `SqlCommand` object's constructor.

Just as with the `AddToWishList` method, the `DeleteFromWishList` method starts with the creation of `SqlConnection` and `SqlCommand` objects. As previously mentioned, the string `"spDeleteFromWishList"` is passed along with the newly created connection object to the `SqlCommand` object's constructor, and the `StoredProcedure.CommandType` is specified.

Next, two `SqlParameter` objects are created. The first one represents the current user's ID, and the second one represents the ID of the product to be removed from the wish list.

Finally, the connection object is opened, and the `SqlCommand` object's `ExecuteNonQuery` method is called.

> **NOTE**
>
> You can find the code for the `WishList` class online.

The User Interface Elements

Three main user interface elements were added to implement wish lists on MyGolfGear.NET. They include the two new pages `AddToWishList.aspx` and `ViewWishList.aspx` as well as additional functionality for the `ProductSelection.aspx` page.

In conjunction with the declarative user interface elements, three code behind classes were used as well. They are named the same as the `.aspx` pages with a `.cs` extension.

The `AddToWishList.aspx.cs` Code Behind Class

The first step in creating a wish list for a user is giving her the ability to add items to her own list. The `AddToWishList` pages provide this functionality. Listing 9.8 shows the `AddToWish List.aspx.cs` code behind page that ties the user interface to the data access class named `Wishlist.cs`.

LISTING 9.8   The *AddToWishList.aspx.cs* Code Behind's *Page_Load* Method

```
protected void Page_Load(object sender, System.EventArgs e)
{
    MyGolfGear.WishList w = new MyGolfGear.WishList( 1 );
    //Get ProductID
    productid = new System.Guid(Request.Params["ProductID"]);
    //Add to WishList
    w.AddToWishList( productid );
    //go to WishList page
    Server.Transfer("viewwishlist.aspx",false);
}
```

The `Page_Load` method of the `AddToWishList.aspx.cs` page uses an instance of the `WishList` class to add items to a user's wish list. First, it creates an instance of the `WishList` class; then it uses the product ID sent as a parameter to the page to call the `WishList` object's

AddToWishList method. Finally, it uses the `Server.Transfer` method to transfer the user to the `ViewWishList.aspx` page.

> **NOTE**
>
> `AddToWishList.aspx` has no visible user interface. We included it in the project simply to tie the user interface to the data access layer.

The `ViewWishList.aspx.cs` Code Behind Class

The `ViewWishList.aspx.cs` class implements two important methods: `Page_Load`, which binds the actual wish list to the user interface elements; and `Delete`, which deletes items from a user's wish list. Listing 9.9 shows the `Page_Load` method for the `ViewWishList.aspx.cs` class.

LISTING 9.9   The *ViewWishList.aspx.cs* Class' *Page_Load Method*

```
protected void Page_Load(object sender, System.EventArgs e) {
    int iUserID = Request.Params["UserID"];
    w = new Wishlist(iUserID);
    SqlDataReader d = w.GetWishList;
    wlDataGrid.DataSource = d;
    wlDataGrid.DataBind();
}
```

The `Page_Load` method simply grabs the user ID from the `parameters` collection and uses it to create a new `WishList` component (the variable used for this task is a protected member variable, so after the page is created, this instance is around for the life of the object). Then it calls the `GetWishList` method, assigns it to the wish list data grid's `DataSource` property, and calls `DataBind` on the `DataGrid` object.

When an item needs to be deleted from a user's wish list, the `Delete` method is used. Listing 9.10 shows what this code looks like.

LISTING 9.10   The *Delete* Method

```
public void Delete(Object sender, DataGridCommandEventArgs e) {
    System.Guid ProductID = (System.Guid)wlDataGrid.DataKeys[e.Item.ItemIndex];
    w.DeleteFromWishList(ProductID);
}
```

The `Delete` method takes the product ID from the wish list data grid and uses it to call the `DeleteFromWishList` method on the protected member `Wishlist` object named w.

The `ViewWishList.aspx` Page

The `ViewWishList.aspx` page was created using the standard MyGolfGear ASP.NET page template. This means that it includes the standard user controls for the category menu, header, footer, and the specials user control. The only thing different about this page is the use of a `DataGrid` object to control the layout and contents of the wish list. Listing 9.11 shows the wish list–specific portion of the `ViewWishList.aspx` page.

LISTING 9.11 The Wish List *DataGrid*

```
<asp:DataGrid id=wlDataGrid BorderColor="black" BorderWidth="1"
➥CellPadding="3" Font-Name="Verdana" Font-Size="8pt" OnDeleteCommand="
➥Delete" datakeyfield="ProductID" AutoGenerateColumns="false" runat=
➥"server" AlternatingItemStyle-BackColor="Beige" FooterStyle-BackColor=
➥"Silver" FooterStyle-ForeColor="White" ItemStyle-BackColor="White"
➥EditItemStyle-BackColor="yellow" HeaderStyle-BackColor="DarkGreen"
➥HeaderStyle-Font-Bold="True" HeaderStyle-ForeColor="Beige">
    <Columns>
        <ASP:TemplateColumn HeaderText="Product">
            <ItemTemplate>
                <%# DataBinder.Eval(Container.DataItem, "ProductName") %>
            </ItemTemplate>
        </ASP:TemplateColumn>
        <asp:ButtonColumn HeaderText="Delete" Text="Delete" CommandName=
➥"Delete" />
        <asp:TemplateColumn HeaderText="Buy Now">
            <ItemTemplate>
                <a href='AddProductsToOrder.aspx?productID=<%# DataBinder.Eval
➥ (Container.DataItem, "ProductID") %>'>Add to cart</a>
            </ItemTemplate>
        </asp:TemplateColumn>
    </Columns>
</asp:DataGrid>
```

We want to point out several important facts about the use of the `DataGrid` object to display wish lists. There are five main parts to the wish list display using the `DataGrid`:

- The `DataGrid` declaration
- The `Columns` collection declaration
- The `TemplateColumn` declarations
- The `ButtonColumn` declaration
- The `ItemTemplate` used for linking to the `AddProductsToOrder.aspx` page

The `DataGrid` declaration is responsible for the way the wish list data is displayed, but it is also the place where the delete method in the code behind class is tied to the grid. When you specify the `OnDeleteCommand="Delete"` attribute, the runtime knows to use the `Delete` method to perform any deletes from the data that is bound to it.

The `Columns` tags simply hold the `TemplateColumn` and `ButtonColumn` declarations. These two types of tags are used to specify columns of data to be displayed as well as buttons to be used with each line item listed. The `ButtonColumn` tag is used in conjunction with the `OnDeleteCommand` attribute in the `DataGrid` declaration to specify what action should be taken when the button is clicked.

The last tag to note is the `ItemTemplate` tag. In this case, the `ItemTemplate` tag is used to create a hyperlink to the `AddProductsToOrder.aspx` page. It allows users to add items in their wish list to their shopping carts. Figure 9.1 shows the `ViewWishList.aspx` page.

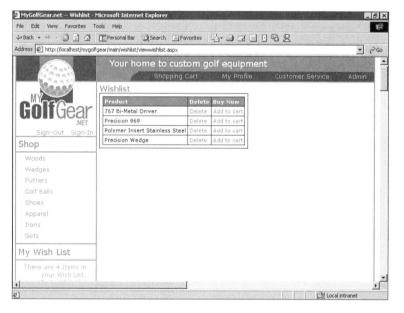

FIGURE 9.1
The View Wish List page.

The `ProductSelection.aspx` Page

The `ProductSelection.aspx` page was modified to allow users to add items to their wish lists. We added a simple anchor tag to the `ItemTemplate` of the `ProductList` data list. The new anchor tag simply links to the `AddToWishList` page. Listing 9.12 shows what this page looks like.

LISTING 9.12   Add to Wish List Anchor

```
<a href='AddToWishList.aspx?productID=<%# DataBinder.Eval(Container.DataItem,
➥"ProductID") %>'><font color="green" size="2"><b>Add To Wish List
</b></font></a>
```

When you use the `DataBinder.Eval` method, the product ID of the current item can be passed to the `AddToWishList.aspx` page. Figure 9.2 shows what the new ProductSelection page looks like.

FIGURE 9.2
The Product Selection page.

Summary

This chapter explained what a wish list is and discussed how this functionality was implemented for MyGolfGear.NET. Specifically, it discussed the necessary additions to the data model, the new stored procedures to support this functionality, a new data access component, and the new user interface elements.

The next chapter, "Using ASP.NET to Implement Product Reviews and Ratings," covers how MyGolfGear.NET implements the capability to accept and display product reviews and ratings.

Self Instruction

Based on what you've learned in this chapter, implement a new user control that lists a logged-in user's wish list. For an idea of what the finished product should look like, check the MyGolfGear.NET Web site at `http://www.MyGolfGear.NET`.

Some Web sites, such as Amazon.com, allow users to search for the wish lists of other registered users. For an extra challenge, try implementing the capability to search and list other user's wish lists.

Using ASP.NET to Implement Product Reviews and Ratings

IN THIS CHAPTER

Objectives

- Learn about the database tables and stored procedures needed to support product reviews and ratings

- Understand how to develop the user interface to support product reviews and ratings

A common feature of some of today's most common Web sites is the capability to view and add product reviews and ratings. MyGolfGear.NET supports this functionality by utilizing some of the common ASP.NET features, such as user controls, data lists, and datasets.

This chapter discusses the MyGolfGear.NET implementation of product reviews and ratings. Specifically, it covers the database changes, new classes, and new the Product Reviews User Control developed for this new functionality.

The Database Changes to Support Product Reviews

To store and retrieve the data needed for product reviews and ratings, we needed to make additions to the MyGolfGear database. For this reason, we added a new table and modified the stored procedure spGetCompleteCatalog.

We created the ProductReviews table to support the new functionality. This table houses a product ID, user ID, a rating, and comments for each item reviewed. Table 10.1 shows the details of this table.

TABLE 10.1 The ProductReviews Table

Column Name	Data Type	Size	Allows Nulls
ReviewID	uniqueid	16	No
ProductID	uniqueid	16	No
UserID	int	4	No
Rating	int	4	No
Comments	varchar	2500	Yes
DateEntered	datetime	8	No

We decided that the CatalogDS class was the most appropriate place to house the code responsible for interacting with this table. To facilitate this, we made a simple addition to the stored procedure spGetCompleteCatalog. Listing 10.1 shows this stored procedure with the new functionality italicized.

LISTING 10.1   The `spGetCompleteCatalog` Stored Procedure

```
CREATE PROCEDURE spGetCompleteCatalog
AS
SELECT    *
FROM    Category

SELECT    *
FROM    Product

SELECT    *
FROM    CategoryProductMapping

SELECT    *
FROM    ProductPrice

SELECT    *
FROM    ProductOptions

SELECT *
FROM ProductSpecial

SELECT *
FROM ProductReviews
ORDER BY DateEntered DESC

GO
```

As you can see, the addition to `spGetCompleteCatalog` simply selects all fields from the
`ProductReviews` table and orders them by the date they were entered. The `CatalogDS` class will be
able to use this information when we make a simple addition to the schema in the next section.

Changes to the `CatalogDS` Class Necessary to Support Product Reviews

We modified the `CatalogDS` class slightly to enable support of product reviews. A simple addition, representing the `ProductReviews` table schema, was made to the `CatalogDS.xsd` file.
Listing 10.2 shows what the new schema looks like, with the new sections italicized.

LISTING 10.2   The `CatalogDS` Schema

```
<?xml version="1.0" encoding="utf-8" ?>
<xsd:schema id="DataSet1" targetNamespace="http://tempuri.org/DataSet1.xsd"
➥elementFormDefault="qualified" xmlns="http://tempuri.org/DataSet1.xsd"
```

LISTING 10.2   Continued

```
➡xmlns:xsd="http://www.w3.org/2001/XMLSchema" xmlns:msdata=
➡"urn:schemas-microsoft-com:xml-msdata">
   <xsd:element name="CatalogDS" msdata:IsDataSet="true">
      <xsd:complexType>
         <xsd:choice maxOccurs="unbounded">
...
            <xsd:element name="ProductReviews">
               <xsd:complexType>
                  <xsd:sequence>
                     <xsd:element name="ReviewID" msdata:DataType=
➡"System.Guid" msdata:DefaultValue="NULL" type="xsd:string"
➡msdata:Ordinal="0" />
                     <xsd:element name="ProductID" msdata:DataType=
➡"System.Guid" msdata:DefaultValue="NULL" type="xsd:string"
➡minOccurs="0" msdata:Ordinal="1" />
                     <xsd:element name="UserID" msdata:DefaultValue="NULL"
➡type="xsd:int" minOccurs="0" msdata:Ordinal="2" />
                     <xsd:element name="Rating" msdata:DefaultValue="NULL"
➡type="xsd:int" minOccurs="0" msdata:Ordinal="4" />
                     <xsd:element name="Comments" msdata:DefaultValue="NULL"
➡type="xsd:string" minOccurs="0" msdata:Ordinal="5" />
                  </xsd:sequence>
               </xsd:complexType>
            </xsd:element>
         </xsd:choice>
      </xsd:complexType>
...
      <xsd:key name="NewDataSetKey12" msdata:PrimaryKey="true">
         <xsd:selector xpath=".//Product" />
         <xsd:field xpath="ProductID" />
      </xsd:key>
      <xsd:key name="NewDataSetKey16" msdata:PrimaryKey="true">
         <xsd:selector xpath=".//ProductReviews" />
         <xsd:field xpath="ReviewID" />
      </xsd:key>
      <xsd:keyref name="ProductReviews" refer="NewDataSetKey12">
         <xsd:selector xpath=".//ProductReviews" />
         <xsd:field xpath="ProductID" />
      </xsd:keyref>
   </xsd:element>
</xsd:schema>
```

> **NOTE**
> _____
>
> You can find the complete listing for the `CatalogDS.xsd` file online.

The only addition necessary for this schema was the italicized section with the name `ProductReviews`. This section describes the database table's `ProductReviews` layout. The next italicized section first defines the primary key of the `ProductReviews DataTable` and then creates a data relationship between the `Product` and `ProductReviews` DataTables. To learn more about XSD Schemas, refer to Appendix D, "ADO.NET Quick Reference."

When used in conjunction with `xsd.exe`, this new schema information creates the `CatalogDS` class product review functionality. Three new classes are generated by this utility: `ProductReviewsDataTable`, `ProductReviewsRow`, and `ProductReviewsRowChangeEvent`. These classes are shown in Listing 10.3.

LISTING 10.3   New Product Review Classes

```
public class ProductReviewsDataTable : DataTable,
➥System.Collections.IEnumerable {
  private DataColumn columnReviewID;
  private DataColumn columnProductID;

  private DataColumn columnUserID;

  private DataColumn columnUserName;

  private DataColumn columnRating;

  private DataColumn columnComments;

  internal ProductReviewsDataTable() :
          base("ProductReviews") {
      this.InitClass();
  }

  [System.ComponentModel.Browsable(false)]
  public int Count {
      get {
          return this.Rows.Count;
      }
  }
```

10

LISTING 10.3   Continued

```
internal DataColumn ReviewIDColumn {
    get {
        return this.columnReviewID;
    }
}

internal DataColumn ProductIDColumn {
    get {
        return this.columnProductID;
    }
}

internal DataColumn UserIDColumn {
    get {
        return this.columnUserID;
    }
}

internal DataColumn UserNameColumn {
    get {
        return this.columnUserName;
    }
}

internal DataColumn RatingColumn {
    get {
        return this.columnRating;
    }
}
internal DataColumn CommentsColumn {
    get {
        return this.columnComments;
    }
}

public ProductReviewsRow this[int index] {
    get {
        return ((ProductReviewsRow)(this.Rows[index]));
    }
}

public event ProductReviewsRowChangeEventHandler ProductReviewsRowChanged;

public event ProductReviewsRowChangeEventHandler ProductReviewsRowChanging;

public event ProductReviewsRowChangeEventHandler ProductReviewsRowDeleted;
```

LISTING 10.3 Continued

```
public event ProductReviewsRowChangeEventHandler ProductReviewsRowDeleting;

public void AddProductReviewsRow(ProductReviewsRow row) {
    this.Rows.Add(row);
}

public ProductReviewsRow AddProductReviewsRow(System.Guid ReviewID,
➥ProductRow parentProductRowByProductReviews, int UserID, string
➥UserName, int Rating, string Comments) {
    ProductReviewsRow rowProductReviewsRow =
➥ ((ProductReviewsRow)(this.NewRow()));
    rowProductReviewsRow.ItemArray = new Object[] {ReviewID,
            parentProductRowByProductReviews[0],
            UserID,
            UserName,
            Rating,
            Comments};
    this.Rows.Add(rowProductReviewsRow);
    return rowProductReviewsRow;
}

public ProductReviewsRow FindByReviewID(System.Guid ReviewID) {
    return ((ProductReviewsRow)(this.Rows.Find(new Object[]
➥{ReviewID})));
}

public System.Collections.IEnumerator GetEnumerator() {
    return this.Rows.GetEnumerator();
}

private void InitClass() {
    this.columnReviewID = new DataColumn("ReviewID",
➥typeof(System.Guid), "", System.Data.MappingType.Element);
    this.columnReviewID.AllowDBNull = false;
    this.columnReviewID.Unique = true;
    this.Columns.Add(this.columnReviewID);
    this.columnProductID = new DataColumn("ProductID",
➥typeof(System.Guid), "", System.Data.MappingType.Element);
    this.Columns.Add(this.columnProductID);
    this.columnUserID = new DataColumn("UserID", typeof(int), "",
➥System.Data.MappingType.Element);
    this.Columns.Add(this.columnUserID);
    this.columnUserName = new DataColumn("UserName", typeof(string), "",
➥System.Data.MappingType.Element);
    this.Columns.Add(this.columnUserName);
    this.columnRating = new DataColumn("Rating", typeof(int), "",
```

10

PRODUCT REVIEWS
AND RATINGS

LISTING 10.3   Continued

```
➥System.Data.MappingType.Element);
        this.Columns.Add(this.columnRating);
        this.columnComments = new DataColumn("Comments", typeof(string), "",
➥System.Data.MappingType.Element);
        this.Columns.Add(this.columnComments);
        this.PrimaryKey = new DataColumn[] {this.columnReviewID};
    }

    public ProductReviewsRow NewProductReviewsRow() {
        return ((ProductReviewsRow)(this.NewRow()));
    }

    protected override DataRow NewRowFromBuilder(DataRowBuilder builder) {
        // We need to ensure that all Rows in the tables are typed rows.
        // Table calls newRow whenever it needs to create a row.
        // So the following conditions are covered by Row newRow(Record
➥record)
        // * Cursor calls table.addRecord(record)
        // * table.addRow(object[] values) calls newRow(record)
        return new ProductReviewsRow(builder);
    }

    protected override System.Type GetRowType() {
        return typeof(ProductReviewsRow);
    }

    protected override void OnRowChanged(DataRowChangeEventArgs e) {
        base.OnRowChanged(e);
        if ((this.ProductReviewsRowChanged != null)) {
            this.ProductReviewsRowChanged(this, new
➥ProductReviewsRowChangeEvent(((ProductReviewsRow)(e.Row)), e.Action));
        }
    }

    protected override void OnRowChanging(DataRowChangeEventArgs e) {
        base.OnRowChanging(e);
        if ((this.ProductReviewsRowChanging != null)) {
            this.ProductReviewsRowChanging(this, new
➥ProductReviewsRowChangeEvent(((ProductReviewsRow)(e.Row)), e.Action));
        }
    }

    protected override void OnRowDeleted(DataRowChangeEventArgs e) {
        base.OnRowDeleted(e);
        if ((this.ProductReviewsRowDeleted != null)) {
            this.ProductReviewsRowDeleted(this, new
```

LISTING 10.3 Continued

```
➡ProductReviewsRowChangeEvent(((ProductReviewsRow)(e.Row)), e.Action));
        }
    }

    protected override void OnRowDeleting(DataRowChangeEventArgs e) {
        base.OnRowDeleting(e);
        if ((this.ProductReviewsRowDeleting != null)) {
            this.ProductReviewsRowDeleting(this, new
➡ProductReviewsRowChangeEvent(((ProductReviewsRow)(e.Row)), e.Action));
        }
    }

    public void RemoveProductReviewsRow(ProductReviewsRow row) {
        this.Rows.Remove(row);
    }
}

public class ProductReviewsRow : DataRow {

    private ProductReviewsDataTable tableProductReviews;

    internal ProductReviewsRow(DataRowBuilder rb) :
            base(rb) {
        this.tableProductReviews = ((ProductReviewsDataTable)(this.Table));
    }

    public System.Guid ReviewID {
        get {
            return ((System.Guid)
➡(this[this.tableProductReviews.ReviewIDColumn]));
        }
        set {
            this[this.tableProductReviews.ReviewIDColumn] = value;
        }
    }

    public System.Guid ProductID {
        get {
            try {
                return ((System.Guid)
➡(this[this.tableProductReviews.ProductIDColumn]));
            }
            catch (InvalidCastException e) {
                throw new StrongTypingException
➡("Cannot get value because it is DBNull.", e);
            }
```

10

PRODUCT REVIEWS
AND RATINGS

LISTING 10.3 Continued

```
        }
        set {
           this[this.tableProductReviews.ProductIDColumn] = value;
        }
    }

    public int UserID {
        get {
           try {
              return ((int)(this[this.tableProductReviews.UserIDColumn]));
           }
           catch (InvalidCastException e) {
              throw new StrongTypingException
➡("Cannot get value because it is DBNull.", e);
           }
        }
        set {
           this[this.tableProductReviews.UserIDColumn] = value;
        }
    }

    public string UserName {
        get {
           try {
              return ((string)
➡(this[this.tableProductReviews.UserNameColumn]));
           }
           catch (InvalidCastException e) {
              throw new StrongTypingException
➡("Cannot get value because it is DBNull.", e);
           }
        }
        set {
           this[this.tableProductReviews.UserNameColumn] = value;
        }
    }

    public int Rating {
        get {
           try {
              return ((int)(this[this.tableProductReviews.RatingColumn]));
           }
           catch (InvalidCastException e) {
              throw new StrongTypingException
➡("Cannot get value because it is DBNull.", e);
           }
```

LISTING 10.3 Continued

```
        }
        set {
            this[this.tableProductReviews.RatingColumn] = value;
        }
    }

    public string Comments {
        get {
            try {
                return ((string)
➥(this[this.tableProductReviews.CommentsColumn]));
            }
            catch (InvalidCastException e) {
                throw new StrongTypingException
➥("Cannot get value because it is DBNull.", e);
            }
        }
        set {
            this[this.tableProductReviews.CommentsColumn] = value;
        }
    }

    public ProductRow ProductRow {
        get {
            return ((ProductRow)
➥(this.GetParentRow(this.Table.ParentRelations["ProductReviews"])));
        }
        set {
            this.SetParentRow(value,
➥this.Table.ParentRelations["ProductReviews"]);
        }
    }

    public bool IsProductIDNull() {
        return this.IsNull(this.tableProductReviews.ProductIDColumn);
    }

    public void SetProductIDNull() {
        this[this.tableProductReviews.ProductIDColumn] =
➥System.Convert.DBNull;
    }

    public bool IsUserIDNull() {
        return this.IsNull(this.tableProductReviews.UserIDColumn);
    }
```

10

PRODUCT REVIEWS
AND RATINGS

LISTING 10.3 Continued

```
    public void SetUserIDNull() {
          this[this.tableProductReviews.UserIDColumn] = System.Convert.DBNull;
    }

    public bool IsUserNameNull() {
          return this.IsNull(this.tableProductReviews.UserNameColumn);
    }

    public void SetUserNameNull() {
          this[this.tableProductReviews.UserNameColumn] =
➥System.Convert.DBNull;
    }

    public bool IsRatingNull() {
          return this.IsNull(this.tableProductReviews.RatingColumn);
    }

    public void SetRatingNull() {
          this[this.tableProductReviews.RatingColumn] = System.Convert.DBNull;
    }

    public bool IsCommentsNull() {
          return this.IsNull(this.tableProductReviews.CommentsColumn);
    }

    public void SetCommentsNull() {
          this[this.tableProductReviews.CommentsColumn] =
➥System.Convert.DBNull;
    }
}

public class ProductReviewsRowChangeEvent : EventArgs {

    private ProductReviewsRow eventRow;

    private System.Data.DataRowAction eventAction;

    public ProductReviewsRowChangeEvent(ProductReviewsRow row,
➥DataRowAction action) {
          this.eventRow = row;
          this.eventAction = action;
    }

    public ProductReviewsRow Row {
```

LISTING 10.3 Continued

```
        get {
            return this.eventRow;
        }
    }

    public DataRowAction Action {
        get {
            return this.eventAction;
        }
    }
}
```

> **NOTE**
>
> You can find the complete listing for the `CatalogDS.cs` file online.

These three classes provide three key pieces of functionality. The first class, `ProductReviewsDataTable`, provides access to each column via internal properties that return references of `DataColumn` type corresponding to each column in the `ProductReview` table. This class not only provides access to each row in the table, but also gives enables us to create new `ProductReview` rows and add those rows to the `ProductReview DataTable`. Additionally, it provides a few useful utility methods such as `FindByReviewID`.

The `ProductReviewsRow` class inherits from the `DataRow` class, so it provides access to all the public `DataRow` methods. Additionally, `xsd.exe` creates `get` and `set` properties to return the values of each column in the given row.

> **NOTE**
>
> For each column in the `ProductReviews` table that allows null values, `xsd.exe` creates `Is[ColumnName]Null` and `Set[ColumnName]Null` methods.

The `ProductReviewsRowChangeEvent` class inherits from the `EventArgs` class.

The Product Review User Control

Because the product review functionality could be viewed from multiple places in the site, it made sense to encapsulate the functionality in a reusable fashion. For this reason, we created the `ProductReview.ascx` user control.

The product review user control is made up of a user interface piece and a code behind class. The user interface portion is called ProductReview.ascx, and the code behind class is called ProductReview.ascx.cs.

ProductReview.ascx controls the basic layout, user interface, of the control. It displays each review and its associated rating. The code for this control is shown in Listing 10.4.

LISTING 10.4   The ProductReview.ascx User Control

```
<%@ Control Language="c#" AutoEventWireup="false" src="ProductReview.ascx.cs"
➥Inherits="MyGolfGear.Main.ProductReview"
➥ CodeBehind="ProductReview.ascx.cs" %>

<table cellspacing=0 cellpadding=0 width=500 border=0>
<tr>
<td class="clsReviewTitle"> <B>Product Reviews</B><br></td>
</tr>
</table>
<br>
<table width="100%" cellpadding=0 cellspacing=0 border=0>
<tr>
<td class="clsReviewCell" >
<asp:Label id="lblNoReview" visible="false" runat="server">
➥This Product has not yet been reviewed.</asp:Label>
<asp:DataList ID="ProdReviewList" ItemStyle-CssClass="clsReviewItem"
➥BackColor="beige" AlternatingItemStyle="Backcolor=white"
➥runat="server" width="500" cellpadding="0" cellspacing="0">
<ItemTemplate>
<img src="images/ReviewRating<%#DataBinder.Eval(Container.DataItem,
➥"Rating")%>.gif">
<br>
<b>
<asp:Label class="TextBold" Text='<%#DataBinder.Eval
➥(Container.DataItem, "UserName")%>' runat="server" ID="Label1"
➥NAME="Label1"/>
<span>  states...  </span></b>
<asp:Label Text='<%#DataBinder.Eval(Container.DataItem, "Comments")%>'
➥runat="server" ID="Label2" NAME="Label2"/><br>
<BR>
</ItemTemplate>
</asp:DataList>
<br>
</td>
</tr>
```

> **NOTE**
>
> You can find the complete listing for the `ProductReviews.ascx` file online.

This code uses simple `DataList` and `ItemTemplate` controls to bind and display the data retrieved in the code behind class. `ItemTemplate` is used to format each record in the `DataList` the same way. The `DataList` is databound to the `ProductReviews DataTable` from the `CatalogDS DataSet`. Listing 10.5 shows the `Page_Load` method from the code behind of `ProductReviews.ascx`.

LISTING 10.5 The `ProductReview.ascx.cs` Code Behind

```
private void Page_Load(object sender, System.EventArgs e)
{
 DataView dv;
 GetCatalog();
 dv = catalogds.ProductReviews.DefaultView;
 dv.RowFilter = "ProductID = '" + ProductID + "'";
 //Populate the Product Review List
 if (dv.Count > 0)
 {
  ProdReviewList.DataSource = dv;
  ProdReviewList.DataBind();
 }
 else
 {
  lblNoReview.Visible = true;
 }
}
```

> **NOTE**
>
> You can find the complete listing for the `ProductReview.ascx.cs` file online.

The `Page_Load` method starts by creating a variable called `dv`, of type DataView. Next, we call the `GetCatalog` method which is responsible for retrieving the `CatalogDS` from the cache, and if it is not found in the cache, it will create the strongly typed dataset and insert it into the cache. Then we set `dv` to ProductReviews' `DefaultView`. We use the `RowFilter` method of the DataView. This allows us to filter the product reviews for the product that is being shown on the product details page. Then we make sure that there are rows in the DataView before we

10

PRODUCT REVIEWS
AND RATINGS

bind it to the DataList, ProdReviewList. If no product reviews were found for this product ID, then we set the Visible property of the No Review label to true. This will display a message to the user that no reviews are available for this product.

Adding the ProductReviews User Control to the Product Details Page

User controls cannot be displayed without a container such as an ASP.NET page. For this reason, we modified the ProductDetails.aspx page to use the product review user control. Listing 10.6 shows the relevant portion of this page.

LISTING 10.6   The ProductDetails.aspx Page

```
...
<%@ Register TagPrefix="MyGolfGear" TagName="ProductReview"
➥Src="../UserControls/ProductReview.ascx" %>
...
<MyGolfGear:ProductReview id=ProductReview runat="server" />
...
```

NOTE

You can find the complete listing for the ProductDetails.aspx file online.

Because the bulk of the product details page was covered in Chapter 6, "Using ASP.NET to Display the Simple Catalog," only the portions necessary to use the ProductReview user control are included in Listing 10.6.

The first line in Listing 10.6 registers the ProductReview user control. Registration associates aliases with namespace and class names for easier, more concise notation. This line declares the MyGolfGear alias as the tag prefix for all controls and then declares MyGolfGear: ProductReview as a TagPrefix:TagName pair for the user control in ProductReview.ascx.

After the tag is registered, the containing page knows where the source is so that it can be incorporated. The other line in Listing 10.6 shows how the ProductReview user control is used. By simply using the TagPrefix:TagName nomenclature defined in the Register line, the page displays the user control.

To populate the user control, you must pass the product ID of the product being displayed on the product details page to the product review. Only a few additional lines are needed to get the product ID and pass it to the product review control. Listing 10.7 shows these additional lines.

LISTING 10.7 Passing the Product ID to the Product Review Control

```
Control ProductReview = this.FindControl("ProductReview");
Type ProductReviewType = ProductReview.GetType();
System.Reflection.FieldInfo ProductReview_ProductID =
➥ProductReviewType.GetField("ProductID");
ProductReview_ProductID.SetValue(ProductReview, ProductID)
```

> **NOTE**
>
> You can find the complete listing for the `ProductDetails.aspx.cs` file online.

This portion of the product detail page first uses the `Control` object's member function `Find` to locate a control with an ID of `ProductReview`. Next, it gets a `Type` instance from the `ProductReview` control's `GetType` method. Finally, it uses `reflection` to populate the `ProductReview` control's `ProductID` property by using the `System.Reflection.FieldInfo.SetValue` method.

Now let's see how the new product details page was transformed. The result is shown in Figure 10.1.

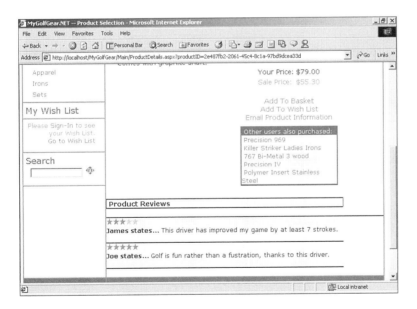

FIGURE 10.1

Product details page with integrated Product Reviews user control.

Summary

This chapter covered the changes necessary to create the product reviews and ratings functionality in MyGolfGear.NET. Specifically, it described the database changes necessary to support this functionality. It also covered the creation of the Product Reviews user control as well as how to integrate this control with the product details page.

Self Instruction

After reading this chapter, you are probably wondering when the product reviews are entered. The answer is after the checkout process has occurred, as part of the order status page. Go to MyGolfGear.NET to view this functionality and then try to create it on your own. Here's a hint: MyGolfGear.NET used a single .aspx page and its corresponding code behind class to input the information into the ProductReviews table. It also relied on the functionality discussed in Chapter 16, "Using .NET Authentication and Authorization for Personalization."

Implementing Gift Certificates in MyGolfGear.NET

IN THIS CHAPTER

Objectives

- Understand the database changes necessary to support gift certificates

- Learn about the OrderDS strongly typed dataset

- Review the new user interface elements needed to support gift certificates on MyGolfGear.NET

Allowing gift certificates to be purchased and redeemed is a simple feature that adds considerable value to a business-to-consumer (B2C) e-Commerce site. Popular sites such as Amazon.com, BarnesAndNoble.com, and Chopshot.com all offer a feature similar to this.

MyGolfGear.NET supports the purchasing and redemption of electronic gift certificates. This chapter discusses the code changes necessary to support this functionality. Specifically, it covers the necessary database changes, the new `GiftCertificate` data access class, changes to the `OrderDS` dataset class, and the necessary user interface changes.

> **NOTE**
>
> Some sites support both gift certificates and coupons. The functionality is similar, so MyGolfGear.NET implemented support only for gift certificates. The biggest difference between the two is that gift certificates are sent on behalf of a customer, whereas coupons are sent on behalf of the company. The redemption and tracking process is virtually identical.

The Database Changes Necessary to Support Gift Certificates

We needed to make only minor additions to the MyGolfGear database schema to support gift certificates. In fact, we needed to add only a single table. The `GiftCertificates` table was added to house the needed information. Table 11.1 shows the layout of this table.

TABLE 11.1 The `GiftCertificates` Table

Column Name	Data Type	Size	Allow Nulls
GiftCertificateID	Int	4	No
Value	Money	8	No

This simple table holds only two values for each record. The first value is a unique ID for each gift certificate, and the second value is the amount the gift certificate can be redeemed for. We also store the gift certificate ID in the Basket table so that when an order is being placed, we can see how much of the gift certificate amount to apply to the order.

For the MyGolfGear.NET implementation, the data in this table is accessed via a new data provider class called GiftCertificate.cs.

> **CAUTION**
>
> Inline SQL is generally frowned upon for two major reasons:
> - Stored procedures are easier to maintain and extend because components don't need to be recompiled and redistributed if the query changes.
> - The execution time of a stored procedure is generally much faster than that of the same inline SQL statement.

The GiftCertificate Data Access Class

The GiftCertificate class serves two main purposes. First, it encapsulates the query necessary to retrieve a gift certificate's value. Second, it houses the query needed to redeem a gift certificate.

The gift certificate value retrieval functionality is implemented in the GetGiftCertificate Value method, which is shown in Listing 11.1.

LISTING 11.1 The GetGiftCertificateValue Method

```
public decimal GetGiftCertificateValue( int GCID )
{
    decimal retval = 0;

    SqlConnection conn = new SqlConnection(ConnectionString);
    SqlCommand myCommand = new SqlCommand("Select * from
➥GiftCertificates where GCID=" + GCID.ToString(), conn);

    // set the command type as a text
    myCommand.CommandType = CommandType.Text;

    // Populate the data reader
    conn.Open();
    SqlDataReader myReader;
    myReader = myCommand.ExecuteReader();
    while( myReader.Read() )
```

LISTING 11.1 Continued

```
    {
            retval = System.Decimal.Parse(myReader["Value"].ToString());
    }

    // return the data reader
    return retval;
}
```

> **NOTE**
>
> You can find the complete listing for the GC.cs file online.

This simple method takes a single parameter of type int, representing the ID of the gift certifi-cate for which you want to retrieve the value. A SqlConnection object is created using the pri-vate member variable ConnectionString. When the connection is made, a SqlCommand object is created using an inline SQL query. This query requests all records with an ID equal to the one passed into the method.

> **NOTE**
>
> This query should never return more than one record because the GiftCertificateID is the primary key of the GiftCertificate table.

When the Command object is created, it returns a SqlDataReader object. This SqlDataReader object, in turn, retrieves the contents of the Value field from the resultset.

When a shopper wants to redeem a gift certificate, the ID of the gift certificate is used in conjunction with the amount being used to update the GiftCertificate table. The GiftCertificate class' UseGiftCertificate method is responsible for this functionality. Listing 11.2 shows this method.

LISTING 11.2 The UseGiftCertificate Method

```
public void UseGiftCertificate(int GCID, decimal amt)
{
    decimal currval = GetGiftCertificateValue(GCID);
    decimal newval = currval - amt;
    if( newval < 0 )
```

LISTING 11.2   Continued

```
        newval = 0;

    SqlConnection conn = new SqlConnection(ConnectionString);
    SqlCommand myCommand = new SqlCommand("Update GiftCertificates
➥set Value=" + newval.ToString() + " where GCID=" + GCID.ToString() , conn);

    myCommand.CommandType = CommandType.Text;

    conn.Open();
    myCommand.ExecuteNonQuery();
}
```

> **NOTE**
>
> You can find the complete listing for the GC.cs file online.

The UseGiftCertificate method accepts a gift certificate ID along with the amount to be used and returns nothing. The ID that is passed in is used to call the GetGiftCertificateValue method. The value returned from this method is used to determine the amount that the Value field should be updated to.

After the amount of the gift certificate is determined, a SqlConnection is created using the private member variable ConnectionString. A SqlCommand object is then created to call the simple update SQL statement necessary to update the GiftCertificate table. Because no value needs to be returned, the command object's ExecuteNonQuery method is used.

> **NOTE**
>
> The ExecuteNonQuery method calls UPDATE, INSERT, and DELETE statements and returns the number of rows affected. Also, bear in mind that although no records are returned, any output parameters or return values mapped to parameter objects will be populated with data.

For the majority of this book, we have discussed most functionality by starting at the database, moving to the classes that interact with the database, and then moving on to discuss other classes. Typically, the user interface elements are the last layer to be discussed. However, in the case of the gift certificate implementation, it makes more sense to jump to a discussion of the user interface and work our way back to this point.

Implementing the Acceptance of Gift Certificates on the Checkout Page

The checkout page offers users a summary of their orders before taking any payment or shipping information. This page is a fairly typical place to accept a gift certifica8te or coupon code, so MyGolfGear followed suit. Figure 11.1 shows what the checkout page looks like.

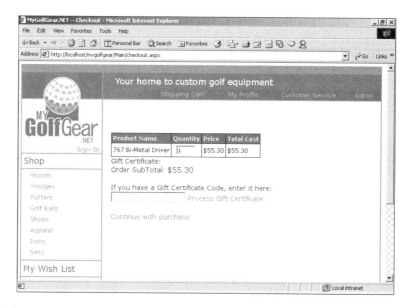

FIGURE 11.1

The Checkout.aspx *page.*

Notice the "process gift certificate" link, which causes the value of the gift certificate to be looked up and deducted from the order's subtotal. The checkout page is made of two parts: an .aspx file and a code behind class. In Chapter 15, "The Checkout Process," the complete functionality of this page and its code behind class will be discussed. For a discussion of how gift certificates are redeemed on MyGolfGear.NET, only the portion of the code necessary to redeem gift certificates will be shown. Listing 11.3 shows the relevant code for the .aspx page.

LISTING 11.3 The Checkout.aspx Page

```
<asp:TextBox ID="txtGC" Runat="server" />
<asp:LinkButton ID="btnDoGC" Runat="server" OnClick="DoGC">
    Process Gift Certificate
</asp:LinkButton>
```

> **NOTE**
>
> You can find the complete listing for the `Checkout.aspx` file online.

Listing 11.3 shows that the only necessary additions to the checkout page are a simple text box and a `LinkButton` control. The `txtGC TextBox` control is the place to enter the gift certificate ID. The `LinkButton` control calls the `DoGC` method in the `Checkout.aspx.cs` code behind class.

The `DoGC` method takes the gift certificate ID, looks up the value associated with that ID, and deducts that value from the current order's subtotal. Listing 11.4 shows this method.

LISTING 11.4   The DoGC Method

```
protected void DoGC( object sender, EventArgs e )
{
    DataAccess.GiftCertificate gc = new DataAccess.GiftCertificate();

    OrderDS orderds = GetOrder();
    decimal temp = gc.GetGCAmount(System.Int32.Parse(txtGC.Text));
    if( temp > System.Decimal.Parse(orderds.Basket.Rows[0]["SubTotal"].
➥ToString()) )
    {
        temp = System.Decimal.Parse(orderds.Basket.Rows[0]["SubTotal"].
➥ToString());
    }
    orderds.Basket.Rows[0]["GiftCertificate"] = temp;
    orderds.Basket.Rows[0]["GiftCertificateID"] = txtGC.Text;

    OrderManager ordermanager = new OrderManager();
    ordermanager.GenOrderTotals(orderds);

    // Save the Order & update the session
    MyGolfGearDP dp = new MyGolfGearDP();
    dp.UpdateOrder((OrderDS)orderds.GetChanges(), orderid);
    orderds.AcceptChanges();
    Session["Order"] = orderds;
    FillCart(orderds);
}
```

NOTE

You can find the complete listing for the `GC.cs` file online.

The `DoGC` method starts by creating an instance of the `GiftCertificate` and `OrderDS` classes. It uses the `GiftCertificate` class to find the amount available on the gift certificate. Then it subtracts the gift certificate amount from the order and adds the gift certificate amount and ID to the basket. Next, it uses the `OrderManager` class to generate the order totals.

When the order totals are generated, the `MyGolfGearDP` data provider class updates the `OrderDS` dataset. After the order is updated, it is reinserted into the session and the basket is filled.

The `OrderManager` Class

The `OrderManager` class is really a utility class used for manipulating product and order information. It is also responsible for calculating shipping, tax, and order total amounts. Most of this functionality will be covered in Chapter 15. This section deals mainly with the order manipulation responsibilities of the `OrderManager` class, especially where the gift certificate functionality is concerned.

Remember that the `OrderManager` class is used in the `Checkout.aspx.cs` code behind class. Order totals are generated by the `OrderManager` class and used on the checkout page.

The `OrderManager.GenOrderTotals` method calculates an order's subtotal and inserts it into the basket. Listing 11.5 shows this method.

LISTING 11.5 The `GenOrderTotals` Method in `OrderManager.cs`

```
public OrderDS GenOrderTotals(OrderDS order)
{
    Decimal subtotal = 0;
    foreach(OrderDS.BasketItemsRow bir in order.BasketItems)
    {
        if (bir.RowState != DataRowState.Deleted)
        {
            subtotal += bir.TotalCost;
        }
    }
    temp1 = order.Basket.Rows[0]["GiftCertificate"].ToString();
    if( temp1 == "" )
    {
        temp = 0;
    }
```

LISTING 11.5   Continued

```
    else
    {
      temp = System.Decimal.Parse(temp1);
    }
    order.Basket.Rows[0]["SubTotal"] = subtotal - temp;
    order.Basket.Rows[0]["OrderTotal"] = subtotal + ((decimal)
➥order.Basket.Rows[0]["ShippingTotal"]) +     ((decimal)
➥order.Basket.Rows[0]["TaxTotal"]);
    return order;
}
```

NOTE

You can find the complete listing for the `OrderManager.cs` file online.

This method takes an instance of an `OrderDS` class as its only parameter. The basket items collection is iterated through, and the `TotalCost` value is summed. Then we determine if a gift certificate was used on this order by retrieving the value of GiftCertificate from within the Basket datatable. Next, we check to see whether anything was returned. If so, we set a temporary variable to 0; otherwise, we change the value to a decimal and set it to a temporary variable. Then, before inserting the value `SubTotal` back into the basket, we deduct the value of the gift certificate. The `ShippingTotal` and `TaxTotal` values are added to the `SubTotal` value to calculate the `OrderTotal`, which is then inserted into the order dataset's basket. After all the values are summed and inserted, the same `OrderDS` object is returned.

Summary

This chapter discussed the steps taken to implement the capability to accept gift certificates on MyGolfGear.NET. It discussed the additional database elements needed, the new data access class `GiftCertificate.cs`, the additions to the `OrderDS` strongly typed dataset, and the modifications made to the user interface elements.

The next chapter, "Automating the E-mailing of Product Information with ASP.NET," shows how MyGolfGear.NET implements the capability to send someone else product information from the product details page. Specifically, it will show the steps necessary for MyGolfGear.NET to support this functionality and discuss the use of the `System.Web.Mail` namespace.

Self Instruction

Gift certificates can be redeemed only if shoppers are allowed to purchase them for others. This chapter showed how MyGolfGear.NET allows for the redemption of a gift certificate. However, we did not explicitly cover how gift certificates are purchased because the implementation is very similar to the implementation of the other products sold.

This implementation is similar to the implementation of a simple part or product. Review Chapters 4, 5, and 6 if necessary to understand how to set up additional products. Follow these steps to tie the purchasing of gift certificates to the redemption process:

- Create a new category and several new parts using the administrative features discussed in Chapter 5. Create three new products corresponding to a $10, $20, and $50 gift certificate.

- As part of the checkout process, the gift certificate ID needs to be generated and inserted into the GiftCertificates table. This ID needs to be unique and not easily spoofed. Alternatively, you may want to modify the table design and all affected components such that the ID can be a GUID.

Automating the E-mailing of Product Information with ASP.NET

IN THIS CHAPTER

Objectives

- Learn how product information e-mailing was implemented in MyGolfGear.NET

- Learn about the System.Web.Mail class

- Understand the changes made to the product details page to support this functionality

- Learn about the e-mail page created to support the e-mailing of product information

An interesting feature of some of today's more popular business-to-consumer (B2C) e-Commerce sites is the capability to e-mail product information to someone. MyGolfGear.NET offers this functionality to its users, and this chapter will cover this feature.

To accomplish this functionality, we took four simple steps. First, we added a new `asp:HyperLink` tag to the `ProductDetails.aspx` page. Second, we modified the `ProductDetails.aspx.cs` code behind page to add functionality to the new `HyperLink` tag. Third, we added a new `Email.aspx` page. Finally, we added an `Email.aspx.cs` code behind page to implement the e-mail functionality.

This chapter covers the four steps taken to implement e-mailing of product information. In addition, it also discusses the use of the `System.Web.Mail` class that was used to implement this functionality.

Modifications to the `ProductDetails.aspx` Page

Two simple modifications were made to the product details section of the MyGolfGear.NET site. We made a change to the `ProductDetails.aspx` page and to the `ProductDetails.aspx.cs` code behind class.

We added a `HyperLink` Web server control to the `ProductDetails.aspx` page. The tag for the new link looks like this:

```
<asp:HyperLink id="Email" runat="server" fontsize=2 forecolor=green/>
```

This tag takes the obligatory `id` and `runat` attributes as well as two others. To allow for a customized look, we also specified font size and forecolor.

To give this link functionality, we added a couple of new lines of code to the `ProductDetails.aspx.cs` code behind class. Listing 12.1 shows this new code.

LISTING 12.1 *ProductDetails.aspx.cs* E-mail Hyperlink Code

```
Email.NavigateUrl = "Email.aspx?productID=" + ProductID.ToString();
Email.Text = "Email Product Information";
```

Two properties are specified in the code behind class. The first one, `NavigateUrl`, is used for specifying the equivalent of an HTML anchor tag's `HREF` property. The second, `Text`, is simply used for specifying the text to display for the link.

> **NOTE**
>
> To reference the `Email` hyperlink object, we added a protected member variable named `Email` to the class definition. This declaration looks like this:
>
> ```
> protected System.Web.UI.WebControls.HyperLink Email;
> ```

After we added the link, we needed to add the actual e-mail functionality.

The `Email.aspx` Page

When a user clicks the e-mail hyperlink on the product detail page, she is taken to the e-mail page. On this page, the user can enter the e-mail address of the person she wishes to receive the specified product's information. This page also displays a preview of the message that will be sent. Figure 12.1 shows what this page looks like.

FIGURE 12.1

The Email.aspx page and input form.

The ASP.NET code necessary to make this page work is shown in Listing 12.2.

LISTING 12.2   *Email.aspx* Code

```
<table border="0" width="428" cellspacing="0" cellpadding="5">
   <tr>
      <td width="428" valign="top">
            <font color="#336699"><B>Email</B></font>
            <BR>
            <table style="BORDER-RIGHT:black 1px solid; BORDER-TOP:black
➡1px solid; FONT:10pt verdana; BORDER-LEFT:black 1px solid;
➡BORDER-BOTTOM:black 1px solid; BACKGROUND-COLOR:white" cellspacing=5>
                  <tr>
                     <td valign=top>
                        Email Address:<br>
                        <asp:TextBox id=EmailAddress runat="server">
                        </asp:TextBox><br>
                        <br>
                        Message:<br><br>
                        <asp:Label id=Label1 runat="server" width="415px"
➡ BorderStyle="Inset">Label</asp:Label><br><br>
                        <asp:LinkButton OnClick=send_OnClick ID="send"
➡Runat="server" Text="send" ></asp:LinkButton>
                     </td>
                  </tr>
               </table>
      </td>
   </tr>
</table>
```

NOTE

Because the Email.aspx page was created using the same basic template as the other pages discussed thus far, Listing 12.2 shows only the code that is specific to the e-mail functionality.

Other than a couple of tables used for layout purposes, the code in Listing 12.2 shows only a few interesting items. The first feature to notice is the TextBox Web server control used to capture the e-mail address of the e-mail recipient.

Two other Web server controls are also used: Label, which displays the e-mail body preview; and LinkButton, which handles the form submission.

> **NOTE**
>
> You can find the code for the `Email.aspx` page online.

System.Web.Mail Namespace

Before discussing the `Email` code behind class, I think it is important to discuss the classes that make this functionality possible. You can find the `System.Web.Mail` namespace within `System.Web.dll`.

The `System.Web.Mail` namespace contains the following three classes:

- `MailAttachment`
- `MailMessage`
- `SmtpMail`

The MailAttachment Class

The `MailAttachment` class contains two public properties: `Encoding` and `Filename`. The `Encoding` property gets and sets the attachment's file type, which can be one of two types. You can specify the type by using the `System.Web.Mail.MailEncoding` enumeration. The possible values for this enumeration are `MailEncoding.Base64` or `MailEncoding.UUEncode`.

The `Filename` property simply specifies the name of the file to attach. This property gets and sets a string value representing the filename and path of the attachment.

This class also contains a single public method named `VerifyFile`. This method tries to open the file specified by the `Filename` property using the `System.IO.File::Open` method. If the file fails to open, the `VerifyFile` method throws an exception of type `HttpException`.

The MailMessage Class

The `MailMessage` class creates the actual message to be sent and can also maintain a list of `MailAttachment` objects. It contains the following 13 public properties:

- `Attachments`—Specifies a list of attachments associated with the mail message
- `Bcc`—Gets and sets a list of e-mail addresses to be sent blind copies of the mail message
- `Body`—Gets and sets the body of the e-mail message
- `BodyEncoding`—Gets and sets the encoding of the body text
- `BodyFormat`—Gets and sets the content type of the body

- Cc—Gets and sets a list of e-mail addresses to be sent a copy of the mail message
- From—Gets and sets the e-mail address of the sender
- Headers—Gets a dictionary specifying any custom headers that are transmitted with the e-mail message
- Priority—Gets and sets the priority of the e-mail message
- Subject—Gets and sets a string representing the subject of the e-mail message
- To—Gets and sets a string representing the address of the e-mail message recipient
- UrlContentBase—Gets and sets the URL base of all relative URLs used within the HTML-encoded body
- UrlContentLocation—Gets and sets a string value representing the location of any URL content

Most of these properties do exactly what you would expect. For instance, the Body property is a string that holds the contents of the e-mail message to be sent. The From and To properties are for specifying the e-mail address of the e-mail sender and receiver, respectively.

The BodyEncoding property can be specified via the System.Text.Endcoding class. This class contains, among other things, properties that represent the possible text encoding supported by the Common Language Runtime (CLR). The possible values are ASCII, UTF7, UTF8, and Unicode.

The BodyFormat property is specified using the MailFormat enumeration. Its possible values are Text and Html.

If an e-mail is HTML-formatted, you can set the UrlContentBase and UrlContentLocation properties. These properties allow images and other content to be downloaded from the given URL.

The SmtpMail Class

The SmtpMail class actually sends the e-mail. It contains the one overloaded static method named Send to do so.

The first version of this method takes a single parameter. An instance of the MailMessage class can be created and populated with the appropriate data before being passed to the MailMessage.Send method.

The other version of the Send method takes four parameters. It allows the programmer to pass in string values representing the e-mail addresses of the sender and recipient as well as the subject and message text.

The `System.Web.Mail` namespace also contains the following enumerations:

- `MailEncoding`
- `MailFormat`
- `MailPriority`

These three enumerations are used in conjunction with the `MailMessage` class. The first two were discussed in the previous sections. The `MailPriority` enumeration sets the `MailMessage` priority property. Its possible values are `Normal`, `Low`, and `High` or `0`, `1`, and `2`, respectively.

The `Email.aspx.cs` Code Behind Class

The `Email.aspx.cs` code behind class is responsible for implementing the functionality displayed in the `Email.aspx` page. This class is responsible for retrieving the product data that is displayed in the e-mail message. In addition, it actually e-mails the message via the `System.Web.Mail` class.

The `Email.aspx.cs` code behind class has two important methods: `Page_Load` and `send_OnClick`.

The `Page_Load` method uses an instance of the `CatalogDS` strongly typed dataset and a protected string member variable to retrieve and display product information. Listing 12.3 shows what this looks like.

LISTING 12.3 The *Page_Load* Method

```
protected void Page_Load(object sender, System.EventArgs e)
{
    ProductID = new System.Guid(Request.Params["ProductID"]);

    GetCatalog();
    //Find the Product row Selected
    CatalogDS.ProductRow ProductRow =
➥catalogds.Product.FindByProductID(ProductID);

    Message = "Hello!!" + "<br><br>";
    Message += "Product Information for " + ProductRow.Name.ToString() +
➥"<br>";
    Message += "<a href=http://www.mygolfgear.net/main/productdetails.aspx?
➥productid=" + ProductID.ToString() + ">
➥Go to Product Page</a><br><br>";
    Message += ProductRow.LongDescription.ToString();

    Label1.Text = Message;
}
```

The first thing that happens in the Page_Load method is that the parameter named ProductID is used to populate the protected member variable named ProductID. Next, the protected method named GetCatalog creates an instance of the CatalogDS class and stores it in the HttpRuntime cache. After CatalogDS is filled, a ProductRow instance can be created using the ProductID variable that was just created. Finally, the protected member string variable named Message is populated using the product information corresponding to the ProductRow object just created.

The other piece of functionality the Email.aspx.cs code behind class implements is the send_OnClick method. This method is responsible for creating and using a MailMessage object as well as an SmtpMail object to send the product information to the recipient specified by the EmailAddress TextBox control. Listing 12.4 shows this code.

LISTING 12.4   The *send_OnClick* Method

```
public void send_OnClick( object sender, EventArgs e )
{
    MailMessage m = new MailMessage();
    m.To = EmailAddress.Text;
    m.From = "webmaster@mygolfgear.net";
    m.Subject = "My Golf Gear product information";
    m.BodyFormat = MailFormat.Html;
    m.Body = Message;

    SmtpMail.Send( m );

    Server.Transfer("productdetails.aspx?productid=" + ProductID.ToString());
}
```

This simple method creates an instance of a MailMessage object and populates its To, From, Subject, BodyFormat, and Body properties. In addition, it also uses the SmtpMail.Send method by passing it the MailMessage object named m. Figure 12.2 shows an example of the mail message that is sent.

After the message is sent, the user is taken back to the ProductSelection page he came from. This action is accomplished by using the Server.Transfer method.

NOTE

You can find the code for the Email.aspx.cs code behind class online.

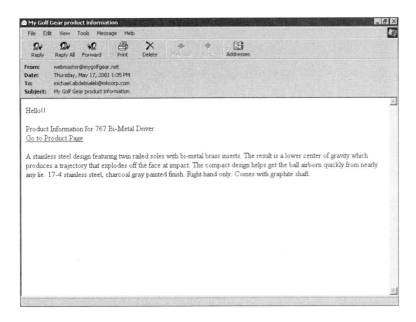

FIGURE 12.2
A sample e-mail output from the form shown in Listing 12.4.

Summary

This chapter covered the four steps taken to allow for the e-mailing of a specific product's information. Specifically, it covered the modifications made to the ProductDetail.aspx page and ProductDetail.aspx.cs class. It also covered the implementation of the new Email.aspx page and its Email.aspx.cs code behind class. In addition, this chapter discussed the System.Web.Mail class and how it was used to achieve the desired functionality.

The next chapter, "Implementing Cross Selling and Up Selling," discusses MyGolfGear.NET's implementation of these two important strategies.

Self Instruction

Based on what you've learned in this chapter, implement a simple e-mail campaign using the System.Web.Mail namespace. First, create a database table to contain the e-mail information. Then create a Campaign class to read and create an e-mail message for each customer in the User table. The User table will be covered in Chapter 16, "Using ASP.NET Authentication and Authorization for Personalization."

Implementing Cross Selling and Up Selling

IN THIS CHAPTER

Objectives

- Explain cross selling

- Show how MyGolfGear.NET integrated cross selling into the site

- Explain up selling

- Show how MyGolfGear.NET integrated up selling into the site

A growing factor in the success of many e-Commerce Web sites is the relationship between the IT and Marketing departments. The IT department is responsible for the technology of the Web site as well as maintaining and enhancing it. In the early years of e-Commerce Web sites, the Marketing department usually took part only in creating the look and feel of Web sites. Now it is getting more involved in ways to bring and keep online customers to the company's Web site.

Some businesses hesitated jumping into the e-Commerce world because they felt that customers would miss the interaction with a salesperson. Also, not having a salesperson means that nobody will try to persuade the consumers to increase their orders. These factors can be described as *cross selling* and *up selling*. As marketing became more of an integral part in making an e-Commerce Web site successful, the Marketing department focused on one area. If it was possible to increase the size of an order without the use of a salesperson, then that meant more income for the company, with a decreased cost associated with that income. For a simple example of how much cross selling or up selling can increase your sales, let's say that in one month we average 1,000 orders with an average total of $50 per order; that gives us sales totaling $50,000. If we are able to increase each order by a low estimate of 5%, that would increase our sales total by $2,500 per month, a $30,000 increase for the year. Continue this scenario with your order totals for a month and see how quickly the numbers add up.

Implementing cross selling and up selling in an e-Commerce site can range from simple to extremely complex, sometimes even more difficult than implementing the e-Commerce Web site itself. In this chapter, we'll use an example to explain how to integrate cross selling and up selling features in the MyGolfGear.NET e-Commerce Web site.

Cross Selling in MyGolfGear.NET

Cross selling and up selling are marketing tactics used to try to increase the size of an order. These two tactics are implemented only slightly differently. An example of cross selling is trying to offer a consumer a similar product to one that she is interested in. Besides, the main objective of increasing the order total, cross selling also provides two more incentives for implementing this feature.

First, when a user is looking at a product that he is extremely interested in, showing a list of similar products may spawn an impulse buy of another product. If you don't show that list, the user may simply proceed to check out. An example would be if a user is looking at a putter; in that case, you may want to show him a list of products that could contain golf balls, a pitching wedge, or even a golf glove.

Second, a user may be simply browsing your catalog without a real desire to purchase anything at this time. However, if while looking at a particular product, the user looks at the cross sell list of products, she may see something that she needs and then go ahead and purchase that product. In this example, you are actually creating an order from a user who really had no intent to buy any products at all.

Cross selling can get complicated very quickly. Another, more specific, level of cross selling includes tracking a user's buying habits and using that information to determine what types of products to show as a cross selling product. When you start down this path, you will quickly find out how many options you have for characterizing a user's behavior and how to associate buying habits to these behaviors.

For MyGolfGear.NET, we took the route of implementing product-to-product cross selling rather than bringing the personalization aspect into the formula. We implemented cross selling only in one location on the site. On the product details page, we added a list of products to display for cross selling. This list is composed of the top five products previously purchased by other users who purchased this product. Although this approach might seem simple, it is very effective and much better than not implementing cross selling at all.

Now let's look at how we implemented cross selling in MyGolfGear.NET.

Database Changes Required for Cross Selling

To implement a cross selling feature, we had to make only one database addition: the SpGetAlsoPurchasedProducts stored procedure, as shown in Listing 13.1.

LISTING 13.1 The SpGetAlsoPurchasedProducts Stored Procedure

```
CREATE PROCEDURE spGetAlsoPurchasedProducts
(
    @ProductID uniqueidentifier
)
AS
SELECT TOP 5
    OI.ProductID,
    P.Name,
    SUM(OI.Quantity) as TotalQty
FROM    OrderItems OI,
    Product P
WHERE P.ProductID = OI.ProductID
```

LISTING 13.1   Continued

```
    and OrderID IN ( SELECT DISTINCT OrderID FROM OrderItems WHERE ProductID =
➥ @ProductID)
    and OI.ProductID != @ProductID
GROUP BY  OI.ProductID, P.Name
ORDER BY  TotalQty DESC
```

Because we are associating products only with the current product on the product details page, only one input parameter is required: the product ID. To make it easier, we'll call the product ID being passed in Product A. The tables required for this stored procedure are `Product` and `OrderItems`. The `OrderItems` table is the place where purchased items for all orders are stored. Notice that immediately after the `SELECT` word, we add `TOP 5` to filter the resultset to only the first 5 rows. You could choose any number such as 3 for a smaller resultset or 10 for a larger one. Then we need to make sure that we sum the quantity for each product in the `OrderItems` table by using the SQL `SUM` function. We name that column `TotalQty`," which will be used later in the `ORDER BY` clause.

The `WHERE` clause of this SQL statement is a little tricky. First, we join the `Product` and `OrderItems` tables by product ID. For an accurate list, we want only the total quantity for those products that were also purchased with Product A. To accomplish this, we add to the `WHERE` clause the condition of order IDs in the resultset returned from the subquery. The subquery returns the `DISTINCT` order ID for each order in which Product A has been purchased. Then the last part of the `WHERE` clause makes sure that the list doesn't contain the product ID being passed in, Product A.

> **NOTE**
>
> When you put the `DISTINCT` keyword in front of a field name in a SQL statement, SQL weeds out any duplicates of that value, returning a value only once.

Finally, we use the `GROUP BY` clause to make sure the resultset does not contain multiple entries of the same product. This step is important; if 100 orders that contained Product A also ordered Product B, Product B would show up in the resultset 100 times. The `Group By` clause makes certain that Product B is displayed only once.

The Cross Selling User Control: `AlsoPurchased.ascx`

We implemented the cross selling feature by creating a user control called `AlsoPurchased.ascx`. In the `AlsoPurchased` class, we had to create only two variables. Listing 13.2 shows the declaration of these two variables.

LISTING 13.2 The Variables Required for the `AlsoPurchased` User Control

```
protected System.Web.UI.WebControls.Repeater alsopurchasedlist;
public System.Guid ProductID;
```

> **NOTE**
>
> You can find the complete listing for the `AlsoPurchased.ascx.cs` file online.

The `alsopurchasedlist` variable is typed as a `Repeater WebControl`. It is declared in the code behind to give us access to the `Repeater` control in the `.ascx` file. With this declaration, we will be able not only to set the data source for the `Repeater` control, but also to have full programmatic control over it. An example would be setting the control's `Visible` property to `false` when there are no items in the `Repeater`. `ProductID` is declared as public, so its value can be set from other classes (`.aspx` pages) that use the `AlsoPurchased` user control.

Listing 13.3 depicts the `Page_Load` method of the `AlsoPurchased` user control. Because this method contains only a few lines of code, we chose not to create a separate method to populate the `Repeater` control. However, if you decide to add more logic—which, of course, means more code—we suggest that you move the code to a separate local method that is called from the `Page_Load` method.

LISTING 13.3 The `Page_Load` Method from the `AlsoPurchased` User Control

```
MyGolfGear.MyGolfGearDP dp = new MyGolfGear.MyGolfGearDP();
System.Data.SqlClient.SqlDataReader dr =
➥dp.GetAlsoPurchasedProducts(ProductID);
alsopurchasedlist.DataSource = dr;
alsopurchasedlist.DataBind();
dr.Close();
// Only show list if there are items to display
if (alsopurchasedlist.Items.Count == 0)
{
  alsopurchasedlist.Visible = false;
}
```

> **NOTE**
>
> You can find the complete listing for the `AlsoPurchased.ascx.cs` file online.

13

IMPLEMENTING
CROSS SELLING
AND UP SELLING

After creating a new instance of the data provider, MyGolfGearDP, we create a SQL Data Reader named dr and set it to the results from the GetAlsoPurchasedProducts method in the MyGolfGearDP class. The GetAlsoPurchasedProducts method is depicted in Listing 13.4, but before we explain that portion of the code, let's complete this method. After the SQL Data Reader, dr, is populated, we make it the data source for the alsopurchasedlist Repeater control. Immediately afterward, we bind that Repeater control and then call the Close method on the SQL Data Reader, dr.

We could end the method here; however, we check to see whether any items are displayed in the alsopurchasedlist Repeater control by checking to see if its Items.Count property is equal to 0. If it is, we set the Visible property of the alsopurchasedlist Repeater control to false.

Now that we've looked at all the code for the AlsoPurchased user control, let's get back to the GetAlsoPurchasedProducts method in the MyGolfGearDP class. This method is shown in Listing 13.4.

LISTING 13.4   GetAlsoPurchasedProducts Method from MyGolfGearDP

```
public SqlDataReader GetAlsoPurchasedProducts(System.Guid productID)
{
NameValueCollection configInfo =
➥ (NameValueCollection)HttpContext.Current.GetConfig("appSettings");
SqlConnection conn = new SqlConnection((String)configInfo["ConnectString"]);
SqlCommand myCommand = new SqlCommand("spGetAlsoPurchasedProducts", conn);

// set the command type as a SP
myCommand.CommandType = CommandType.StoredProcedure;

// Add Parameters
SqlParameter parameterProductID = new
➥ SqlParameter("@ProductID", SqlDbType.UniqueIdentifier, 16);
parameterProductID.Value = productID;
myCommand.Parameters.Add(parameterProductID);

// Populate the data reader
conn.Open();
SqlDataReader myReader;
myReader = myCommand.ExecuteReader();
// return the data reader
return myReader;
}
```

> **NOTE**
>
> You can find the complete listing for the `MyGolfGearDP.cs` file online.

First, we retrieve the application settings from `HttpContext` and insert them into a `NameValueCollection` called `configInfo`. Then we use the named index, `"ConnectString"`, to create a SQL connection. Afterward, we set `SqlCommand` to use `spGetAlsoPurchasedProducts`, discussed earlier.

After we create a new parameter to contain the product ID, we set its value to that of the product ID being passed into the method. Then we add that parameter to the `SqlCommand` object using the `Add` method. When this step is complete, we open the connection and then create a `SqlDataReader` called `myReader`. Next, we set `myReader` equal to the results from executing the `ExecuteReader` method on the `SqlCommand` object and then return `myReader` to the calling function.

Using the `AlsoPurchased` User Control

Now that we have created this user control, we need to add it to the ProductDetails page. Doing so will send the product ID of the item being viewed by the user to the `AlsoPurchased` user control. Then, if any products are associated with the one being viewed, they will be displayed in a list. Note that the product names of the products in the user control are links to their specific product details page.

Listing 13.5 shows the cope snippet used to insert the user control into the `ProductDetails.aspx` page.

LISTING 13.5 Registering and Referencing the `AlsoPurchased` User Control on the `ProductDetails.aspx` Page

```
...
<%@ Register TagPrefix="MyGolfGear" TagName="AlsoPurchased" Src=
➥ "../UserControls/AlsoPurchased.ascx" %>
...
<MyGolfGear:AlsoPurchased id="AlsoPurchased" runat="server"
➥ NAME="AlsoPurchased" />
...
```

The first line registers the control on the page. Registration is required so that, during the processing of this page, it knows where the source for this user control is located. The source attribute, `Src`, is used to set the location of the user control. The values of the `TagPrefix` and `TagName` attributes are used to help create the custom tag that depicts where the user control will be inserted on the page. This is shown in the next line of this code snippet. The values of `TagPrefix` and `TagName` combined with a colon create the custom tag. It then has attributes of the ID, used by the code behind, `runat`, and `NAME`.

Now let's look at the code behind the `ProductDetails.aspx` page. Listing 13.6 shows the code snippet necessary to set the product ID of the `AlsoPurchased` User Control.

LISTING 13.6 Setting the `ProductId` Property on the `AlsoPurchased` User Control from the `ProductDetails` Page

```
//Populate the AlsoPurchased user control
Control AlsoPurchased = this.FindControl("AlsoPurchased");
Type AlsoPurchasedType = AlsoPurchased.GetType();
System.Reflection.FieldInfo AlsoPurchased_ProductID =
➥AlsoPurchasedType.GetField("ProductID");
AlsoPurchased_ProductID.SetValue(AlsoPurchased, ProductID);
```

What we must do first is locate the `AlsoPurchased` control. We do so by creating a variable called `AlsoPurchased` of type `Control` and using the `FindControl` method of the `this` object, passing it the ID of the control we are looking for, `AlsoPurchased`. Next, we create a `Type` variable called `AlsoPurchasedType` and set it to the type of the `AlsoPurchased` control by using its `GetType` method. We then use reflection to get to the public field (property) called `ProductID` and set its value using the `AlsoPurchased_ProductID.SetValue` method.

Figure 13.1 shows an example of the `AlsoPurchased` user control in action.

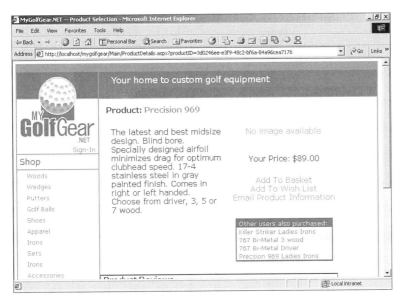

FIGURE 13.1

The `ProductDetails.aspx` *page with the* `AlsoPurchased` *user control.*

Up Selling in MyGolfGear.NET

Up selling is similar to the cross selling marketing tactic. It has many of the same benefits. The main difference is that, in up selling, the sole purpose is to increase the size of the order. This is mainly done by looking at what the user is getting ready to purchase and then offering products that are upgrades to any of the items in the user's order.

Say a user is getting ready to check out and has a $90 driver in his shopping cart. We could then offer him a better driver that costs $150. Just as in cross selling, we could bring in the user's preferences and buying habits to determine which products to up sell.

In MyGolfGear.NET, we give the ability to the administrator to associate an `UpSell` product for a given product. For example, any time a user has Product A in her shopping cart, an administrator can up sell Product E to her. We also give the administrator the ability to set start and end dates for each up sell record.

Database Changes Required for Up Selling

To implement an up selling feature in MyGolfGear.NET, we needed to make two database additions. First, we created the `ProductUpSell` table, shown in Table 13.1. Then we created the other, the stored procedure named `spGetUpSellProducts`, shown in Listing 13.7.

TABLE 13.1 The ProductUpSell Table

Column Name	Data Type	Size	Allow Nulls
ProductID	Uniqueidentifier	16	No
ProdUpSellID	Uniqueidentifier	16	Yes
StartDate	Datetime	8	Yes
EndDate	Datetime	8	Yes

LISTING 13.7 The spGetUpSellProducts Stored Procedure

```
CREATE    PROCEDURE dbo.spGetUpSellProducts
(
    @OrderID uniqueidentifier,
    @OrderDate datetime = NULL
)
AS
--Set a Default value for Order Date if a value is not given.
IF @OrderDate IS NULL
BEGIN
    SELECT @OrderDate = CONVERT(datetime, GETDATE())
END

SELECT    PUS.ProdUpSellID,
       P.Name
FROM        ProductUpSell PUS, Product P, BasketItems BI
WHERE    BI.OrderID = @OrderID
       AND PUS.ProdUpSellID Not In  (Select Distinct ProductID
➥ from BasketItems where OrderID = @OrderID)
       AND PUS.ProductID = BI.ProductID
       AND PUS.ProdUpSellID = P.ProductID
       AND PUS.StartDate <= @OrderDate
       AND PUS.EndDate >=@OrderDate
```

The spGetUpSellProducts stored procedure accepts two parameters: the order ID and order date. Our first task is to verify that the order date is not null. If it is, we set it to the SQL's data by using the GETDATE function and converting it to SQL's datetime data type using the CONVERT function.

We need only two fields, so we select the UpSell product ID, ProdUpSellID, and the product's name, Name. The tables necessary for this code to work are ProductUpSell, Product, and BasketItems. Now we get to the tricky part: the WHERE clause.

The purpose of this WHERE clause is to return only UpSell product IDs and their product names for all products in the BasketItems and ProductUpSell tables. The first part filters only the rows in the BasketItems table for the order ID that was passed in. Then we want to make sure that the UpSell product ID is not already in the order by executing a subquery and making sure that the UpSell product ID is *not* in the resultset. Next, we join the ProductUpSell and BasketItems tables by the product ID. Then we join the ProductUpSell and Product tables by using the UpSell product ID to retrieve the name of the product we are trying to up sell. Finally, the last two lines of the WHERE clause make certain that only up sells within valid start and end date ranges are displayed.

The Up Selling User Control: UpSellProducts.ascx

We implemented the up selling feature by creating a user control called UpSellProducts.ascx, similar to the AlsoPurchased user control. In the UpSellProducts class, we had to create only three variables, as shown in Listing 13.8.

LISTING 13.8   The Variables Required for the UpSellProducts User Control

```
protected System.Web.UI.WebControls.Repeater UpSellList;
private OrderManager ordermanager = new OrderManager();
private System.Guid orderid;
```

13

IMPLEMENTING
CROSS SELLING
AND UP SELLING

> **NOTE**
>
> You can find the complete listing for the UpSellProducts.ascx.cs file online.

First, we create UpSellList, which gives us access to the UpSellList Repeater control. Next, we create a new instance of OrderManager and then the orderid variable. Notice that both of them are declared as private, meaning that only code within the UpSellProducts class is aware of them.

Listing 13.9 depicts the Page_Load method of the UpSellProducts user control. Because this method contains only a few lines of code, we chose not to create a separate method to populate the Repeater control. However, if you decide to add more logic—which, of course, means more code—we suggest that you move the code to a separate local method that is called from the Page_Load method.

LISTING 13.9 The `Page_Load` Method from the `UpSellProducts` User Control

```
OrderDS orderds = GetOrder();
if (orderds == null)
{
  UpSellList.Visible = false;
}
else
{
  MyGolfGearDP dp = new MyGolfGearDP();
  System.Data.SqlClient.SqlDataReader dr = dp.GetUpSellProducts(
➥ orderds.Basket[0].OrderID,orderds.Basket[0].OrderDate);
  // Only show list if there are items to display
  UpSellList.DataSource = dr;
  UpSellList.DataBind();
  dr.Close();
}
if (UpSellList.Items.Count == 0) {UpSellList.Visible = false;}
```

> **NOTE**
>
> You can find the complete listing for the `UpSellProducts.ascx.cs` file online.

First, we populate `orderds` by calling the `GetOrder` method and determine whether an order exists. We don't need to begin executing the up sell code if there are no items in the order. The `GetOrder` method is shown in Listing 13.10.

LISTING 13.10 The `GetOrder` Method from the `UpSellProducts` User Control

```
private OrderDS GetOrder()
{
  MyGolfGear.DataAccess.OrderDS orderds =
➥(MyGolfGear.DataAccess.OrderDS)Session["Order"];
  OrderManager ordermanager = new OrderManager();
  if (orderds == null)
  {
   LoginInformation loginInfo = new LoginInformation();
   int userid = loginInfo.GetUserID( Request.ServerVariables["REMOTE_USER"] );
   orderid = ordermanager.OrderExists(userid);
   if (orderid != System.Guid.Empty)
```

LISTING 13.10   Continued

```
 {
   //Retrieve existing order
   MyGolfGearDP dp = new MyGolfGearDP();
   orderds = new OrderDS();
   dp.FillBasketOrder(orderds,orderid);
   return orderds;
 }
 else
 {
   return null;
 }
 }
 return orderds;
}
```

> **NOTE**
>
> You can find the complete listing for the UpSellProducts.ascx.cs file online.

The GetOrder method first checks to see whether there is an order in the session. If so, it simply returns that order. If there is no order in the session, we get the user's ID by creating an instance of LoginInformation and calling the GetUserID method, passing it the "REMOTE USER" value from the Server Variables collection. If there is no user ID, we return null; otherwise, we try to see whether an order exists for this user by calling the OrderExists method on the ordermanager object. This call returns a GUID. If it's an empty GUID, we return null because no order was found. Otherwise, we create a new instance of an order and populate it by calling MyGolfGearDP's FillBasketOrder method.

Now let's return to the code in Listing 13.9. We check to see whether orderds, the order dataset, is null. If it is null, we set the UpSellList's Visible property to false. If an order does exist, we begin our up sell code. We now must retrieve the products to up sell on the shopping cart page. First, we create a SQL Data Reader called dr and populate it by calling the GetUpSellProducts method on the MyGolfGearDP class. We pass to this method the order ID and order date, which are then passed to and used by the spGetUpSellProducts stored procedure. This method is similar to the GetAlsoPurchasedProducts method of MyGolfGearDP, so we won't explain the code. Then we set the DataSource property of the UpSellList Repeater control to dr, followed by calling the DataBind method of UpSellList and closing the SQL Data Reader.

Next, we check to see whether the UpSellList has any items in it by checking its Items.Count property. If it's equal to zero, we set the UpSellList's Visible property to false.

Using the UpSellProducts User Control

We'll use the UpSellProducts user control similarly to the AlsoPurchased user control. We'll insert this user control on the basket page exactly like we inserted the AlsoPurchased user control. This procedure is shown in Listing 13.11.

LISTING 13.11   Registering and Referencing the AlsoPurchased User Control on the Basket.aspx Page

```
...
<%@ Register TagPrefix="MyGolfGear" TagName="UpSellProducts" Src=
➡ "../UserControls/UpSellProducts.ascx" %>
...
<MyGolfGear:UpSellProducts id="UpSellProductsUC" runat="server"
➡ NAME="UpSellProducts" />
...
```

> **NOTE**
>
> You can find the complete listing for the Basket.aspx file online.

Because this user control doesn't have any fields (properties) to set like the AlsoPurchased user control, that's all we have to do to get it working.

Figure 13.2 shows an example of the UpSellProducts user control on the basket page.

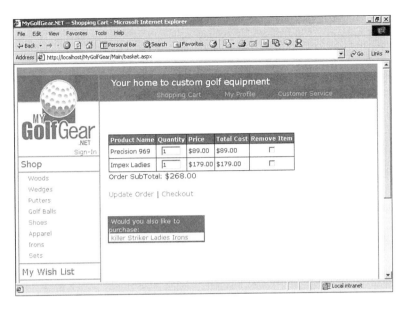

FIGURE 13.2

The `Basket.aspx` *page with the* `UpSellProducts` *user control.*

Summary

This chapter described the importance of implementing some level of cross selling or up sell-ing in your e-Commerce Web site. The Return On Investment (ROI) can be very high. The way we implemented these features in MyGolfGear.NET is just the beginning. From here, you can begin creating complex formulas to improve your chances of the cross sell or up sell causing an impulse buy. Another hidden point we made in this chapter was showing two very good uses of user controls and how powerful this ASP.NET feature can make your Web site.

Self Instruction

In the "Up Selling in MyGolfGear.NET" section, I referred to the administrator having the ability to manage which products can be associated with up sell products and the time frame, start date to end date, that the up sell is valid. Create an admin `.aspx` page that will allow an administrator to update, add, and delete records in the `ProductUpSell` table.

Using ASP.NET to Build the Shopping Cart

IN THIS CHAPTER

Objectives

- Review ASP.NET state management options

- Understand the data model necessary to implement a shopping cart

- Learn how MyGolfGear.NET creates and manages an order

- Learn how to add, update, and delete items within a MyGolfGear.NET order

- Create a shopping cart page where the products within an order are displayed

The heart of an e-Commerce site is the shopping cart. Users can build their orders in this area by selecting various products and adding them to their orders. Usually, this process is described as "adding items to your basket," just as you would do at a grocery store. This chapter discusses the steps necessary to build a fully functional shopping cart. We'll discuss creating an order, managing items in an order, and viewing the items within an order.

State Management in ASP.NET

Before we get into the details of building a shopping cart, I first want to explain the role of state management in ASP.NET sites. It is important to understand the options that are available for state management before you create your shopping cart. This will allow you to determine how the order and other information can and should be stored. State management has two forms in ASP.NET: application state and session state. In the following sections, I'll explain the powerful options that ASP.NET gives Web developers to manage state. Although application and session state have been greatly improved, they are similar to the features that ASP developers use today. Then I'll detail how state management was implemented in MyGolfGear.NET.

Application State

Storing data in an application is like storing data in a global variable. That data can then be accessed by all objects within that application. In an ASP.NET Web site, an application consists of files under the top-level virtual directory. This data is shared through the use of the `HttpApplicationState` class. To utilize this class, you must use the `System.Web` namespace.

An instance of the `HttpApplicationState` class is created the first time a client requests any resource within the virtual directory. Just like in ASP 3.0, the `Application` class provides a key-value dictionary of objects. This dictionary object allows you to store any type of data within the application.

NOTE

Application state is available only on a per Web server basis. It is not accessible across Web servers. This means that it is best not to store user-specific information in a server environment that is being load balanced. Store only data that is used by the application or is valid for all users. Each virtual directory has its own application state for each Web server.

Listing 14.1 shows how to put a value in an application and then retrieve that same value.

LISTING 14.1 Accessing Application Objects

```
string ServerName;
string WebServerName;
ServerName = "LocalHost";
Application.Lock();
Application["Server"] = ServerName;
Application.Add("Server", ServerName);
Application.UnLock();
WebServerName = Application.Get("Server");
```

Notice how to use the Lock and UnLock methods of the application. We use them this way to make certain that no one else can write to these application variables while we are. If you don't write them like this, you may have some deadlock issues. After the Lock method is called, the next two lines of code perform the same action—adding an object into the application. Finally, we use the Get method of the application to retrieve the value that is stored in the variable named "Server".

Even though you can store anything you want in the application state, be careful not to go overboard. Remember, everything that is stored in the application is really being stored in memory on that server. Always ask yourself whether it is truly necessary to insert this object into the application. You should weigh the performance gains against the consumption of memory.

Storing data in the application can be a great performance boost to your Web application. However, you must make certain that you're storing read-only type data, not critical data. Storing critical data within the application is not safe because the application can be cleared or restarted, causing all the data to be recycled. If this is the case, you would be better off storing that data in the database.

14

USING ASP.NET TO BUILD THE SHOPPING CART

As in ASP 3.0, application state in ASP.NET provides methods that you can hook into when the application changes. These methods include `Application_Start`, `Application_End`, `Application_BeginRequest`, and `Application_EndRequest`. `Start` and `End` are used for application startup and cleanup code, respectively. `BeginRequest` and `EndRequest` are used for application code to execute at the beginning of every request and end of every request, respectively. An example of the `Application_Start` method is shown in Listing 14.2.

LISTING 14.2 `Application_Start` from `Global.asax.cs`

```
protected void Application_Start(Object sender, EventArgs e)
{
 // Insert the catalog into the Cache
 MyGolfGearDP dp = new MyGolfGearDP();
 CatalogDS catalogds = new CatalogDS();
 dp.FillCatalog(catalogds);
 HttpRuntime.Cache.Insert("Catalog",catalogds,null,System.DateTime.MaxValue,
➥System.TimeSpan.FromHours(24),CacheItemPriority.High,
➥CacheItemPriorityDecay.Never,null);
}
```

NOTE

You can find the complete listing for the `Global.asax.cs` file online.

The code snippet in Listing 14.2 is from the code behind of MyGolfGear.NET's `global.asax` file. It shows how to insert the catalog into the `HttpRuntime` cache. This procedure greatly improves the performance of the site because each page doesn't have to make a database call to retrieve product information.

Session State

Using session state in ASP 3.0 became taboo over the years as developers tried to develop more scalable Web applications. Session state didn't work at all if your Web application was in a Web farm using a load-balancing tool, unless you had *stickiness* turned on. Also, in the beginning of ASP 3.0, developers started to put all types of data into the session without understanding the circumstances. This approach worked well for small sites with few users, but when that site began to achieve some load, Web servers started crashing. This happened because all the data stored in the session is stored in memory, causing the Web servers to run out of memory on their machines. After this situation became apparent, many Web applications abandoned the session and reverted to storing everything in the database.

> **NOTE**
>
> The basis of a load-balancing tool is to direct Web requests to multiple servers in a Web farm. Using this tool allows redundancy, as well as makes sure that all servers are efficiently being utilized. When a load-balancing tool has *stickiness* turned on, the users' Web requests continue to be directed to the same server. This allowed some sites to still utilize the ASP 3.0 `Session` object.

In ASP.NET, the session is back with a vengeance. The session allows you to store data for each individual user to your e-Commerce site. An example of information you might store in the session object could be the user's ID or name. ASP.NET's session state enables you to identify a user requesting content from your site and to create a session specific for that user. This session lasts over many continuous requests. You therefore can store information in the session to be used across multiple pages without having to access that information from the database. Session state also can clear a session after a specified period of time, which allows you to have only active sessions alive.

ASP.NET session state now can withstand IIS restarts because session state is no longer stored in the same process as inetinfo, which is the name of ISS's process. As a result, you can restart IIS without losing any of your session data. ASP.NET session state is also more scalable because it works in a load-balanced Web server environment and allows you to scale your servers "up" instead of "out" by adding more processors to a Web server for a Web application. Next, we will discuss the options available to determine where to store session state.

Another benefit of ASP.NET's session state management is the capability to specify the type of mode you want the session to run in. This mode, called `SessionStateMode`, has four possible values; they are described in Table 14.1. We will discuss each available option in detail in the following sections.

TABLE 14.1 `SessionStateMode` Values

SessionStateMode	*Description*
`Off`	Disables session state.
`InProc`	In process with the ASP.NET process (default). Similar to ASP 3.0; very efficient but not as robust as the other options.
`StateServer`	Allows for out-of-process session state. This can be on the same Web server as the Web application or another Web server.
`SQLServer`	Stores the state in `tempdb` tables in a SQL database.

In-Process Session Management

The in-process mode of session state, called `InProc`, runs in the same process as the ASP.NET process. This is very similar to ASP 3.0, except that you can restart IIS without having to sacrifice the session data because ASP now has its own process, `aspnet_wp.exe`. If you restart the ASP.NET process, however, all session data will be lost if you have it stored in-process. This is the price you must pay for choosing the most efficient session state mode. Listing 14.3 depicts the configuration necessary.

LISTING 14.3   `InProc` Session State, Taken from `web.config`

```
<sessionState
  mode="InProc"
  cookieless="false"
  timeout="30"
>
```

NOTE

You can find the complete listing for the `web.config` file online.

This setting in the `config.web` file belongs within `<System.Web></System.Web>`. You specify that session state will run in-process with the ASP.NET process by setting the `mode` attribute to `"InProc"`. In this case, we want to use cookies, so we set the `cookieless` attribute to `"false"` and then set the session timeout to 30 minutes.

Out-of-Process Session Management

With out-of-process session state management, you can really begin to understand the improvements that ASP.NET has made to the session. To make your session out-of-process, set `Mode` attribute to `StateServer`, as shown in Listing 14.4.

LISTING 14.4   `StateServer` Session State, Taken from `web.config`

```
<sessionState
  mode="StateServer"
  stateConnectionString="tcpip=127.0.0.1:42424"
  server="127.0.0.1"
  port=42424
  cookieless="false"
  timeout="30"
/>
```

> **NOTE**
>
> You can find the complete listing for the `web.config` file online.

As you can see, this state is similar to the `InProc` mode except for a few more attributes. Notice how `StateConnectionString` is actually a combination of the next two lines, which depict the name of the server that will house the state and the port number used to access that server. In this example, we used server `127.0.0.1`, which is our localhost. This is still a benefit to us because it makes our session data more standalone. Now we will be able to recycle the ASP.NET process without losing any of our session data. Just remember that you take a performance hit by retrieving objects across processes. However, in some cases, the stability may be worth the performance decrement. Also, if you want to move this server into a Web farm, you could easily change this configuration so that you use a session state server. All you would have to alter is the server name and port number.

> **NOTE**
>
> For the `StateServer` mode to work, you must start the ASP.NET state service, `aspnet_state.ex`. You can do so by going to the Services Management console and selecting the service named ASP.NET State, right-clicking, and then selecting Start. While here, you might want to set the startup type to automatic.

SQL-Based Solution

The SQL-based solution is probably the most stable when you're concerned about losing any session data. Rather than store the session data in-memory, like the two options described in the preceding sections, you store the data in a SQL database. Listing 14.5 shows the configuration necessary in the `config.web` file to make this approach work.

LISTING 14.5 Session State Stored in SQL Server, Taken from `web.config`

```
<sessionState
  mode="SQLServer"
  sqlConnectionString="data source=127.0.0.1;user id=sa;password="
  cookieless="false"
  timeout="30"
/>
```

> **NOTE**
>
> You can find the complete listing for the `web.config` file online.

Notice how to set the mode to `SQLServer` and set the connection string for which SQL Server contains the ASP.NET state database.

> **NOTE**
>
> For the `SQLServer` mode to work, you must run a SQL script named `InstallSqlState.sql` to create a set of tables in the `tempdb` database. You can find this script in the `WINNT\Microsoft.NET\Framework\<Version Number>` directory. The script creates the `ASPStateTempApplications` and `ASPStateTempSessions` tables. The session also uses several stored procedures to insert and retrieve data from these tables. The actual data in the session is stored in the `SessionItemShort` field of the `ASPStateTempSessions` table.

Although you won't lose data by using this option, it will cause a good amount of load on your SQL Server. The decision to use this option should be made by both your company's technology and business teams. The business team will most often fight for no loss of data, whereas the technology team will most likely choose the option that performs the best.

The Data Model and Stored Procedures

For MyGolfGear.NET, we created several tables to hold orders while they are being created and manipulated by the users. We called these "Basket" tables. For now, we will focus on two of those tables: `Basket` and `BasketItems`. The `Basket` table, described in Table 14.2, contains high-level information about orders, such as order totals and user IDs.

TABLE 14.2   The `Basket` Table

Field Name	Data Type	Description
OrderID (PK)	uniqueidentifier	The unique ID of an order.
OrderDate	Datetime	The date and time the order is being placed.
UserID	uniqueidentifier	The ID of the user who is creating this order.
Status	Int	Status of the order; for future growth. Examples are `Creation`, `Product Selection`, and `Submission`.

TABLE 14.2 Continued

Field Name	Data Type	Description
ShippingTotal	Money	Total shipping cost of the order.
TaxTotal	Money	Total tax charged for this order.
SubTotal	Money	Subtotal of the order; does not include shipping or tax costs.
OrderTotal	Money	Final cost of the order; to be paid by the purchaser.

The BasketItems table, described in Table 14.3, stores product information for products the users have selected.

TABLE 14.3 The BasketItems Table

Field Name	Data Type	Description
OrderID (PK)	uniqueidentifier	The unique ID of an order.
ProductID (PK)	uniqueidentifier	The unique ID that represents a product.
Quantity	Int	The quantity requested by the user.
Price	Money	Price of a single product.
TotalCost	Money	Total cost for this product. (Price * Quantity.)
Bonus	Smallint	Depicts whether this item is a bonus item, in other words, free of charge.

Several stored procedures manage the information in the Basket tables. For now, we will focus on the ones that affect the Basket and BasketItems tables. These stored procedures are used by the SQL Data Adapter in the UpdateOrder method of the MyGolfGearDP component. As you read on, you'll notice that we didn't use these stored procedures to update the dataset; we used them only after all changes were applied to the dataset and ready to be submitted to the database.

Stored Procedure Used to Create an Order

The insert stored procedure spCreateNewOrder, shown in Listing 14.6, is used only one time on an order—that is, when it's first created. This stored procedure takes only a user ID and an order ID as parameters and inserts the data into the Basket table. Notice that it uses the SQL GetDate() function to get the current SQL Server date to use as the order date.

LISTING 14.6 The spCreateNewOrder Stored Procedure

```
CREATE PROCEDURE spCreateNewOrder
        (
        @UserID uniqueidentifier,
                @OrderID uniqueidentifier
        )
AS
INSERT INTO Basket
                (
        OrderID,
        UserID,
        OrderDate
        )
VALUES
        (
        @OrderID,
        @UserID,
        GETDATE()
        )
```

Stored Procedure Used to Update an Order

The update stored procedure spUpdateBasketOrder, shown in Listing 14.7, updates any data element of the Basket table. The accepted parameters are order ID, order date, user ID, status, shipping total, tax total, subtotal, and order total. Notice that we limited the number of rows that are updated to the specific order that we are working on by specifying a where clause based on order ID.

LISTING 14.7 The spUpdateBasketOrder Stored Procedure

```
CREATE PROCEDURE spUpdateBasketOrder
        (
        @OrderID uniqueidentifier,
        @OrderDate datetime,
        @UserID uniqueidentifier,
                @Status int,
                @ShippingTotal money,
                @TaxTotal money,
                @SubTotal money,
                @OrderTotal money
        )
```

LISTING 14.7 Continued

```
AS
UPDATE Basket
SET             OrderID = @OrderID,
                OrderDate = @OrderDate,
                UserID = @UserID,
                Status = @Status,
                ShippingTotal = @ ShippingTotal,
                TaxTotal = @TaxTotal,
                SubTotal = @SubTotal,
                OrderTotal = @OrderTotal
WHERE
        (
        OrderID = @OrderID
        )
```

Stored Procedure Used to Delete an Order

The delete stored procedure spDeleteBasketOrder, shown in Listing 14.8, deletes the entire header record of an order in the Basket table. The SQL where clause must be set for a specific order. The only parameter accepted is the order ID.

LISTING 14.8 The spDeleteBasketOrder Stored Procedure

```
CREATE PROCEDURE spDeleteBasketOrder
        (
        @OrderID uniqueidentifier
        )
AS
DELETE
FROM Basket
WHERE
        (
        OrderID = @OrderID
        )
```

Stored Procedure Used to Insert an Item in an Order

The insert stored procedure spInsertBasketItems, shown in Listing 14.9, is used the first time a product is added to an order. It inserts a record into the BasketItems table. This stored procedure takes an order ID, product ID, quantity, price, total cost, and bonus as parameters.

14

USING ASP.NET TO BUILD THE SHOPPING CART

LISTING 14.9   The spInsertBasketItems Stored Procedure

```
CREATE PROCEDURE spInsertBasketItems
        (
        @OrderID uniqueidentifier,
                @ProductID uniqueidentifier,
                @Quantity int,
                @Price money,
                @TotalCost money,
                @Bonus smallint
        )
AS
INSERT INTO BasketItems
                (
        OrderID,
        ProductID,
        Quantity,
                Price,
                TotalCost,
                Bonus
        )
VALUES
        (
        @OrderID,
        @ProductID,
        @Quantity,
                @Price,
                @TotalCost,
                @Bonus
        )
```

Stored Procedure Used to Update an Item in an Order

The update stored procedure spUpdateBasketItems, shown in Listing 14.10, updates data in
the BasketItems table. The accepted parameters are order ID, product ID, quantity, price, total
cost, and bonus. Notice that we used both the order ID and product ID as criteria for the where
clause to ensure that we are updating only one record.

LISTING 14.10   The spUpdateBasketItems Stored Procedure

```
CREATE PROCEDURE spUpdateBasketItems
        (
        @OrderID uniqueidentifier,
        @ProductID uniqueidentifier,
```

LISTING 14.10 Continued

```
            @Quantity int,
            @Price money,
            @TotalCost money,
            @Bonus smallint
        )
AS
UPDATE BasketItems
SET         OrderID = @OrderID,
            ProductID = @ProductID,
            Quantity = @Quantity,
            Price = @ Price,
            TotalCost = @TotalCost,
            Bonus = @Bonus
WHERE
        (OrderID = @OrderID )
            AND (ProductID = @ProductID)
```

Stored Procedure Used to Delete an Item in an Order

The delete stored procedure spDeleteBasketItems, shown in Listing 14.11, deletes only a single product from the BasketItems table. The only parameters accepted are order ID and product ID.

LISTING 14.11 The spDeleteBasketItems Stored Procedure

```
CREATE PROCEDURE spDeleteBasketItems
        (
        @OrderID uniqueidentifier,
        @ProductID uniqueidentifier
        )
AS
DELETE
FROM BasketItems
WHERE
        (OrderID = @OrderID )
            AND (ProductID = @ProductID)
```

Management of a MyGolfGear.NET Order

At the center of the MyGolfGear.NET Web application is the order. This, of course, is the place where we keep information pertaining to what the consumers want, where to ship the products, how much the order will cost them, and how they will pay for the merchandise.

Because this logic is so important, rather than have this code spread throughout our .aspx pages, we created a component named OrderManager to manage a MyGolfGear.NET order.

All manipulation of an order is done through the OrderManager component. For example, instead of having several .aspx pages contain the code and logic to create an order, we created the CreateNewOrder method within the OrderManager component. This method helps us in many ways. It organizes the code in a central location, which allows us to make a change in one section of code that gets implemented everywhere that method is called. As long as the parameters to that method do not change, the client code, the .aspx pages, do not have to be touched. In the following sections, we will focus on the methods of OrderManager used to create the order as well as those that manage the items within the order.

Creating an Order

The creation of an order brings us to our first look at the OrderManager component. It also provides an interaction between the OrderManager component and the MyGolfGearDP component, which is the data provider component. This means all data access to and from our SQL database is done through this component.

First, let's look at the CreateNewOrder method of MyGolfGearDP, shown in Listing 14.12.

LISTING 14.12 MyGolfGearDP.CreateNewOrder() Method

```
public OrderDS CreateNewOrder(System.Guid UserID, System.Guid OrderID)
{
   NameValueCollection configInfo =    (NameValueCollection)
➡HttpContext.Current.GetConfig("appSettings");
   SqlConnection con = new SqlConnection((String)configInfo["ConnectString"]);
   SqlCommand com = new SqlCommand("spCreateNewOrder", con);
   com.CommandType = CommandType.StoredProcedure;
   com.Parameters.Add(new SqlParameter("@UserID", SqlDbType.UniqueIdentifier,
➡16,"UserID"));
   com.Parameters["@UserID"].Value = UserID;
   com.Parameters.Add(new SqlParameter("@OrderID", SqlDbType.UniqueIdentifier,
➡16,"OrderID"));
   com.Parameters["@OrderID"].Value = OrderID;
   con.Open();
   com.ExecuteNonQuery();
   OrderDS order = new OrderDS();
   FillBasketOrder(order, OrderID);
   con.Close();
   return order;
}
```

This method accepts a user ID and an order ID. It creates a database connection and then executes the `spCreateNewOrder` stored procedure. Notice that we use the `ExecuteNonQuery` method of the `SqlCommand` object because we don't need any records returned. All we are accomplishing here is the creation of the "header" record of the order in the `Basket` table. After the query is executed, we then call the `FillBasketOrder` method.

The `FillBasketOrder` method, shown in Listing 14.13, creates the order dataset that is used throughout the site code and the `OrderManager` component.

LISTING 14.13   `MyGolfGearDP.FillBasketOrder()` Method

```
public void FillBasketOrder(OrderDS ds, System.Guid OrderID)
{
  NameValueCollection configInfo = NameValueCollection)
➥HttpContext.Current.GetConfig("appSettings");
  SqlConnection con = new SqlConnection((String)configInfo["ConnectString"]);
  SqlDataAdapter sda = new SqlDataAdapter("spGetOrder", con);
  sda.SelectCommand.CommandType = CommandType.StoredProcedure;
  sda.SelectCommand.Parameters.Add("@OrderID",SqlDbType.UniqueIdentifier,16,
➥"OrderID");
  sda.SelectCommand.Parameters["@OrderID"].Value = OrderID;
  con.Open();
  sda.TableMappings.Add("Table", "Basket");
  sda.TableMappings.Add("Table1", "BasketItems");
  sda.TableMappings.Add("Table2", "BasketShippingInfo");
  sda.TableMappings.Add("Table3", "BasketPaymentInfo");
  sda.Fill(ds);
  con.Close();
}
```

14

USING ASP.NET
TO BUILD THE
SHOPPING CART

At the start of this method, we create a connection to the database and then create a `SqlDataAdapter` based on the `SpGetOrder` stored procedure. This stored procedure has a select statement for each of the Basket tables, along with a where clause that uses the order ID passed in. This means that only the records for the specified order are retrieved. These tables are then mapped to the order dataset. The second parameter of the TableMappings.Add method defines the datatable's name. You may wonder why we are retrieving data that we know does not exist because this order was just created. We do so because this same method also is used when we are retrieving an order that already has data.

Now that we have looked at the data access side of creating an order, let's get back to the OrderManager component. This component contains a method called CreateNewOrder, as shown in Listing 14.14. This method is called from .aspx pages whenever an order needs to be generated for the first time.

LISTING 14.14   OrderManager.CreateNewOrder() Method

```
public OrderDS CreateNewOrder(System.Guid userid, System.Guid orderid)
{
  MyGolfGearDP dp = new MyGolfGearDP();
  OrderDS order = dp.CreateNewOrder(userid,orderid);
  //Default some of the totals
  OrderDS.BasketRow brow = order.Basket.FindByOrderID(orderid);
  brow.BeginEdit();
  brow.OrderTotal = 0;
  brow.ShippingTotal = 0;
  brow.TaxTotal = 0;
  brow.SubTotal = 0;
  brow.EndEdit();
  return order;
}
```

NOTE

You can find the complete listing for the OrderManager.cs file online.

The only parameters required here are the user ID and order ID because they are passed through to the data provider methods. After the order dataset is created and passed back, we then set the default for the totals of the order to 0. Setting the totals to 0 helps us out for any totaling as well as any display features.

Storing and Retrieving an Order

After an order is created, we must address two issues: where we are going to store the order and how we go about retrieving the order. These decisions are very important because they affect how we write our site code. At the beginning of this chapter, we discussed the different options available for storing objects in ASP.NET. For MyGolfGear.NET, we chose to store the order dataset in the session. If, however, someone made a business decision that under no possible circumstances could data ever be lost, we would have either reverted to storing the session data in SQL or updating the database on every page whenever a change is made to the order.

Any time you store data in a session, you must always check to make sure the data is there before you retrieve it. Otherwise, an exception will occur. The following two code snippets show how we check to make sure the order exists in the session and also how easily we can insert objects into the session. Both of these examples are taken from the `Basket.aspx` page. The first code snippet, in Listing 14.15, shows how to retrieve the order from the session, but first we validate that the order already exists in the session.

LISTING 14.15 GetOrder() Method from `Basket.aspx.cs`

```
private OrderDS GetOrder()
{
 MyGolfGear.DataAccess.OrderDS orderds = (MyGolfGear.DataAccess.OrderDS)
➥Session["Order"];
 OrderManager ordermanager = new OrderManager();
 if (orderds == null)
 {
   System.Guid userid;
   userid = new System.Guid(ordermanager.GetShoppingCartUserID());
   orderid = ordermanager.OrderExists(userid);
   if (orderid != System.Guid.Empty)
   {
    //Retrieve existing order
    MyGolfGearDP dp = new MyGolfGearDP();
    orderds = new OrderDS();
    dp.FillBasketOrder(orderds,orderid);
    orderid = new System.Guid(orderds.Basket.Rows[0]["OrderID"].ToString());
    return orderds;
   }
   else
   {
    lblwelcome.Text = "Currently your order is empty.";
    lblsubtotal.Text = String.Format("{0:c}",0);
    updateorder.Enabled = false;
    return null;
   }
 }
 return orderds;
}
```

> **NOTE**
>
> You can find the complete listing for the `Basket.aspx.cs` file online.

First, we create a variable called orderds of type `MyGolfGear.DataAccess.OrderDS`; it is the strongly typed order dataset. (For more information about strongly typed datasets, see Appendix D, "ADO.NET Quick Reference.") It then sets that value to the Order variable in the session, after casting it to a strongly typed dataset. Then we determine whether an order actually was in the session. We need to make sure it exists before our code tries to access the order. If it exists, we simply return the order dataset to the calling code; otherwise, we execute the contents of that if statement, which determines whether an order for this user already exists in the database. If it does, we then retrieve that order; otherwise, we display some messages stating that the order is empty. Remember that an order is created only when a user tries to add a product to an order.

Now that we have looked at how to retrieve an order, let's look at a code snippet that inserts an order into the session. Listing 14.16 shows the code necessary for this action.

LISTING 14.16   Code Snippet from the `UpdateBtn_Click()` Method in `Basket.aspx.cs`.

```
// Save the Order & update the session
MyGolfGearDP dp = new MyGolfGearDP();
dp.UpdateOrder((OrderDS)orderds.GetChanges(), orderid);
orderds.AcceptChanges();
Session["Order"] = orderds;
```

> **NOTE**
>
> You can find the complete listing for the `Basket.aspx.cs` file online.

The first line of this code snippet creates an instance of MyGolfGear.NET's data provider, `MyGolfGearDP`. We then call the `UpdateOrder` method, passing in only the changes that were made to the order dataset and the orderid. We are able to send the changes of the dataset only by using the GetChanges method, which returns a generic dataset of changed data. This generic dataset is then cast to our OrderDS before being sent. The UpdateOrder method is responsible for updating the database with all changes that were made to the order. Finally, all that we need to put the order dataset into the session is that last line of code. It's that simple.

Adding Items to an Order

Adding items to an order connects the product selection portion of an e-Commerce application to the order processing portion of the application. On all product selection pages and the product details page, we have positioned an "Add to Cart" link. When users decide that they want to purchase a product, they click this link, which sends them to the AddProductToOrders.aspx page. We'll spend most of our time on this page in this section of the chapter.

We'll begin with the Page_Load method, which is shown in Listing 14.17.

LISTING 14.17   Page_Load() Method in AddProductsToOrder.aspx.cs

```
protected void Page_Load(object sender, System.EventArgs e)
{
  int quantity;
  ordermanager = new MyGolfGear.OrderManager();
  dp = new MyGolfGear.MyGolfGearDP();
  //Get ProductID
  System.Guid productid = new System.Guid(Request.Params["ProductID"]);
  //Get Quantity. Left it like this in case you wanted the user to be able to
  // input a quantity
  if (Request.Params["Quantity"] == null)
  {
   quantity = 1;
  }
  else
  {
   quantity = Convert.ToInt32(Request.Params["Quantity"]);
  }
  //Get Order
  GetOrder();
  //Add Product to the order
  ordermanager.AddProducts(orderds,orderid,productid,quantity);
  // Total the order   — · calling order manager
  ordermanager.GenOrderTotals(orderds);
  // Save the Order & update the session
  dp.UpdateOrder(orderds, orderid);
  orderds.AcceptChanges();
  Session["Order"] = orderds;
  // Navigate to basket page.
  Server.Transfer("basket.aspx",false);
}
```

14

NOTE

You can find the complete listing for the `AddProductsToOrder.aspx.cs` file online.

In Listing 14.17, we instantiate both `OrderManager` and `MyGolfGearDP` components. Next, we use the request object to retrieve the product ID, passed to us by the hyperlink the user clicked to add to the order. This value is then inserted into the `productid` variable. Immediately afterward, we look for the quantity request parameter. Currently, we do not send this information from either the product selection or product details page. We left this functionality in for future improvements to the site. The `GetOrder` method was described in Listing 14.15.

Next, we call the `AddProducts` method of the `OrderManager` component. The code for this method is shown in Listing 14.18.

LISTING 14.18 OrderManager.AddProducts() Method

```
public void AddProducts(OrderDS orderds, System.Guid orderid, System.Guid
➥productid, int quantity)
{
 decimal price = 0;
 decimal promoprice = 0;
 //Determine if this part has already been added to the order
 OrderDS.BasketItemsRow productrow =orderds.BasketItems.FindByOrderIDProductID
➥(orderid,productid);
 if (productrow != null)
 {
  //Update the quantity and the total cost
  productrow.BeginEdit();
  //Determine if product is on sale
  price = GetPromoPrice(productid,productrow.Price);
  if (price == 0)    { price = productrow.Price; }
  productrow.Quantity = productrow.Quantity + quantity;
  productrow.TotalCost = productrow.Quantity * price;
  productrow.EndEdit();
 }
 else
 {
  //Add Product to the order
  productrow = orderds.BasketItems.NewBasketItemsRow();
  productrow.OrderID = orderid;
  productrow.Quantity = quantity;
  productrow.ProductID = productid;
  productrow.Bonus = 0;
```

LISTING 14.18 Continued

```
//Locate Price
price = GetProductPrice(productid);
//Find price and multiply by quantity to determine cost. First determine if
//on sale.
promoprice = GetPromoPrice(productid,price);
if (promoprice > 0)     { price = promoprice; }
productrow.Price = price;
productrow.TotalCost = price * quantity;
orderds.BasketItems.AddBasketItemsRow(productrow);
//Determine if a bonus part should be awarded, if so add to the order.
System.Guid promopart = GetPromoPart(productid);
if (promopart != System.Guid.Empty)
{
OrderDS.BasketItemsRow bonusrow = orderds.BasketItems.NewBasketItemsRow();
bonusrow.OrderID = orderid;
bonusrow.Quantity = 1;
bonusrow.ProductID = promopart;
bonusrow.Price = 0;
bonusrow.TotalCost = 0;
bonusrow.Bonus = 1;
orderds.BasketItems.AddBasketItemsRow(bonusrow);
}
}
}
```

NOTE

You can find the complete listing for the `OrderManager.cs` file online.

The primary function of this method is, of course, to add products to an order. However, we added some logic in this method to make this process more robust. First, we check to see whether this product already exists in the order; that way, if a user adds a product to an order twice, we increment only the quantity and adjust the total cost of the product. We do so by using the `FindByOrderIDProductID` method, which provides one of the benefits of using a strongly typed dataset. If a row is found, meaning that `productrow` is not equal to `null`, we just alter the product information for this row where necessary. We do so by first determining whether a promotion currently running will cause the user to receive a sale price on the selected product; we do so by calling the `GetPromoPrice` method of the `OrderManager` component. This method was described in Chapter 8, "Using ASP.NET to Implement Discount Specials." Then we adjust the quantity and alter the total cost of the product.

When productrow is null, meaning that this is the first time this product has been added to the order, we execute the else portion of the if statement. We create a new row in the BasketItems datatable and populate the order ID, quantity, product ID, and bonus elements. Then we call the GetProductPrice method, described in Listing 14.19, to determine the current price of the product.

LISTING 14.19 The OrderManager.GetProductPrice() Method

```
public decimal GetProductPrice(System.Guid productid)
{
 decimal price = 0 ;
 // Load the catalog to get part price information from
 CatalogDS catalogds = (CatalogDS)HttpRuntime.Cache.Get("CatalogDS");
 if (catalogds == null)
 {
  // Re-insert catalog into the cache
  MyGolfGearDP dp = new MyGolfGearDP();
  catalogds = new CatalogDS();
  dp.FillCatalog(catalogds);
  HttpRuntime.Cache.Insert("Catalog",catalogds,null,System.DateTime.MaxValue,
➡System.TimeSpan.FromHours(24),CacheItemPriority.High,
➡CacheItemPriorityDecay.Never,null);
 }
 CatalogDS.ProductRow pr = catalogds.Product.FindByProductID(productid);
 CatalogDS.ProductPriceRow[] ppr = pr.GetProductPriceRows();
 //Determine the current price
 foreach(CatalogDS.ProductPriceRow r in ppr)
 {
  if ((r.IsStartDateNull() && r.IsEndDateNull()) || ((r.StartDate <
➡System.DateTime.Today) && (r.EndDate >
➡System.DateTime.Today)) )
  {
   price = r.Price;
  }
 }
 return price;
}
```

NOTE

You can find the complete listing for the OrderManager.cs file online.

Listing 14.19 shows the code necessary to return the current price of a product. All that is passed to the GetProductPrice method is the partid. First, we create a variable to hold the price of the product, called price. Then we retrieve the product catalog from the cache. If it is not in the cache, we regenerate the catalog and then insert it into the cache. Next, we use the FindByProductID method to retrieve the row for this specific product. We use this row to iterate through all the associated product price rows. Then we retrieve the price valid for today's date and return that value.

This call is then followed by a call to the GetPromoPrice method of the OrderManager component to determine whether that price should be reduced to a lower sale price. After we find the current price, we compute the total cost of the product. Immediately afterward, we add BasketItemsRow to the BasketItems table.

After the product is added to the order, we must determine whether a bonus product should also be added to the order in conjunction with the current product being added to the order. If a promotional, or bonus, part exists, it is added to the order just like a normal item, except that price and total cost are 0 and the bonus data element is set to 0.

Let's get back to the Page_Load method of the Basket.aspx page. We left off our description by going into the AddProducts method. After the selected product is added to the order, we then need to update the totals of the order. We do so by calling the OrderManager component's GenOrderTotals method. The code for the GenOrderTotals method is shown in Listing 14.20.

LISTING 14.20 OrderManager.GenOrderTotals() Method

```
public OrderDS GenOrderTotals(OrderDS order)
{
  // Generate the subtotal
  Decimal subtotal = 0;
  foreach(OrderDS.BasketItemsRow bir in order.BasketItems)
  {
    if (bir.RowState != DataRowState.Deleted)
    {
      subtotal += bir.TotalCost;
    }
  }
  order.Basket.Rows[0]["SubTotal"] = subtotal;
  order.Basket.Rows[0]["OrderTotal"] = subtotal + ((decimal)order.Basket.Rows
  [0]["ShippingTotal"])        + ((decimal)order.Basket.Rows[0]["TaxTotal"]);
  return order;
}
```

> **NOTE**
>
> You can find the complete listing for the `OrderManager.cs` file online.

This method iterates through all the rows in the `BasketItems` table and increments the subtotal variable by the total cost associated with each product. The subtotal value is then used to update the `SubTotal` element in the `Basket` datatable. Immediately afterward, we update the total for the order. The order dataset is then returned to the client that called this method.

> **NOTE**
>
> Notice how we first determine the state the `BasketItem` row is in before we use its total cost in the calculation for the order subtotal. We do not want to add a product that the user has just deleted. We do so by making sure `RowState` is not equal to `DataRowState.Deleted`. Remember, the users can add, remove, and update products. Therefore, we could have a combination of both an add and a delete.

After the totals have been updated in the order, we need to save the order both to the database and to the session. To do so, we implement a call to the `UpdateOrder` method on the `MyGolfGearDP` component sending the order dataset as well as the order ID. Here, we'll show only the code snippets associated with applying changes to the `BasketItems` table. However, the same piece of functionality also executes on the `Basket`, `BasketShippingInfo`, and `BasketPaymentInfo` tables. This `UpdateOrder` method is called whenever you want your changes to the dataset saved to the database. You don't even have to specify the changes; you can simply send in your order dataset, and all updates, deletes, and inserts will be applied to the database tables that comprise the order dataset. Listing 14.21 shows the code used to implement this functionality.

LISTING 14.21   `MyGolfGearDP.UpdateOrder()` Method

```
public void UpdateOrder(OrderDS ds, System.Guid OrderID)
{
 NameValueCollection configInfo = (NameValueCollection)
➥HttpContext.Current.GetConfig("appSettings");
 SqlConnection con = new SqlConnection((String)configInfo["ConnectString"]);
 SqlDataAdapter sda = new SqlDataAdapter("spGetOrder", con);
 sda.SelectCommand.Parameters.Add("@OrderID",SqlDbType.UniqueIdentifier,16,
➥"OrderID");
 sda.SelectCommand.Parameters["@OrderID"].Value = OrderID;
```

LISTING 14.21 Continued

```
con.Open();
SqlTransaction t = con.BeginTransaction();
try
{
  //Insert BasketItems
  sda.InsertCommand = new SqlCommand("spInsertBasketItems", con, t);
  sda.InsertCommand.CommandType = CommandType.StoredProcedure;
  sda.InsertCommand.Parameters.Clear();
  sda.InsertCommand.Parameters.Add("@OrderID", SqlDbType.UniqueIdentifier,
➡4,"OrderID");
  sda.InsertCommand.Parameters.Add("@ProductID", SqlDbType.UniqueIdentifier,
➡4,"ProductID");
  sda.InsertCommand.Parameters.Add("@Quantity", SqlDbType.Int, 4,
➡ "Quantity");
  sda.InsertCommand.Parameters.Add("@Price", SqlDbType.Money,8 , "Price");
  sda.InsertCommand.Parameters.Add("@TotalCost", SqlDbType.Money,8 ,
➡ "TotalCost");
  sda.InsertCommand.Parameters.Add("@Bonus", SqlDbType.SmallInt,2 , "Bonus");
  //Update BasketItems
  sda.UpdateCommand = new SqlCommand("spUpdateBasketItems", con, t);
  sda.UpdateCommand.CommandType = CommandType.StoredProcedure;
  sda.UpdateCommand.Parameters.Clear();
  sda.UpdateCommand.Parameters.Add("@OrderID", SqlDbType.UniqueIdentifier,
➡4,"OrderID");
  sda.UpdateCommand.Parameters.Add("@ProductID", SqlDbType.UniqueIdentifier,
➡4,"ProductID");
  sda.UpdateCommand.Parameters.Add("@Quantity", SqlDbType.Int, 4,
➡"Quantity");
  sda.UpdateCommand.Parameters.Add("@Price", SqlDbType.Money,8 , "Price");
  sda.UpdateCommand.Parameters.Add("@TotalCost", SqlDbType.Money,8 ,
➡"TotalCost");
  //Delete BasketItems
  sda.DeleteCommand = new SqlCommand("spDeleteBasketItems", con, t);
  sda.DeleteCommand.CommandType = CommandType.StoredProcedure;
  sda.DeleteCommand.Parameters.Clear();
  sda.DeleteCommand.Parameters.Add("@OrderID", SqlDbType.UniqueIdentifier,
➡4,"OrderID");
  sda.DeleteCommand.Parameters.Add("@ProductID", SqlDbType.UniqueIdentifier,
➡4,"ProductID");
  // Update BasketItems table w/ changes
  sda.Update(ds, "BasketItems");
  ...more code for the rest of the "Basket" tables
  //Commit transactions
  t.Commit();
```

LISTING 14.21 Continued

```
  }
  catch( Exception e )
  {
   t.Rollback();
   throw new Exception("SQL Update Failed" + e.ToString());
  }
  finally
  {
   con.Close();
  }
 }
```

> **NOTE**
>
> You can find the complete listing for the MyGolfGearDP.cs file online.

After a SQL connection is made, a SQL Data Adapter is created, passing it the spGetOrder stored procedure, to match the schema of the Basket tables that are about to be updated with the datatables in the dataset. Then we call the BeginTransaction method of the connection object. This ensures that if any of the updates fail, all other changes will be rolled back. Doing so ensures that the data in SQL is always valid data. Afterward, we set the insertcommand of the SQL Data Adapter to the spInsertBasketItems stored procedure. Also, each parameter in the stored procedure is mapped to a data element within the BasketItems datatable. This same process is repeated for the update and delete stored procedures. Then the Update method of the SQL Data Adapter is called, passing it the order dataset and the name of the table to be updated. The line more code for the rest of the "Basket" tables indicates that this process is also repeated for the other Basket tables. Finally, we commit the transaction. This process applies all updates to the database. If this database update fails, an exception is thrown.

To finish the description of the Page_Load method of the Basket.aspx page, we can resume where we call the AcceptChanges() method on the order dataset to ensure that the order dataset and data in the Basket tables are in sync. Then we can update the order in the session and transfer the user back to the basket page.

Updating and Deleting Items in an Order

On the shopping cart page, Basket.aspx, users can not only view items in their orders, but also update and delete them. Here, we will detail what is done to update items within the orders. Listing 14.22 shows the UpdateOrder method on the Basket.aspx page.

LISTING 14.22 `UpdateOrder()` Method in `Basket.aspx.cs`.

```
protected void UpdateOrder(OrderDS orderds)
{
 int idx = 0;
 // iterate the rows in the datagrid
 foreach (DataGridItem item in itemslist.Items)
 {
  // Get references to the quantity box and the delete checkbox
  int qty = Int32.Parse(((TextBox)item.FindControl("Quantity")).Text);
  bool deleterow = ((CheckBox)item.FindControl("delete")).Checked;
  // if quantity was altered or remove item was checked
  if ((qty != Int32.Parse(itemslist.DataKeys[idx].ToString())) || deleterow
➡ == true)
  {
   System.Guid productid=new System.Guid(((Label)item.FindControl
➡("ProductID")).Text.ToString());
   // Determine if we need to update or delete the item.
   try
   {
    if ((qty == 0)||(deleterow == true))
    {
     ordermanager.DeleteProduct(orderds,productid);
    }
    else
    {
     ordermanager.UpdateProduct(orderds,productid,qty);
    }
   }
   catch
   {
    lblerror.Text = "You incorrectly entered a quantity, please verify.";
   }
  }
  idx++;
 }
}
```

14

NOTE

You can find the complete listing for the `Basket.aspx.cs` file online.

When the user clicks the Update Order link, we call the `UpdateOrder` method, which iterates through all the items in the data grid. Then, for each iteration, we populate a qty integer variable and a `deleterow` Boolean variable. Next, we check to see whether the user changed anything. First, we see whether the quantity from the text box is different from the quantity hidden in the data grid. Then we check to see whether the delete check box was selected. If either one of these situations is true, we continue. After grabbing the actual product ID, we determine whether we need to update or delete the product. If the item is to be updated, we call the `UpdateProduct` method on the `OrderManager` component. The code for this method is displayed in Listing 14.23. It is similar to the first portion of the `AddProducts` method when a product already exists in the order.

LISTING 14.23 OrderManager.UpdateProduct() Method

```
public void UpdateProduct(OrderDS order, System.Guid productid, int quantity)
  {
   decimal price;
   DataRow r = order.Basket.Rows[0];
   System.Guid orderid = new System.Guid(r["OrderID"].ToString());
   OrderDS.BasketItemsRow productrow =
➥order.BasketItems.FindByOrderIDProductID(orderid,productid);
   //Update the quantity and the total cost
   productrow.BeginEdit();
   //Determine if product is on sale
  price = GetPromoPrice(productid,productrow.Price);
  if (price == 0)     { price = productrow.Price; }
  productrow.Quantity = quantity;
  productrow.TotalCost = quantity * price;
  productrow.EndEdit();
 }
```

> **NOTE**
>
> You can find the complete listing for the `OrderManager.cs` file online.

When the user checks the delete box or sets the quantity to 0, we need to delete that product from the order. Listing 14.24 shows how to call the `DeleteProduct` method of the `OrderManager` component..

LISTING 14.24 OrderManager.DeleteProduct() Method

```
public void DeleteProduct(OrderDS order, System.Guid productid)
{
 DataRow r = order.Basket.Rows[0];
```

LISTING 14.24   Continued

```
System.Guid orderid = new System.Guid(r["OrderID"].ToString());
OrderDS.BasketItemsRow bir =
➥ order.BasketItems.FindByOrderIDProductID(orderid,productid);
bir.Delete();
//Determine if there was a bonus item w/ this product and delete it as well
System.Guid bonuspart = GetPromoPart(productid);
if (bonuspart != System.Guid.Empty)
{
  OrderDS.BasketItemsRow br =
➥ order.BasketItems.FindByOrderIDProductID(orderid,bonuspart);
  br.Delete();
}
}
```

> **NOTE**
>
> You can find the complete listing for the `OrderManager.cs` file online.

First, we locate the `BasketItems` row by using the `FindByOrderIDProductID` method of the `OrderDS` and then immediately afterward call the `Delete()` method. Next, we call the `GetPromoPart` method to determine whether a bonus item was also added to the order. If so, it is also deleted from the order. If a user receives a bonus part for ordering a specific product and then deletes that product, we should also delete the bonus part.

Displaying Items in an Order (The Shopping Cart)

After users add an item to an order or click the Shopping Cart link on the header navigation bar, they are sent to the shopping cart page, `Basket.aspx`. The shopping cart page displays the products in the order, along with the product name, quantity, price, and total cost. Then the order subtotal is displayed. An example of the basket page is shown in Figure 14.1.

In the code behind of the `Basket.aspx` page, we created a `FillCart` method, which accepts an order dataset, to populate the data grid of items as well as the subtotal of the order. This method is shown in Listing 14.25.

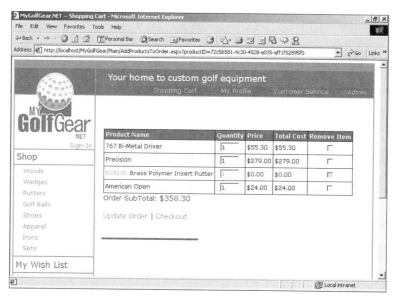

FIGURE 14.1

Basket.aspx *page displaying a bonus part.*

LISTING 14.25   FillCart() Method of Basket.aspx.cs.

```
private void FillCart(OrderDS orderds)
{
 // Load the catalog from cache
 GetCatalog();
 DataTable dt = new DataTable("Items");
 dt.Columns.Add("ProductID");
 dt.Columns.Add("Name");
 dt.Columns.Add("Price");
 dt.Columns.Add("Quantity");
 dt.Columns.Add("TotalCost");
 dt.Columns.Add("Bonus");
 foreach(OrderDS.BasketItemsRow bir in orderds.BasketItems)
 {
  DataRow tempRow = dt.NewRow();
  tempRow["ProductID"] = bir.ProductID;
  if (bir.Bonus == 1)
  {
    tempRow["Name"] = "<font color=red>BONUS: </font>" +
➡catalogds.Product.FindByProductID(bir.ProductID).Name.ToString();
  }
  else
```

LISTING 14.25 Continued

```
  {
   tempRow["Name"] = catalogds.Product.FindByProductID(bir.ProductID).
➥Name.ToString();
  }
  tempRow["Bonus"] = bir.Bonus;
  tempRow["Price"] = String.Format("{0:c}",bir.Price);
  tempRow["Quantity"] = bir.Quantity;
  tempRow["TotalCost"] = String.Format("{0:c}",bir.TotalCost);
  //Add row
  dt.Rows.Add(tempRow);
 }
 itemslist.DataSource = dt.DefaultView;
 itemslist.DataBind();
 // Disable the Quantity textbox & delete checkbox for bonus items
 foreach (DataGridItem item in itemslist.Items)
 {
  if ( ((Label)item.FindControl("Bonus")).Text == "1")
  {
   ((TextBox)item.FindControl("Quantity")).Enabled = false;
   ((CheckBox)item.FindControl("delete")).Enabled = false;
  }
 }
 // Get the order subtotal
 lblsubtotal.Text = String.Format("{0:c}",orderds.Basket.Rows[0]["SubTotal"]);
}
```

> **NOTE**
>
> You can find the complete listing for the Basket.aspx.cs file online.

We start by retrieving the catalog dataset from the HttpRuntime cache. The GetCatalog method is shown in Listing 14.26.

LISTING 14.26 GetCatalog() Method in Basket.aspx.cs.

```
protected void GetCatalog()
{
 // Load the catalog from cache
 catalogds = (CatalogDS)HttpRuntime.Cache.Get("Catalog");
 if (catalogds == null)
 {
```

LISTING 14.26   Continued

```
// Re-insert catalog into the cache
MyGolfGearDP dp = new MyGolfGearDP();
catalogds = new CatalogDS();
dp.FillCatalog(catalogds);
HttpRuntime.Cache.Insert("Catalog",catalogds,null,System.DateTime.MaxValue,
➥ System.TimeSpan.FromHours(24),
CacheItemPriority.High,CacheItemPriorityDecay.Never,null);
  }
}
```

NOTE

You can find the complete listing for the `Basket.aspx.cs` file online.

Notice how we still make sure that the catalog is in the session before we try to use it. If it's not found, meaning it's equal to `null`, the catalog is retrieved and then reinserted into the cache.

Let's get back to the `FillCart` method. We begin the creation of a data table that will be the basis for the data grid on the `.aspx` page. We can't just use the `BasketItems` datatable from the order dataset because we need more information about the products than what is stored in the `BasketItems` datatable. So we create a datatable called `Items` and then define the columns of the datatable. We then iterate through all the rows in the `BasketItems` datatable, creating a new row for the `dt` datatable. After creating `tempRow`, we populate the data elements of the table. Next, we determine whether the product is a bonus. If it is, we add the red text `"Bonus"` to the product name. Then we bind the newly created datatable to the data grid. We iterate through the data grid to disable the quantity text box and the deletion check box. This is so the user has no control over removing a bonus product or deleting a bonus. Last, we set the value `lblsubtotal`, which is displayed under the data grid.

Now we get to display the data grid, which is shown in Figure 14.1. Listing 14.27 displays the ASP.NET code responsible for the layout of the data grid.

LISTING 14.27   Data Grid in `Basket.aspx` to Display Items in an Order

```
<asp:DataGrid id="itemslist" AutoGenerateColumns="false" AlternatingItemStyle-
➥BackColor="beige" BorderColor="black" BorderWidth="1" CellPadding="3"
➥Font-Name="Verdana" Font-Size="10pt"
HeaderStyle-BackColor="DarkGreen" HeaderStyle-Font-Bold="True" HeaderStyle-
```

LISTING 14.27   Continued

```
➥ForeColor="Beige"
DataKeyField="Quantity" runat="server">
 <Columns>
  <asp:BoundColumn HeaderText="Product Name" DataField="Name" />
  <asp:TemplateColumn HeaderText="Quantity">
  <ItemTemplate>
   <center>
   <asp:label id="ProductID" visible="false" runat="server" Text=
➥'<%# DataBinder.Eval(Container.DataItem, "ProductID") %>' />
   <asp:label id="Bonus" visible="false" runat="server" Text=
➥'<%# DataBinder.Eval(Container.DataItem, "Bonus") %>' />
   <asp:TextBox id="Quantity" runat="server" Columns="3" Text=
➥'<%# DataBinder.Eval(Container.DataItem, "Quantity") %>' width="40px" />
   </center>
  </ItemTemplate>
  </asp:TemplateColumn>
  <asp:BoundColumn HeaderText="Price" DataField="Price" />
  <asp:BoundColumn HeaderText="Total Cost" DataField="TotalCost"  />
  <asp:TemplateColumn HeaderText="Remove Item">
  <ItemTemplate>
  <center>
  <asp:CheckBox id=delete runat="server" />
  </center>
  </ItemTemplate>
  </asp:TemplateColumn>
  </Columns>
</asp:DataGrid>
```

> **NOTE**
>
> You can find the complete listing for the Basket.aspx file online.

Now let's look at all the attributes that were set to give the data grid its pleasant appearance. In this data grid, we have normal bound columns such as the product name and price columns. We use TemplateColumns for the quantity text box and the delete check box. The Quantity Template Column allows us to define a column heading such as Quantity and use the ItemTemplate to specify the objects that will make up that column for each item. We add a label control to store the product ID of the row being displayed. This label is not displayed; it's used to associate the altered quantity in the text box to the product it belongs to.

Summary

This chapter described some important topics that play a big part in both the ASP.NET world and in the MyGolfGear.NET Web application. First, we discussed the new options available for state management in .NET, especially those associated with the session. Next, we described the stored procedures used to manage the order data in the database. Then we described the creation and management of a MyGolfGear.NET order, in particular, adding, updating, and removing items from an order as well as displaying the items of an order on the shopping cart page. We hope that this chapter will give you a good foundation in using the strongly typed dataset order, which will continue to be manipulated by our `OrderManager` component for pages to come.

Self Instruction

Some e-Commerce sites allow users to enter quantities for multiple items at a time on a product selection page and add all of them to the order at one time. To add this functionality, alter the product selection and product detail pages with quantity text boxes next to each product. This will allow the users to enter their desired quantity. Then alter the code in Listing 14.17 to iterate through the forms collection and, when the `Quantity` control has a value greater than zero, add that product to the order.

The Checkout Process

IN THIS CHAPTER

Although the shopping cart may be the heart of an e-Commerce application, it means nothing if users cannot check out. Similar to a grocery store, if shoppers put items in their shopping carts but never make it through the checkout lane, that company doesn't make any money. This makes the checkout process an extremely important part of an e-Commerce application. Many business rules are applied to the order in this process.

Examples of business rules that might be applied to an order are shipping costs, tax amounts, approval, and acceptance of payment. All these features will be described in this chapter as well as how we implemented them in MyGolfGear.NET using the .NET Framework.

Beginning the Checkout Process

The checkout process begins with the shipping page, which collects all necessary information required to ship the product. In the beginning of this checkout process for MyGolfGear.NET, we made a business rule that anyone who submits an order must first be registered with the site. If the user is not logged on, he cannot continue with the checkout process. Listing 15.1 shows the code necessary to implement this feature.

LISTING 15.1   The Page_Load Method of ShippingInfo.aspx.cs

```
...
private void Page_Load(object sender, System.EventArgs e)
{
  // Make sure the user has logged in, before they proceed w/ checkout
  LoginInformation l = new LoginInformation();
  int id = l.GetUserID( Request.ServerVariables["REMOTE_USER"] );
  if (id < 1)
  {
  lblwelcome.Text = "You must log in, before you continue the checkout
➡ process.  Please click on the sign-in link to the left.";
  lblwelcome.ForeColor = System.Drawing.Color.Red;
```

LISTING 15.1   Continued

```
btnCheckOut.Visible = false;
 }
}
...
```

NOTE

Listing 15.1 is only a code snippet. Go online to view all the code in `ShippingInfo.aspx`.

In Listing 15.1, we first create a new instance of the `LoginInformation` component. Then we set the value of the `id` variable to the return value of the `GetUserID` method of the `Login Information` component. This method requires the username, which we obtain by looking in the `ServerVariables` collection of the `Request` object. If the user has already been authenticated by the site, this collection would be populated. If the ID returned is greater than 0, the user has already been authenticated and she can continue with the checkout process. Otherwise, we create an error message by setting the text of `lblwelcome` and changing the text color to red. To stop the user from checking out, we set the `Visible` property of the checkout link to `false`. The result of this code is shown in Figure 15.1.

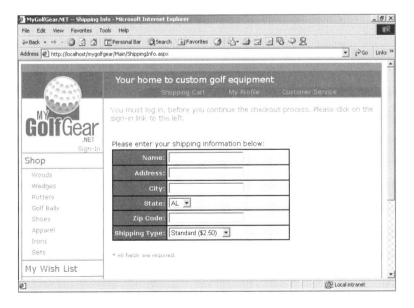

FIGURE 15.1

The `ShippingInfo.aspx` *page with an anonymous user trying to check out.*

Figure 15.1 shows what the user will see if he tries to check out before being authenticated. When this situation occurs, the user must go through the authentication process explained in Chapter 16, "Using ASP.NET Authentication and Authorization for Personalization." However, we had to make some adjustments to this code. The problem is that if an anonymous user who already has items in her basket logs in to the site, the user ID associated with that order is no longer correct. To ensure that the order is updated with the correct user ID when an anonymous user logs in to the site or when a new user account is created, we had to make some changes to two methods. The first change occurs when a new user is being created. This code is shown in Listing 15.2.

LISTING 15.2   The DoJoin method of join.aspx.cs

```
...
protected void DoJoin( object sender, EventArgs e )
{
 LoginInformation l = new LoginInformation();
 if( l.GetUserID(Email.Text) != 0 )
 {
   message.Text = "That user already exists.  Please try again.";
   return;
 }
 else
 {
   if(l.Create(FirstName.Text,LastName.Text,Email.Text,Password.Text))
   {
    message.Text = "User Successfully Created.";
    // If there is an order in the session, update the userid.
    if (Session["Order"] != null)
    {
     MyGolfGear.DataAccess.OrderDS orderds =
➥(MyGolfGear.DataAccess.OrderDS)Session["Order"];
     orderds.Basket[0].UserID = l.GetUserID(Email.Text);
     MyGolfGearDP dp = new MyGolfGearDP();
     dp.UpdateOrder((OrderDS)orderds.GetChanges(),orderds.Basket[0].OrderID);
     orderds.AcceptChanges();
     Session["Order"] = orderds;
    }
   }
   else
   {
    message.Text = "Please Enter all information and try again.";
   }
 }
}
```

> **NOTE**
>
> Listing 15.2 is only a code snippet. Go online to view all the code in `join.aspx.cs`.

We added the new portion of code directly under the place where the message text was being set to indicate that the new user was successfully created. Immediately afterward, we check to see whether there is an order in the session. If there isn't, no action is taken; otherwise, we update the user ID element of the order. First, we create a new order dataset called `orderds` and set it to the order that is already in the session. We then set the `UserID` element of the `Basket` datatable to the return value of the `GetUserID` method of the `LoginInformation` component, passing it the e-mail address entered by the user. When that task is complete, we must update the order in the database. We do so by creating a new instance of `MyGolfGearDP` and calling the `UpdateOrder` method, passing it only the changes that were made to the order dataset and the `OrderID`. Now that the database is updated, we can accept the changes in the dataset by calling the `AcceptChanges` method of `orderds`. Finally, we update the order that is in the session with the order that was just updated. Now the user will be able to continue the checkout process with no problems.

The next piece of authorization code that had to be altered affects when an existing user hasn't yet logged in to the site but tries to check out. He will get the same error as the anonymous user but will only have to sign in as opposed to create a new user account, which we just discussed. The code section that we had to alter is the `DoSubmit` method in `login.aspx.cs`. This code is shown in Listing 15.3.

LISTING 15.3 The `DoSubmit` method of `login.aspx.cs`

```
protected void DoSubmit( object sender, EventArgs s )
{
  if( Verify(Email.Text, Password.Text) )
  {
   FormsAuthenticationTicket ticket = new FormsAuthenticationTicket(Email.Text,
➡ false, 5000);
   //If there is an order in the session, update the userID
   if (Session["Order"] != null)
   {
    MyGolfGear.DataAccess.OrderDS orderds = (MyGolfGear.DataAccess.OrderDS)
➡Session["Order"];
    LoginInformation l = new LoginInformation();
    orderds.Basket[0].UserID = l.GetUserID(Email.Text);
    MyGolfGearDP dp = new MyGolfGearDP();
    dp.UpdateOrder((OrderDS)orderds.GetChanges(),orderds.Basket[0].OrderID);
```

LISTING 15.3 Continued

```
  orderds.AcceptChanges();
  Session["Order"] = orderds;
 }
 FormsAuthentication.RedirectFromLoginPage(Email.Text, saveinfo.Checked);
}
else
{
 loginmessage.Text= "There was a problem with your login.  Please try again";
}
}
```

NOTE

Listing 15.3 is only a code snippet. Go online to view all the code in `login.aspx.cs`.

In Listing 15.3, we added the new code segment immediately after the `FormsAuthentication Ticket` was created. This code segment is similar to the one added in `join.aspx.cs`. We verify that an order exists in the session, and if it does, we retrieve the user ID of the logged-in user and update the order dataset accordingly.

Retrieving Shipping Information

Now that the user has been successfully authenticated, she can continue with the checkout process. This time when she enters the ShippingInfo page, an error message will not be displayed. The display of the shipping page is rather basic. It has input boxes for the ShipTo Name, Address, City, State, Zip Code, and Shipping Type. Currently, MyGolfGear.NET provides two shipping methods: standard and overnight. At the bottom of these input boxes are a checkout link and a text message stating that all fields are required.

To make the form input boxes required in ASP 3.0, you had to write the JavaScript to make sure that each input box had a value before the form was submitted or check these values on the server in your ASP page. This coding effort was simple but very tedious. Now in ASP.NET, you use Validator controls. Validator controls are easy to implement as well as very powerful. You have several Validator controls to choose from, including `RequiredFieldValidator`, `CompareValidator`, `RangeValidator`, `CustomValidator`, and `RegularExpressionValidator`. I highly recommend that you become familiar with these controls because they can save you a lot of coding time and make form field validation easy to maintain. Another nice feature of Validator controls is that they support both client-side and server-side code generation, depending on the target browser level.

On the `ShippingInfo.aspx` page, we implemented the `RequiredValidator` control. The implementation of this control is similar to the other Validator controls. Listing 15.4 shows `RequiredValidator` in action.

LISTING 15.4   The `RequiredValidator` Control from `ShippingInfo.aspx`

```
...
<tr>
    <td class="clsFormCell">City:</td>
    <td class="clsFormInput">
        <asp:TextBox ID="txtCity" Runat="server" maxlength=30/>
        <asp:RequiredFieldValidator
            id="reqtxtCity"
            ControlToValidate="txtCity"
            Display="Static"
            Width="20%" runat=server >
            *
        </asp:RequiredFieldValidator>
    </td>
</tr>
...
```

> **NOTE**
>
> Listing 15.4 is only a code snippet. Go online to view all the code in `ShippingInfo.aspx`.

Listing 15.4 shows how to use the `RequiredValidator` control to make sure that the user enters a value in the City input box. First, we use the ASP.NET `TextBox` control to create the input box and set its `runat` attribute to `Server` and its `maxlength` attribute to `30`. Next, we insert our `RequiredValidator` control. This control has many attributes that we must set. We first set the `id` attribute, followed by the `ControlToValidate` attribute. This attribute, as its name states, determines which `TextBox` control on the page to mark as required. The next attribute, `Display`, is set to `Static`, which means that when the `TextBox` control does not have a value, the error text has already allocated space for this message. Make sure that your table cells have enough width to encompass both the `TextBox` control and error message. The `Width` attribute determines how much of the available space will be used by the error message. Finally, we set the `runat` attribute to `"server"`. After we set all the attributes for the `RequiredValidator` control, we close the opening tag of the control and then insert our error message text. In this case, all we have is an asterisk. We could put some text, such as `"The city field requires a value"`, but we have found that the page looks cleaner if we put an asterisk after each TextBox and then insert "* All fields are required." at the bottom of the page. Figure 15.2 shows the output of the ShippingInfo page when a user forgets to insert a value in the City input box.

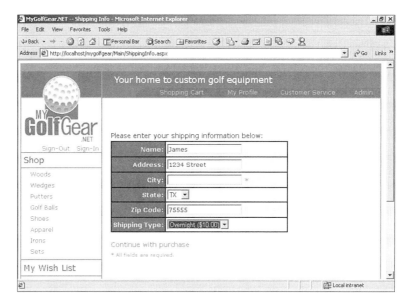

FIGURE 15.2
The ShippingInfo.aspx *page, with missing required value.*

When the user inserts a value in the City input box, the page will be processed normally. Let's look at what happens behind the scenes when a user clicks the Continue with Purchase button. This CheckOut method of ShippingInfo.aspx.cs is shown in Listing 15.5.

LISTING 15.5   ShippingInfo.aspx.cs

```
...
public void CheckOut(Object sender, EventArgs e)
{
 OrderDS order = GetOrder();
 OrderDS.BasketRow br = (OrderDS.BasketRow) order.Basket.Rows[0];
 OrderDS.BasketShippingInfoRow bsi =
➥order.BasketShippingInfo.NewBasketShippingInfoRow();
 bsi.OrderID = br.OrderID;
 bsi.ShipToName = txtName.Text;
 bsi.ShipToAddress = txtAddress.Text;
 bsi.ShipToCity = txtCity.Text;
 bsi.ShipToState = lstState.SelectedItem.Value;
 bsi.ShipToZipCode = txtZip.Text;
```

LISTING 15.5 Continued

```
 br.ShippingTotal = Decimal.Parse(lstShippingType.SelectedItem.Value);
 MyGolfGear.localhost.taxService t = new MyGolfGear.localhost.taxService();
 br.TaxTotal = (decimal)t.GetTax((double)br.SubTotal,
➥bsi.ShipToState.ToString());
 order.BasketShippingInfo.Rows.Clear();
 order.BasketShippingInfo.AddBasketShippingInfoRow(bsi);
 OrderManager o = new OrderManager();
 o.GenOrderTotals( order );
 Session["Order"] = order;
 Response.Redirect("payment.aspx");
}
...
```

> **NOTE**
>
> Listing 15.5 is only a code snippet. Go online to view all the code in
> ShippingInfo.aspx.cs.

In Listing 15.5, the CheckOut method is executed as soon as the user clicks the Continue with Purchase button. The method starts by retrieving the order. Then we create two data rows, one to contain the first row of the Basket datatable and the other to contain a new BasketShippingInfo row. The next set of lines sets the field elements of the BasketShippingInfo row with the values that the user entered in the Shipping form. After that, we set the ShippingTotal element of the Basket row to the selected value from the ShippingType drop-down list, after it is converted to a decimal. When that task is complete, we call our Tax Web service to retrieve the tax total for the order. This process is explained in greater detail later in this chapter.

After the tax total is calculated, it is inserted into the TaxTotal element of the Basket row. Next, we want to add the newly created BasketShippingInfo row to the BasketShippingInfo datatable; however, before we execute that statement, we clear all the rows in this table by calling the Clear method on order.BasketShippingInfo.Rows. Now we must update the order total, which is composed of the subtotal, shipping total, and tax total, by calling the GenTotals method of the OrderManager component. When these steps are complete, the shipping information and all totals are updated in the order. Next, we take this updated order dataset and reinsert it into the session. Finally, the user is redirected to the Payment page to complete the checkout process.

Reviewing Options for Calculating Tax

Any time you are dealing with a retail company of any type, one responsibility that is unavoidable is the application of sales tax. Sales tax on the Internet has lately become an important topic for both state and federal governments. Currently, the law states that sales tax needs to be collected only if the company has a business entity located where the order is being shipped. For example, say that MyGolfGear.NET's main office is in Dallas, Texas, and a user on the site is purchasing an order to be shipped to New Orleans, Louisiana. In this situation, sales tax does not have to be charged as long as MyGolfGear.NET does not have a business office in the New Orleans area.

With the current law, those companies that have business entities throughout the country have an extremely more complex tax issue than those that conduct business in only a couple of cities. For these companies, it's certainly worthwhile to look into a tax package to assist in the calculation of sales tax.

Now let me briefly inform you why determining a tax rate for a specific location can be difficult. A sales tax rate can be a combination of state, city, jurisdiction, and other tax rates. Also, depending on the type of product, tax rates differ from location to location. For example, tax rates for a cosmetic product may be different depending on state and local tax laws. To add just a little more difficulty, tax rates can change as often as every month.

In situations like the one just described, it is usually easier to integrate with a tax package rather than maintain all the tax rules for your various places of business. Although the actual integration may be challenging in the beginning, when it is complete, you will start to see the benefits of having such a package. Today, you can choose from a number of tax packages.

> **NOTE**
>
> My coauthor Jason and I have worked with the Vertex package (`http://www.Vertexinc.com`) with pleasing results. Another widely used package is Taxware (`http://www.Taxware.com`); however, you have many packages to choose from. Keep in mind that every company will have a different "best" solution because each company's requirements are usually different.

Currently, these packages or any that I'm aware of as of this writing have yet to move to the .NET platform. Be aware that this means that a portion of your e-Commerce application may have to interoperate with some COM components.

As for MyGolfGear.NET, we kept tax calculations simple so that we could focus on the technology, not the hundreds of different sales tax laws.

Using the Tax Web Service

For MyGolfGear.NET, we implemented our tax calculations as a Web service. You can find a brief overview of SOAP and Web services in Chapter 2, ".NET Overview."

> **NOTE**
>
> For more specifics on this concept, read Robert Tabor's book, *Microsoft .NET Web Services* (ISBN: 0-672-32088-6).

We had to consider several pros and cons when deciding between creating a tax component or a Tax Web service. The reasons we chose to create a Web service are simple yet very powerful. Using a Web service allowed us to separate all the tax processing from the rest of our site. Even though MyGolfGear.NET's tax implementation is simple today, this may not be the case in two months or two years from now. If we see that the tax laws are changing and becoming more complex, we can simply change our tax service to integrate with a tax package without having to change any of the site code. This makes a major change such as moving to a tax package or from one tax package to another seamless to the Web site. Another reason to create this part of the application as a Web service is that if other departments or subsidiaries of our company also need to calculate tax, they will be able to use our Tax Web service no matter what platform their system is running on.

Now let's look at the code used to create this Web service. Listing 15.6 displays the code necessary to create the Tax Web service for MyGolfGear.NET.

LISTING 15.6   The `taxService` Web Service

```
public class taxService : System.Web.Services.WebService
{
 private System.Data.SqlClient.SqlConnection Con;
 private System.Data.SqlClient.SqlCommand cmdGetTaxRate;
 public string ConnectionString;

 public taxService()
 {
  NameValueCollection configInfo = (NameValueCollection)
➥HttpContext.Current.GetConfig("appSettings");
  ConnectionString = ((String)configInfo["ConnectString"]);
  InitializeComponent();
 }
```

LISTING 15.6   Continued

```csharp
private void InitializeComponent()
{
 // Create Sql Connection
 ...
 // cmdGetTaxRate
 this.cmdGetTaxRate.CommandText = "dbo.spGetTaxRate";
 this.cmdGetTaxRate.CommandType = System.Data.CommandType.StoredProcedure;
 this.cmdGetTaxRate.Connection = this.Con;
 this.cmdGetTaxRate.Parameters.Add(new System.Data.SqlClient.SqlParameter
➥("@RETURN_VALUE", System.Data.SqlDbType.Int, 4,
➥System.Data.ParameterDirection.ReturnValue, true, ((System.Byte)(10)),
➥ ((System.Byte)(0)), "", System.Data.DataRowVersion.Current, null));
 this.cmdGetTaxRate.Parameters.Add(new System.Data.SqlClient.SqlParameter(
➥"@State", System.Data.SqlDbType.Char, 2,
➥System.Data.ParameterDirection.Input, true, ((System.Byte)(0)),
➥((System.Byte)(0)), "",  System.Data.DataRowVersion.Current, null));
 }

 [WebMethod]
 public double GetTax(double Amount, string StateCode)
 {
  Con.Open();
  cmdGetTaxRate.Parameters["@State"].Value = StateCode;
  Object o = cmdGetTaxRate.ExecuteScalar();
  double rate;
  If( o == null )
   rate = 0;
  else
   rate = (double) o;
  Con.Close();
  return Amount * rate;
 }
 ...
}
```

> **NOTE**
>
> Listing 15.6 is only a code snippet. Go online to view all the code in the taxService.
> asmx.cs Web service.

The .NET Framework makes creating Web services painless. Let's walk through the code so that I can prove this point to you. Our first task is to make sure that this class inherits from `System.Web.Services.WebService` by using the : indicator after the class name. After this task is complete, we declare variables that will be used throughout this class. Next, we create our main method, `taxService`. This method accomplishes two tasks: First, it sets our `ConnectionString` variable and then calls the `InitializeComponent` method. The `InitializeComponent` method creates a `SqlConnection` object and prepares our `SqlCommand` object to execute the `spGetTaxRate` stored procedure. This simple stored procedure accepts only a state and returns the tax rate.

The important piece of this code snippet is the `GetTax` method. Notice that we give it a `WebMethod` attribute by adding `[WebMethod]` above the method declaration. This method accepts two parameters: an amount and a state code. The first two lines of this method open the SQL connection and set the `@State` parameter of the `cmdGetTaxRate` command created in the `InitializeComponent` method. Next, we execute the command by calling its `ExecuteScalar` method. We used this method because it returns only the value of the first column of the first row. We then check to see whether this value is null. If it is, we set the rate variable to 0; otherwise, we set it to the value returned from the stored procedure. Then we close the connection and return the amount passed in multiplied by the rate variable.

Calling the Tax Web Service from the Web

Now let's look at the Tax Web service in action. First, let's see what is required to call and interact with the Web service from a Web page. To call the Web service from a Web page, download the code for this chapter and, insert `http://localhost/MyGolfGear/WebServices/taxservice.asmx` into your URL address bar, and press Enter. You can replace `localhost` with the name of your local machine name. The page that appears is displayed in Figure 15.3.

The page in Figure 15.3, `taxservice.asmx`, is generated automatically by .NET. When this page is displayed, click the `GetTax` link, and the page shown in Figure 15.4 will be displayed. This link will activate the `GetTax` method of the `taxService` class.

The link activates the method and then automatically prompts you with input boxes to insert values that will be passed to the parameters of the `GetTax` method. Also on this page are samples of different ways to call the Web service. Again, this functionality is provided by .NET. After these values are entered and you click the Invoke button, the `GetTax` method is executed and the results are returned, as shown in Figure 15.5.

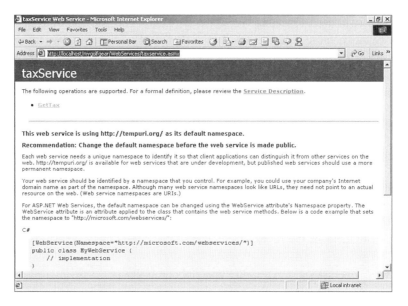

FIGURE 15.3

The taxservice.asmx *page.*

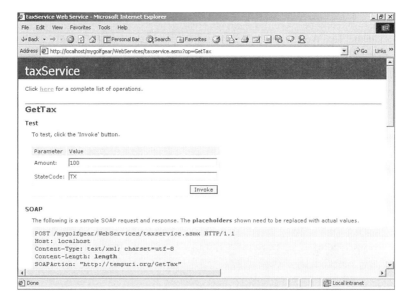

FIGURE 15.4

The taxservice.asmx *page, after clicking the* GetTax *link.*

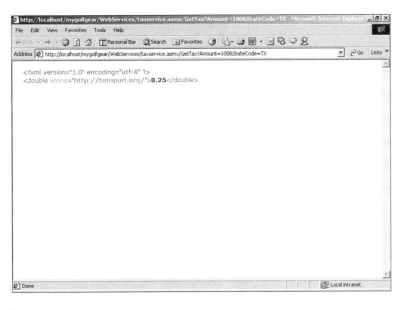

FIGURE 15.5
The taxservice.asmx *page, after invoking the* GetTax *Web method.*

After the method is executed, the results are returned in XML format, as shown in Figure 15.5.

Calling the Tax Web Service from a Component

In MyGolfGear.NET, we don't need to call the Tax Web service from the Web; instead, we can call it from the code behind of the Shipping.aspx page. Listing 15.7 shows how this call is made.

LISTING 15.7 Calling the taxService Web Service

```
...
MyGolfGear.localhost.taxService t = new MyGolfGear.localhost.taxService();
br.TaxTotal = (decimal)t.GetTax( (double)br.SubTotal,
➥bsi.ShipToState.ToString() );
...
```

> **NOTE**
>
> Listing 15.7 is only a code snippet. Go online to view all the code in the
> ShippingInfo.aspx.cs code behind.

To call the Web service, we create a new instance of the tax service. Then we execute the `GetTax` method, passing it the Order subtotal and the Ship To state. We then cast this value to a decimal and insert it into the `TaxTotal` field of the `Basket` datatable.

Reviewing Options for Authorizing Payment

If you ask any business owner about which part of an online store is the most important, most will answer the acceptance of payment. Arguing with that answer is very difficult because it doesn't matter how user-friendly the site is or the type of products being offered; if you can't successfully accept payment, the business will fail.

Even though online stores have been accepting payments for some time now, you may be surprised at the methods in which these payments are accepted. Even today many e-Commerce sites don't have real-time payment methods. They may accept your credit card number online; however, it is not approved while you're online. That order may be printed out and given to a real person who sits behind a desk and calls the credit card company to get a credit card pre-authorization for the amount of the order.

That being said, more and more e-Commerce sites are moving toward getting real-time credit card pre-authorizations, which are extremely more efficient than having an individual call over the phone. Also, getting pre-authorization ensures that before we accept payment, the business is assured that the user has enough funds to pay for the complete order total.

Now let's look at the steps necessary to accomplish this task. First, you must seek out a bank that handles online credit card transactions and get a merchant code. These banks are responsible for making sure that customers have enough funds available to complete the purchase of their orders.

After a pre-authorization code is given from the bank, we still haven't received payment. A pre-authorization code simply means that the user's credit card has enough available credit that will allow this purchase to be charged; no funds are transferred at this point. Funds cannot be transferred until the goods are actually shipped. Therefore, after the order is shipped, we can do a post-authorization. This process actually depletes the user's credit card account for the pre-authorized total and inserts that amount into our bank account.

This process is not free, of course. The bank will charge a transaction fee for each pre-authorization and post-authorization. Some banks consider them one transaction, therefore acquiring only a single transaction fee. This fee differs depending on the number of transactions that are normally processed. There is a way to get this cost down. Most banks offer a discount if you use some level of Address Verification Service (AVS). AVS makes you retrieve more information about the credit card holder, such as the billing address. Also, AVS is a fraud deterrent because it increases the knowledge a fraudulent user must have besides just a credit card number and name.

Now that you understand the process of accepting payments online, you may be thinking that it's a lot to manage. Well, that's where third-party payment packages come into play. These credit card packages can assist you in accepting payment, thus achieving pre-authorization, post-authorization, reporting, and reconciliation. Payment is very important to a business; the business must always know how much money is coming in. Most of these packages also have very good fraud features. for example, if three requests come in with the same credit card number for a specific order total, that user can be blocked by the payment package. Another plus to using a payment package is communication with the bank for both pre- and post-authorizations. These transactions are very important, and most banks expect the payment information, sent in packets, in a specific format. Most third-party payment packages already have agreements with most banks, so you won't have to worry about this issue.

> **NOTE**
>
> Jason and I have worked with the ClearCommerce package (`http://www.ClearCommerce.com`). Another popular package is CyberCash (`http://www.CyberCash.com`); however, you have many packages to choose from. Keep in mind that each third-party package has different features with different costs associated with them. Make certain you spend the time researching the right package for your business needs.

Retrieving Payment Information

MyGolfGear.NET's payment page, `PaymentInfo.aspx`, serves two purposes. One is to display a summary of the order, including the order subtotal, shipping total, tax total, and finally the order total. The other allows users to enter their payment information.

Before we get into the details of how this page was created, let's discuss payment pages in general. Most online purchases are made using credit cards. Therefore, users are careful, as they should be, as to which online sites they will use for credit card purchases. Most Internet users want to make sure that the payment page is secure. By this, we mean using the Secure Sockets Layer (SSL).

SSL is the most widely used method for secure transactions on the Internet today. Under IIS, the default HTTP port used for SSL is port 443. However, this port is adjustable within IIS. Not only must you set up this port correctly on your IIS servers, but also in your code. Normal hyperlinks on a Web page use `http://` to send data back and forth; however, when this data needs to be encrypted, you must use `https://`. The *s* notifies the client browser that it should communicate back to the server using SSL.

Currently, two levels of encryption, 40 bit and 128 bit, are supported by most browsers. You also need to be aware of many other issues when configuring your environment for SSL, so I recommend using the IIS help files or Microsoft's Web site (http://www.microsoft/iis).

We didn't get an SSL certificate for MyGolfGear.NET's servers because it is a fictitious e-Commerce site. So let's get back to our payment page. Figure 15.6 shows what our payment page looks like.

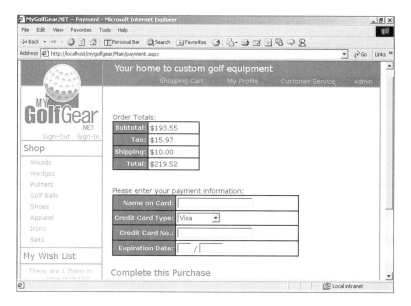

FIGURE 15.6
The PaymentInfo.aspx *page.*

The payment page uses RequiredValidator controls, just like our ShippingInfo page. For information on Validator controls, review the "Retrieving Shipping Information" section earlier in this chapter. Now that we know what the final output of the page will look like, let's examine the code that populates the first half of the page. Listing 15.8 shows code responsible for the output of the order totals.

LISTING 15.8   The Page_Load and FillOrderTotals Methods from Payment.aspx.cs

```
...
protected System.Web.UI.WebControls.Label lblSubtotal;
protected System.Web.UI.WebControls.Label lblTax;
protected System.Web.UI.WebControls.Label lblShipping;
protected System.Web.UI.WebControls.Label lblTotal;
...
```

LISTING 15.8 Continued

```
private void Page_Load(object sender, System.EventArgs e)
{
 if (!IsPostBack)
 {
  OrderDS orderds = GetOrder();
  if (orderds != null)
  {
   FillOrderTotals(orderds);
  }
 }
}
...
private void FillOrderTotals(OrderDS orderds)
{
 OrderDS.BasketRow br = (OrderDS.BasketRow) orderds.Basket.Rows[0];
 lblSubtotal.Text = br.SubTotal.ToString("C");;;
 lblShipping.Text = br.ShippingTotal.ToString("C");
 lblTax.Text = br.TaxTotal.ToString("C");
 lblTotal.Text = br.OrderTotal.ToString("C");
}
...
```

> **NOTE**
>
> Listing 15.8 is only a code snippet. Go online to view all the code in the
> `Payment.aspx.cs` code behind.

In the `Page_Load` function in Listing 15.8, we first check the value of the `IsPostBack` property. This property returns a Boolean value indicating if this is the user's first time to this page or if it's being posted back from the client. We want to execute this page only the first time the page is accessed; therefore, we want to execute this section of code only if `IsPostBack` is `false`. Once inside that condition, we retrieve the order by calling the `GetOrder` method, which returns the order from the session, if one exists. Next, we make sure that the order returned is not empty by making sure it doesn't equal null. Finally, we call the `FillOrderTotals` method, passing it the order dataset.

The `FillOrderTotals` method is responsible for setting the values of each total label in the `PaymentInfo.aspx` page. Notice that the `Label` controls are declared at the beginning of this listing. We create a `Basket` row variable called `br` and populate it with the first row of the `Basket` datatable. Then we set the `Text` property of the `lblSubTotal` `Label` control to the

SubTotal element of the Basket row, but first we convert it to a string. Notice that in the ToString method, we pass "C" as a parameter to format the value as currency, automatically formatting the value with a dollar sign and a two-digit placeholder for cents. This is done for each total.

The next part of the payment page has to do with collecting the payment information, including the name on the credit card, type of credit card, the credit card number, and finally the credit card's expiration date. This is the only information required by MyGolfGear.NET's payment process; however, if you want a higher level of protection from fraud, you may have to alter this page to accept the billing address of the credit card as well. Listing 15.9 displays the code that is executed after a user successfully enters his payment information and clicks the Complete This Purchase link.

LISTING 15.9 The CheckOut Method from Payment.aspx.cs

```
public void CheckOut(Object sender, EventArgs e)
{
 OrderDS order = GetOrder();
 OrderDS.BasketRow br = (OrderDS.BasketRow) order.Basket.Rows[0];
 orderid = br.OrderID;
 OrderDS.BasketPaymentInfoRow bpi = order.BasketPaymentInfo.
➥NewBasketPaymentInfoRow();
 bpi.NameOnCard = txtName.Text;
 bpi.CCtype = lstCCType.SelectedItem.Value;
 bpi.CCnumber = txtCCNum.Text;
 bpi.OrderID = orderid;
 order.BasketPaymentInfo.Rows.Clear();
 order.BasketPaymentInfo.AddBasketPaymentInfoRow(bpi);
 MyGolfGear.OrderManager o = new MyGolfGear.OrderManager();
 o.PreAuthPayment(order);
 bpi = (OrderDS.BasketPaymentInfoRow) order.BasketPaymentInfo.Rows[0];
 if( bpi.PreAuthCode.ToString() == "APPROVED" )
 {
  MyGolfGearDP dp = new MyGolfGearDP();
  dp.UpdateOrder((OrderDS)order.GetChanges(), orderid);
  order.AcceptChanges();
  o.SubmitOrder(order, orderid);
  Session["Order"] = null;
  Response.Redirect("confirmation.aspx?OrderID=" + orderid.ToString().
➥Substring(0,11));
 }
 else
 {
```

LISTING 15.9 Continued

```
lblerror.Text = "There was a problem with your Credit Card Information.
➥Please check the information you entered and try again";
 }
}
...
```

> **NOTE**
>
> Listing 15.9 is only a code snippet. Go online to view all the code in the
> `Payment.aspx.cs` code behind.

The first matter of business for the method in Listing 15.9 is to retrieve the order from the session. We do so by calling the `GetOrder` method and inserting into the order variable of type `OrderDS`, the strongly typed order dataset. Next, we create `br`, a `Basket` row, and populate it with the first row of the `Basket` table within the order. We then take the `OrderID` element of `br` and use it to populate `OrderID`. Now we must create a new `BasketPaymentInfo` row to insert the information entered by the user. Then we populate each element of the `BasketPaymentInfo` row with the actual values entered by the user. Next, we must add that row to the order dataset by passing the newly created row to the `AddBasketPaymentInfoRow` method; however, before we do that, we call the `Clear` method on `BasketPaymentInfo.Rows`. The next section of the code retrieves a pre-authorization for the credit card being used and then the order submission process is started. Both of these topics will be discussed in the following sections.

Using the Payment Web Service

Just as we did with MyGolfGear.NET's Tax Web service, we also decided to create a Payment Web service. The reasons are really the same. MyGolfGear.NET will most likely begin using a third-party payment package when the company gets off the ground. Until then, we'll do basic payment validation before accepting orders. Listing 15.10 shows the code necessary to create this Web service.

LISTING 15.10 Creating the `ccService` Web Service

```
public class ccService : System.Web.Services.WebService
{
 ...
 public bool LundCheck( string ccNum )
 {
```

LISTING 15.10 Continued

```csharp
    int iSum = 0;
    int iLength = ccNum.Length;
    int iOddEven = iLength & 1;
    char[] sCardNumber = ccNum.ToCharArray();
    for(int i = 0; i < iLength; i ++)
    {
     int iDigit = System.Int32.Parse(sCardNumber[i].ToString());
     if (!(((i & 1) ^ iOddEven)==0))
     {
      iDigit *= 2;
      if(iDigit > 9)
      {
       iDigit -= 9;
      }
     }
     iSum += iDigit;
    }
    if (iSum % 10 == 0)
     return true;
    else
     return false;
}

[WebMethod]
public string GetAuthorization(string ccNum)
{
  if( LundCheck( ccNum ) )
   { return "APPROVED"; }
  else
   { return "DECLINED"; }
}
...
```

> **NOTE**
>
> Listing 15.10 is only a code snippet. Go online to view all the code in the
> ccService.asmx.cs Web service.

The Web service in Listing 15.10 is similar to the Tax Web service; therefore, we'll walk through only the code relevant to the validation of the credit card number. Let's start with the GetAuthorization method. Before the declaration of the method, we insert the [WebMethod] attribute, which indicates that we want this method exposed as a Web service. This method accepts only one parameter: the credit card number. When it is received, we call the LundCheck method, which is a standardized formula to determine whether the credit card number is valid. This process is not a pre-authorization, simply a process to determine whether the credit card number is valid. The digits of the credit card are added together with some special logic; then the method makes sure the total is divisible by 10 with no remainder. This calculation is accomplished by using the modulus, %, operator. If the remainder is 0, the method returns an "APPROVED" string; otherwise, it returns "DECLINED".

Calling the Payment Web Service

We won't go over how to call the Payment Web service because it involves the same steps as calling the Tax Web service, except that you need to navigate to the ccService.asmx file.

Let's look at how we call the Payment Web service from our code. Listing 15.11 shows the code required to call the Web service.

LISTING 15.11   Calling the ccService Web Service

```
...
// Get PreAuth
public OrderDS PreAuthPayment(OrderDS order)
{
 OrderDS.BasketPaymentInfoRow bpi = (OrderDS.BasketPaymentInfoRow)
➥order.BasketPaymentInfo.Rows[order.BasketPaymentInfo.Rows.Count - 1];
 MyGolfGear.localhost1.ccService cc = new MyGolfGear.localhost1.ccService();
 bpi.PreAuthCode = cc.GetAuthorization(bpi.CCnumber.ToString());
return order;
}
...
```

> **NOTE**
>
> Listing 15.11 is only a code snippet. Go online to view all the code in
> OrderManager.cs.

When the site code needs to interact, we make it go through the PreAuthPayment method in the OrderManager component. This method receives the strongly typed dataset, OrderDS. It then retrieves the first row from the BasketPaymentInfo datatable and inserts it into the bpi variable. Next, we create a new instance of the ccService Web service and then set the PreAuthCode element of the bpi row to the return value GetAuthorization. We pass the

CCnumber element of the bpi row to the method, first converting the value to a string. Finally, we return the updated OrderDS.

Submitting Orders

Order submission is the process of moving an order from our Basket tables to their final resting place, the Order tables. The Order tables, which have the same schema as the Basket tables do, include OrderHeader, OrderItems, OrderShippingInfo, and OrderPaymentInfo.

When we left off, we were trying to get a credit card pre-authorized by making a call from the code behind of the payment page. Listing 15.12 shows a portion of that code.

LISTING 15.12   Payment.aspx Code Behind (Beginning Order Submission)

```
...
if( bpi.PreAuthCode.ToString() == "APPROVED" )
{
 MyGolfGearDP dp = new MyGolfGearDP();
 dp.UpdateOrder((OrderDS)order.GetChanges(), orderid);
 order.AcceptChanges();
 o.SubmitOrder(order, orderid);
 Session["Order"] = null;
 Response.Redirect("confirmation.aspx?OrderID=" +
➥orderid.ToString().Substring(0,11));
}
else
{
 lblerror.Text = "There was a problem with your Credit Card Information.
➥Please check the information you entered and try again";
}
...
```

> **NOTE**
>
> Listing 15.12 is only a code snippet. Go online to view all the code in payment.
> aspx.cs.

The section of code in Listing 15.12 comes from the CheckOut method in the code behind of payment.aspx. This section comes immediately after calling the Payment Web service to receive a pre-authorization for the order. The first thing we do is determine whether the PreAuthCode is "APPROVED"; if it isn't, we display an error message to the user. Otherwise, we create a new instance of MyGolfGearDP and call the UpdateOrder method. This method was discussed in Chapter 14, "Using ASP.NET to Build the Shopping Cart." It updates the order in the database. When this step is complete, we call the AcceptChanges method on the order dataset. Because these two steps are back to back, we are assured that the order that we are working with is identical to the one in the Basket tables in our database. Next, we call the SubmitOrder method of the OrderManager component. We pass this method the order dataset and the order ID. We'll discuss the SubmitOrder method next, but first let's finish this method. After the SubmitOrder method is complete, we clear out the order that is in the session by setting it to null. Finally, we redirect the user to the payment.aspx page, passing the first 11 digits of the order ID.

The SubmitOrder method is responsible for moving the order from the Basket tables to the Order tables and then deleting the order from the Basket tables. Listing 15.13 shows the code for this method.

LISTING 15.13   The SubmitOrder Method from OrderManager.cs

```
...
public  void SubmitOrder(OrderDS order, System.Guid OrderID)
{
 //"consume" gift certificate, if any
 string temp = order.Basket.Rows[0]["GCID"].ToString();
 if( temp != "" )
 {
  MyGolfGear.DataAccess.GC gc = new MyGolfGear.DataAccess.GC();
  gc.UseGC(System.Int32.Parse(order.Basket.Rows[0]["GCID"].ToString()),
➡System.Decimal.Parse(order.Basket.Rows[0]["GiftCertificate"].
➡ToString()));
 }
 NameValueCollection configInfo = (NameValueCollection)HttpContext.Current.
➡GetConfig("appSettings");
 SqlConnection con = new SqlConnection((String)configInfo["ConnectString"]);
 SqlCommand com = new SqlCommand("spSubmitOrder",con);
 com.CommandType = CommandType.StoredProcedure;
 com.Parameters.Add(new SqlParameter("@OrderID",SqlDbType.UniqueIdentifier,
➡16,"OrderID" ));
 com.Parameters["@OrderID"].Value = OrderID;
 con.Open();
 com.ExecuteNonQuery();
 con.Close();
}
...
```

15

> **NOTE**
>
> Listing 15.13 is only a code snippet. Go online to view all the code ins
> `OrderManager.cs`.

In the `SubmitOrder` method in Listing 15.13, before we begin moving the order into the `Order` tables, we must first determine whether a gift certificate was used on this order. To accomplish this task, we retrieve the gift certificate ID, `GCID`, from the first row of the `Basket` table and insert it into the `temp` variable. Then we determine whether `temp` is an empty string. If it is, we just continue with the submission process; otherwise, we create a new instance of the gift certificate component, `GC`. When this task is completed, we execute the `UseGC` method, passing it the gift certificate ID and the amount of the gift certificate. This method updates the `GiftCertificates` table to show that a specific amount has been used.

After we finish processing the gift certificate, we move to the section of code responsible for the submission of the order. First, we retrieve the `connection` string and use it to create a new `SqlConnection` object, con. Then we create a `SqlCommand` object, passing it the stored procedure spSubmitOrder and the con object. Next, we set the `CommandType` of the `SqlCommand` to `StoredProcedure`. Then we need to create a `SqlParameter` to send the `OrderID` to the stored procedure. When this step is complete, we set the parameter's value to `OrderID`. Finally, we open the connection using the `Open` method, call the `ExecuteNonQuery` method on `SqlCommand`, and then call the `Close` method of the `SqlConnection` object. The `ExeceuteNonQuery` method is used because no records are returned from this stored procedure.

Now let's look at the `spSubmitOrder` stored procedure shown in Listing 15.14.

LISTING 15.14 spSubmitOrder Stored Procedure

```
CREATE PROCEDURE spSubmitOrder
(
    @OrderID uniqueidentifier
)
AS
delete from OrderItems where orderid = @OrderID
delete from OrderPaymentInfo where orderid = @OrderID
delete from OrderShippingInfo where orderid = @OrderID
delete from OrderHeader where orderid = @OrderID

declare @temp uniqueidentifier
declare    @OrderDate datetime
declare    @UserID int
```

LISTING 15.14   Continued

```
declare     @Status int
declare     @ShippingTotal money
declare     @TaxTotal money
declare     @SubTotal money
declare     @OrderTotal money
declare     @GiftCertificate money
declare     @GCID int
...
--Declare the rest of the variables used

declare OrderHeaderCursor cursor for Select * from Basket where orderid =
➥@OrderID
open OrderHeaderCursor
FETCH NEXT FROM OrderHeaderCursor into @temp, @OrderDate, @UserID, @Status,
➥ @ShippingTotal, @TaxTotal, @SubTotal, @OrderTotal, @GiftCertificate,
➥ @GCID
WHILE @@FETCH_STATUS = 0
BEGIN
insert into OrderHeader values( @OrderID, GetDate(), DATEADD(day,5,GetDate()),
➥ @UserID, @Status, @ShippingTotal, @TaxTotal, @SubTotal, @OrderTotal,
➥@GiftCertificate, @GCID)
FETCH NEXT FROM OrderHeaderCursor into @temp, @OrderDate, @UserID, @Status,
➥@ShippingTotal, @TaxTotal, @SubTotal, @OrderTotal, @GiftCertificate,
➥ @GCID
END
CLOSE OrderHeaderCursor
DEALLOCATE OrderHeaderCursor


...
--Move the data of the other Basket tables

delete from BasketItems where orderid = @OrderID
delete from BasketPaymentInfo where orderid = @OrderID
delete from BasketShippingInfo where orderid = @OrderID
delete from Basket where orderid = @OrderID
```

NOTE

Listing 15.14 is only a portion of the stored procedure. Go online to view the complete contents of the spSubmitOrder stored procedure.

spSubmitOrder is a complicated stored procedure that utilizes SQL cursors to move the records from one table to another. Listing 15.14 is just a snippet of the real stored procedure. Because the data is moved from a Basket table to an Order table in the same manner, we'll discuss the beginning of the stored procedure, an example of moving the data to an Order table, and then the closing of the stored procedure.

The stored procedure begins by creating the @OrderID parameter; it is the order ID that we want to move from the Basket tables and insert into the Order tables. The next set of lines makes sure that, for any reason, this order does not exist in the Order tables by executing delete statements on each Order table using @OrderId as part of the where clause. Next, we declare all the variables used in this stored procedure. Only the ones used for the OrderHeader table are shown here. Next, we declare OrderHeaderCursor as a cursor and insert into it the result of a select statement on the OrderHeader table by using a where clause with the @OrderID passed in.

> **NOTE**
>
> Cursors allow you to work with either a row or a subset of rows from a resultset. A cursor allows data modification as well as transact-SQL statements within stored procedures, triggers, and script. We used cursors in this stored procedure so that we could use the row in one cursor as insert values for an insert statement for a different table.

After the OrderHeaderCursor is declared, we open the cursor to execute the select statement that the cursor is based on and populate it with the results of that select statement, whether it is one or many rows. Next, we iterate through the rows in the cursor, implementing an insert statement into the OrderHeader table for each row. We do so by first calling the FETCH NEXT FROM command on OrderHeaderCursor, putting the results into the variables that were declared at the beginning of the stored procedure. We then begin a while loop using the WHILE @@FETCH command. We loop through the rows until the status is equal to 0. A status of 0 means that the FETCH statement was successful, meaning that a row did exist in the cursor. When that equation is true, the statements within the keywords BEGIN and END are executed. In this example, we are inserting the values put into the variables from the FETCH NEXT statement into the VALUES clause of the insert command. This will insert the record that was in the Basket table into the OrderHeader table. When this task is complete, we close OrderHeaderCursor and then deallocate it. Deallocating a cursor means that the data structures that comprised that cursor are now released.

That same logic is then executed for the OrderItems, OrderShippingInfo, and OrderPayment Info tables. Finally, we execute delete statements on the Basket tables using the where clause with the @OrderID to delete only this order because it is now successfully inserted into the Order tables.

Developing the Confirmation Page

The confirmation page is usually one of the simplest pages of the site to develop, and for MyGolfGear.NET, this held true. The purpose of the confirmation page is to ensure the users that their orders have been successfully submitted. Confirming the order, combined with showing the order on the order status page, is a great way to ease the worries of your users. Our confirmation page shows the users a Your order has been received... message, the order ID for the order, and a link that will take the users to the order status page.

The confirmation page does not have much code associated with it. Listing 15.15 shows the code necessary to produce the page.

LISTING 15.15 The Page_Load Method of confirmation.aspx.cs

```
...
protected System.Web.UI.WebControls.Label lblOrderID;
...
private void Page_Load(object sender, System.EventArgs e)
{
  lblOrderID.Text = Request.Params["OrderID"];
}
...
```

> **NOTE**
>
> Listing 15.15 is only a portion of the code. Go online to view the complete contents of confirmation.aspx.cs.

The only purpose of the code for the confirmation page is to receive the order ID that is passed in from payment.aspx.cs and set the text for the OrderID label that is displayed on the page. The output of this page is shown in Figure 15.7.

Although the confirmation page is very basic in nature, it plays an important role in the placement of an online order. It shows the final completion point in the creation and submission of an order.

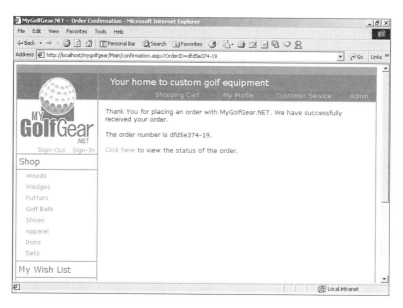

FIGURE 15.7

The confirmation.aspx *page.*

Summary

In this chapter, we discussed all the features of the checkout process. This is an extremely important part of an e-Commerce application because it encompasses many areas in which the business usually has a high degree of interest and/or concern. The checkout process for MyGolfGear.NET is similar to many of the e-Commerce sites that you will find on the Internet. It includes the retrieval of shipping information, calculation of shipping and tax costs, retrieval of payment information, authorization of that payment information, and then the order submission process.

Also, within these key areas, we were able to showcase many reasons why Microsoft's .NET technology is such a powerful development platform. This includes but is not limited to Validator controls and Web services.

I recommend that you spend lots of time planning this part of your e-Commerce site—not only to help you overcome technology issues, but also to work with the business to make sure that you provide the functionality that your company expects.

Self Instruction

One piece of functionality that to add to the Checkout process for this exercise is the management of inventory. Although some e-Commerce sites implement a real-time inventory management system, others don't even worry about it for their online sites. This can cause some aggravation for your users because now they can pay for a product that may be out of stock or on back order and not even know about it.

Not only should you add the depletion logic for the quantity on hand when a product is ordered, but you also should inform the user of products that are either out of stock or on back order. This information can either be displayed on the product selection pages or in a stage during the checkout process.

At a minimum, you need a `PartQtyAvailable` table that should have fields named `productid`, `QtyOnHand`, and `BackOrderFlag`. The first two are self-explanatory. `BackOrderFlag` can be a quick way to determine whether a product is on back order or is out stock if you use a different indicator for each. After this, develop an inventory component to manage the inventory data.

Using ASP.NET Authentication and Authorization for Personalization

IN THIS CHAPTER

Objectives

- Learn how the User and UserType tables are used in MyGolfGear.NET to implement authentication

- Understand the login process and the role the LoginInformation class plays in the implementation of the MyGolfGear.NET authentication and authorization

- Discover the process by which new users can join MyGolfGear.NET and how this process fits into its authentication, authorization, and personalization strategy

To supply targeted content to visitors of MyGolfGear.NET, we need to know who a given user is and which features that user is allowed to access. We employed the built-in .NET authentication and authorization mechanisms for personalization, as well as a single new class to achieve this functionality.

Specifically, MyGolfGear.NET uses two tables, a single data provider component, a `login.aspx` page, a `login.aspx.cs` code behind class, a `join.aspx` page, and a `join.aspx.cs` code behind class to implement the login process. ASP.NET provides `FormsAuthenticationTicket` and `FormsAuthentication` classes.

This chapter covers the ASP.NET authentication and authorization features as well as the custom class used to implement personalization for MyGolfGear.NET.

NOTE

Authentication is the process of accepting a username and password from a user and comparing them against a known authority.

Authorization is the process of determining whether a given user should be given access to a particular resource.

The authentication and authorization features available in ASP.NET and the .NET Framework can be used to personalize a user's experience. This can take the form of simply greeting return customers, to allowing access to personal information. Many sites use personalization as a means of providing features such as order status and account history (the MyGolfGear.NET implementation of this functionality is covered in Chapter 17, "Tracking the Status of Orders.")

Additions to the MyGolfGear Data Model Used to Support Authentication, Authorization, and Personalization

As part of the implementation of the MyGolfGear.NET login process, we needed additional tables in the MyGolfGear database so we added new `User` and `UserType` tables. These two tables form the basis of the authentication and authorization process used by MyGolfGear.NET.

Users are authenticated against the `User` table. The `UserType` table is then used to authorize the authenticated users so only users of the appropriate type are allowed access to various resources within the site.

The `User` Table

To store basic information about a registered user, we created the `User` table. This simple table houses an auto-generated user ID, a user type ID, the user's first and last names, and the user's e-mail address and password. As you will see later, the most important aspects of this table, for authentication, are the e-mail address and password. Table 16.1 shows the layout of the `User` table.

TABLE 16.1   The `User` Table

Column Name	Data Type	Size	Allow Nulls
UserID	Int	4	No
UserTypeID	Int	4	No
FirstName	Varchar	50	Yes
LastName	Varchar	50	Yes
EmailAddress	Varchar	50	No
Password	Varchar	16	No

> **NOTE**
>
> A better design—one for a real business—would be more normalized. We included the first and last names in this table for convenience only.

After we created a place to store user information, we needed a way to distinguish user types.

The `UserType` Table

The `UserType` table holds the metadata that describes each type of user allowed in the site. Examples of user types are customers and administrators. To describe a user type, we used only two fields. One field is for the auto-generated `UserTypeID`, and one field is for the name of the user type. Table 16.2 shows the layout of the `UserType` table.

TABLE 16.2   The `UserType` Table

Column Name	Data Type	Size	Allow Nulls
UserTypeID	Int	4	No
Name	Varchar	50	No

Implementing the `LoginInformation` Class to Facilitate Authentication in MyGolfGear.NET

The `LoginInformation.cs` class performs the bulk of the work for authenticating a user. This class has two main methods: `GetUserID` and `Login`.

The `GetUserID` method looks up users by username and returns user IDs. Listing 16.1 shows the code for the `GetUserID` method.

LISTING 16.1   The `LoginInformation.GetUserID` Method

```
public int GetUserID( string Username )
{
    int retval=0;

    SqlConnection conn = new SqlConnection(connectionstring);
    SqlCommand myCommand = new SqlCommand("Select * from [User] where
➥EmailAddr='" + Username + "'", conn);

    myCommand.CommandType = CommandType.Text;

    conn.Open();

    SqlDataReader r;
    r = myCommand.ExecuteReader();
    while( r.Read() )
        retval = (int) r["UserID"];

    return retval;
}
```

> **NOTE**
>
> You can find the complete listing for the `LoginInformation.cs` file online.

The `GetUserID` method uses `SqlConnection`, `SqlCommand`, and `SqlDataReader` objects. This method first opens a connection to the database by passing in the private member connectionstring, which is populated in the `LoginInformation` class' constructor. Next, a `SqlCommand` object is created by passing the raw SQL statement to fetch all information for a given username and password. Finally, `SqlDataReader` is created by executing the command. `SqlDataReader` is, in turn, used to retrieve the `UserID` of the given user.

The `Login` method logs in the user by verifying that the username and password match those in the `User` table. Listing 16.2 shows the code for the `Login` method.

LISTING 16.2 The `LoginInformation.Login` Method

```
public bool Login( string Username, string Password )
{
    bool retval = false;

    SqlConnection conn = new SqlConnection(connectionstring);
    SqlCommand myCommand = new SqlCommand("Select * from [User] where
➥EmailAddr='" + Username + "'", conn);

    myCommand.CommandType = CommandType.Text;

    conn.Open();

    SqlDataReader r;
    r = myCommand.ExecuteReader();
    while( r.Read() )
    {
        if( r["Password"].ToString() == Password )
        {
            retval = true;
        }
    }
    return retval;
}
```

> **NOTE**
>
> You can find the complete listing for the `LoginInformation.cs` file online.

The `Login` method is similar to the `GetUserID` method—with two exceptions. The first is that the `Login` method returns a Boolean, whereas `GetUserID` returns an `int`. The second is that `SqlDataReader` compares the value of the `Password` field to that of the password passed into the method. If a password is found and it matches for the given user, the return value is `true`. Otherwise, the `Login` method returns `false`.

Using the Login Page for Authentication

After we established the data model and created a data provider to communicate with the database, we needed a way to interact with the user. The user interface elements for this example are split into the usual `.aspx` page and an associated code behind class.

The `Login.aspx.cs` Code Behind Class

The `Login.aspx.cs` code behind class is responsible for using both the customer `LoginInformation` class as well as the built-in ASP.NET forms-based authentication classes. The real job of the `Login.aspx.cs` code behind class is to tie the two pieces of functionality together.

Two methods are all that we need in the `Login.aspx.cs` code behind class to tie the information provided in the standard form to the `LoginInformation` class and the ASP.NET authentication classes.

When a user submits a login form, the `DoSubmit` method is called. This method calls the `Verify` method and uses the ASP.NET authentication classes if the user is found in the `User` table. Listing 16.3 shows the code for the `DoSubmit` method.

LISTING 16.3 The `DoSubmit` Method

```
protected void DoSubmit( object sender, EventArgs s )
{
    if( Verify(Email.Text, Password.Text) )
    {
        FormsAuthenticationTicket ticket = new FormsAuthenticationTicket(Email
➡.Text, false, 5000);
        FormsAuthentication.RedirectFromLoginPage(Email.Text,
➡saveinfo.Checked);
    }
```

Using ASP.NET Authentication and Authorization for Personalization

CHAPTER 16

315

16

AUTHENTICATION
AND
AUTHORIZATION

LISTING 16.3   Continued

```
    else
    {
        loginmessage.Text= "There was a problem with your login.
➡Please try again";
    }
}
```

> **NOTE**
>
> You can find the complete listing for the `Login.aspx.cs` file online.

As we stated earlier, this method calls the `Verify` method by passing in the e-mail address and password from the ASP.NET form. If the `Verify` method returns `true`, the user was found, the correct password was provided, and the user needs to be "marked" as authenticated. This marking is done via the `FormsAuthenticationTicket` class.

> **NOTE**
>
> The `FormsAuthenticationTicket` class represents the authentication cookie, which is used by the `FormsAuthenticationModule` class. When this class is created, a name for the cookie is passed, along with a timeout period. Additionally, the cookie can be marked as *persistent*, which means a user could remain authenticated after her browser is closed or some other action ends her session.

When we know who the user is, the `FormsAuthentication` class' `RedirectFromLoginPage` method is called. Calling this static method causes the user's browser to redirect to the page that was originally requested.

> **CAUTION**
>
> The format of the e-mail address should probably be validated to minimize the likelihood of erroneous data being given.

The only other piece of functionality we need to discuss is the `Verify` method. As we previously stated, this method uses the `LoginInformation` class to determine whether the user's credentials are valid. Listing 16.4 shows the code for this class.

LISTING 16.4 The Verify Method

```
private bool Verify( string Username, string Password )
{
    LoginInformation l = new LoginInformation();
    return l.Login( Username, Password );
}
```

NOTE

You can find the complete listing for the Login.aspx.cs file online.

The Verify method is really just a wrapper. It simply creates an instance of the LoginInformation class and calls its Login method.

Implementing the Login.aspx Page for Authentication

The Login.aspx page was created to display the form for gathering the user's e-mail address and password. When displayed, it looks like the form shown in Figure 16.1.

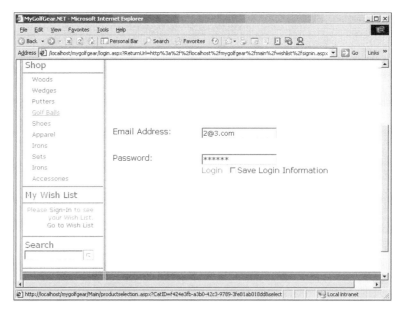

FIGURE 16.1

The Login.aspx page.

Using ASP.NET Authentication and Authorization for Personalization

CHAPTER 16

317

16

AUTHENTICATION
AND
AUTHORIZATION

To create the login form, we used two `TextBox` server controls and one `LinkButton` server control. Listing 16.5 shows the definition of these controls.

LISTING 16.5 The `Login.aspx` Server Controls

```
<TR>
   <TD vAlign="top">Email Address: </TD>
   <TD vAlign="top">
<asp:TextBox id="Email" Runat="server"></asp:TextBox><BR></TD>
   <TD width="176">  </TD></TR>
<TR>
<TR>
   <TD vAlign="top">Password: </TD>
   <TD vAlign="top" colSpan="2">
<asp:TextBox id="Password" Runat="server" TextMode="Password">
</asp:TextBox><BR>
<asp:LinkButton id="Submit" onclick="DoSubmit" Runat="server" Text="Login">
</asp:LinkButton> 
<asp:CheckBox id="saveinfo" Runat="server"></asp:CheckBox>Save
   Login Information
</TD>
</TR>
```

NOTE

You can find the complete listing for the `Login.aspx` file online.

The definition of these controls is pretty straightforward. The only thing to note is the `TextMode` property on the `Password` `TextBox` control's definition. Notice that the `Email` `TextBox` control does not specify a `TextMode` property. This causes the control to default to `SingleLine`.

NOTE

The `TextMode` property accepts one of the three `TextBoxMode` enumeration values: `MultiLine`, `Password`, or `SingleLine`.

Implementing the Join Page So New Users Can Join MyGolfGear.NET

At this point, you are probably thinking, "How do users get added to the User table so they can log in?" The answer is, users can register with MyGolfGear.NET via the Join page. The Join page is made up of the standard .aspx page and a code behind class.

The `Join.aspx.cs` Code Behind Class

The `Join.aspx.cs` code behind class communicates with the `LoginInformation` class. The actual addition of new member information is performed by this class' `Create` method.

The action of the form used to add new members is performed by the `DoJoin` method in the `Join.aspx.cs` code behind class. The `DoJoin` method is shown in Listing 16.6.

LISTING 16.6   The `Join.aspx.cs` `DoJoin` Method

```
protected void DoJoin( object sender, EventArgs e )
{
    LoginInformation l = new LoginInformation();
    if( l.GetUserID(Email.Text) != 0 )
    {
        message.Text = "That user already exists.  Please try again.";
        return;
    }
    else
    {
        if(l.Create(FirstName.Text,LastName.Text,Email.Text,Password.Text))
        {
            message.Text = "User Successfully Created.";
        }
        else
        {
            message.Text = "Please Enter all information and try again.";
        }
    }
}
```

NOTE

You can find the complete listing for the `Join.aspx.cs` file online.

Using ASP.NET Authentication and Authorization for Personalization

CHAPTER 16

319

16

AUTHENTICATION
AND
AUTHORIZATION

The DoJoin method creates an instance of the LoginInformation class and calls its GetUserID method. If any number other than 0 is returned, a user with the given ID already exists and a message is displayed to the user. If no user is found, the LoginInformation class' Create method is called—passing in the user's first and last name, along with his e-mail address and a password. If the addition fails for some reason, the Create method returns false, and a message is displayed to the user.

Implementing the Join.aspx Page

To gather the information necessary to create a new user, we used a simple form on the Join.aspx page. Figure 16.2 shows what the Join page looks like.

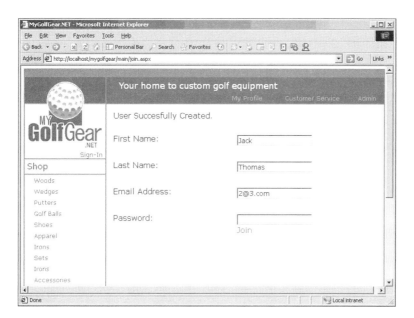

FIGURE 16.2
The Join.aspx *page.*

To implement this functionality, we used simple TextBox and LinkButton controls again. Listing 16.7 shows the relevant code for this form.

LISTING 16.7   The Join.aspx Form

```
<TD vAlign="top">First Name: </TD>
<TD vAlign="top">
<asp:TextBox id="FirstName" Runat="server"></asp:TextBox><BR></td></tr><tr>
```

LISTING 16.7 Continued

```
<TD vAlign="top">Last Name: </TD>
<TD vAlign="top">
<asp:TextBox id="LastName" Runat="server"></asp:TextBox><BR></TD></tr><tr>
<TD vAlign="top">Email Address: </TD>
<TD vAlign="top">
<asp:TextBox id="Email" Runat="server"></asp:TextBox><BR></TD></tr><tr>
<TD vAlign="top">Password: </TD>
<TD vAlign="top" colSpan="2">
<asp:TextBox id="Password" Runat="server" TextMode="Password"></asp:TextBox>
<BR>
<asp:LinkButton id="Submit" Runat="server" OnClick="DoJoin" Text="Join">
</asp:LinkButton>
```

> **NOTE**
>
> You can find the complete listing for the `Join.aspx` file online.

> **CAUTION**
>
> The `Join.aspx` form does not contain the usual double password fields. We didn't add them for simplicity's sake. You should always provide a second password field and verify that both are the same before recording the value.

This simple form does not need much explanation. As with the login form, notice the use of the `TextMode` property for the `Password TextBox` control.

Summary

This chapter covered MyGolfGear.NET's implementation of authentication and authorization so that personalization could be provided. It also discussed the development of the data model, the `LoginInformation` class, and the user interface elements used to implement the login functionality. Finally, it discussed how using them together provides the authentication, authorization, and personalization functionality for the site.

The next chapter, "Tracking the Status of Orders," discusses how the functionality in this chapter provides users access to their order status and history.

Self Instruction

Given what you have learned in this chapter, add two new stored procedures to replace the inline SQL statements in the LoginInformation class. Then change the GetUserID and Login methods, from the LoginInformation class, to use the two new stored procedures.

For practice with ASP.NET validation controls, re-create the join form adding a second Password TextBox control and implement the CompareValidator control to ensure that a new user's password is the same.

Tracking the Status of Orders

IN THIS CHAPTER

Objectives

- **Explain the order status features of the MyGolfGear.NET site**

- **Learn how to make the order status page restricted**

- **Illustrate how to retrieve and display orders**

- **Learn how to optimize order status**

After placing an order in MyGolfGear.NET, users will be able to check the status of their orders. This feature is common in e-Commerce applications. It provides a comfort level for the users in that they can see that the order was correctly received by the e-Commerce application and is on its way to be fulfilled.

The purpose of the order status page is to allow users to view details about orders they have placed in the past. This page also shows all the products that make up the order. To increase the comfort level of our users, we also provide the shipping date of the order. This information tells users when they should expect their orders to arrive.

Restricting Access to the Order Status Page

Because an order is specifically tied to a user, we must make sure that the user has logged in to the site and has been authenticated. Doing so ensures us that the user will see only the order she placed on the site and not be able to look at anyone else's orders.

To implement this functionality, we must ensure that the order status page is protected from anonymous users. An anonymous user is one who has not been authenticated, meaning the application doesn't know the identity of the user. In ASP.NET, limiting access on a page to only authenticated users is actually a simple task.

The page that we restrict to only authenticated users is actually `MyProfile.aspx`. Listing 17.1 shows the settings required in the `web.config` file to restrict anonymous users access to the `MyProfile.aspx` page.

LISTING 17.1 Updating the `web.config` file to restrict access to the `MyProfile.aspx` page.

```
<location path="main/MyProfile.aspx">
  <system.web>
```

LISTING 17.1 Continued

```
    <authorization>
        <deny users="?" />
    </authorization>
  </system.web>
</location>
```

NOTE

You can find the complete listing for the `web.config` file online.

Notice that we set the `path` attribute of the `location` tag to the page we want to restrict access to. Then, within the `authorization` tag, we insert the `deny` tag and set its `users` attribute to `"?"`. The question mark represents anonymous users. By making this addition to the `web.config` file, we restrict access to the `MyProfile.aspx` page to anonymous users.

In the future, if you have several pages that require users to be authenticated before they can access those pages, I recommend that you create a directory named protected. Then you can put all the pages you want to restrict access to in this directory. After you complete this task, you can set the `path` attribute of the `location` tag to `protected` to apply the restriction to all pages in that folder.

We restrict access to the MyProfile page because users must go through this page to get to the order status page. To get to the order status page, users can click the My Profile link at the top of the page. When a user clicks this link, if he is not already authenticated, he is forced to log in to the site after being redirected to the sign-in page. To learn more about authentication, refer to Chapter 16, "Using ASP.NET Authentication and Authorization for Personalization."

After a user signs in, she is sent to the `MyProfile.aspx` page, shown in Figure 17.1, where she is given two options. One is a link to update her user profile; the other is a link to view her order history. The user must click the View My Order History link to get to the order status page.

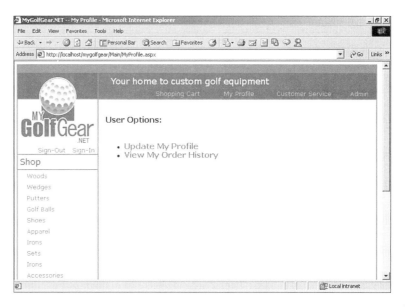

FIGURE 17.1
The MyProfile.aspx *page.*

Accessing the Order Status Page

When a user first accesses the order status page, all previous orders placed by the logged-in user are displayed. A couple of tasks must be completed in order to successfully display the status of the user's orders. These tasks include determining the user ID, retrieving the orders, and finally displaying the orders. Figure 17.2 shows the information displayed to the user when he first arrives at the order status page, OrderStatus.aspx.

Determining the User ID

The first item we'll look at is how to get the user ID. The user ID is required because it is used to determine which orders to retrieve. Listing 17.2 shows the code used in the Page_Load method of the OrderStatus.aspx page.

LISTING 17.2   Retrieving the User ID

```
private void Page_Load(object sender, System.EventArgs e)
{
  LoginInformation l = new LoginInformation();
  int userid = l.GetUserID(Request.ServerVariables["REMOTE_USER"]);
  ...
}
```

Tracking the Status of Orders

CHAPTER 17

327

17

TRACKING THE
STATUS OF
ORDERS

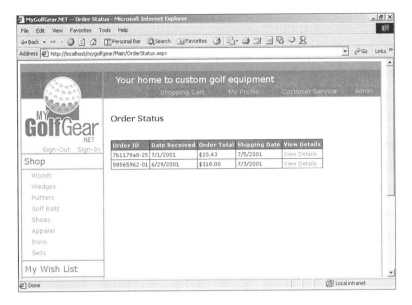

FIGURE 17.2
The OrderStatus.aspx *page.*

NOTE

You can find the complete listing for the OrderStatus.aspx.cs file online.

The first line inside the Page_Load method creates an instance of the LoginInformation class. Then we set the value of userid to the return value of the GetUserID method in Login Information. This method requires that the username be passed in order to determine the user ID. We get the username by accessing REMOTE_USER of the server variables. The REMOTE_USER value is set when the user logs in to the site.

Retrieving the Orders

After we have the user ID, we can begin the retrieval process. Listing 17.3 shows the code used to retrieve the orders for this user.

LISTING 17.3 Retrieving Orders for the Authenticated User

```
private void Page_Load(object sender, System.EventArgs e)
{
```

LISTING 17.3 Continued

```
   ...
MyGolfGearDP dp = new MyGolfGearDP();
ds = dp.GetOrderStatus(userid);
   ...
}
```

NOTE

You can find the complete listing for the `OrderStatus.aspx.cs` file online.

After creating an instance of `MyGolfGearDP`, we set ds, a dataset, to the return value of the `GetOrderStatus` method of `MyGolfGearDP`. Then we pass the user ID to the `GetOrderStatus` method.

Listing 17.4 shows the stored procedure used to return all the orders for the logged-in user.

LISTING 17.4 The `spGetOrderHistory` Stored Procedure

```
CREATE PROCEDURE spGetOrderHistory @UserID int
AS
SELECT          OrderID,
          OrderDate,
          OrderTotal,
          ShippingDate
FROM          OrderHeader
WHERE          UserID = @UserID
ORDER   BY      OrderDate DESC

SELECT          OI.OrderID,
          OI.Price,
          OI.Quantity,
          OI.TotalCost,
          OI.Bonus,
          P.Name
FROM          OrderItems OI,
          OrderHeader OH,
          Product P
WHERE          OH.USerID = @UserID
          And OH.OrderID = OI.OrderID
          And OI.ProductID = P.ProductID
```

This stored procedure returns two resultsets. The first SELECT statement returns all the orders placed by the user. It contains the order ID, order date, order total, and the shipping date. The orders are returned in descending order on the date the order was received. The second SELECT statement returns all the products ordered for the associated orders. The first part of this WHERE clause is the same as the one in the first SELECT statement. The second part combines the OrderHeader table to the OrderItems table by order ID. Finally, we combine the product ID of the OrderItems table with the product ID of the product table to return the name of the products.

This stored procedure is called by the GetOrderStatus method of MyGolfGearDP. This method is shown in Listing 17.5.

LISTING 17.5   The GetOrderStatus Method of MyGolfGearDP

```
public DataSet GetOrderStatus(int UserID)
{
  NameValueCollection configInfo = (NameValueCollection)HttpContext.Current.
GetConfig("appSettings");
  SqlConnection con = new SqlConnection((String)configInfo["ConnectString"]);
  SqlDataAdapter sda = new SqlDataAdapter("spGetOrderHistory", con);
  sda.SelectCommand.CommandType = CommandType.StoredProcedure;
  // Add Parameters
  SqlParameter paramUserID = new SqlParameter("@UserID", SqlDbType.Int, 4);
  paramUserID.Value = UserID;
  sda.SelectCommand.Parameters.Add(paramUserID);
  con.Open();
  sda.TableMappings.Add("Table", "OrderHeader");
  sda.TableMappings.Add("Table1", "OrderItems");
  DataSet ds = new DataSet();
  sda.Fill(ds);
  con.Close();
  // return the dataset
  return ds;
}
```

> **NOTE**
>
> You can find the complete listing for the MyGolfGearDP.cs file online.

This method accepts the user ID as a parameter and creates a DataSet filled with orders and their associated order items. As in most of the methods for MyGolfGearDP, we start by retrieving the connection string. After that, we create a new instance of the SqlConnection object, followed by a new instance of a `SqlDataAdapter` passing the name of the stored procedure we want to execute, `spGetOrderHistory`, and the connection object we just created. Next, we must set the `CommandType` property of `SelectCommand` to `StoredProcedure`. Then we create a new `SqlParameter`, `paramUserID`, and set its `Value` property to the user ID that was passed into this method. After we add the parameter to the `parameters` collection of the `Select Command`, we open the connection by calling the `Open` method of the `connection` object. When the connection is open, we use `TableMappings` to map the source table—for example, `Table`—with the `DataTable` name. The `DataTable` name is important because it is used to identify this table in the `DataSet`.

After we set the `TableMappings`, we create a `DataSet` and then call the `Fill` method of the `SqlDataAdapter` passing in the `DataSet`. This takes the results from executing the stored procedure and populates the `DataTables` in the `DataSet`. When that step is complete, we close the connection and then return the `DataSet`.

Displaying the User's Orders

The two major parts to displaying the user's orders are the `OrderHeader` data grid and `OrderDetail` data grid. The `OrderHeader` data grid displays summary information about each order placed by the user. An example of this page is shown in Figure 17.3.

Listing 17.6 shows the ASP.NET code used to create the data grid.

LISTING 17.6   The `OrderHeader` Data Grid

```
<asp:DataGrid id=OrderHeaderDataGrid  BorderColor="black" BorderWidth="1"
        CellPadding="3" Font-Name="Verdana" Font-Size="8pt"
        datakeyfield="OrderID" AutoGenerateColumns="false"
        runat="server" AlternatingItemStyle-BackColor="Beige"
        FooterStyle-BackColor="Silver" FooterStyle-ForeColor="White"
        ItemStyle-BackColor="White" EditItemStyle-BackColor="yellow"
        HeaderStyle-BackColor="DarkGreen" HeaderStyle-Font-Bold="True"
        HeaderStyle-ForeColor="Beige">
  <Columns>
    <ASP:TemplateColumn HeaderText="Order ID">
    <ItemTemplate>
      <%# DataBinder.Eval(Container.DataItem,
➥"OrderID").ToString().Substring(0,11) %>
    </ItemTemplate>
    </ASP:TemplateColumn>
    <ASP:TemplateColumn HeaderText="Date Received">
      <ItemTemplate>
      <%# DataBinder.Eval(Container.DataItem, "OrderDate","{0:d}") %>
      </ItemTemplate>
```

Tracking the Status of Orders

CHAPTER 17

331

17

TRACKING THE
STATUS OF
ORDERS

LISTING 17.6   Continued

```
  </ASP:TemplateColumn>
  <ASP:TemplateColumn HeaderText="Order Total">
    <ItemTemplate>
    <%# DataBinder.Eval(Container.DataItem, "OrderTotal","{0:c}")%>
    </ItemTemplate>
  </ASP:TemplateColumn>
  <ASP:TemplateColumn HeaderText="Shipping Date">
    <ItemTemplate>
      <%# DataBinder.Eval(Container.DataItem, "ShippingDate","{0:d}")%>
    </ItemTemplate>
  </ASP:TemplateColumn>
  <asp:ButtonColumn HeaderText="View Details" Text="View Details"
➡CommandName="Select" />
  </Columns>
</asp:DataGrid>
```

NOTE

You can find the complete listing for the `OrderStatus.aspx` file online.

With the use of ASP.NET's `DataGrid` control, displaying data in a grid format is a simple task. We also get some rich display options with which we can customize the layout. In the `DataGrid` tag, besides all the layout attributes, the `id` attribute is important because it enables us to identify this control on the code behind page, `OrderStatus.aspx.cs`. Next, we populate the `Columns` tag with `TemplateColumns`. Each `TemplateColumn` then contains an `ItemTemplate`. Within the `ItemTemplate`, we use the `DataBinder.Eval` method, which binds a column in the `DataGrid` with a field in the data source of the control. We pass the `Eval` method two values: The first is the `Container.DataItem`, and the second is the name of the field to display. In some places, notice that we pass a third parameter, which is used to format the value before it is displayed.

The code to populate the `DataGrid` is shown in Listing 17.7.

LISTING 17.7   The `Page_Load` Method in `OrderStatus.aspx.cs`

```
...
protected System.Web.UI.WebControls.DataGrid OrderHeaderDataGrid;
protected System.Web.UI.WebControls.Panel detailsPanel;
protected System.Web.UI.HtmlControls.HtmlGenericControl HeaderText;
...
```

LISTING 17.7 Continued

```
private void Page_Load(object sender, System.EventArgs e)
{
  LoginInformation l = new LoginInformation();
  int userid = l.GetUserID( Request.ServerVariables["REMOTE_USER"] );
  MyGolfGearDP dp = new MyGolfGearDP();
  ds = dp.GetOrderStatus(userid);
  If (ds.Tables["OrderHeader"].Rows.Count > 0)
  {
    OrderHeaderDataGrid.DataSource = ds.Tables["OrderHeader"].DefaultView;
    OrderHeaderDataGrid.DataBind();
  }
  else
  {
    HeaderText.InnerText = "No Orders to display";
    OrderHeaderDataGrid.Visible = false;
    OrderDetailDataGrid.Visible = false;
    OrderID.Visible = false;
  }
}
```

NOTE

You can find the complete listing for the `OrderStatus.aspx.cs` file online.

The first task at hand is to make sure that we can access the `DataGrid` created in the `OrderStatus.aspx` page so that we can set the data source. To do so, we create the `OrderHeaderDataGrid` variable of type `System.Web.UI.WebControls.DataGrid`. After we call the `GetOrderStatus` method, we check to make sure that the `OrderHeader` datatable has at least one row. If it doesn't, we change the header display text to indicate that no orders were found and then hide the other controls on the page by setting their `Visible` property to `false`. Otherwise, we set the data source of the `OrderHeader` data grid to the `DefaultView` of the `OrderHeader` datatable.

We need to discuss one last column in the `OrderHeader` data grid. It is a button column that contains a button named View Details. The purpose of this button is to allow users to view the details of their orders, including the product name, price, quantity, and total cost of each product ordered.

We hook into the event of this button being clicked by updating the `InitializeComponent` method of `OrderStatus.aspx.cs`, as shown in Listing 17.8.

LISTING 17.8   The InitializeComponent Method in OrderStatus.aspx.cs

```
private void InitializeComponent()
{
  OrderHeaderDataGrid.ItemCommand += new System.Web.UI.WebControls.
➥DataGridCommandEventHandler (this.Select);
  this.Load += new System.EventHandler(this.Page_Load);
}
```

> **NOTE**
>
> You can find the complete listing for the OrderStatus.aspx.cs file online.

To hook into the event of one of the records being selected by a user, we tie the OrderHeaderDataGrid's ItemCommand event to the local Select method. As a result, any time the View Details button is clicked, the Select method is executed. The Select method is shown in Listing 17.9.

LISTING 17.9   The Select Method in OrderStatus.aspx.cs

```
public void Select(Object sender, DataGridCommandEventArgs e)
{
if ( IsValid )
 {
  System.Guid orderid = (System.Guid)OrderHeaderDataGrid.DataKeys
➥[e.Item.ItemIndex];
  OrderID.InnerText = "Order Details for order " +
➥orderid.ToString().Substring(0,11);
  detailsPanel.Visible = true;
  DataView dv;
  dv = ds.Tables["OrderItems"].DefaultView;
  dv.RowFilter = "OrderID = '" + orderid + "'";
  OrderDetailDataGrid.DataSource = dv;
  OrderDetailDataGrid.DataBind();
 }
}
```

> **NOTE**
>
> You can find the complete listing for the OrderStatus.aspx.cs file online.

After we check that the page is valid, we then need to retrieve the order ID for the order selected. We do so by taking the index of the row selected, `e.Item.ItemIndex`, and using it for the `DataKeys` property of the `OrderHeaderDataGrid`. So, if the user clicks the second row, the index will be 1 and the `orderid` variable will be set with the order ID of the second row. We then use that `orderid` to display a message above the `OrderDetailsDataGrid` so that the user knows which order she is seeing the details for. Next, we set the `Visible` property to `true` for the ASP.NET `Panel` control, which contains the `OrderDetailDataGrid`. Next, we create a `DataView` and populate it with the `DataSet`'s `OrderItems` table.

Because the `OrderItems` datatable contains items for all orders, we must filter it for the selected order by using the `RowFilter` property of the `DataView`. The filter keeps only rows where the `orderid` in the `DataTable` equals the `orderid` we got from the `OrderHeaderDataGrid`'s selected row. After the `DataView` is filtered, we set the data source of the `OrderDetailDataGrid` to the `DataView` and then call the `DataBind` method. The final output is displayed in Figure 17.3.

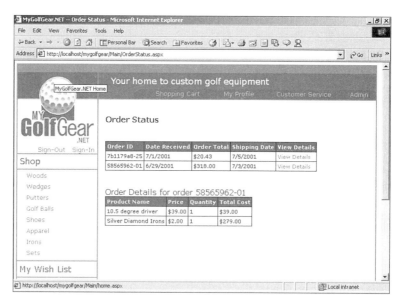

FIGURE 17.3
The `OrderStatus.aspx` *page with the detail order view.*

The ASP.NET code to display the products ordered is shown in Listing 17.10.

LISTING 17.10   Displaying the Item Detail of the Selected Order

```
<asp:Panel id="detailsPanel" runat="server" Visible="false">
<span id="OrderID" EnableViewState="false" runat="server"></span>
 <asp:DataGrid id=OrderDetailDataGrid BorderColor="black"
      BorderWidth="1" CellPadding="3" Font-Name="Verdana" Font-Size="8pt"
      datakeyfield="OrderID" AutoGenerateColumns="false" runat="server"
      AlternatingItemStyle-BackColor="Beige" FooterStyle-BackColor="Silver"
      FooterStyle-ForeColor="White" ItemStyle-BackColor="White"
      EditItemStyle-BackColor="yellow" HeaderStyle-BackColor="DarkGreen"
      HeaderStyle-Font-Bold="True" HeaderStyle-ForeColor="Beige">
  <Columns>
    <ASP:TemplateColumn HeaderText="Product Name">
      <ItemTemplate>
        <%# DataBinder.Eval(Container.DataItem, "Name")%>
      </ItemTemplate>
    </ASP:TemplateColumn>
    <ASP:TemplateColumn HeaderText="Price">
      <ItemTemplate>
        <%#String.Format("{0:c}",DataBinder.Eval(Container.DataItem,"Price"))%>
      </ItemTemplate>
    </ASP:TemplateColumn>
    <ASP:TemplateColumn HeaderText="Quantity" >
      <ItemTemplate>
        <%# DataBinder.Eval(Container.DataItem, "Quantity")%>
      </ItemTemplate>
    </ASP:TemplateColumn>
    <ASP:TemplateColumn HeaderText="Total Cost">
      <ItemTemplate>
        <%# String.Format("{0:c}",DataBinder.Eval(Container.DataItem,
➥"TotalCost"))%>
      </ItemTemplate>
    </ASP:TemplateColumn>
  </Columns>
 </asp:DataGrid>
</asp:Panel>
```

17

**TRACKING THE
STATUS OF
ORDERS**

NOTE

You can find the complete listing for the OrderStatus.aspx file online.

This `DataGrid` is similar to the `OrderHeaderDataGrid` data grid. Note that the `DataGrid` is inside an ASP.NET `Panel` control. This allows us to hide and show the `DataGrid` when needed. The default is to hide the panel; only when the user chooses to see the details of an order do we make the panel visible.

Summary

This chapter described how to add an order status page to your e-Commerce application. We also discussed how to protect a page so that only an authenticated user can view the page. The order status page displays all the orders for the user as well as allows the user to view the products that were ordered.

Self Instruction

When creating the order status page, we kept some optimization techniques in mind. This page pulls all the data that is needed in a single database call by using a `DataSet`. Now to really take advantage, you can cache the dataset that contains the orders by putting it into the session.

First, create a private method called `GetOrders` in the `OrderStatus.aspx.cs` page. Make this method responsible for calling `MyGolfGearDP` to retrieve the orders and populate the dataset. Then insert that dataset into the session so that whenever the page is loaded, it calls this method to get the orders. It first looks in the session for the `DataSet`. If the `DataSet` is not in the session, it calls the data provider, populates the `DataSet`, and then inserts it into the session.

Implementing this optimization raises one issue. If the user checks order status and then immediately places an order and goes back to the order status page, the newly placed order will not show up in the user's order status. For most sites, not showing this information would be all right because users usually don't place multiple orders in a single day. However, you should make customers aware of this functionality before implementing; doing so will save you lots of customer service calls. A workaround for this problem would be to provide an Update Order Status button on the page; when this button is clicked, it would repopulate the dataset in the session, which would then include the latest orders placed.

Delivering and Keeping the Site Going

IN THIS PART

Maintaining MyGolfGear.NET's User Information

IN THIS CHAPTER

Objectives

- Learn about the UserDS class

- Understand how the Users.aspx.cs code behind class uses the UserDS class

- Learn how the User.aspx page was created and what purpose it serves

Administrative users of Web sites like MyGolfGear.NET need tools to manage user information. At a minimum, administrators need the ability to assign users to groups and edit user information.

This chapter discusses how basic user management was implemented for MyGolfGear.NET. Specifically, it reviews the pertinent database objects, discusses the creation of a new strongly typed dataset class, and describes the new user interface elements created to support this functionality.

The User Tables Revisited

To better understand how the user administrative features for MyGolfGear.Net were implemented, we need to revisit the user-related portion of the data model. For this discussion, we'll focus on the User and UserType tables.

The User table holds basic username, password, and contact information. Specifically, it holds first and last names, e-mail addresses, and user passwords. Table 18.1 shows the specifics for this table.

TABLE 18.1   The User Table

Name	Data Type	Size	Allow Nulls
UserID	int	4	No
UserTypeID	int	4	No
FirstName	varchar	50	Yes
LastName	varchar	50	Yes
EmailAddress	varchar	50	No
Password	varchar	50	No

CAUTION

It is not a good idea to store passwords or other sensitive data as a varchar in a SQL Server table without first encrypting that data. The .NET Framework provides a rich set of cryptographic services that you can use for this purpose. For more information, check out the System.Security.Cryptography namespace.

The User table's primary key is UserID. This field is an autogenerated integer created by specifying the field as an Identity field. The identity was seeded with a value of 1 and set to increment by one every time a new record is added.

Using an Identity Field in SQL Server

After a new record is inserted into a SQL Server database table, the variable @@IDENTITY contains the last identity value generated. If the table does not contain an Identity column, @@IDENTITY will return NULL. This can be useful when you need to know the value of the key upon insertion of a new record. For example, the @@IDENTITY variable could be used if a stored procedure were needed to add new users to the User table, and the user ID was needed at the time of insertion. Rather than create a separate stored procedure and undergo the overhead of a second round trip to the database, the value could be returned as part of the insert stored procedure. Listing 18.1 shows this procedure.

LISTING 18.1 The spAddNewUser Stored Procedure

```
CREATE PROCEDURE spAddNewUser

@UserTypeID int,
@FName varchar(50),
@LName varchar(50),
@EmailAddress varchar(50),
@Password varbinary(15)

 AS

INSERT INTO [User] (UserTypeID, FirstName, LastName, EmailAddress,Password
)
VALUES (@UserTypeID, @FName, @LName, @EmailAddress, @Password)

SELECT @@IDENTITY
GO
```

The spAddNewUser stored procedure, shown in Listing 18.1, takes as parameters all the needed fields for the User table except UserID. UserID is returned with the SELECT @@IDENTITY statement at the bottom of the listing.

The UserType table was created to hold metadata describing the different types of users allowed to use MyGolfGear.NET. For example, MyGolfGear.NET supports administrative users and "normal" users. These user types are used in conjunction with the User table to

18

MAINTAINING USER INFORMATION

determine what actions the users are allowed to perform. This simple table requires only two fields: UserTypeID and Type. Table 18.2 shows the details for this table.

TABLE 18.2   The UserType Table

Name	Data Type	Size	Allow Nulls
UserTypeID	Int	4	No
Type	varchar	50	Yes

The UserTypeID field is the primary key for the UserType table. For this table, like the User table, the primary key was set up as an Identity column. The Type field simply holds a string value that can be used to describe the record. For example, for MyGolfGear.NET, the two values Normal and Admin are used.

Access to these two tables is made possible by two stored procedures. One retrieves the initial set of users and their user types, and the other is designed to update an existing user's information.

To construct a DataSet containing all the user and user type information, we need to retrieve all records from the User and UserType tables. The preferred way to do so is to use a stored procedure that can later be used by a data provider class. We created the spGetUsers stored procedure to provide MyGolfGear.NET with this capability. Listing 18.2 shows the code for this stored procedure.

LISTING 18.2   The spGetUsers Stored Procedure

```
CREATE PROCEDURE spGetUsers
AS
SELECT    *
FROM UserType

SELECT    *
FROM    [User]
GO
```

The stored procedure in Listing 18.2 selects all the rows from the UserType table and then selects all the rows from the User table. Two resultsets get returned. These two resultsets are used to create a DataSet for manipulating the user data. This functionality is discussed in detail in the section titled "The UserDS DataSet."

When information about a particular user needs to be updated, the User table needs to be updated with the appropriate data. The preferred way to accomplish this is to use a stored procedure. For the MyGolfGear.NET implementation, we created the spUpdateUser stored procedure, as shown in Listing 18.3.

LISTING 18.3 The spUpdateUser Stored Procedure

```
CREATE PROCEDURE spUpdateUser
(
    @UserID int,
    @UserTypeID int,
    @EmailAddr varchar(50),
    @UserFName varchar(50),
    @UserLName varchar(50),
    @Password varchar(50)
)
AS
UPDATE [User]
SET
UserTypeID = @UserTypeID,
EmailAddr = @EmailAddr,
UserFName = @UserFName,
UserLName = @UserLName,
Password = @Password
WHERE
UserID = @UserID

GO
```

Listing 18.3 shows how we implemented the spUpdateUser stored procedure. It accepts a user's ID, user type, first and last name, e-mail address, and password. It then uses a simple UPDATE command to set the User table's values for the particular user ID.

TIP

In the real world, this functionality might be more robust. For instance, the password field should probably be updated separately and the old password verified before the new one is replaced. This stored procedure could also be made to allow the different fields to be updated independently. We chose this implementation for simplicity and ease of explanation.

When a user needs to be removed from the MyGolfGear system, a row in the User table corresponding to that user must be deleted. To accomplish this task, we created the spDeleteUser store procedure, as shown in Listing 18.4.

18

MAINTAINING
USER
INFORMATION

LISTING 18.4   The spDeleteUser Stored Procedure

```
CREATE PROCEDURE [spDeleteUser]
(
    @UserID int
)
 AS


DELETE FROM [User] WHERE UserID = @UserID
```

The spDeleteUser stored procedure, shown in Listing 18.4, takes a user's ID as its only para-meter. It uses that ID to delete any record (there should be only one) with the UserID equal to the ID passed in.

> **NOTE**
>
> Use of the [] brackets around the User table name is necessary because User is a SQL Server reserved keyword.

The UserDS DataSet

To gain access to the information stored in the User and UserType tables, we created a new strongly typed dataset class by first creating an XML schema file. The UserDS.xsd file was created by describing, in XML, the layout and makeup of the User and UserType database tables. Listing 18.5 shows this schema.

LISTING 18.5   The UserDS.xsd Schema

```
<?xml version="1.0" encoding="utf-8" ?>
<xsd:schema id="UserDS" targetNamespace="http://tempuri.org/UserDS.xsd"
➥elementFormDefault="qualified" xmlns=http://tempuri.org/UserDS.xsd
➥ xmlns:xsd="http://www.w3.org/2001/
➥XMLSchema" xmlns:msdata="urn:schemas-microsoft-com:xml-msdata">
   <xsd:element name="UserDS" msdata:IsDataSet="true">
      <xsd:complexType>
         <xsd:choice maxOccurs="unbounded">
            <xsd:element name="User">
               <xsd:complexType>
                  <xsd:sequence>
                     <xsd:element name="UserID" type="xsd:int" />
                     <xsd:element name="UserTypeID" type="xsd:int"
➥minOccurs="0" />
```

LISTING 18.5 Continued

```xsd
                              <xsd:element name="UserFName" type="xsd:string"
➥minOccurs="0" />
                              <xsd:element name="UserLName" type="xsd:string"
➥minOccurs="0" />
                              <xsd:element name="EmailAddr" type="xsd:string"
➥minOccurs="0" />
                              <xsd:element name="Password" type="xsd:string" />
                          </xsd:sequence>
                       </xsd:complexType>
                    </xsd:element>
                    <xsd:element name="UserType">
                       <xsd:complexType>
                          <xsd:sequence>
                              <xsd:element name="UserTypeID" type="xsd:int"
➥minOccurs="0" />
                              <xsd:element name="Type" type="xsd:string"
➥minOccurs="0" />
                          </xsd:sequence>
                       </xsd:complexType>
                    </xsd:element>
                </xsd:choice>
            </xsd:complexType>
            <xsd:key name="UserKey" msdata:PrimaryKey="true">
                <xsd:selector xpath=".//User" />
                <xsd:field xpath="UserID" />
            </xsd:key>
            <xsd:key name="UserTypeKey" msdata:PrimaryKey="true">
                <xsd:selector xpath=".//UserType" />
                <xsd:field xpath="UserTypeID" />
            </xsd:key>
            <xsd:keyref name="UserTypeUser" refer="UserTypeKey">
                <xsd:selector xpath=".//User" />
                <xsd:field xpath="UserTypeID" />
            </xsd:keyref>
        </xsd:element>
</xsd:schema>
```

18

MAINTAINING
USER
INFORMATION

NOTE

You can find the complete listing for the UserDS.xsd file online.

The schema definition file in Listing 18.5 first describes the User table. The description starts just after the first xsd:complexType tag. A name and a type specify each field. The varchar fields are represented as strings, and the int fields remain int fields. The second set of xsd:complexType tags contains the description of the UserType table. Its data types are string and int as well.

After the schema definition file is created, the xsd.exe tool is used to generate the UserDS.cs class. When we specify the name of the .xsd file to use (in this case, UserDS.xsd), along with the switch /d or /dataset, a class that derives from DataSet will be generated.

> **NOTE**
>
> Chapter 6, "Using ASP.NET to Display the Simple Catalog," contains a sidebar on using the xsd.exe utility.

The result of running the xsd.exe utility and specifying the UserDS.xsd file is the UserDS.cs class. This class provides a rich object model for the XML data being represented. Listing 18.6 shows the result of using the UserDS.xsd file with xsd.exe.

LISTING 18.6 The UserDS Class

```
namespace MyGolfGear.DataAccess {
    using System;
    using System.Data;
    using System.Xml;
    using System.Runtime.Serialization;


    [Serializable()]
    [System.ComponentModel.DesignerCategoryAttribute("code")]
    public class UserDS : System.Data.DataSet {

        private UserDataTable tableUser;

        private UserTypeDataTable tableUserType;

        private DataRelation relationUserTypeUser;

        public UserDS() {
            this.InitClass();
        }
```

LISTING 18.6   Continued

```
        private UserDS(SerializationInfo info, StreamingContext context) {
            this.InitClass();
            this.GetSerializationData(info, context);
        }

        [System.ComponentModel.Browsable(false)]
        [System.ComponentModel.DesignerSerializationVisibilityAttribute(System.
➥ComponentModel.DesignerSerializationVisibility.Content)]
        public UserDataTable User {
            get {
                return this.tableUser;
            }
        }

        [System.ComponentModel.Browsable(false)]
        [System.ComponentModel.DesignerSerializationVisibilityAttribute(System.
➥ComponentModel.DesignerSerializationVisibility.Content)]
        public UserTypeDataTable UserType {
            get {
                return this.tableUserType;
            }
        }

        protected override bool ShouldSerializeTables() {
            return false;
        }

        protected override bool ShouldSerializeRelations() {
            return false;
        }

        protected override void ReadXmlSerializable(XmlReader reader) {
            this.ReadXml(reader, XmlReadMode.IgnoreSchema);
        }

        protected override System.Xml.Schema.XmlSchema GetSchemaSerializable()
➥{
            System.IO.MemoryStream stream = new System.IO.MemoryStream();
            this.WriteXmlSchema(new XmlTextWriter(stream, null));
            stream.Position = 0;
            return System.Xml.Schema.XmlSchema.Read(new XmlTextReader(stream)
➥, null);
        }
```

18

MAINTAINING
USER
INFORMATION

LISTING 18.6 Continued

```
        private void InitClass() {
            this.DataSetName = "UserDS";
            this.Namespace = "http://tempuri.org/UserDS.xsd";
            this.tableUser = new UserDataTable();
            this.Tables.Add(this.tableUser);
            this.tableUserType = new UserTypeDataTable();
            this.Tables.Add(this.tableUserType);
            this.tableUser.Constraints.Add(new System.Data.
➥ForeignKeyConstraint("UserTypeUser", new DataColumn[] {
                            this.tableUserType.UserTypeIDColumn},
➥new DataColumn[] {
                            this.tableUser.UserTypeIDColumn}));
            this.relationUserTypeUser = new DataRelation("UserTypeUser",
➥ new DataColumn[] {
                        this.tableUserType.UserTypeIDColumn}, new
➥DataColumn[] {
                        this.tableUser.UserTypeIDColumn}, false);
            this.Relations.Add(this.relationUserTypeUser);
        }

        private bool ShouldSerializeUser() {
            return false;
        }

        private bool ShouldSerializeUserType() {
            return false;
        }

        public delegate void UserRowChangeEventHandler(object sender,
➥UserRowChangeEvent e);

        public delegate void UserTypeRowChangeEventHandler(object sender,
➥UserTypeRowChangeEvent e);

        public class UserDataTable : DataTable, System.Collections.
➥IEnumerable {

            private DataColumn columnUserID;

            private DataColumn columnUserTypeID;

            private DataColumn columnUserFName;

            private DataColumn columnUserLName;
```

LISTING 18.6 Continued

```
private DataColumn columnEmailAddr;

private DataColumn columnPassword;

internal UserDataTable() :
        base("User") {
    this.InitClass();
}

[System.ComponentModel.Browsable(false)]
public int Count {
    get {
        return this.Rows.Count;
    }
}

internal DataColumn UserIDColumn {
    get {
        return this.columnUserID;
    }
}

internal DataColumn UserTypeIDColumn {
    get {
        return this.columnUserTypeID;
    }
}

internal DataColumn UserFNameColumn {
    get {
        return this.columnUserFName;
    }
}

internal DataColumn UserLNameColumn {
    get {
        return this.columnUserLName;
    }
}

internal DataColumn EmailAddrColumn {
    get {
        return this.columnEmailAddr;
    }
}
```

LISTING 18.6 Continued

```
            internal DataColumn PasswordColumn {
                get {
                    return this.columnPassword;
                }
            }

            public UserRow this[int index] {
                get {
                    return ((UserRow)(this.Rows[index]));
                }
            }

            public event UserRowChangeEventHandler UserRowChanged;

            public event UserRowChangeEventHandler UserRowChanging;

            public event UserRowChangeEventHandler UserRowDeleted;

            public event UserRowChangeEventHandler UserRowDeleting;

            public void AddUserRow(UserRow row) {
                this.Rows.Add(row);
            }

            public UserRow AddUserRow(int UserID, UserTypeRow
➥parentUserTypeRowByUserTypeUser, string UserFName, string
➥UserLName, string EmailAddr, string Password) {
                UserRow rowUserRow = ((UserRow)(this.NewRow()));
                rowUserRow.ItemArray = new object[] {
                        UserID,
                        parentUserTypeRowByUserTypeUser[0],
                        UserFName,
                        UserLName,
                        EmailAddr,
                        Password};
                this.Rows.Add(rowUserRow);
                return rowUserRow;
            }

            public UserRow FindByUserID(int UserID) {
                return ((UserRow)(this.Rows.Find(new object[] {
                        UserID})));
            }
```

LISTING 18.6 Continued

```
        public System.Collections.IEnumerator GetEnumerator() {
            return this.Rows.GetEnumerator();
        }

        private void InitClass() {
            this.columnUserID = new DataColumn("UserID", typeof(int),
➥"", System.Data.MappingType.Element);
            this.columnUserID.AllowDBNull = false;
            this.columnUserID.Unique = true;
            this.Columns.Add(this.columnUserID);
            this.columnUserTypeID = new DataColumn("UserTypeID",
➥typeof(int), "", System.Data.MappingType.Element);
            this.Columns.Add(this.columnUserTypeID);
            this.columnUserFName = new DataColumn("UserFName",
➥typeof(string), "", System.Data.MappingType.Element);
            this.Columns.Add(this.columnUserFName);
            this.columnUserLName = new DataColumn("UserLName",
➥typeof(string), "", System.Data.MappingType.Element);
            this.Columns.Add(this.columnUserLName);
            this.columnEmailAddr = new DataColumn("EmailAddr",
➥typeof(string), "", System.Data.MappingType.Element);
            this.Columns.Add(this.columnEmailAddr);
            this.columnPassword = new DataColumn("Password",
➥typeof(string), "", System.Data.MappingType.Element);
            this.columnPassword.AllowDBNull = false;
            this.Columns.Add(this.columnPassword);
            this.PrimaryKey = new DataColumn[] {
                    this.columnUserID};
        }

        public UserRow NewUserRow() {
            return ((UserRow)(this.NewRow()));
        }

        protected override DataRow NewRowFromBuilder(DataRowBuilder
➥builder) {
            return new UserRow(builder);
        }

        protected override System.Type GetRowType() {
            return typeof(UserRow);
        }
```

LISTING 18.6   Continued

```
            protected override void OnRowChanged(DataRowChangeEventArgs e) {
                base.OnRowChanged(e);
                if ((this.UserRowChanged != null)) {
                    this.UserRowChanged(this, new UserRowChangeEvent(
➥ ((UserRow)(e.Row)), e.Action));
                }
            }

            protected override void OnRowChanging(DataRowChangeEventArgs e) {
                base.OnRowChanging(e);
                if ((this.UserRowChanging != null)) {
                    this.UserRowChanging(this, new UserRowChangeEvent(
➥ ((UserRow)(e.Row)), e.Action));
                }
            }

            protected override void OnRowDeleted(DataRowChangeEventArgs e) {
                base.OnRowDeleted(e);
                if ((this.UserRowDeleted != null)) {
                    this.UserRowDeleted(this, new UserRowChangeEvent(
➥ ((UserRow)(e.Row)), e.Action));
                }
            }

            protected override void OnRowDeleting(DataRowChangeEventArgs e) {
                base.OnRowDeleting(e);
                if ((this.UserRowDeleting != null)) {
                    this.UserRowDeleting(this, new UserRowChangeEvent(
➥ ((UserRow)(e.Row)), e.Action));
                }
            }

            public void RemoveUserRow(UserRow row) {
                this.Rows.Remove(row);
            }
        }

        public class UserRow : DataRow {

            private UserDataTable tableUser;

            internal UserRow(DataRowBuilder rb) :
                    base(rb) {
                this.tableUser = ((UserDataTable)(this.Table));
            }
```

LISTING 18.6 Continued

```
            public int UserID {
                get {
                    return ((int)(this[this.tableUser.UserIDColumn]));
                }
                set {
                    this[this.tableUser.UserIDColumn] = value;
                }
            }

            public int UserTypeID {
                get {
                    try {
                        return ((int)(this[this.tableUser.UserTypeIDColumn]));
                    }
                    catch (InvalidCastException e) {
                        throw new StrongTypingException("Cannot get value
➥because it is DBNull.", e);
                    }
                }
                set {
                    this[this.tableUser.UserTypeIDColumn] = value;
                }
            }

            public string UserFName {
                get {
                    try {
                        return ((string)(this[this.tableUser.
➥UserFNameColumn]));
                    }
                    catch (InvalidCastException e) {
                        throw new StrongTypingException("Cannot get value
➥because it is DBNull.", e);
                    }
                }
                set {
                    this[this.tableUser.UserFNameColumn] = value;
                }
            }

            public string UserLName {
                get {
                    try {
                        return ((string)(this[this.tableUser.
➥UserLNameColumn]));
```

LISTING 18.6   Continued

```
                }
                catch (InvalidCastException e) {
                    throw new StrongTypingException("Cannot get value
➥because it is DBNull.", e);
                }
            }
            set {
                this[this.tableUser.UserLNameColumn] = value;
            }
        }

        public string EmailAddr {
            get {
                try {
                    return ((string)(this[this.tableUser.
➥EmailAddrColumn]));
                }
                catch (InvalidCastException e) {
                    throw new StrongTypingException("Cannot get value
➥because it
➥is DBNull.", e);
                }
            }
            set {
                this[this.tableUser.EmailAddrColumn] = value;
            }
        }

        public string Password {
            get {
                return ((string)(this[this.tableUser.PasswordColumn]));
            }
            set {
                this[this.tableUser.PasswordColumn] = value;
            }
        }

        public UserTypeRow UserTypeRow {
            get {
                return ((UserTypeRow)(this.GetParentRow(this.
➥Table.ParentRelations[
➥"UserTypeUser"])));
            }
            set {
```

LISTING 18.6   Continued

```
                this.SetParentRow(value, this.Table.
ParentRelations["UserTypeUser"]);
            }
        }

        public bool IsUserTypeIDNull() {
            return this.IsNull(this.tableUser.UserTypeIDColumn);
        }

        public void SetUserTypeIDNull() {
            this[this.tableUser.UserTypeIDColumn] = System.Convert.DBNull;
        }

        public bool IsUserFNameNull() {
            return this.IsNull(this.tableUser.UserFNameColumn);
        }

        public void SetUserFNameNull() {
            this[this.tableUser.UserFNameColumn] = System.Convert.DBNull;
        }

        public bool IsUserLNameNull() {
            return this.IsNull(this.tableUser.UserLNameColumn);
        }

        public void SetUserLNameNull() {
            this[this.tableUser.UserLNameColumn] = System.Convert.DBNull;
        }

        public bool IsEmailAddrNull() {
            return this.IsNull(this.tableUser.EmailAddrColumn);
        }

        public void SetEmailAddrNull() {
            this[this.tableUser.EmailAddrColumn] = System.Convert.DBNull;
        }
    }

    public class UserRowChangeEvent : EventArgs {

        private UserRow eventRow;

        private System.Data.DataRowAction eventAction;
```

LISTING 18.6 Continued

```csharp
        public UserRowChangeEvent(UserRow row, DataRowAction action) {
            this.eventRow = row;
            this.eventAction = action;
        }

        public UserRow Row {
            get {
                return this.eventRow;
            }
        }

        public DataRowAction Action {
            get {
                return this.eventAction;
            }
        }
    }

    public class UserTypeDataTable : DataTable, System.Collections.
➥IEnumerable {

        private DataColumn columnUserTypeID;

        private DataColumn columnType;

        internal UserTypeDataTable() :
                base("UserType") {
            this.InitClass();
        }

        [System.ComponentModel.Browsable(false)]
        public int Count {
            get {
                return this.Rows.Count;
            }
        }

        internal DataColumn UserTypeIDColumn {
            get {
                return this.columnUserTypeID;
            }
        }
```

LISTING 18.6 Continued

```csharp
        internal DataColumn TypeColumn {
            get {
                return this.columnType;
            }
        }

        public UserTypeRow this[int index] {
            get {
                return ((UserTypeRow)(this.Rows[index]));
            }
        }

        public event UserTypeRowChangeEventHandler UserTypeRowChanged;

        public event UserTypeRowChangeEventHandler UserTypeRowChanging;

        public event UserTypeRowChangeEventHandler UserTypeRowDeleted;

        public event UserTypeRowChangeEventHandler UserTypeRowDeleting;

        public void AddUserTypeRow(UserTypeRow row) {
            this.Rows.Add(row);
        }

        public UserTypeRow AddUserTypeRow(int UserTypeID, string Type) {
            UserTypeRow rowUserTypeRow = ((UserTypeRow)(this.NewRow()));
            rowUserTypeRow.ItemArray = new object[] {
                    UserTypeID,
                    Type};
            this.Rows.Add(rowUserTypeRow);
            return rowUserTypeRow;
        }

        public UserTypeRow FindByUserTypeID(int UserTypeID) {
            return ((UserTypeRow)(this.Rows.Find(new object[] {
                    UserTypeID})));
        }

        public System.Collections.IEnumerator GetEnumerator() {
            return this.Rows.GetEnumerator();
        }

        private void InitClass() {
            this.columnUserTypeID = new DataColumn("UserTypeID", typeof
➥ (int), "", System.Data.MappingType.Element);
```

LISTING 18.6   Continued

```
                this.columnUserTypeID.AllowDBNull = false;
                this.columnUserTypeID.Unique = true;
                this.Columns.Add(this.columnUserTypeID);
                this.columnType = new DataColumn("Type", typeof(string), "",
➥System.Data.MappingType.Element);
                this.Columns.Add(this.columnType);
                this.PrimaryKey = new DataColumn[] {
                        this.columnUserTypeID};
        }

        public UserTypeRow NewUserTypeRow() {
            return ((UserTypeRow)(this.NewRow()));
        }

        protected override DataRow NewRowFromBuilder(DataRowBuilder
➥builder) {
            // We need to ensure that all Rows in the tables are typed
rows.
            // Table calls newRow whenever it needs to create a row.
            // So the following conditions are covered by
            // Row newRow(Record record)
            // * Cursor calls table.addRecord(record)
            // * table.addRow(object[] values) calls newRow(record)
            return new UserTypeRow(builder);
        }

        protected override System.Type GetRowType() {
            return typeof(UserTypeRow);
        }

        protected override void OnRowChanged(DataRowChangeEventArgs e) {
            base.OnRowChanged(e);
            if ((this.UserTypeRowChanged != null)) {
                this.UserTypeRowChanged(this, new UserTypeRowChangeEvent(
➥ ((UserTypeRow)(e.Row)), e.Action));
            }
        }

        protected override void OnRowChanging(DataRowChangeEventArgs e) {
            base.OnRowChanging(e);
            if ((this.UserTypeRowChanging != null)) {
                this.UserTypeRowChanging(this, new UserTypeRowChangeEvent(
➥ ((UserTypeRow)(e.Row)), e.Action));
            }
        }
```

LISTING 18.6 Continued

```
              protected override void OnRowDeleted(DataRowChangeEventArgs e) {
                  base.OnRowDeleted(e);
                  if ((this.UserTypeRowDeleted != null)) {
                      this.UserTypeRowDeleted(this, new UserTypeRowChangeEvent(
➡ ((UserTypeRow)(e.Row)), e.Action));
                  }
              }

              protected override void OnRowDeleting(DataRowChangeEventArgs e) {
                  base.OnRowDeleting(e);
                  if ((this.UserTypeRowDeleting != null)) {
                      this.UserTypeRowDeleting(this, new UserTypeRowChangeEvent(
➡ ((UserTypeRow)(e.Row)), e.Action));
                  }
              }

              public void RemoveUserTypeRow(UserTypeRow row) {
                  this.Rows.Remove(row);
              }
          }

      public class UserTypeRow : DataRow {

          private UserTypeDataTable tableUserType;

          internal UserTypeRow(DataRowBuilder rb) :
                  base(rb) {
              this.tableUserType = ((UserTypeDataTable)(this.Table));
          }

          public int UserTypeID {
              get {
                  return ((int)(this[this.tableUserType.UserTypeIDColumn]));
              }
              set {
                  this[this.tableUserType.UserTypeIDColumn] = value;
              }
          }

          public string Type {
              get {
                  try {
                      return ((string)(this[this.tableUserType.TypeColumn]));
                  }
```

Listing 18.6   Continued

```
                    catch (InvalidCastException e) {
                        throw new StrongTypingException("Cannot get value
➥because it is DBNull.", e);
                    }
                }
                set {
                    this[this.tableUserType.TypeColumn] = value;
                }
            }

            public bool IsTypeNull() {
                return this.IsNull(this.tableUserType.TypeColumn);
            }

            public void SetTypeNull() {
                this[this.tableUserType.TypeColumn] = System.Convert.DBNull;
            }

            public UserRow[] GetUserRows() {
                return ((UserRow[])(this.GetChildRows(this.Table.
➥ChildRelations["UserTypeUser"])));
            }
        }

        public class UserTypeRowChangeEvent : EventArgs {

            private UserTypeRow eventRow;

            private System.Data.DataRowAction eventAction;

            public UserTypeRowChangeEvent(UserTypeRow row, DataRowAction
➥action) {
                this.eventRow = row;
                this.eventAction = action;
            }

            public UserTypeRow Row {
                get {
                    return this.eventRow;
                }
            }

            public DataRowAction Action {
                get {
```

LISTING 18.6 Continued

```
                return this.eventAction;
            }
        }
    }
}
}
```

> **NOTE**
>
> You can find the complete listing for the UserDS.cs class online.

The UserDS class provides access to the columns and rows in both the User and UserType tables. Additionally, it provides access to the relationship between these two tables as well as some utility methods and common properties. These methods include a FindByUserID method that returns a UserRow representing a single record in the User table corresponding to the ID passed in. Also included are the NewUserRow method, which adds a new row to the User table, and the RemoveLastUserRow method, which deletes the last user record in the data table representing user data.

Internal properties that return references to DataColumn objects corresponding to each column in the User and UserType tables are standard as well. These DataColumns are the building blocks for creating schemas for DataTable objects.

> **NOTE**
>
> An *internal* property is accessible only within files in the same assembly. Internal members are like friends or protected members, but on the assembly level.

The MyGolfGearDP Data Access Class

The UserDS strongly typed dataset class is useful only after it is filled with the appropriate data. Because it inherits directly from the DataSet class, it can be filled just as any other DataSet class can be. Filling a DataSet requires the use of a DataAdapter. For the MyGolfGear. NET implementation, we encapsulated this functionality in a data provider class called MyGolfGearDP.

The `MyGolfGearDP` class handles all the interaction between other `DataSet` classes and the data these classes provide access to. Typically, this consists of a `get` method and an `update` method. These methods return a newly filled dataset or update a dataset passed in.

The `GetUsers` method takes reference to a `UserDS` class and uses a `DataAdapter` to fill it. As we will see in the next section, the `UserDS` class is passed into this method to be filled with user data when the `User.aspx` page is first called. Listing 18.7 shows the `MyGolfGearDP.GetUsers` method.

LISTING 18.7   The `GetUsers` Method

```
public void GetUsers(UserDS ds)
{
    SqlConnection con = new SqlConnection(ConnectString);
    SqlDataAdapter sda = new SqlDataAdapter("spGetUsers", con);
    sda.SelectCommand.CommandType = CommandType.StoredProcedure;

    con.Open();
    sda.TableMappings.Add("Table", "UserType");
    sda.TableMappings.Add("Table1", "User");
    sda.Fill(ds);
    con.Close();
}
```

The `GetUsers` method, shown in Listing 18.7, first creates a `SqlConnection` object using the private member variable `ConnectString`. After the connection object is created, a `SqlDataAdapter` object is created by passing the stored procedure `spGetUsers` and the connection object just created into the constructor. The `SqlDataAdapter`'s `SelectCommand.CommandType` property is set to `StoredProcedure`, indicating that a stored procedure rather than inline SQL is to be used to retrieve the user data. Next, `TableMappings` classes are added by specifying the foreign key table first and then the main table. Last, the `Fill` method is called.

NOTE

Select, Update, Insert, and Delete commands can all be assigned to `SqlDataAdapter` classes. These classes represent the set of commands and database connections used to fill `DataSet` objects and update SQL Server databases. These classes are said to bridge the gap between a `DataSet` and the SQL Server database.

Besides retrieving a list of all users and their respective information, the MyGolfGearDP class also provides a method for updating the user's DataSet. The UpdateUsers method, shown in Listing 18.8, was created for this purpose.

LISTING 18.8 The UpdateUsers Method

```
public void UpdateUsers( UserDS ds )
{
    SqlConnection con = new SqlConnection(ConnectString);
    SqlDataAdapter sda = new SqlDataAdapter("spGetUsers", con);
    sda.SelectCommand.CommandType = CommandType.StoredProcedure;
    con.Open();

    sda.DeleteCommand = new SqlCommand("spDeleteUser",con);
    sda.DeleteCommand.CommandType = CommandType.StoredProcedure;
    sda.DeleteCommand.Parameters.Clear();
    sda.DeleteCommand.Parameters.Add(new SqlParameter("@UserID",
➥SqlDbType.Int,4,"UserID"));

    sda.UpdateCommand = new SqlCommand("spUpdateUser", con);
    sda.UpdateCommand.CommandType = CommandType.StoredProcedure;
    sda.UpdateCommand.Parameters.Clear();
    sda.UpdateCommand.Parameters.Add(new SqlParameter("@UserID",
➥SqlDbType.Int,4,"UserID"));
    sda.UpdateCommand.Parameters.Add(new SqlParameter("@UserTypeID",
➥SqlDbType.Int,4,"UserTypeID"));
    sda.UpdateCommand.Parameters.Add(new SqlParameter("@EmailAddr",
➥SqlDbType.VarChar,50,"EmailAddr"));
    sda.UpdateCommand.Parameters.Add(new SqlParameter("@UserFName",
➥SqlDbType.VarChar,50,"UserFName"));
    sda.UpdateCommand.Parameters.Add(new SqlParameter("@UserLName",
➥SqlDbType.VarChar,50,"UserLName"));
    sda.UpdateCommand.Parameters.Add(new SqlParameter("@Password",
➥SqlDbType.VarChar,50,"Password"));

    sda.Update(ds, "User");

}
```

18

MAINTAINING
USER
INFORMATION

Like the GetUsers method, the UpdateUsers method in Listing 18.8 accepts an instance of the UserDS class as its only parameter. It creates and opens a SqlConnection object and a SqlDataAdapter class. The SqlDataAdapter class used in the UpdateUsers method is passed a connection and the name of the same stored procedure as the GetUsers method.

Because this method is intended to update the UserDS DataSet class with *any* changes made to it, Update and Delete commands are also provided. The spDeleteUser and spUpdateUser stored procedures are provided to create the new UpdateCommand and DeleteCommand that the SqlDataAdapter needs. In both cases, new Parameter objects are created and added to the appropriate command's Parameters collection.

Finally, the SqlDataAdapter's Update method is called. The two parameters used are the DataSet instance to apply the changes to and the name of the data source (in this case, the User table).

> **NOTE**
>
> The SqlDataAdapter's Update method calls each Insert, Update, and Delete statement for each row that is added, updated, or deleted from the DataSet parameter passed in.

The Users.aspx.cs Code Behind Class

For the user management of MyGolfGear.NET, we needed something to tie the data provider class to the user interface. The built-in ASP.NET mechanism for doing this is the code behind class. We created the Users.aspx.cs code behind class for this purpose; it ties the User.aspx page to the MyGolfGearDP and UserDS classes.

The functionality encapsulated by the Users code behind class can be broken down into four main areas. First, it provides a means of retrieving a list of all users in the UserDS DataSet (and the User table). Next, it provides details about the currently selected user and the ability to update or delete that user's information. Last, it provides the ability to add a new user.

The Page_Load method provides the functionality for displaying the list of all users. It uses the MyGolfGearDP and UserDS classes along with a data-bindable DataList. Listing 18.9 shows the code for this method.

LISTING 18.9   The Page_Load Method

```
private void Page_Load(object sender, System.EventArgs e)
{
    ds = (UserDS) Session["UserDS"];
    if( ds == null )
    {
        MyGolfGearDP dp = new MyGolfGearDP();
        ds = new UserDS();
        dp.GetUsers(ds);
        Session["UserDS"] = ds;
```

LISTING 18.9 Continued

```
    }

    if( !Page.IsPostBack )
    {
            lstUsers.DataSource = ds.User.DefaultView;
            lstUsers.DataTextField = "EmailAddr";
            lstUsers.DataValueField = "UserID";
            lstUsers.DataBind();
            lstUserType.DataSource = ds.UserType.DefaultView;
            lstUserType.DataTextField = "Type";
            lstUserType.DataValueField = "UserTypeID";
            lstUserType.DataBind();
            DisplayUser(int.Parse(lstUsers.SelectedItem.Value));
    }
}
```

The `Page_Load` method in Listing 18.9 takes the usual code behind event method parameters. The first one is a reference to the object that raised the event. The second one is a reference to an object that can contain event-specific information.

A private field called ds is used to hold the `UserDS DataSet`. The `Page_Load` method first looks for a reference to this class in the `Session` object. If one is not available, it creates a new one, along with a new `MyGolfGearDP` data provider object, and fills it using the `MyGolfGearDP`. `GetUsers` method. Then it puts the `User DataSet` back in the `Session` object for easy retrieval later.

> **NOTE**
>
> Developers who are familiar with ASP 2.0 or 3.0 may question the use of the `Session` object. In ASP.NET, the scalability and performance issues associated with the use of the `Session` object have been addressed. It is no longer considered bad practice to use the `Session` object for state management.

Next, two drop-down boxes are populated. The first one contains the e-mail addresses of all the users in the `DataSet`. The second one contains all the user types in the `UserDS DataSet` class. Both are `DropDownList` controls. Next, both `DropDownList` controls are data bound to the `UserDS DataSet` instance. The `User DataTable`'s default view is bound to the first one, and the `UserType DataTable`'s default view is bound to the second one. Finally, the `DisplayUser` method, which is discussed next, is displayed.

The user's details corresponding to the e-mail address in the `lstUsers` `DropDownList` instance are displayed on the `Users.aspx` page when the `DisplayUser` method is called. Listing 18.10 shows this method.

LISTING 18.10   The `DisplayUser` Method

```
public void DisplayUser( int UserID )
{
   UserDS.UserRow r = ds.User.FindByUserID(UserID);
   txtEmail.Text = r.EmailAddr;
   txtFirstName.Text = r.UserFName;
   txtLastName.Text = r.UserLName;
   txtPassword.Text = r.Password;
   foreach( ListItem l in lstUserType.Items )
   {
      l.Selected = false;
      if( l.Value == r.UserTypeID.ToString() )
         l.Selected = true;
   }
}
```

The `DisplayUser` method accepts a single integer value representing a user's ID as its only parameter. It uses this value to call the `User` `DataTable`'s `FindByUserID` method. This method returns a `UserRow` object, which is derived from the generic `DataRow` class. The class allows for the referencing of each column in the table, corresponding to the current row, by name. This, along with Visual Studio's statement completion, makes programming .NET even more intuitive and easy.

> **NOTE**
>
> An `xsd.exe`-generated `DataSet` class will contain a `FindByX` method (where X represents the `DataTable`'s primary key) for every `DataTable` in the `DataSet`.

When an administrator needs to navigate through users or view the details of a different user, she can select a different user's e-mail address from the `lstUser` `DropDownList` control. When she does so, the `ChangeUser` method is called. The code for this event method is shown in Listing 18.11.

LISTING 18.11 The `ChangeUser` Method

```
public void ChangeUser( object sender, EventArgs e )
{
    int UserID = int.Parse(lstUsers.SelectedItem.Value);
    DisplayUser( UserID );
}
```

The `ChangeUser` method in Listing 18.11 takes the typical object and `EventArgs` method parameters that most event methods accept. They are the same types accepted by the `Page_Load` method, which was discussed previously. The value of the selected user's ID is parsed using the `System.Int32.Parse` static method, which converts the string representation of a number to a 32-bit integer and returns it. This integer value is then used to call the `DisplayUser` method.

When the `Delete LinkButton` is clicked on the `Users.aspx` page, the `Delete` method is called. This event method removes the specified user from the current `DataSet`. Listing 18.12 shows the code for this method.

> **NOTE**
>
> A more robust implementation would allow the administrator to verify that he really intended to delete the specified user. This would prevent accidental deletions and the ensuing customer service issues associated with losing customer records.

18

MAINTAINING USER INFORMATION

LISTING 18.12 The `Delete` Method

```
public void Delete( object sender, EventArgs e )
{
    UserDS.UserRow r = ds.User.FindByUserID(int.Parse
➥(lstUsers.SelectedItem.Value));
    r.Delete();
    MyGolfGearDP dp = new MyGolfGearDP();
    dp.UpdateUsers( (UserDS) ds.GetChanges() );
    ds.AcceptChanges();
    lstUsers.DataSource = ds.User.DefaultView;
    lstUsers.DataTextField = "EmailAddr";
    lstUsers.DataValueField = "UserID";
    lstUsers.DataBind();
    DisplayUser(int.Parse(lstUsers.SelectedItem.Value));
}
```

The Delete method takes the standard event method arguments as parameters. It uses the User DataTable's FindByUserID method to retrieve the row corresponding to the selected e-mail address in the lstUsers DropDownList control. Then it calls the DataRow's Delete method, which removes the row from the DataSet it belongs to. Next, an instance of the MyGolfGearDP data provider class is created, and its UpdateUsers method is called.

> **NOTE**
>
> Notice that the DataSet's GetChanges method is called. It returns a copy of the DataSet with any changes made to it since it was filled.

Next, the AcceptChanges method is called, committing all changes made to it since it was filled or the last time the AcceptChanges method was called. Finally, the updated DataSet is rebound to the lstUsers DropDownList instance, and the DisplayUser method is called.

When the Update LinkButton control on the Users.aspx page is clicked, the Update event method is called. This method ensures that the selected user's information is updated in the DataSet and the User table in the MyGolfGear database. Listing 18.13 shows the code for this method.

LISTING 18.13 The Update Method

```
public void Update( object sender, EventArgs e )
{
    UserDS.UserRow r = ds.User.FindByUserID(int.Parse(lstUsers.
➥SelectedItem.Value));
    r.EmailAddr = txtEmail.Text;
    r.UserFName = txtFirstName.Text;
    r.UserLName = txtLastName.Text;
    r.Password = txtPassword.Text;
    r.UserTypeID = int.Parse(lstUserType.SelectedItem.Value);
    MyGolfGearDP dp = new MyGolfGearDP();
    dp.UpdateUsers( (UserDS) ds.GetChanges() );
    ds.AcceptChanges();
    lstUsers.DataSource = ds.User.DefaultView;
    lstUsers.DataTextField = "EmailAddr";
    lstUsers.DataValueField = "UserID";
    lstUsers.DataBind();
    DisplayUser(int.Parse(lstUsers.SelectedItem.Value));
}
```

The signature for the Update method in Listing 18.13 is identical to the other event methods discussed in this section. Like the Delete method, it retrieves a reference to a DataRow object corresponding to the user's ID currently selected in the Users DropDownList control. It passes the text values directly from the TextBox controls to the UserRow instance for each column in the row. The exception is the UserTypeID, which uses the System.Int32 static method named Parse to convert the text representation of the user's ID to an integer. Next, it creates an instance of the MyGolfGearDP class to update the changes to the UserDS DataSet instance and calls the DataSet's AcceptChanges method. Finally, it rebinds the Users DropDownList control and calls DisplayUser to ensure that the information is consistent between the database and the .aspx page.

> **NOTE**
>
> You can find the complete listing for the Users.aspx.cs code behind class online.

Accessing User Information via the Users.aspx Page

Administrators of MyGolfGear.NET can navigate to the Users.aspx page to perform user management. The ASP.NET page allows administrators to view a list of all users, enter new users into the system, modify existing users' information, and delete existing users from the MyGolfGear database. This page uses the Users code behind class, discussed in the preceding section, to "wire up" the events needed by this page to handle the needed actions. The code for this page is shown in Listing 18.14.

LISTING 18.14   The Users.aspx Page

```
<%@ Page language="c#" Codebehind="Users.aspx.cs" AutoEventWireup="false"
➥Inherits="MyGolfGear.Admin.Users" %>
<%@ Register TagPrefix="MyGolfGear" TagName="LeftNav" Src="../UserControls
➥/LeftNav.ascx" %>
<%@ Register TagPrefix="MyGolfGear" TagName="Header" Src="../UserControls
➥/Header.ascx" %>
<%@ Register TagPrefix="MyGolfGear" TagName="Footer" Src="../UserControls
➥/Footer.ascx" %>

<HTML>
<HEAD>
```

LISTING 18.14   Continued

```
<title>MyGolfGear.net -- Manage Users
</title>
<LINK href="../css_mygolfgear.css" type=text/css rel=stylesheet >
</HEAD>
<body text=#000000 aLink=#336699 link=#336699 bgColor=#ffffff>
<!--START MAIN TABLE-->
<div align=center>
<center>
<table cellSpacing=0 cellPadding=0 width=790 border=0>
<tr>
<td width=2 bgColor=#808080><IMG height=2 src="../images/spacer_clear.gif"
➥width=2 border=0 > </td>
<td width=786 bgColor=#808080><IMG height=2 src="../images/spacer_clear.gif"
➥width=786 border=0 > </td>
<td width=2 bgColor=#808080><IMG height=2 src="../images/spacer_clear.gif"
➥width=2 border=0 > </td></tr>
<tr>
<td vAlign=top width=2 bgColor=#808080></td>
<td vAlign=top width=786>
<table cellSpacing=0 cellPadding=0 width=786 border=0>
<tr>
<td vAlign=top width=172>
<!--START LEFT COLUMN CONTENT MASTR TABLE--><MYGOLFGEAR:LEFTNAV id=LeftNav
➥runat="server"></MYGOLFGEAR:LEFTNAV>
<!--END LEFT COLUMN CONTENT-->
<!--</center>
--></td>
<td vAlign=top width=2 bgColor=#808080></td>
<td vAlign=top align=left width=616>
<!-- Insert Top Nav --><MYGOLFGEAR:HEADER id=Header runat="server">
</MYGOLFGEAR:HEADER>
<!--MAIN CONTENT-->
<table cellSpacing=0 cellPadding=5 width="100%" border=0>
<tr>
<td vAlign=top width="100%">
<form id=Form1 method=post
runat="server"><font color=#336699><B>
User Manager - Select a User to Administer</B></font> <BR>
<asp:dropdownlist id=lstUsers Runat="server" OnSelectedIndexChanged=
➥"ChangeUser" AutoPostBack="True">
</asp:dropdownlist>
<table>
<tr>
```

LISTING 18.14   Continued

```
<td>Email:</td>
<td><asp:TextBox ID="txtEmail" Runat="server" /></td>
</tr>
<tr>
<td>First Name: </td>
<td><asp:textbox id=txtFirstName Runat="server"></asp:textbox>
</td>
</tr>
<tr>
<td>
Last Name:
</td>
<td>
<asp:TextBox ID="txtLastName" Runat="server" /></td></tr>
<tr>
<td>
Password:
</td>
<td>
<asp:TextBox ID="txtPassword" Runat="server" />
</td>
</tr>
<tr>
<td>
User Type:
</td>
<td>
<asp:DropDownList ID="lstUserType" Runat="server" />
</td>
</tr>
<tr>
<td>
<asp:LinkButton ID="btnDelete" Runat="server" OnClick="Delete">Delete
➥</asp:LinkButton> |
<asp:LinkButton ID="btnUpdate" Runat="server" OnClick="Update">Update
➥</asp:LinkButton> |
<a href="../Main/join.aspx">Add New</a>
</td>
</tr>
</table></form>
<!-- END OF MAIN CONTENT --></td></tr></table>
<!--END MAIN CONTENT-->
```

Listing 18.14   Continued

```
<p>
</p></td></tr>
<!-- Insert Footer -->
<MyGolfGear:Footer id=Footer runat="server" /></table>
<DIV>
</DIV>
<!--END MASTER TABLE-->
<p>
</p></td></tr></table></center></div>
</body>
</HTML>
```

Note

You can find the complete listing for the `Users.aspx` page online.

The `Users.aspx` page uses several Web Server controls to implement the user administration functionality. Specifically, it uses two instances of the `LinkButton` control, two instances of the `DropDownList` control, and four instances of the `TextBox` control.

One `LinkButton` control calls the `Delete` method. The other `LinkButton` control calls the `Update` method in the code behind class. Both of these methods were discussed in the section titled "The `Users.aspx.cs` Code Behind Class."

The `TextBox` controls provide a means to input a user's e-mail address, first and last name, and password.

Caution

The `RequiredFieldValidator` control should be used for the e-mail address and password because the `User` table requires them. Additionally, a second password text box should be used along with a `CompareValidator` control.

The two `DropDownList` controls hold the list of all users and all available user types. Be aware that for a site with many registered users, an alternative means of navigating the entire list of users should be developed. Figure 18.1 shows what this page looks like.

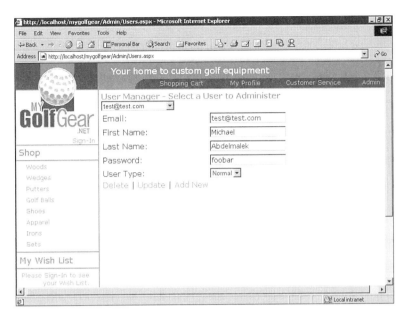

FIGURE 18.1
The Users.aspx *page.*

Summary

This chapter discussed the administrative features of MyGolfGear.NET that were developed to allow the addition and modification of user information. It reviewed the pertinent database objects and explored the data access techniques used to support this functionality. It showed how the UserDS strongly typed dataset class was created and the portions of the MyGolfGearDP data provider class that use the UserDS class. It also showed how the Users.aspx page and Users.aspx.cs code behind class were implemented and discussed their role in supporting the user administration functionality.

The next chapter, "Debugging and Optimizing the Site," will cover the use of ASP.NET debugging, monitoring, and logging. In addition, it also will discuss stress testing as an important step in deploying the MyGolfGear.NET site.

Self Instruction

Based on the information covered in this chapter, add the ability to disable user accounts. Modify the User table by adding an additional boolean field called active. Modify the Users.aspx page and supporting classes as well. You will also need to modify Users.xsd and regenerate the UsersDS class using xsd.exe.

After reading this chapter, you should recognize that MyGolfGear.NET supports two types of users: Normal and Admin. The current implementation requires a developer to manually enter a row in the UserType table when a new user type is desired. Create another administrative screen that allows administrators to add new user types to the UserType table. At a minimum, you need to create the following:

- A UserType.aspx page
- A UserType.aspx.cs code behind class
- A new stored procedure for updating the UserType table called something like spAddUserType

Debugging and
Optimizing the Site

IN THIS CHAPTER

Objectives

- Learn what stress testing is and examine some of the available tools

- Understand some of the profiling and debugging services available with .NET, including performance monitoring

- Explore some of the programmatic practices that can improve performance

- Discover some of the IIS and networking optimizations that you can make to improve a site's performance

As with any software development, throughout the course of building MyGolfGear.NET, we found many occasions for debugging. Fortunately, the .NET Framework offers many useful and easy-to-use features for debugging. This chapter covers the debugging techniques used when creating MyGolfGear.NET.

Often you need to squeeze a little more performance out of an application. Usually, you do so in an attempt to make the site speedier or to enable it to service more users simultaneously. MyGolfGear.NET was built with this functionality in mind. Therefore, this chapter will also cover the steps and considerations taken when developing MyGolfGear.NET.

In addition to debugging and optimizing, I think it is necessary to discuss a few other important topics. Therefore, this chapter also covers topics such as stress testing, monitoring, and logging, all of which become important after the bulk of the code has been written.

Stress Testing

As I mentioned previously, this chapter is mostly about optimization and debugging. So, why does it open with a discussion about stress testing? The answer is that stress testing is one of the most important and yet often overlooked steps in developing Internet applications before going live.

> **NOTE**
>
> *Stress testing* refers to the practice of simulating high traffic on a Web site via some programmatic means.

Stress testing is important because it can uncover hidden weaknesses and undiscovered bugs as well as identify an application's breaking points. Therefore, I think it makes sense to discuss stress testing before delving into debugging and optimizing.

To stress test an application, you must place a load on it. All too often, Web sites are stress tested by the production environment. In other words, developers and the organizations they work for determine an application's capability to perform by opening the site to their users. Although this approach is a sure-fire way to determine whether an application can handle a true load, it is very risky.

There are alternatives, however. The approach that makes the most sense is to simulate the expected load (or more than the expected load just to be safe). So, how is this done? You could get hundreds or thousands of your friends to simultaneously use the application in your staging environment (not likely!), or you can use automated tools.

Using Stress Testing Tools

You have more than a couple of options when it comes to stress-testing tools. One of the easiest and most common practices is to build a *test harness*.

A test harness is just what it sounds like—a simple "home grown" application that makes multiple (possibly simultaneous) requests to a specific piece of an application. While we were building MyGolfGear.NET, any time we built a component, we used a test harness to determine whether it was functioning properly before plugging it into the rest of the site. This procedure was also part of the basic unit testing.

You can take a couple of approaches here. First, you could create a separate test method for every corresponding method in the component to be tested. Alternatively, to test the component as a whole, you could write a test method that makes method calls similarly to how the real system will operate. When we created test harnesses for MyGolfGear.NET, we took this approach most often.

Listing 19.1 shows the code for a simple test harness we created to test the `MyGolfGearDP` data provider component.

LISTING 19.1 *MyGolfGearDP* Test Harness

```
using System;
using MyGolfGear;
using MyGolfGear.DataAccess;

class MyGolfGearDPTester{

    public static void Main(){
        Console.WriteLine("Begin MyGolfGearDP tester.");
        //Create the CatalogDS strongly-typed DataSet
        CatalogDS catDS = new CatalogDS();
        //Create the data provider component we wish to test.
        MyGolfGearDP dp = new MyGolfGearDP();
```

LISTING 19.1   Continued

```
// Loop and call multiple times.
for(int i=0; i<10; i++){
  // Call the first data provider method
  dp.FillCatalog(catDS);

  // Add and populate a new row to the DataSet
  CatalogDS.CategoryRow categoryRow = catDS.Category.NewCategoryRow();

  categoryRow.CategoryID = System.Guid.NewGuid();
  categoryRow.Name = "Name" + i.ToString();
  categoryRow.ParentCategoryID = System.Guid.NewGuid();
  categoryRow.Description = "Description" + i.ToString();
  categoryRow.DisplaySeq = Convert.ToInt16(i);
  categoryRow.Display = Convert.ToInt16(i);

  catDS.Category.AddCategoryRow(categoryRow);

  // Call the second data provider method
  dp.UpdateCatalog((CatalogDS)catDS.GetChanges());

  // have the DataSet accept the changes.
  catDS.AcceptChanges();
    }
  }
}
```

Even though Listing 19.1 is a simple example, it illustrates my point. The code in this listing calls the `MyGolfGearDP` data provider component similarly to the way the `CategoryManager` code behind calls it. This similarity ensures that it is tested in a meaningful way.

As it happens, the functionality tested in Listing 19.1 will not be put under undue stress during normal use because only administrators will add and update categories.

If a piece of functionality were to be used by every visitor of the site, we could create a multi-threaded client of this test class. It would allow multiple instances, running on separate threads, to exercise the data provider component.

> **NOTE**
>
> This same type of test harness can be modified to be free threaded. Appendix A, "C# Language Reference," contains a section on free threading that will be useful.

Although this approach is quick and easy, it has limited value. This approach allows us to place a load only on a particular piece of functionality instead of on the application as a whole. To place a load on the whole application, we could build an application that requests specific pages, passing or posting parameters as necessary. We could then create multiple instances of this application and hope to put enough stress on the site to really tax it. This approach would be a lot of work, and the results would be difficult to track and analyze.

What we need is a tool that allows users to place a load on any site that can be viewed from a browser as well as simulate different numbers of users. The capability to simulate different client connection speed and load would also be helpful. A good stress-testing tool should also provide reports with detail results such as page load time and Performance Monitor counters.

Using the Web Application Stress Tool

Fortunately, many stress-testing tools already out there do exactly what we need. WebHammer, LoadRunner, and Microsoft's Web Application Stress (WAS) tools are a few. (I'm sure many more are available, but these are the ones I've heard about) Other available systems might be better suited for enterprise-level testing and monitoring, but Microsoft's WAS is free, so it was the obvious choice for me.

> **NOTE**
>
> The Microsoft Web Application Stress (WAS) tool can be downloaded for free at `http://webtool.rte.microsoft.com/download.asp`.

The WAS tool was created to simulate multiple simultaneous users hitting a Web site. It allows you to gather performance data and assess the stability of a Web site before you put it into production.

The WAS tool makes it easy to get started if you are unfamiliar with load testing tools. Creating a new test script is easy; just follow these simple steps:

1. Select Scripts, Create, Record.
2. Choose whether you want to record the delay between requests, cookies, or host headers.
3. Type the URL of the site you want to load test into the browser's address bar that is opened for you.
4. Navigate the site in the manner in which you want to test.
5. Click the Stop Recording button on the WAS tool's Recording tab.

19

DEBUGGING AND
OPTIMIZING
THE SITE

After you stop recording, you can run the newly recorded script either by clicking the Run Script button on the toolbar or selecting Scripts, Run from the menu bar. You can modify scripts manually by choosing Create, Manual from the Scripts menu.

After you run the script, you can view reports based on the results of the test scrip. You can view these reports either by selecting View, Reports from the menu bar or clicking the Reports button on the toolbar. Figure 19.1 shows the types of reports generated by the WAS tool.

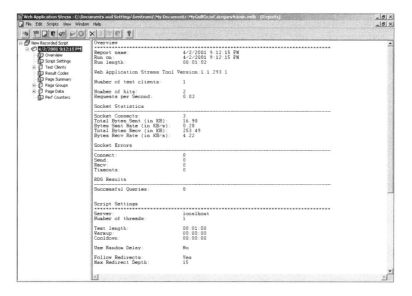

FIGURE 19.1

Sample WAS report.

Several reports are available. They include an overview, which details the number of clients, the number of socket connections, and the number of hits; a report on the script settings; a report for each test client; result codes encountered; a page summary; a page group report; page data reports for each page called; and a report detailing each Performance Monitor counter recorded during the test period.

Performance Considerations

Before you decide on a stress-testing strategy, consider the following:

- How many users do you expect to visit the site at one time?
- How long should each page take to load?
- If you've created a shopping site, how long should it take an average user to place an order?

It is important to make a determination about the number of users you expect to visit your site so that you have a target to shoot for when you're load testing. For instance, suppose that I expect to get between 10,000 and 20,000 visitors per day to my site. I know that I need to simulate, at least, a 20,000-user-per-day load. I say *at least* because, like anything else, it is better to err on the side of caution.

Knowing how long a page should take to load is important because this easily captured metric can be used as a gauge for how much stress a site is under. In other words, if a given page normally takes less than 5 seconds to load but takes 15 seconds to load with 15,000 users, you know that you have some work to do on the page and/or the process that generates the page (stored procedures, components, and so on).

Knowing how long it should take the average user to go through your site and purchase something is helpful also. The number of orders that can be purchased in a given period of time is sometimes referred to as *throughput*. As you will see later in the chapter, you can take several steps to increase throughput. You need to define a throughput baseline so that changes made in an attempt at optimization can be realized.

You also need to be aware of a couple of other points. First, if your load testing environment does not closely resemble that of your production environment, the results you obtain from stress testing will not accurately reflect your application's behavior under load. Similarly, if the load scripts created by the tool don't accurately simulate the "typical" user behavior on your site, your stress-testing results won't be as valid.

No one wants to use a slow Web site, just as no developer wants to develop a slow Web site. For this reason, performance tuning is very important. The question is this: How can we pinpoint exactly where a site's bottleneck is? Fortunately, the .NET Framework provides a host of profiling and debugging services that are ideally suited for answering this question.

Profiling and Debugging Services

Used in conjunction with stress-testing data, the performance data gathered via profiling can prove to be invaluable in determining where an application needs performance improvement. You can gather performance data in two ways. One is to use the Performance Monitor counters discussed briefly in the next section. The other, and the one I will spend the most time discussing, is to use the .NET Performance Counter API.

Performance Monitor

To use the Windows 2000 Performance Monitor, choose Start, Administrative Tools and then click the Performance icon, or simply type `perfmon` in the Run dialog or at a command prompt.

To select specific counters to monitor, simply click the Add button on the toolbar. Clicking this button opens a dialog that allows you to choose which computer to monitor, which type of object to monitor, and specifically what counters of that type to monitor. Figure 19.2 shows the Performance Monitor and the Add Counters dialog.

FIGURE 19.2
The Performance Monitor and Add Counters dialog.

In the figure, notice that several .NET CLR–specific performance objects are listed. They include the ability to monitor exceptions, interop, JIT, loading, locks, memory, remoting, security, and threads. You can select individual counters within each group, or you can select the All Instances option, which adds every counter for the object.

In addition to the .NET CLR performance counter objects, two ASP.NET performance objects also are available. They are the ASP.NET System object and the ASP.NET Application object.

The ASP.NET System object gives you access to counters such as the number of applications running, the number of worker processes running, Requests Queued, and three or four others.

The ASP.NET Application object provides many more counters than the ASP.NET System object. In fact, you can choose from about 50 ASP.NET Application object counters. They include Authentication Anonymous Requests, about 10 cache counters, 5 error counters, the normal Request and Session counters, and 5 transaction counters, as well as a few others. Figure 19.3 shows Performance Monitor's report view of all the ASP.NET Application counters.

All these Performance Monitor counters are great after the fact, but what we really need is a more penetrating or customized approach. Fortunately, the .NET Framework provides a performance counter API.

The .NET Performance Counter API

As mentioned in the "Profiling and Debugging Services" section, Windows 2000 comes with a built-in monitoring tool called Performance Monitor. You can monitor literally hundreds of counters, but the important ones to watch for Web-based applications are Available Memory, Connections Per Second, CPU Utilization, Current Anonymous Users, and Requests Queued.

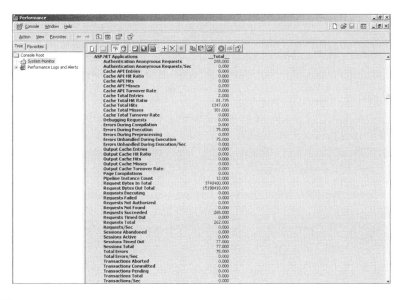

FIGURE 19.3
ASP.NET Application counters.

The available memory should remain somewhat constant as long as no additions or changes are made to the applications running on a Web server. It is important to monitor your Web server's available memory because a sudden or unexpected increase in memory utilization can signify a memory leak. A memory leak can be caused by code that does not close down properly or that does not release system resources when done.

Thanks to the built-in caching services available with the .NET runtime, the Connections Requested Per Second counter is not as necessary as it was in the Active Server Pages days. Basically, a Web server can handle a limited number of requests per second because the server has to decide with each request whether code needs to be executed or a static page simply needs to be served up. For this reason, it is still important to keep any static pages as HTML pages.

When a component or components perform such CPU-intensive processing that the Web server is no longer able to keep up with requests, performance of the application will suffer. Keeping an eye on CPU utilization will help identify when you need to offload some processing to application servers.

Monitoring the Current Anonymous Users count, in conjunction with all the other counts mentioned here, will help determine the threshold at which you need to plan for additional hardware. In other words, when used along with CPU Utilization, Available Memory, Requests Queued, and Connections Requested, the Current Anonymous Users count can serve as an indicator of when to scale up and/or out.

When IIS cannot execute the code in a page as fast as the requests are coming in, it queues requests. Therefore, monitoring the Requests Queued count can be a good indicator that an external resource or process is overloaded. Even one significantly slow page on a site can slow down the entire site by consuming all available requests and forcing IIS to queue the remaining incoming requests.

To monitor these counters, open Performance Monitor by typing `perfmon` in the Run dialog, which you open from the Start menu. Click the Add button on the toolbar to open the Add Counters dialog. From the Add Counters dialog, select the appropriate objects from the Performance Object drop-down list.

For current anonymous users, select the Web Service performance object. For requests per second, select the ASP.NET Application performance object. For Requests Queued, select the ASP.NET System performance object. For CPU Utilization, select the Processor performance object, and for Available Memory, select the Memory performance object.

Several other performance counters may be worth monitoring periodically, depending on the environment. I suggest that you pay particular attention to the ASP.NET Application objects' Errors During Execution and Errors Unhandled During Execution counters because some overhead is associated with the cleanup of such errors—not to mention the user impact of running into unhandled exceptions.

Some of the Network Interface object's counters can give you valuable insight into the Web server's health from a network perspective. Counters such as Current Bandwidth, Bytes Sent and Received, and Packets Received Errors can all help you identify difficult-to-track-down network problems that can bring an otherwise screaming application to a halt.

The .NET Framework provides an API that allows developers to create custom performance counters that can be viewed in Performance Monitor. It also allows for access to the built-in ASP.NET and .NET CLR counters discussed in the preceding section.

This API allows developers to write specific counters to help pinpoint bottlenecks and other bugs within their systems. For example, a developer might create a counter that records how long a critical process takes, such as a tax calculation or credit card processing. Alternatively, a developer might use a custom counter to help debug one of these disconnected services.

Creating a custom Performance Monitor counter is as easy as creating a new `PerformanceCounterCategory` object and an instance of the `PerformanceCounter` class. Listing 19.2 shows how to create the `MyCategory` class and a single counter called `MyCounter`.

LISTING 19.2   A Custom Performance Monitor Counter

```
using System;
using System.Diagnostics;
```

LISTING 19.2 Continued

```
class MyClass{
   public static void Main(){

   try{
       PerformanceCounterCategory pcc =PerformanceCounterCategory.Create
➡("MyCategory","MyCategoryHelp","MyCounter","MyCounterHelp");
   }catch(System.InvalidOperationException ioe){
      Console.WriteLine(ioe.Message);
   }finally{

      PerformanceCounter pc = new PerformanceCounter("MyCategory",
➡"MyCounter", false);

      for(int i=0; i< 10; i++){
        pc.Increment();
      }
   }
  }
}// End of Class
```

NOTE

You can find the complete code listing for this class online.

The simple class in Listing 19.2 shows the creation of a `PerformanceCounterCategory` object at the beginning of the `try` block. Notice that it is surrounded by a `try`-`catch` block, which prevents an exception from being thrown when this class is executed more than once.

In the `finally` block, starting on line 11, a `PerformanceCounter` object is created by specifying the category and counter names. The Boolean parameter in the constructor means the instance will not be read-only.

Line 16 shows the actual use of the `PerformanceCounter` object. I stuck it in a simple `for` loop, but this example illustrates exactly how it would be used to record an order being placed, a tax calculation being made, an inventory reservation call being made, or a credit card being authorized.

By creating custom counters in this manner, developers can track meaningful data in key locations of their applications. These counters allow them to pinpoint the areas that need optimizing.

19

DEBUGGING AND OPTIMIZING THE SITE

Trace and Debug Classes

After an application is released for testing, debugging problems can be cumbersome at best. This is especially true with very large applications. Fortunately, the .NET Framework provides a couple of tools to help you debug applications without having to step through your code line by line.

The System.Diagnostics namespace contains Debug and Trace classes, which are very similar. They both provide several static methods that can be used in your code to gather detailed information about what is happening.

> **NOTE**
>
> Because the Debug and Trace classes are so similar, this section will focus on the Trace class.

To use the Trace class, follow these steps:

1. Define the TRACE symbol in your code.
2. Create an instance of a Listener object (such as the OutputDebugString Windows API).
3. Add calls to the Trace object within your code.

Listing 19.3 shows a simple method using the Trace class.

LISTING 19.3   Using the Trace Class

```
using System;
using System.Diagnosi
class Foo{
    public Foo(){
        Trace.WriteLine("Initializing Foo.");
    }
}
```

Listing 19.3 shows a constructor using the Trace method. When an instance of the Foo class is created, if a Listener is connected, the words "Initializing Foo." will be displayed.

The WriteLine method is by no means the only method available for developers to use. Four properties and about 10 static methods are also available. Table 19.1 shows all the Trace class properties, and Table 19.2 shows all its methods.

TABLE 19.1 The *Trace* Class Properties

Property	Description
AutoFlush	Gets and sets a Boolean value determining whether Flush should be called on the Listener objects after each call
IndentLevel	Gets and sets an integer value representing the number of indents a tracing message will contain
IndentSize	Gets and sets an integer value representing the number of spaces per indent
Listeners	Returns a collection of Listener objects monitoring the output

TABLE 19.2 Static Methods

Method	Description
Assert	Tests for a condition and displays a message if the condition is false
Close	Closes all listeners and flushes the output buffer; useful when writing to a file
Fail	Forces an error message to be written to the listener
Flush	Causes any buffered data to be written to the listeners and flushes the output buffer
Indent	Increments the IndentLevel by one
Unindent	Decrements the IndentLevel by one
Write	Writes a message to all the listeners
WriteIf	Writes a message to all the listeners if a condition is true
WriteLine	Writes a message to all the listeners and includes a new line
WriteLineIf	Writes a message to all the listeners and includes a new line if a condition is true

Optimizing the Site

When you need to make an Internet application more scalable, reliable, and faster, you can do many things to optimize the site. These optimizations fall into roughly two groups: .NET-intrinsic optimizations and optimizations that are outside the realm of the .NET Framework.

The available .NET-specific features include .NET finalization and garbage collection, managed code, speedier value types, and a built-in StringBuilder class. In addition, you can optimize code by simply using the /optimize command-line argument when compiling (this command is turned on by default).

.NET Finalization and Garbage Collection

One of the easiest ways to optimize a .NET Web-based application is to take advantage of the built-in garbage collection system. Even though this system operates entirely without input or direction from the developer, there are ways to make optimal use of it.

Let me add a few caveats, however. First, objects that implement a `Finalize` method take longer to deallocate. Second, if many objects must be finalized at once, the process can be resource-intensive and can even slow down performance. Third, not all finalizable objects will be finalized. This is the case when a finalizable object points to another object that is not finalizable. Last, finalization does not occur in any particular order, and it cannot be forced. In other words, there is no deterministic finalization.

So, the message here is that finalization is a good thing when used responsibly. Here are a few guidelines to help determine whether finalization is appropriate:

- Don't implement `Finalize` if a class has only managed references.
- Do not call any other object's `Finalize` method except `base.Finalize`.
- Implement `Finalize` only in classes that need it.
- Because you have no guarantee that the `Finalize` method will be called, implement the `Dispose` design pattern on objects that contain resources that must be freed.

Given all these guidelines, how is the `Finalize` method implemented? If an object holds references to other resources—for example, a database connection—`Finalize()` should be overridden so that these resources can be freed before the object is destroyed by the garbage collector. Listing 19.4 shows a class that implements the `Finalize()` method.

LISTING 19.4   The `Finalize` Method

```
using System;

class Foo{
  public Foo(){
    Console.WriteLine("Constructor called.");
  }

    protected override void Finalize(){
     // Do some clean up here.
    Console.WriteLine("Finalize called.");
    base.Finalize();
  }
}
```

LISTING 19.4 Continued

```
class MyClass{
   public static void Main(){
      Foo foo = new Foo();
      System.GC.Collect();
      System.GC.WaitForPendingFinalizers();
   }
}
```

> **NOTE**
>
> You can find the complete code listing for this class online.

Listing 19.4 shows a simple class named Foo that implements a constructor and overrides the base class object's Finalize() method. If Foo actually used resources, such as the file system or a database connection, the Console.WriteLine call in the Finalize method could be replaced with a statement or statements that freed these resources.

Managed-Unmanaged Code Transitions

As robust as the .NET Framework is, sometimes a developer will still need to make API calls or interact with COM objects. In the case of COM interop, this will most likely be in an attempt to take advantage of previously written functionality. Although taking advantage of this functionality seems like a good idea from a code reuse perspective, it can create a potential performance bottleneck.

When managed code must interact with unmanaged code, some overhead is associated with the transition (between 10 and 40 instructions per call). When you are making the decision to use unmanaged code, follow these tips:

- Use API calls that perform several functions instead of several API calls that perform a single task.
- Resist the temptation to simply replace the user interface of existing Internet applications with an ASP.NET UI that makes COM interop calls to existing components.
- Limit the number of *transitions*. The transition is expensive, not the COM/API call.

.NET Value Types Versus Reference Types

The Common Language Runtime (CLR) supports value types and reference types. Value types describe actual primitive types such as integers and floating-point variables, whereas reference types point to the memory location of data. Classes, structs, and interfaces are all examples of reference types.

Small pieces of data that can be held in value types have performance advantages over a similar reference type. This is true because value types are allocated on the stack and reference types are allocated on the garbage collection heap. Reference types also have the overhead of needing a constructor called for each instance. If the garbage collector must call a `Finalize` method, this adds to the overhead as well.

For instance, when given the option of creating an integer as a value type `int` or as a reference type `System.Int32`, choose the `int`. In other words,

```
int i;
```

should perform better than

```
System.Int32 i = new System.Int32();
```

Using the .NET `StringBuilder` Class

If you're performing multiple string manipulations, use the `System.Text.StringBuilder` class instead of making changes to a `String` variable directly. You should do so because changes to a `String` variable force the CLR to create a copy of the original string with the changes made to it. In other words, any modifications to a `String` variable don't actually modify the existing `String` instance. This means you have the overhead of creating and destroying an object for every modification.

Fortunately, the .NET runtime offers a baked-in solution. The `StringBuilder` class, located in the `System.Text` namespace, allows you to modify string variables without creating a new object. You can use the `StringBuilder` class to remove, replace, insert, append, and delete characters within a string without the overhead of creating a new `String` object. Listing 19.5 shows how to use the `StringBuilder` class.

> **NOTE**
>
> The term *baked-in* is sometimes used to emphasize the point that a feature or set of features is part of the .NET core. This is in contrast to something like Microsoft Transaction Server (MTS) being "bolted-on" to COM.

LISTING 19.5 Using the `StringBuilder` Class

```
1: using System;
2: using System.Text;
```

LISTING 19.5   Continued

```
3:
4: class MyClass{
5:
6:     public static void Main(){
7:         StringBuilder sb = new StringBuilder("My StringBuilder");
8:         String myString = " my String.";
9:
10:         sb.Append(myString);
11:         Console.WriteLine(sb);
12:
13:         sb.Replace("My", "A");
14:         Console.WriteLine(sb);
15:
16:         sb.Insert(16, " class uses an existing ", 1);
17:         Console.WriteLine(sb);
18:
19:         sb.Remove(sb.Length - 10, 3);
20:
21:         Console.WriteLine(sb);
22:
23:         sb.Insert(sb.Length - 1, " class");
24:         Console.WriteLine(sb);
25:     }
26: }
```

> **NOTE**
>
> You can find the complete code listing for this class online.

The MyClass class in Listing 19.5 shows how to use some of the more common properties and methods of the StringBuilder class. It starts by creating a new StringBuilder class and a new String instance on lines 7 and 8. Line 10 uses the Append method, and line 11 prints the results to the console window. The example goes on to use the Replace, Insert, and Remove methods as well as the Length property. The results of compiling and running an .exe created from this class would look like this:

```
A StringBuilder my String.
A StringBuilder  class uses an existing my String.
A StringBuilder  class uses an existing String.
A StringBuilder  class uses an existing String class.
```

Internet Information Server (IIS) Optimization

Another option for squeezing performance out of an Internet-based application is to take advantage of the Internet Information Server (IIS) 5.0 optimizations that are available. These optimizations are broken down into two main groups: IIS Metabase settings and Registry settings.

You can tune Web servers running IIS 5.0 by using the Active Directory Service Interface (ADSI) to alter the IIS Metabase. Some of the more important Metabase changes you can make are `ServerSize`, `ServerListenBackLog`, `ConnectionTimeout`, `CacheISAPI`, and `MaxEndPointConnections`.

> **NOTE**
>
> Most IIS Metabase changes do not take effect until you restart the Web service.

The `ServerSize` Metabase setting is perhaps the easiest to change. You can change it on the Properties sheet of any Web site on the IIS admin console. In general terms, this property affects the number of clients expected to be served per day; it adjusts the number of resources dedicated to the IIS service. The settings range from 0 to 2, which translates to 10,000 or fewer clients; 10,000 to 100,000; and more than 100,000. This setting has a direct impact on the `ServerListenBackLog` setting. Figure 19.4 shows the Properties sheet used to adjust the `ServerSize` setting.

FIGURE 19.4

Performance tuning Properties sheet.

The `ServerListenBackLog` setting specifies the number of sockets that can be queued. The value of the `MaxEndPointConnections` property is used in conjunction with this property to set the number of sockets queued by the server. If the `ServerSize` Metabase property is set to `0`, the default `ServerListenBackLog` value is `5`. If the `ServerSize` is `1`, the default is `40`, and if the `ServerSize` is `2`, the default `ServerListenBackLog` property value is `100`. You can adjust this property value as low as `5` to as great as `1000`.

The `ConnectionTimeout` property specifies the number of seconds the server will wait before disconnecting idle clients. This property defaults to 15 minutes (900 seconds). Decreasing the value of this property can improve performance because open connections consume resources that could not otherwise be used to perform work.

The `MaxEndPointConnections` property specifies the total number of "listen" sockets that can be aggregated on a single port. The default value for this property is `100`. This number, in conjunction with the `ServerListenBackLog` property, determines the number of sockets pooled on a server.

The `CacheISAPI` property tells the server whether to cache ISAPI DLLs in memory after each use. This property defaults to `TRUE`, which means any ISAPI DLLs loaded into memory will remain there until the server is stopped. It might be useful to set this property to `FALSE` for debugging purposes. Setting this property to `TRUE` on all production servers is best, however, because loading and unloading an ISAPI DLL between every request would be very expensive. The `aspnet_isapi.dll` file is the ASP.NET ISAPI DLL, so having this property set to `FALSE` while running ASP.NET applications could significantly slow an application.

Several Registry settings, when altered, can improve performance, but the two most important are `ProcessorThreadMax` and `RequestQueueMax`. The `ProcessorThreadMax` setting sets the maximum number of threads per processor, whereas the `RequestQueueMax` setting, as the name suggests, sets the maximum size of the request queue. You can find them at `HKEY_LOCAL_MACHINE\SYSTEM\CurrentControlSet\Services\W3SVC\ASP`.

As with any significant changes you make to an Internet application, you should validate changes to the Metabase or the Registry by performing additional stress-testing. This testing ensures that changes made to IIS do not have detrimental performance effects. This somewhat trial-and-error approach to performance tuning is the reason that IIS tuning is sometimes called an art.

Windows 2000 Optimizations

You can take a few steps to take advantage of some of the Windows 2000–specific optimizations. We also could have mentioned some of these suggestions with the IIS optimizations in the preceding section.

One of the easiest optimizations is to allow applications to run in medium protection mode, which is the default. This mode allows applications to share the same process, which cuts down on memory overhead and also offers more protection than the low protection, or in-process, mode.

Performing disk defragmentation periodically on Web servers is another easy Windows 2000 optimization. Defragmenting the disk helps minimize the number of disk reads necessary for a Web server to access files and directories.

Checking the event logs for service failures also can help increase performance because the IISRest utility often restarts applications without needing to be told. Overhead is involved, so identifying and preventing these service failures will result in better performance.

You should use SSL only when completely necessary. A great deal of overhead is associated with encrypting and decrypting every request made to a Web server, so you should limit the use of SSL to credit card processing pages and other highly sensitive areas of a Web site.

Networking Optimizations

You can make several optimizations at the networking layer to ensure optimal performance of a Web-based application. Three of the common, Internet server-related optimizations involve bandwidth throttling, HTTP Keep-Alives, and connection limits.

> **NOTE**
>
> An HTTP *Keep-Alive* connection is a connection that is not closed after a request-response exchange is complete.

Bandwidth throttling allows administrators to define how much network bandwidth the IIS service can consume. This can help ensure that plenty of network bandwidth is available for other pieces of a distributed application, such as a database server or application servers.

Enabling HTTP Keep-Alives tells IIS to keep a connection after a client's request is made. This same connection can be used for subsequent requests, thereby reducing the overhead associated with creating and destroying connections. Note, however, that this means more server resources will be tied up, but the client's perceived performance should be enhanced. The HTTP Keep-Alive feature is enabled by default in IIS 5.0. This feature keeps connections active and available for subsequent request. Note that the client *and* the server must support this feature for it to take effect. Internet Explorer 2.0 and later and Netscape Navigator 2.0 and later support HTTP Keep-Alives. IIS 1.0 and later support this feature on the server side.

You also can limit the number of client connections IIS serves. If you decide to let IIS make unlimited connections, it will do so until all server resources are maxed, which will result in poor performance.

All these IIS-specific network optimizations can be made via the IIS Properties sheet. Figure 19.5 shows the Web Site tab on which you can set the connection timeout and limit the number of connections.

FIGURE 19.5
Setting connection limits.

After you make any of the optimizations mentioned in this chapter, you need to monitor the site to ensure that the changes have the desired effect.

Logging in .NET

The .NET runtime provides access to the Windows 2000 event log system. This access eases your ability to record, audit, and troubleshoot problems and other events that occur during application execution. You can use four main Event Log events: application, system, security, and custom events.

The .NET runtime allows developers to create instances of the EventLog class to log events. The EventLog class also overloads the WriteEntry() method with static versions, so you can make entries without creating an instance of the EventLog class. The syntax looks like this:

```
EventLog.WriteEntry("Source goes here.", "A message goes here." ,
➥ EventLogEntryType.Information);
```

Figure 19.6 shows how the preceding code line would appear in the Event Viewer after it is executed.

FIGURE 19.6

An Application event log entry.

Alternatively, you can use an instance of the `EventLog` class to create Application and System type event entries. You can use an instance of the `EventLog` class to write to the System log like this:

```
EventLog el = new EventLog("System", "MachineName", "BogusSource");
el.WriteEntry("Test entry");
```

Writing to the Application log is the same except that you use `"Application"` as the first parameter.

Note that the Security log is read-only (unless the code runs as an Administrator role or the local system; you'll find more details on this topic in the next chapter). Therefore, substituting `"Security"` for `"System"` in the preceding example would result in a runtime error.

Creating Custom Events

Sometimes you need to create custom event logs. For instance, suppose you want to easily record and aggregate the errors that occur in a specific application. Rather than just write to the Application log, which could be more difficult to locate all errors that occurred in your application, you could create a custom event log. This way, tracking errors specific to your application would be as easy as looking in one spot. Listing 19.6 shows how to create and use a new event log.

LISTING 19.6   Creating a Custom Event Log

```
using System;
using System.Diagnostics;

class MyClass{
```

LISTING 19.6 Continued

```
public static void Main(){
    EventLog el = new EventLog("System", " MyMachine, "BogusSource");
    el.WriteEntry("Test entry");

    try{
        EventLog.CreateEventSource("MyApplication", "MyNewSource");
    }catch(System.ArgumentException ae){
        Console.WriteLine("Event source already exists." + ae.Message);
    }finally{
        el = new EventLog("MyApplication", " MyMachine", "NewBogusSource");
        el.WriteEntry("New test entry.");
    }
}
}
```

The MyClass.Main method shown in Listing 19.6 first creates a new instance of the EventLog class. It initializes the new class by passing in the name of the event log to use, along with the machine name and source of the event that is to be logged. The source can be a class name, method name, or anything else that would aid in diagnosing a problem.

Next, the CreateEventSource method attempts to create a new event source based on the application name and source name passed in. If an event source with the same name already exists, an exception is thrown.

In the `finally` section of the `try-catch-finally` block, another instance of the EventLog class is created using the new event source.

Summary

This chapter primarily focused on optimizing and debugging tactics, such as writing to the event log, monitoring with Performance Monitor, and using stress-testing tools, for the MyGolfGear.NET site. Specifically, regarding optimization, this chapter covered garbage collection; issues with using unmanaged code; differences in performance for value types versus reference types; the `StringBuilder` class; and a few operating system, IIS, and networking considerations.

With respect to debugging, this chapter covered profiling and other debugging services as well as stress testing and logging in .NET.

The next chapter will cover securing the MyGolfGear.NET site. It will cover some key concepts such as permissions, authorization, and authentication before moving on to role-based security, code-access security, and how ASP.NET security works.

Self Instruction

For a better understanding of how load testing tools work, try downloading the WAS tool from Microsoft and create a test script of your own. The WAS tool can be downloaded from `http://homer.rte.microsoft.com`.

Securing the Site

IN THIS CHAPTER

Objectives

- Learn about the basic concepts of security

- Explain the benefits of role-based and code access security

- Understand the many ways to encrypt data in the .NET Framework

- Learn about the available options for securing your ASP.NET site

Securing an Internet-based application is a complex and involved process that, for the most part, is beyond the scope of this book. This chapter does, however, discuss the available .NET security features and some of the techniques used to ensure the security of MyGolfGear.NET.

Specifically, this chapter will cover key .NET security concepts such as permission objects, authentication and authorization, type safety, and role-based security. In addition, it will discuss code access and role-based security as well as the security implications of COM+ interoperability, data encryption, and the ASP.NET security model.

Key Concepts

.NET security protects code from misuse and damage by other code by enforcing certain restrictions on managed code. Managed code can request the permissions it needs, and security policy (managed by an administrator) can determine whether to allow the code to run. The .NET Framework provides two types of security: code access and role-based.

Before we delve into the details of the .NET security model, it will be helpful to discuss some key concepts. At a high level, .NET security can be divided into five different areas: permissions, authentication and authorization, principal objects, type safety, and security policy.

Permissions

In a .NET application, managed code can do only what the Common Language Runtime (CLR) allows it to. In other words, the runtime allows managed code to perform the actions it has permission to. Permissions objects actually implement the enforcement of restrictions on managed code.

Three types of permissions exist: code-access, identity, and role-based permissions. Code-access permissions are used for performing protected operations or accessing protected resources.

The CLR provides several built-in permissions classes and also allows for the implementation of custom permissions. Following is a list of the available code-access permissions classes:

- DirectoryServicesPermission
- DnsPermission

- EnvironmentPermission
- EventLogPermission
- FileDialogPermission
- FileIOPermission
- IsolatedStorageFilePermission
- IsolatedStoragePermission
- MessageQueuePermission
- OleDbPermission
- PerformanceCounterPermission
- PrintingPermission
- ReflectionPermission
- RegistryPermission
- SecurityPermission
- ServiceControllerPermission
- SocketPermission
- SqlClientPermission
- UIPermission
- WebPermission

Each code-access permission object is fairly self-explanatory. Each represents permission to use the specified resource; for example, `FileIOPermission` specifies the actions that can be taken on a file or folder.

To create a custom code-access permissions class, you must create a class that inherits from `System.Security.CodeAccessPermissions`. Listing 20.1 shows a simple example of a custom `CodeAccessPermissions` class.

LISTING 20.1   Custom `CodeAccessPermissions` Class

```
using System;
using System.Security;
using System.Security.Permissions;

namespace MyCodeAccessPermissions
{

    class MyCodeAccessPermissions : CodeAccessPermission
    {
```

LISTING 20.1   Continued

```
//Creates and returns an identical copy
// of the current IPermission object
public override IPermission Copy()
{
    return new MyCodeAccessPermissions();
}

//Creates a security object from the given XML encoding
// provided.
public override void FromXml(SecurityElement el)
{
}

//Creates and returns an IPermission object that
// is the intersection of the current object
// and the IPermission object passed in.
public override IPermission Intersect(IPermission perm)
{
    return perm;
}

public override bool IsSubsetOf(IPermission perm)
{
    return true;
}

//Creates an XML encoding of
// the object and its current state.
public override SecurityElement ToXml()
{
    return new SecurityElement("MySecurityElement");
}

}
}
```

The code in Listing 20.1 shows an example of a simple custom CodeAccessPermissions class called MyCodeAccessPermissions. Although this class does not perform any useful work, it does implement all required methods to inherit from the CodeAccessPermissions class. Above each method is an explanation of what each should do.

Role-based security permissions are used to determine if a user has a particular identity or is a member of a particular group. The only role-based security permission object supplied by the

.NET runtime is `PrincipalPermission`. This object can be used to determine if a user has a specified identity or is a member of a given role. Listing 20.2 shows the syntax for using the `PrincipalPermission` object.

Listing 20.2   `PrincipalPermission` Object

```
using System;
using System.Security.Permissions;

class MyClass{

    public static void Main(){
        PrincipalPermission pp = new PrincipalPermission("Jason", "SiteAdmin");
        pp.Demand();

        //...
    }
}
```

NOTE

You can find the complete listing for the `PrincipalPermission.cs` file online.

In Listing 20.2, if the current principal does not match the user Jason in the SiteAdmin role, the code is not allowed to run. Calling `Demand()` in this manner determines whether the current principal matches the one specified.

Identity permissions indicate whether a particular piece of code has appropriate credentials. They allow security checks based on the identity of code via digital signature, URL, and so on. When developers use the `StrongNameIdentityPermissionAttribute` like this, they can demand during just-in-time (JIT) compilation that client code has `StrongNameIdentityPermission`:

```
[StrongNameIdentityPermissionAttribute(SecurityAction.LinkDemand,
PublicKey="00240000048000009400000006020000000...")]
```

This attribute is used with code that will execute only if a client has the corresponding private key.

Authentication and Authorization

Before any security measures can be applied, the identity of a user must be discovered and verified. In conjunction with identifying the user, the user's limits must be determined. In other words, the runtime needs to know who a user is and what that user is allowed to do. This is the crux of authentication and authorization.

Authentication is the process of verifying that a user is who he claims to be. This process involves comparing a user's credentials to some authoritative datastore. In .NET, this is the point at which role-based security can be used to determine whether a user should have access to a piece of managed code.

Developers can implement authentication in many ways. Some of them include Passport, basic, digest, NT LAN Manager (NTLM), and Kerberos. Many of these authentication mechanisms can be used with role-based security. The use of MS Passport is discussed later in this chapter.

Authorization is the process of deciding whether a user has the rights needed to perform a given task. This happens after authentication because it requires the user's identity and any associated roles in order to determine what actions the user can take. Authorization can be implemented with .NET role-based security.

Principal Objects

In the preceding discussion about authentication and authorization, I made reference to "users" multiple times, but security operations are typically more complicated than just user-based operations. The idea of a *principal* encapsulates the identity *and* role or roles of a user and can act in the interest of that user.

Three types of principals are supported by the .NET runtime: generic, Windows, and custom. If a principal exists independent of Windows users and roles, it is said to be *generic*. Developers can create generic principals by using the `GenericIdentity` and `GenericPrincipal` classes.

Using these classes would be useful if you need to "role your own" authentication and authorization schema. You could require users to present a username and password, verify them against a database, and then create your own identity and principal objects based on the values retrieved from the database.

To use the `GenericPrincipal` class, you must follow three steps. First, you need to create an `Identity` object. Second, you need to create an instance of the `GenericPrincipal` class and initialize it with the `Identity` object created in the first step. The last step is to attach the newly created `GenericPrincipal` object to the current thread. Listing 20.3 uses a generic principal, following these three steps.

LISTING 20.3 Using the `GenericPrincipal` Class

```
using System;
using System.Security.Principal;
using System.Threading;
```

LISTING 20.3   Continued

```csharp
public class Class1 {
    public static void Main(string[] args) {
        GenericIdentity oGenericIdentity = new GenericIdentity
➥("MyGenericIdentity");

        String[] aRoles = {"SiteAdmin", "Developer", "User"};
        GenericPrincipal oGenericPrincipal = new GenericPrincipal
➥(oGenericIdentity, aRoles);

        Thread.CurrentPrincipal = oGenericPrincipal;

        Console.WriteLine("Identity name is:   " +
➥oGenericPrincipal.Identity.Name);
        Console.WriteLine("IsAuthenticated is:   " +
➥oGenericPrincipal.Identity.IsAuthenticated);
        Console.WriteLine("IsInRole 'Developer':   " +
➥oGenericPrincipal.IsInRole("Developer"));
        Console.Write ("Type any key to continue.");
        int i = Console.Read();
    }
}
```

> **NOTE**
>
> You can find the complete listing for the GeneralPrincipal.cs file online.

The code in Listing 20.3 creates a GenericIdentity class that initializes the name value to "MyGenericIdentity". This is followed by the creation of a GenericPrincipal object that passes in the previously created Identity object and an array of the Identity's roles. Then the CurrentPrincipal property of the current Thread object is set to the newly created oGenericPrincipal object. When this is done, the principal object can be used. Figure 20.1 shows the output that results from executing the code in Listing 20.3.

If a principal does represent Windows users and roles, it is said to be a *Windows* principal and can impersonate other users and access resources on their behalf.

Developers can create applications that require all users to be validated against a Windows NT or Windows 2000 domain. You could use the WindowsPrincipal object to do this.

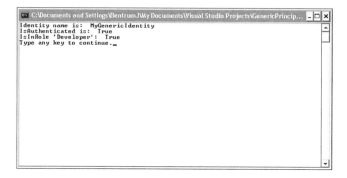

FIGURE 20.1
Results from executing the code in Listing 20.3.

You create and use the WindowsPrincipal object similarly to the way you create and use the GenericPrincipal object. One exception is that you don't need to attach it to the current thread. Listing 20.4 uses the WindowsPrincipal and WindowsIdentity objects.

LISTING 20.4   Using the WindowsPrincipal Class

```
using System;
using System.Threading;
using System.Security.Principal;
public class Class1 {

    public static void Main(string[] args) {
        WindowsPrincipal oWindowsPrincipal = new WindowsPrincipal(
➡WindowsIdentity.GetCurrent());
        Console.WriteLine(oWindowsPrincipal.Identity.Name);
        Console.WriteLine(oWindowsPrincipal.Identity.IsAuthenticated.
➡ToString());
        // Print out the current WindowsIdentity object's properties.
        Console.WriteLine(WindowsIdentity.GetCurrent().Name);
        Console.WriteLine(WindowsIdentity.GetCurrent().IsAuthenticated.
➡ToString());
        Console.WriteLine(WindowsIdentity.GetCurrent().IsAnonymous.ToString());
        Console.WriteLine(WindowsIdentity.GetCurrent().IsGuest.ToString());
        Console.WriteLine(WindowsIdentity.GetCurrent().IsSystem.ToString());
        Console.WriteLine(WindowsIdentity.GetCurrent().Token.ToString());
        int i = Console.Read();
    }
}
```

NOTE

You can find the complete listing for the `WindowsPrincipal.cs` file online.

Listing 20.4 shows how to create and use the `WindowsPrincipal` and `WindowsIdentity` objects. To get a reference to the current `WindowsIdentity` object, simply use the `WindowsIdentity`'s static method `GetCurrent()`.

Applications can extend the concept of principals in any way needed. When this is done, these applications are said to use *custom* principals. You can create custom principal objects by implementing the `IPrincipal` interface and any custom properties or methods necessary to achieve the desired behavior. Listing 20.5 shows an example of a custom principal class.

LISTING 20.5 Creating a Custom Principal Class

```
using System;
using System.Security;
using System.Security.Principal;

namespace CustomPrincipal
{
   class MyCustomPrincipal: IPrincipal {
      private IIdentity m_Identity;

      public MyCustomPrincipal(IIdentity oIdentity){
         m_Identity = oIdentity;
      }

      public bool IsInRole(String sRole){
         // look up role info here.
         return true;
      }

      public IIdentity Identity{
         get{
            return m_Identity;
         }
      }

   }
}
```

The code in Listing 20.5 shows a custom principal class called `MyCustomPrincipal`. Notice that to create a custom principal class, you have to implement only the `IPrincipal` interface, which consists of the `IsInRole()` method and an `Identity` property. If any other user information is needed for authorization purposes, it can be added to the class.

Type Safety

Type safety means that a managed class cannot access the memory of another managed class unless authorized to do so. In other words, type-safe code can access only the memory it has authorization to access.

This type safety means that components with different trust levels can operate in the same process without fear of being adversely affected by other code. Although type-safe code is not mandatory, the CLR can completely isolate assemblies from one another when necessary.

Security Policy

The CLR enforces configurable rules set by administrators; these rules decide what code should be allowed to do. So the CLR compares the code's credentials to the security policy to determine whether it should have access to a given requested resource.

Information, known as *evidence*, is examined at runtime to tell the security policy what permissions to grant to a given assembly. This evidence consists of the software publisher's signature, code's site of origin, code's zone of origin, strong name of the assembly, code's URL of origin, code's hash algorithm, application directory, and whether to skip a code's verification. Security policy grants every assembly that is loaded permissions based on the trust that is "earned" given the code's evidence.

Security permissions can be modified by calling permissions classes or by supplying security permissions attributes. You can apply security permissions attributes to a method to enable the calling of unmanaged code like this:

```
[SecurityPermission(SecurityAction.Deny, Flags =
➥SecurityPermissionFlag.UnmanagedCode)]
```

Because the `SecurityAction.Deny` value is used, the method that this attribute is applied to will not be able to call unmanaged code. You can achieve the same effect by creating a `SecurityPermission` object like this:

```
SecurityPermission perm = new SecurityPermission
➥(SecurityPermissionFlag.UnmanagedCode);
```

Calling `perm.Deny()` would then remove the method's capability to call unmanaged code.

So, when a security policy is in place, how exactly does it get enforced? Role-based security is one option. The next section deals entirely with implementing role-based security.

Role-Based Security

Internet applications such as MyGolfGear.NET sometimes need to provide access to certain functionality based on who the user is. Many applications handle this access from the role level rather than on a case-by-case basis. So, a user's role can be checked and resources can be shared based on the role of the user. The .NET CLR supports role-based security based on Windows accounts or custom identities.

Overview of Roles

Roles can be used to enforce policy or restrict functionality. For instance, MyGolfGear.NET could implement a role called SiteAdmin. Users who are members of this role would have the ability to add, remove, update, and delete categories, parts, users, and other application-related data.

The .NET CLR implements role-based security by making information about a principal available to a calling thread. Principal objects are created based on an identity object. An identity object can be based on a Windows account, or it can be custom constructed.

> **NOTE**
>
> *Principals* encapsulate the identity and roles of users and can act on their behalf.

A .NET application can authorize users based on their identity, their role in a membership group, or both. Principals can be members of multiple roles. This way, .NET applications can use the fact that a principal is a member of a particular role to grant or deny access to any given resource or requested action.

> **NOTE**
>
> A *role* is a specific group of users who have the same security rights. For example, the SiteAdmin group is a role.

Using Role-Based Security

An application can authenticate a user and provide role and identity information to the CLR. The runtime can then provide that information to code at runtime. The CLR can use APIs and permission demands to do so. Listing 20.6 shows how to use role-based security to determine whether the current user is in the SiteAdmin group.

LISTING 20.6   Role-Based Security

```
public bool IsSiteAdmin(){
  AppDomain.CurrentDomain.SetPrincipalPolicy
➥(PrincipalPolicy.WindowsPrincipal);
  WindowsPrincipal user = Thread.CurrentPrincipal as WindowsPrincipal;
  return user.IsInRole("SiteAdministrator");
}
```

Listing 20.6 shows a simple class that returns true if the current thread is executing as a user in the SiteAdministrator role. Because the default principal is unauthenticated, you need to tell the CLR to use Windows authentication. The WindowsPrincipal object returns true when the IsInRole method is called and the current principal is in the given role.

Alternatively, you can achieve the same effect by using the PrincipalPermission attribute, as shown in Listing 20.7.

LISTING 20.7   The PrincipalPermission Attribute

```
[PrincipalPermission(SecurityAction.Demand, Role="SiteAdministrator")]
public void DoSomethingProtected(){
  // Do something important...
}
```

Because the PrincipalPermission attribute is placed before the declaration of the DoSomethingProtected() method, the method will execute only if the current user is in the specified role (in this case the SiteAdministrator role).

COM+ Interoperability

The CLR enables you to integrate managed code with COM+ role-based security. This functionality is available with Windows 2000. Identity is based on a Windows NT token that is associated with executing code.

To enable the use of COM+ security, the CLR provides a wrapper class. This wrapper provides for easier access to the COM+ IsecurityContext.

Code-Access Security

Code-access security controls access to protected resources and operations, such as unmanaged code and file I/O. .NET code-access security performs many functions. For instance, .NET code-access security defines the permissions that allow access to system resources and enables administrators to manage and configure security policy.

Some of the most important functions .NET code-access security performs are allowing code to specify any permissions it requires to run and enabling code to demand which permissions its clients must have. It also compares a client's permissions to the permissions it must have and grants permission to loaded assemblies based on requested permissions and those set by the security policy.

So how does all this work? The CLR's security system walks the call stack and compares the permissions that have been granted to each client with the permissions being demanded by the code that is being called. Security exceptions are thrown if the client's permissions are not sufficient. This design prevents luring attacks.

> **NOTE**
>
> *Luring attacks* can occur when code with lesser permissions calls code with greater permissions and then uses the highly trusted code to perform illegal operations.

Why would a developer use code-access security? One common example is the case in which an application can download controls from a host Web site. In this scenario, an administrator could require any downloaded code to have a particular digital signature, and at runtime, the CLR's security system would determine whether the downloaded code could execute based on the existence of this digital signature.

Using Code-Access Security

Code-access security can be applied in two ways when using the .NET Framework. Developers can use *declarative* or *imperative* security calls to interact with the .NET runtime security system.

> **NOTE**
>
> *Declarative* security calls are those made by using attributes. *Imperative* security calls involve using instances of certain security classes within code.

Imperative security demands can be made by code to impose certain security restrictions on its access. When you create an object that represents the desired permissions and then call Demand(), code can ensure that any code that uses it meet the specified permissions. Listing 20.8 shows the skeleton of a simple custom code-access security class that could be used for imperative security syntax.

LISTING 20.8   A Custom Code-Access Security Class

```
class MyPermission : CodeAccessPermission{

    public override IPermission Copy(){
       return this;
    }

    public override IPermission Intersect (IPermission perm){
       return perm;
    }

    public override bool IsSubsetOf(IPermission perm){
       return true;
    }

    public override SecurityElement ToXml(){
       return new SecurityElement("<Foo>");
    }

    public override void FromXml(SecurityElement el){
    // Implementation goes here.
    }
    public override IPermission Union(IPermission perm){
       return perm;
    }
  }
}
```

NOTE

You can find the complete listing for the MyPermission.cs file online.

Listing 20.8 shows the skeleton of the simple code-access security class MyPermission. The stubbed-out methods are required to be overridden when creating a custom code-access security class by deriving from CodeAccessPermission. With the exception of the Copy() method, which simply returns a reference to the current class, none of the methods are really implemented. This example will compile, so it could be used for an imperative demand, as in Listing 20.9.

LISTING 20.9 An Imperative Demand Using `MyPermission` Class

```
public void Foo(){
        MyPermission myPerm = new MyPermission();
        myPerm.Demand();
        // do something interesting
}
```

Listing 20.9 shows how to use the `MyPermission` object to implement an imperative demand in the method `Foo()`. When you create an instance of a permission object and call its `Demand()` method in this manner, the CLR will determine at runtime whether all callers higher in the stack have been granted the permissions specified by the `MyPermission` object.

You could use declarative syntax to achieve the same result as the code in Listing 20.9. The difference is that declarative syntax uses attributes to place extra security information into the metadata of a piece of code. Imperative syntax can be used at the assembly, class, or method level. Listing 20.10 shows how to use declarative syntax to achieve the same result as Listing 20.9.

LISTING 20.10 Declarative Security Syntax

```
using System;
using System.Security;
using System.Security.Permissions;
using System.IO;
using System.IO.IsolatedStorage;

namespace MyDeclarativeSecurity
{
    class MyClass{
         static void Main(string[] args){
         Bar();
    }

    [FileIOPermission(SecurityAction.Demand)]
    public static void Bar(){
        IsolatedStorageFile isf =  IsolatedStorageFile.GetStore
➥(IsolatedStorageScope.User | IsolatedStorageScope.Assembly, null, null);
        StreamWriter sw = null;
```

20

LISTING 20.10 Continued

```
        sw = new StreamWriter(new IsolatedStorageFileStream("Bar.txt",
➥FileMode.CreateNew,isf));
        sw.WriteLine("Foo bar baz quirk.  Ipsum dolor sit amet.");
        sw.Close();
    }
  }// End of class
}// End of Namespace
```

> **NOTE**
>
> You can find the complete listing for the `MyDeclarativeSecurity.cs` file online.

The code in Listing 20.10 uses declarative syntax to ensure the appropriate permissions are available when the `Bar()` method is called. Using the `FileIOPermission` attribute with the `SecurityAction.Demand` constructor parameter ensures that all callers higher in the call stack have the appropriate permission to write to isolated storage; otherwise, the CLR will throw an exception.

Encrypting Data

The .NET runtime offers a complete set of cryptographic services via the `System.Security.Cryptography` namespace. This namespace allows secure encoding, decoding, hashing, random number generation, and a number of other functionalities.

Two main types of cryptographic algorithms are available in .NET: *symmetric* and *asymmetric*. Symmetric algorithms use one secret key to encrypt and decrypt data, whereas asymmetric algorithms use two keys, one private and one public. Asymmetric algorithms are also called *public-key* algorithms. To create a new public-key algorithm, you need to inherit from AsymmetricAlgorithm. The private key is kept secret by the receiver, and the public key is kept (and made public) by the sender (and encrypter) of the data.

The `HashAlgorithm`, hashing, is an essential part of today's cryptography. It is composed of hash functions that map binary strings of some unknown length to smaller binary strings of a set length, which are known has *hash values*. It is almost impossible to find two different values that would hash to the same value. Hash algorithms are widely used for data integrity and digital signatures.

At the core of the CLR's cryptography design is the `CryptoStream` object. This is important because objects that implement the `CryptoStream` class can stream encrypted data from one object to another. The `HashAlgorithm` is an example of a class that implements `CryptoStream`.

ASP.NET Security

From a security perspective, an online store such as MyGolfGear.NET is similar to a real-world store in many respects. Think about your local supermarket for a minute. Anyone can enter the store, browse for merchandise, place items in a shopping cart, and the local supermarket will certainly take anyone's money. However, access to inventory data, financial resources, and the ability to add or remove products from the shelves is restricted to a few groups of store employees.

An online store needs to protect sensitive information—for example, a user's billing information and catalog inventory data. Fortunately, the ASP.NET security features help address these concerns and many others.

ASP.NET and Internet Information Services (IIS) can authenticate users via basic, digest, NTLM or Kerberos (Windows Authentication), Passport, or Forms authentication.

Access to site information in ASP.NET can be controlled in two ways. One way is to authenticate users against the NT File System permissions, and the other is to authenticate them against an XML file that specifies authorized users and roles.

How ASP.NET Security Works

Internet application security with ASP.NET involves performing three main actions: authentication, authorization, and impersonation. As previously discussed, authentication is the process of ensuring that a user is who she claims to be, and authorization is the act of granting or denying permission to access a given resource. *Impersonation* is the act of giving an application a user's identity when a request is made via IIS. In this case, access can be granted or denied based on the assumed identity.

ASP.NET Security Architecture

All Web-based clients access ASP.NET applications through IIS. It is IIS that authenticates and, if appropriate, finds and returns the requested item or items. Figure 20.2 shows what this architecture looks like conceptually.

As Figure 20.2 suggests, ASP.NET applications can use ASP.NET security features or lower-level CLR security features (such as code access, which was discussed earlier).

As I said earlier, site access can be controlled via authentication against the NT File System permissions or against an XML file. The NT File System's Permissions method is nothing new, so I won't spend much time covering it. The XML-based authentication is of significant interest, however.

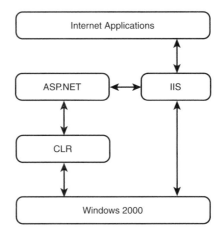

Figure 20.2
ASP.NET security architecture.

Configuration data for ASP.NET applications is kept in XML files named `web.config`. These configuration files are the basis of the ASP.NET hierarchical configuration architecture and are stored in an application's root directory. All directories under the directory that contains the `web.config` file will inherit the same configuration data unless overridden by providing another `web.config` file for that directory.

The security section of a `web.config` file is broken down into the three main action categories: authentication, authorization, and identity. Listing 20.11 shows the default configuration of the `machine.config` file.

Listing 20.11   Default `machine.config` File

```
<!-- security -->
        <authentication mode="Windows">
                            <!-- mode="[Windows, Forms, Passport, None]" -->

            <forms name=".ASPXAUTH" loginUrl="login.aspx" protection="all"
➥timeout="30" path="/" >
                    <!-- protection="[All|None|Encryption|Validation]"   -->
                <credentials passwordFormat="SHA1"> <!-- passwordFormat=
➥"[Clear, SHA1, MD5] -->
                    <!-- <user name="UserName" password="password"/> -->
                </credentials>

            </forms>
            <passport redirectUrl="internal" />
```

LISTING 20.11 Continued

```
        <!-- Specify the page to redirect to, if the page requires
          authentication, and the user has not signed on with passport -->

    </authentication>

    <identity impersonate="false" />

    <authorization>
        <allow users="*" /> <!-- Allow all users -->

            <!--  <allow     users="[comma separated list of users]"
                             roles="[comma separated list of roles]"/>
                  <deny      users="[comma separated list of users]"
                             roles="[comma separated list of roles]"/>
            -->
    </authorization>
```

> **NOTE**
>
> The machine.config file is the highest level at which configuration changes can be
> made. It is located in the Winnt\Microsoft.NET\Framework\buildnumber\config
> directory.

The values for each of the above sections are typically overridden at the application level in a
web.config file.

Authentication

Authentication is the process of collecting a username and password (or other identification
credentials) from a user and validating that information against an "authority." Assuming the
credentials supplied are valid, the user is granted an authenticated status.

ASP.NET authentication is implemented through three types of providers: Windows, Passport,
and Forms. Windows authentication works with IIS to perform authentication by using either
basic, digest, or Integrated Windows Authentication. ASP.NET can use the authenticated identity to authorize access.

The WindowsAuthenticationModule can be used to implement site security with a minimum
amount of coding because the WindowsAuthenticationModule constructs an Identity object

and a `Principal` object and attaches them to the application context. This `WindowsPrincipal` object can map identities to Windows groups.

Mapping identities to Windows groups could be useful if an impersonation schema is needed. To use such a schema, simply set the `mode` attribute of the authentication element to `"Windows"` and the `impersonate` attribute of the identity element to `"true"` in the application's `web.config` file.

Passport, a centralized authentication service provided by Microsoft, provides profiling services with a single sign-in point. It is a cookie-based authentication schema that works in the following way. If a client requests a protected resource and does not have a valid passport cookie, the user is redirected to the Passport login service. An encrypted version of the original request URL is passed along as well, and when the client logs in with the Passport service and is authenticated, the user is issued a cookie and redirected to the originally requested URL.

Forms authentication is usually used for home-grown authentication schemas. The flow of events for Forms authentication is similar to Passport. In this scenario, a user requests a protected resource, and if a cookie with the appropriate identification is not present, the client is redirected to a simple login form. When the application authenticates the user, he is issued a cookie and redirected to the original URL.

Authorization

Authorization is the process of determining whether a user should gain access to a given resource. File authorization or URL authorization can be used with ASP.NET.

File authorization is used in conjunction with Windows authentication. The `FileAuthorizationModule` class performs an ACL check to determine whether a given user should have access to a requested resource.

URL authorization is performed by the `URLAuthorizationModule` class. This class maps users and roles to a given URI namespace and can be used with either positive or negative assertions. In other words, it can be used to allow or deny users and/or groups to any given resource.

When you place the `<allow users="*" />` tag inside the `authorization` tags of a given `web.config` file, all users will be allowed. Likewise, a list of users and/or roles could be allowed or denied if you specify a comma-separated list like this:

```
<authorization>
  <allow users="Jason, James, Michael"/>
  <deny  users="Bob, Barry, David"/>
</authorization>
```

Placing this code in the `web.config` file of any ASP.NET directory would allow authenticated users Jason, James, and Michael to access, while denying access to everything in the current directory and below to Bob, Barry, and David.

Impersonation

ASP.NET supports impersonation, so an ASP.NET application can execute code on the behalf of someone else. If impersonation is enabled, IIS will pass a token to the ASP.NET application after authentication. From then on, the application will access resources based on the identity of the impersonation, and authentication will take place as normal.

Summary

This chapter covered security from the perspective of using the .NET built-in features and some of the techniques used in building MyGolfGear.NET. It also covered key concepts such as authentication and authorization, role-based and code-access security, and ASP.NET security. In addition, it discussed some of the data encryption capabilities of .NET.

The next chapter will cover deployment. Specifically, it will cover a high-level discussion of server farms, Application Center, and file copy deployment; it also will cover packaging a site to be hosted externally and moving databases.

Self Instruction

The best way to get a better understanding of these different types and methods of security in the .NET Framework is to implement them. Give all three types of authentication methods in ASP.NET a try. Take the `web.config` file and change its authentication mode to use `WindowsAuthenticationModule`. Then, after you see how this mode works, try Forms Authentication, which is used by MyGolfGear.NET. Finally, try using Microsoft's Passport for a more centralized authentication service.

Deploying the Site

IN THIS CHAPTER

Objectives

- Understand, from a high level, what Application Center 2000 is and how it can be used to deploy and monitor a Web site

- Learn what a Web farm is

- Explore other Web site content deployment options

- Learn about deploying a database, including the movement of database data and associated objects

After you code and test an Internet application, you need to move it to an environment its intended users will have access to. This step is often easier said than done.

In the COM+ world, moving an application involved copying ASP, HTML, JavaScript, images, and other user interface elements to the presentation tier server or servers and then copying Distributed Component Object Model (DCOM) DLLs to the business tier servers and configuring them to run remotely, configuring Universal Data Links (UDLs) and/or Data Source Names (DSNs), and then moving any database objects to the data tier server.

Even though a few tools were available to make this task easier (such as the Microsoft Site Server Publish tool), these tools were awkward and moved files only from server to server. These tools did nothing for configuring or setting up the application, and if COM components already existed on a server, things were even worse. The old components often had to be unregistered and then deleted before the new ones could be moved successfully.

This Content Replication System (CRS) could handle tasks such as creating Registry entries, creating ODBC entries, and configuring COM+ applications only by writing custom scripts that would run before or after the content was replicated. The more complicated an application got, the more complicated and error prone these CRS scripts became. Clearly, we needed a better solution.

Microsoft Application Center 2000 greatly simplifies the deployment of .NET (and COM+) applications. Application Center allows IIS Metabase settings, COM+ applications, Registry entries, ODBC entries, as well as application files to be replicated easily and accurately.

A large portion of this chapter is devoted to Application Center 2000 because I feel it is going to play a critical part in the deployment and management of .NET Web farms. However, this chapter also covers some fundamentals, such as deploying file copies and packaging an application to be hosted externally, as well as using Web server farms and moving databases.

A Few Words About Server Farms

As traffic on a Web site grows or the number of a particular Web-based application's users grows, the only way to handle the load is to increase the number of machines servicing the application or Web site or to increase the power of the existing machines.

Often it is not feasible to *scale up* (increase the number or clock speed of the processors in existing servers) when the machine resources in a server farm are taxed beyond the point they are able to process incoming requests. The price or even the availability of faster processors can be limiting factors, as can the hardware's capability to accept more or different components. In other words, existing motherboards may not be able to accept more or faster chips or memory. Therefore, it is often more feasible to *scale out*, which means adding more servers to a Web farm. When administrators choose to scale out an application, they create *Web server farms*.

> **NOTE**
>
> *Web server farms* are a group of independent servers that act as a unit and share the load, thereby creating the illusion of one giant server.

Although scaling out may provide a cost-effective means of increasing an Internet-based application's or Web site's capability to serve content and perform, doing so can seriously complicate its deployment and maintenance. A typical Web farm has two or more Web servers, two or more application servers, and two or more database servers. Large Web farms could have as many as 50 or more Web servers, 10 application servers, and 4 or more database servers. Figure 21.1 shows a schematic of such a Web farm to help you put things in perspective.

As Figure 21.1 suggests, deploying a complicated Web application is further complicated when you have to deploy to a large and complicated environment. Two things will make your life easier if you're a .NET developer: Application Center 2000 and the inherently easy nature with which you can deploy .NET applications.

> **NOTE**
>
> Web farm servers often come in pairs. The reason for this is redundancy and fail-over. For example, if one of the two Web servers fails, the other can continue to serve the Web site's needs so that the users' experience is not interrupted.

The next section will cover some of the many benefits of using Application Center 2000 to deploy Web-based applications.

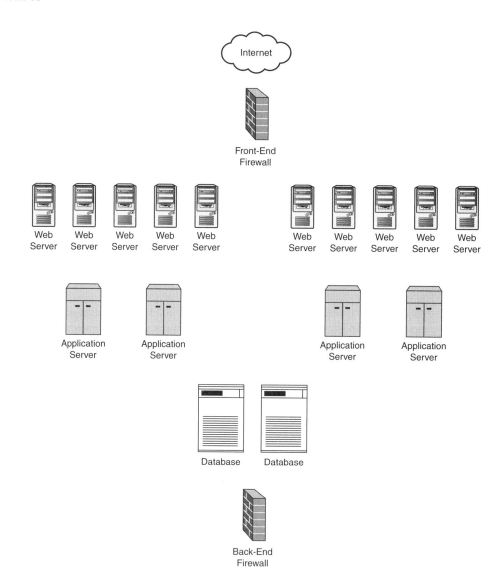

FIGURE 21.1

A large Web farm.

Application Center

Application Center 2000 is a robust and feature-rich application used to ease deployment and maintenance of large-scale Web applications. A great deal has been written about Application Center, so this section will provide only a high-level overview of the product and focus on a couple of the features that are useful for deployment.

> ## Deploying and Managing .NET Web Farms
>
> Deploying and managing large .NET Web applications can be very complicated. A single chapter in this book cannot possibly do justice to the subject. For a more comprehensive look at managing and deploying .NET applications, see Barry Bloom's excellent book *Deploying and Managing .NET Web Farms* (ISBN: 0672320576) from Sams Publishing.

Application Center was designed to manage clusters of servers. In Application Center terms, a *cluster* is a set of servers that offer the same content to clients. This content could be Web pages or COM+ applications. To manage clusters, Application Center offers the following services:

- Clustering
- Load balancing
- Monitoring
- Synchronization and deployment

Application Center Clustering

Application Center's clustering services can be broken down into three types of clusters. The first is the General or Web-Tier Cluster. A General Cluster uses one or more servers to process client requests. It is the most widely used cluster for .NET developers.

Another type of Application Center cluster is the COM+ Application Cluster. This type of cluster exists solely to handling COM+ application requests. COM+ application clusters can load balance calls to COM+ components across multiple application servers.

The other type of Application Center cluster is the COM+ Routing Cluster. Although rarely used, this type of cluster can route requests from a General Cluster to a COM+ Application Cluster.

Load Balancing

Load balancing is a term used to describe the distribution of work across members in a cluster. Application Center supports two main types of load balancing, although it can be used in conjunction with other load balancing mechanisms. Application Center's built-in load balancing consists of Network Load Balancing (NLB) and Component Load Balancing (CLB).

Windows 2000 Advanced Server and Windows 2000 Data Center include NLB. Application Center also includes NLB so that Windows 2000 Server can support it.

NLB is an IP-load balancing technology that allows Transmission Control Protocol (TCP), User Datagram Protocol (UDP), and Generic Routing Encapsulation (GRE) requests to be balanced between members of a cluster.

CLB, which is included as part of Application Center, allows for the load-balanced activation of COM+ components. CLB can do so because of the location-transparent nature of COM+ components.

Application Center's Built-In Monitoring

Application Center provides a robust set of monitoring features that allows administrators to monitor and detect cluster performance and availability issues before they become a major problem.

Each member of a cluster stores event and performance data in an *MSDE* database. From here, performance data can be rolled up for each of the cluster members and viewed in a consolidated form, or each member's data can be viewed independently. This data can be viewed in real-time or from a historical perspective in increments of 15 minutes, 2 hours, 1 day, 1 week, or 3 months.

> **NOTE**
>
> *MSDE* is the SQL Server 2000 runtime environment packaged for deployment to the desktop. MSDE can be used on a local server just like SQL Server can. For example, you can use tables, stored procedures, views, and other SQL Server objects you are already familiar with.
>
> You are probably asking yourself whether you can use MSDE instead of SQL Server for all your applications. The answer is probably not. MSDE falls short of SQL Server in many ways. For example, MSDE supports only 2GB worth of data and lacks support for symmetrical multiprocessing.
>
> MSDE was actually designed to replace the Access data engine for use by small workgroups. It is ideal for local data access where using a distributed data store would degrade performance.

Additionally, Health Monitor 2.1 is bundled with Application Center 2000. It allows administrators to set thresholds on event logs, service failures, and HTTP calls, for example. This functionality can be used to alert the necessary resources so that potential problems can be quashed before they get out of hand.

Synchronization and Deployment

As far as this chapter goes, the most compelling feature of Application Center 2000 is its synchronization and deployment functionality. A single object or "image" is used to represent a single application and all its required files, components, and settings.

In Application Center terms, *deployment* is the act of moving an application object from one cluster to another. In most environments, this process involves moving an application from a testing or staging environment to the production environment, where real users will have access to the application. During this phase, the *cluster controller* receives the new content and is responsible for synchronization.

> **NOTE**
>
> A *cluster controller* is responsible for synchronizing its content to all the members of a cluster. It is the member that maintains the most up-to-date content.

In this scenario, if new content is received during the deployment of a new or updated application, the cluster controller automatically synchronizes each member with the new or updated content. Optionally, an administrator or Webmaster may choose to perform synchronization manually. Manual, or on-demand, synchronizations can be used to update the entire cluster, a subset of the entire cluster, or individual cluster members. This type of synchronization might be useful when you're adding additional servers to a cluster. Rather than synchronize the entire cluster, you can target the new members, thus saving time and resources.

To manually synchronize a cluster, right-click the cluster controller in the Application Center MMC snap-in and select the Synchronize Cluster option from the context menu, as shown in Figure 21.2.

FIGURE 21.2
The Synchronize Cluster option.

File Copy Deployment

File copy deployment is made possible thanks to the .NET Framework. Because applications built using the .NET Framework are self-contained and don't rely on Registry entries or other dependencies, you can deploy them from one environment to another by simply copying the necessary files.

File copy deployment allows multiple versions of an application to run side-by-side without interfering with one another. The .NET runtime also allows applications to be updated without being shut down so that clients of current components don't have to experience an interruption while code is updated.

Configuration data, such as how and which database to connect to, can be stored in .xml files known as *Config files*. For example, Web sites all have a Web.config file associated with them. This means that you no longer need to store database connectivity information in a DSN.

You have a few options when it comes to how you want to package a .NET application for deployment. You can create a single assembly or a collection of assemblies using the DLLs and/or EXEs as they were built. You can choose to create CAB files, which means all the necessary application files are compressed (using these files can make distribution faster). You may also choose to create an installer program via the Windows Installer (this creates .MSI files) or some other installer such as Install Shield. I will describe some of the packaging options in the next section, "Packaging a Site to Be Hosted Externally."

When the application files are packaged, the application can be file copy deployed in several ways. The most obvious way is simply to use the XCOPY command or FTP. Thanks to the self-describing nature of .NET applications, they can simply be copied to the appropriate directory of each target machine and run.

NOTE

Using Application Center, as described in the previous section, is really just a fancy way of deploying using XCOPY.

Bear in mind that a client can also download code. In this scenario, a client that requests an application can automatically have the application downloaded to its machine. This is usually appropriate for distribution on an intranet or extranet, where the client already knows who the application is coming from. This scenario may also be necessary if custom Forms Controls need to be downloaded for a particular application.

If an application needs to repair an installation of the .NET Framework on a target machine or update the global assembly cache or other private folders, an .MSI file or other distribution package might be appropriate.

Packaging a Site to Be Hosted Externally

Not all developers deploy .NET Web applications in a corporate environment. Applications may be co-located on rented server space or some other offsite location. In these cases, it is unlikely that Application Center 2000 will be available for deployment.

As a developer, you have a few options when it comes to these scenarios. For simple .NET applications, files can simply be copied to an appropriate directory via FTP, as mentioned before. For more complicated applications, a packaged deployment might be the best way to go.

If an application needs to be packaged for deployment, you have a few options. You can use a third-party installation program such as Install Shield. Windows Installer can be downloaded as part of the Platform SDK from the MSDN site. Optionally, if you have access to it, you can use Visual Studio .NET, which offers various packaging and setup projects to help ease the deployment of complex applications. Figure 21.3 shows Visual Studio .NET and the setup projects that are available.

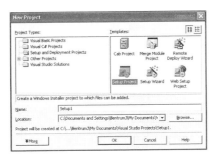

FIGURE 21.3
Visual Studio .NET setup and deployment projects.

Creating a Windows Installer .MSI file for a Web application by using Visual Studio .NET is easy. First, select New, Project from the File menu. A dialog then prompts you for an application type (see Figure 21.4). Click the Setup and Deployment Projects folder in the Project Types list box and click the Setup Wizard icon in the Templates list box.

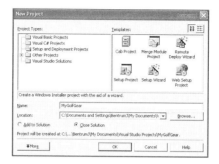

FIGURE 21.4
Visual Studio .NET New Project dialog.

After you choose a location for your Setup application and click OK, the Setup Wizard takes you through the following four steps:

- A typical Welcome screen
- The Choose a Project Type screen
- The Choose Files to Include screen
- A Create Project summary screen

As you can see, the wizard really has only two steps. The first one involves choosing the project type. The options for this step include creating a setup for a Windows application, a Web application, a *merge module* for Windows Installer, or creating a downloadable CAB file. Figure 21.5 shows this step.

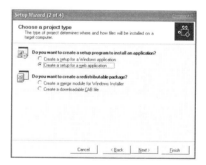

FIGURE 21.5
The Choose a Project Type screen.

NOTE

A *merge module* is a feature of the MSI Installer that allows the delivery of updates and additions to an existing `.MSI` file. Merge modules cannot be delivered alone, but are an excellent way to deliver additional versions or updates to your existing applications without your having to completely rebuild the installation project.

For this example, I chose the Create a Setup for a Web Application option.

On the Choose Files to Include screen, you can add additional files to the installation. This step is appropriate for including any Readme file or other documentation that needs to go along with the application. Figure 21.6 shows this step.

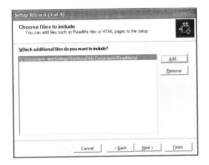

FIGURE 21.6
The Choose Files to Include screen.

On this screen, you can click the Add button to open a standard File Open dialog titled Add Files. Simply browse to any files you want to include and click the Open button.

The last screen is simply a summary that shows the type of project created, any project groups that were included, any additional files included (Readme files and so on), and the Project directory. Figure 21.7 shows this screen.

When you're finished, choose the File System Editor. From here, you can add all the necessary files by right-clicking the Web Application Folder icon and choosing Add, File from the context menu. You can add the entire directory structure for an application in this manner. Components and new folders can be added in this way, too. Figure 21.8 shows Component Selector dialog that you can use to include .NET components.

After a component is added to a setup project, the Visual Studio .NET setup project automatically includes any dependencies. Figure 21.9 shows the dependencies added to my sample setup project.

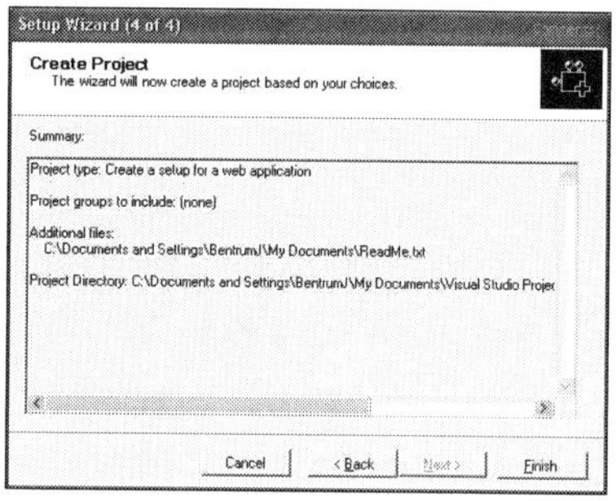

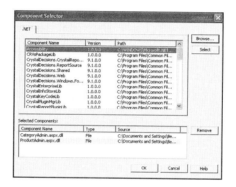

FIGURE 21.7

The Create Project summary screen.

FIGURE 21.8

The Component Selector.

After you add all the necessary files to the setup project, simply press Ctrl+Shift+B to build the project. Visual Studio creates an .MSI file that can then be used to deploy the application.

At this point, you could FTP the .MSI file to a directory and launch it remotely using pcAnywhere or Terminal Services client. Doing so would allow the deployer to walk through a standard installation wizard. The only thing left to do would be to move the database objects and any needed data.

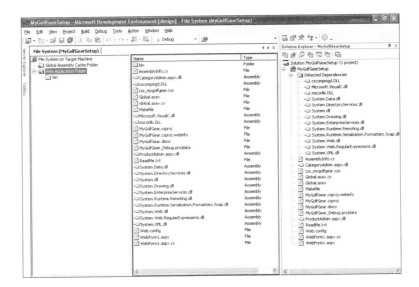

FIGURE 21.9
Detected dependencies.

Moving the Database

After the application code is deployed to the target machines, a copy of the database needs to be moved for the application to function properly. You can copy data between SQL Servers in several ways. You can back up the source database and restore it on the new server, use the Copy Database Wizard, use the Data Transformation Services (DTS) Import/Export Wizard, use the Bulk Copy Program (BCP), or use the INSERT command along with a distributed query to select data from another source. For our scenario, two methods make sense: the backup and restore method and the DTS Import/Export Wizard.

Backing Up and Restoring Databases

Three general steps are involved in copying a database via the backup and restore method:

- Backing up the source database
- Creating backup devices on the source (optional; not covered here)
- Restoring the database on the destination computer

> **NOTE**
>
> A *device* is a logical or physical entity for data in a database to be backed up to.
>
> A *physical backup device* is the name used by the operating system to specify the location of the backup—for example, C:\Backups\MyGolfGear.bak.
>
> A *logical device* is an alias for a physical device that is stored in a system table within SQL Server.

Creating a Database Backup

You can use the BACKUP DATABASE statement to back up a database. By simply specifying the name of the database to be backed up and the device to write the backup to, you can back up an entire database. Listing 21.1 shows how to back up the Pubs database.

LISTING 21.1   Backing Up the Pubs Database

```
BACKUP DATABASE pubs
TO DISK='C:\temp\PubsBackup.dat'
```

Alternatively, you can use the TO TAPE clause to back up the database to a specified tape device. Listing 21.2 shows the syntax for backing up to tape.

LISTING 21.2   Backing Up to Tape

```
BACKUP DATABASE pubs
TO TAPE='\\.\TAPE0'
```

When you use the BACKUP DATABASE command, two important statements can affect how the database is backed up. Using the INIT clause causes the backup to overwrite the backup media. You can use the FORMAT clause when using media for the first time. This clause initializes the media and rewrites any existing media header.

> **CAUTION**
>
> The FORMAT and INIT clauses destroy all backups on the backup media.

After you back up the database, you can restore it on another server. At this point, you could create backup devices on the source, but this step is optional.

Restoring the Database

Restoring a database from a backup re-creates the backed-up database and all its associated files. Any incomplete transactions are automatically rolled back to ensure consistency.

You can restore databases by using the RESTORE DATABASE command. Listing 21.3 shows the syntax for restoring the Pubs database.

LISTING 21.3   Restoring the Pubs Database

```
RESTORE DATABASE pubs
FROM DISK='C:\temp\PubsBackup.dat'
```

The syntax for restoring a database is remarkably similar to that of backing one up. Simply specify the name of the database to back up and the source of the backup. As with the BACKUP command, the backup device can be either a tape or disk.

Using the DTS Import/Export Wizard

Another common way to move an entire database is to use the DTS Import/Export Wizard. This wizard walks you through the following steps:

- Opening a typical wizard welcome screen
- Specifying the data source
- Specifying the destination (and allowing for the creation of a new database)
- Specifying whether to copy tables and views, objects and data, or using a query to specify the data to move
- Specifying the specific objects to copy, whether to replace or append existing data, and whether to create new objects on the destination server
- Specifying when and how to run the replication
- Viewing a typical wizard summary screen

For example, you could use the DTS Import/Export Wizard to copy the Northwind database. Say your computer is not part of a network right now, so you can simply make a copy of the database on your local machine.

First, you start the wizard by right-clicking the Databases folder on your local SQL Server instance in SQL Server Enterprise Manger and selecting All Tasks, Export Data (see Figure 21.10). Selecting these options launches the wizard and displays a typical wizard welcome screen describing what the wizard does.

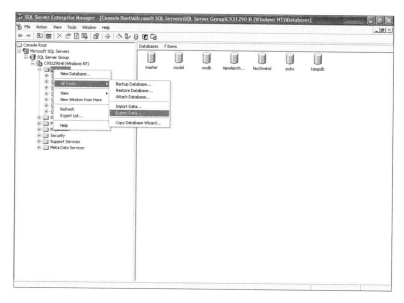

FIGURE 21.10

Starting the DTS Import/Export Wizard.

Clicking the Next button opens the Choose a Data Source screen (see Figure 21.11). From here, you can choose the database server name from a drop-down box or type it in. You can also specify what form of authentication to use (Windows or Mixed), specifying a username and password if Mixed mode is to be used. Last, you can pick the database from which you want to copy.

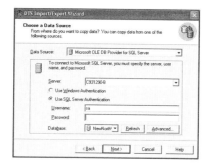

FIGURE 21.11

Choosing a data source.

The next step is specifying the destination. The Choose a Destination screen, shown in Figure 21.12, is similar to the Choose a Data Source screen, except for one thing. The drop-down menu used to specify the database has the option <new>, which allows you to create a new database (given the right authorization).

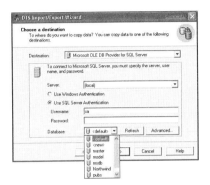

FIGURE 21.12

Choosing a destination.

Selecting the <new> option brings up the Create Database dialog in which you can specify a name for the new database as well as the default data and log file sizes. Figure 21.13 shows this dialog.

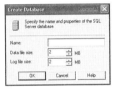

FIGURE 21.13

The Create Database dialog.

Clicking Next takes you to the Specify Table Copy or Query screen (see Figure 21.14). Here, you can specify whether to copy just tables and views, create a query to move the data, or copy objects and data between servers. For this example, I chose the Copy Objects and Data Between SQL Server Databases option.

Choosing the Copy Objects and Data Between SQL Server Databases option opens the Select Objects to Copy screen (see Figure 21.15). On this screen, you can specify whether database objects should be created, existing objects should be dropped, and whether you want to include dependent objects. In addition, you can specify whether the data should be appended or replaced as well as specify whether you want to copy all objects or specify specific ones.

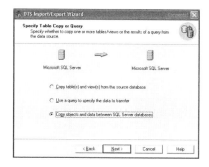

FIGURE 21.14

The Specify Table Copy or Query screen.

FIGURE 21.15

The Select Objects to Copy screen.

For this example, I accepted the default options and clicked the Next button. On the next screen, titled Save, Schedule, and Replicate Package, you can specify when and how the data and objects are to be moved (see Figure 21.16). Specifying Run Immediately, as I did, makes the database move occur at the completion of the wizard. If you select the Use Replication to Publish Destination Data, you use SQL Server's replication features to move the data. This screen also allows you to save the DTS package for later use as well as schedule a saved package for later execution.

Here, I accepted the default option, Run Immediately, and clicked the Next button. Clicking this button takes you to the summary screen, which lists all the options selected through the course of the wizard. Because I chose to run the DTS package immediately, clicking the Finish button starts the copying process.

When the DTS package is launched, the Executing Package dialog is displayed (see Figure 21.17). This dialog displays the progress and status of each step in the DTS package and alerts you when the copy is complete.

FIGURE 21.16
The Save, Schedule, and Replicate Package screen.

FIGURE 21.17
The Executing Package dialog.

When the Executing Package dialog's progress indicator reaches 100%, a message box is displayed, informing you that the process is complete. Clicking the Done button on the dialog completes the process and the data is moved.

Summary

This chapter began with a brief discussion about Web server farms and then presented a high-level overview of Application Center 2000. It also covered some fundamentals such as using file copy deployment to move a .NET application and packaging a .NET Web site to be hosted externally. Finally, it discussed the steps required to move a SQL Server database to deploy an application.

Following this chapter is a set of appendixes I thought would be useful if you're a .NET developer creating a B2C e-Commerce site. These appendixes include a C# language reference, a VB.NET language reference, an ASP.NET object model, and an ADO.NET quick reference.

Self Instruction

Based on what you've learned in this chapter, download some of the code examples from some of the other chapters and create a setup project. You should be able to follow the same steps outlined in the section titled "Packaging a Site to Be Hosted Externally."

Appendixes

PART
V

IN THIS PART

C# Language Reference

This appendix provides a brief overview of the language features available in the new Microsoft C# language and covers the features most likely to be used in this book. However, C# is a feature-rich and complicated language and can't be fully covered in an appendix.

> **NOTE**
>
> You can find the code listings for this appendix online.

Data Types

C# supports two kinds of data types: Value and Reference.

Value Types

Value types in C# are made up of either a struct or an enumeration. Simple types are provided as a set of predefined structs subdivided into integral, numeric, and floating-point types.

Value types are *sealed* and are derived indirectly from the base class `Object`. A type is sealed if it can't be inherited from. Using the `sealed` modifier prevents a class from being inherited from.

Variables of value types can't contain a `null` value and must contain a value of the same type. In other words, a variable of type `byte` can't contain a floating-point value.

Struct Types

In C#, the `struct` keyword declares value types that are either stack allocated or allocated inline. Later in this appendix, the `class` keyword is used to declare reference types, which are heap allocated.

Simple Types

C# provides simple types in a set of predefined structs. Reserved keywords identify these simple types. These reserved keywords are actually aliases for the struct types in the `System` namespace. Table A.1 shows the keyword, runtime alias, and size of some of the more common simple types.

Using the keyword `float` is exactly the same as using `System.Single` to declare a float variable.

Because these simple types are aliases for structs that inherit from `Object`, they have access to member properties and methods. For instance, every type that inherits from `Object` has a `ToString()` method. So, the syntax in Listing A.1 is valid.

Table A.1   Simple Types

Keyword	Alias	Size (in Bytes)
byte	Byte	1
short	Int16	2
int	Int32	4
long	Int64	8
char	Char	2
float	Single	4
double	Double	8
bool	Boolean	1
decimal	Decimal	8

Listing A.1   Simple Types

```
int myInteger = 123;
String myString = myInteger.ToString();
myString = 456.ToString();
```

Enums

Enumerators can declare a related set of constants. Listing A.2 shows an example of a simple enumerator. Enumerators are covered in greater depth later in the section "Enumerators."

Listing A.2   The *Nonsense* Enumerator

```
enum Nonsense{
    foo,
    bar,
    baz,
    quirk
}
```

Reference Types

As previously mentioned, C# uses the `class` keyword for reference types but also supports arrays, interfaces, and delegates (each of which is covered in greater detail later in this appendix).

The value of a reference type is a reference to an instance of that type (also known as an object). A `null` value is used when no instance exists.

Boxing

C# enables you to treat *any* type as an object in a process known as *boxing*. To achieve this effect, a wrapper object is allocated to the heap, and the value type's value is copied to it. Reversing this process is known as *unboxing*. Listing A.3 shows a simple boxing example.

LISTING A.3   Simple Boxing Example

```
using System;
public class SimpleBoxingExample{
    public static int Main(){
        Console.WriteLine(1000.ToString());
        return 1000;
    }
}
```

When you compile and run the code in Listing A.3, the value 1000 is printed to the screen. This example shows that the integer value 1000 gets wrapped, or boxed, so that the base class' ToString() method can be used to print its value to the screen.

Classes

Classes are data structures that contain data (or fields) and methods and properties to manipulate this data. Classes support inheritance, so one class can be derived from another and extend the base class' functionality or simply take advantage of the work previously done. Listing A.4 shows a simple Point class.

LISTING A.4   A Simple *Point* Class Declaration

```
1: using System;
2:3: class Point{
4:    public double X = 0;
5:    public double Y = 0;
6:7:    public void print(){
8:        Console.WriteLine("(" + X + ", " + Y + ")" );
9:    }
10:
11: }// End of Point Class
```

Listing A.4 shows a very simple Point class. Lines 4 and 5 show the two public fields X and Y, which are double value types.

Lines 7 through 9 show the Point class, which contains a print() function for printing a formatted representation of the Point class' X and Y fields onscreen.

> **NOTE**
>
> If you don't specify a constructor, C# assumes a default constructor taking no parameters. However, if you specify an overloaded constructor that does take at least one parameter, you must explicitly specify that the default constructor be available to any client of the class.

Structs

Structs are similar to classes, except that classes are reference types and structs are value types. In other words, if an instance of a struct is passed to a method, a copy is made and passed. If an instance of a class is passed to a method, a reference to that object is passed. So, structs are useful for creating user-defined types that behave like built-in types. Listing A.5 shows a simple struct example.

LISTING A.5   A Simple *Point* Struct Declaration

```
 1: using System;
 2:
 3: struct Point{
 4:     public double X;
 5:     public double Y;
 6:
 7:     public void print(){
 8:        Console.WriteLine("(" + X + ", " + Y + ")" );
 9:     }
10:
11: }// End of Point struct
12:
13: public class PointStructTester{
14:     public static void Main(){
15:        Point p;
16:        p.X = 2;
17:        p.Y = 5;
18:        p.print();
19:     }
20: }
```

Notice a few things about Listing A.5:

- Lines 4 and 5 don't initialize the X and Y fields. C# doesn't allow instance field initializers in structs.

- As I pointed out earlier, an instance of the `Point` struct is created on the stack, whereas the `Point` class is heap allocated.
- Lines 13 through 20 show a simple driver class that instantiates and uses the `Point` struct. In line 15, note that an instance of `Point` p is declared but doesn't use the `new` keyword, although that is permitted.

Enumerators

Enumerators improve the readability of code in situations in which a value can have only a certain set of values. Listing A.6 shows a simple enumeration in the `UserAccess` class. In this example, different processing occurs depending on the user type.

LISTING A.6   *UserAccess* Class

```
using System;

class UserAccess{

   public enum UserType{
      Administrator,
      Registered,
      Anonymous
   }

   public static void AssignAccess(UserType userType){
      switch(userType){
         case UserType.Administrator:
            // do some processing
         break;

         case UserType.Registered:
            // do some processing
         break;

         case UserType.Anonymous:
            // do some processing
         break;
      }
   }

   // Driver method
   public static void Main(){
      AssignAccess(UserType.Administrator);
   }

}// End of Class
```

Initialization

If no values are specified, the default value of the first enum member is 0, and each subsequent member is incremented by 1. You can set specific values, however, as shown in Listing A.7.

Listing A.7   Initializing the *UserType* Enum

```
public enum UserType{
   Administrator = 2,
   Registered = 4,
   Anonymous = 6
}
```

In this example, the UserType enum specifies the values 2, 4, and 6 for its members.

Base Types

The amount of storage allocated for an enumeration is determined by the enum's base type. In C#, if no base type is specified, the default is int. Listing A.8 shows how to specify an enum's base type.

Listing A.8   *UserType* Enum with Long Base Type

```
public enum UserType:long {
   Administrator=2000000000,
   Registered=4000000000,
   Anonymous=6000000000
}
```

C# supports the following base types for enums: byte, sbyte, short, ushort, int, uint, long, and ulong. You can't use type char as an underlying type for an enum in C#.

Statements and Execution Flow

C# provides many statements similar to those found in C, C++, and Java. The statement types discussed in this appendix are selection statements, looping statements, and jump statements.

Selection Statements

Selection statements control the flow of execution based on an expression's value. C# supports two types of selection statements: if and switch.

if

The if statement controls program execution based on the outcome of a Boolean expression. Listing A.9 shows a simple example of an if statement in C#.

LISTING A.9   The *if* Statement

```
using System;

class MyClass{

    public static void Main(){

        int x = 1;
        int y = 2;

        if(x == y){
            Console.WriteLine("x has the same value as y.");
        }
    }
}
```

The else statement is used with if to denote an alternative flow of execution based on the out-come of the Boolean expression evaluated in the if statement immediately preceding it. Listing A.10 illustrates the use of an else statement.

LISTING A.10   The *else* Statement

```
using System;

class MyClass{

    public static void Main(){

        int x = 1;
        int y = 2;

        if(x == y){
            Console.WriteLine("x has the same value as y.");
        }else{
            Console.WriteLine("x has a different value than y.");
        }
    }
}
```

You could have written the if statement in Listing A.10 and the else statement in Listing A.11 without the { and } characters because the result of both statements was the execution of only a single line of code. In C#, as in C, C++, and Java, only multiple lines of execution need to be enclosed in { and }.

switch

Often you need to decide between multiple variables. In such cases, the if and if else statements can be cumbersome. C# provides the switch statement to make such selections easier to code and easier to read. If you are familiar with Visual Basic, the switch statement is akin to the Select Case. Listing A.11 illustrates the use of the switch statement.

LISTING A.11   The *switch* Statement

```
using System;

class MyClass{

    public static void Main(String[] args){
        Console.Write ("Enter the developer: ");
        String developer = Console.ReadLine();

        switch(developer.ToUpper()){
            case "DAVID":
            Console.WriteLine("The developer is David.");
            break;

            case "BOB":
            Console.WriteLine("The developer is Bob.");
            break;

            case "JAMES":
            Console.WriteLine("The developer is James.");
            break;

            case "JASON":
            Console.WriteLine("The developer is Jason.");
            break;

            case "BARRY":
            Console.WriteLine("The developer is Barry.");
            break;

            case "MICHAEL":
            Console.WriteLine("The developer is Michael.");
            break;

            default:
                Console.WriteLine("Invalid developer specified.");
            break;
        }
    }
}
```

Listing A.11 illustrates a simple console application that asks for a developer's name and simply repeats that name to the user or notifies him that he has entered an invalid developer name.

The *switch expression* is the string variable `"developer"`. A call to `String.ToUpper()` is made in the select expression, so each case of the input isn't a factor in comparing the string values.

Switch statements aren't allowed to "fall through" as they are in C and C++. Instead, C# requires either a `break` statement after each `case` or a `goto` statement. This requirement forces developers to choose to implement the "fall-through" behavior, which is usually an exception anyway.

Looping Statements

Looping or iteration statements repeatedly execute code based on set criteria. C# supports the `do`, `while`, `for`, and `foreach` statements.

do

In C#, a do statement executes based on the outcome of a Boolean statement. Execution of the do statement stops when either a `break` statement is reached or the Boolean expression is evaluated as `false`. Listing A.12 shows a simple example of a do statement. A do statement executes at least once.

LISTING A.12   The *do* Statement

```
int x = 0;
do{
    Console.WriteLine("x=" + x++);
}while(x<=10);
```

Listing A.12 shows a simple do loop that writes the value of the variable x to the screen, as long as it is less than or equal to 10, and then increments the x variable by 1.

while

while loops execute as long as a given expression resolves to `true`. Execution of the statements inside a while loop stop when a `break` statement is reached or the while expression evaluates to `true`. Listing A.13 shows a simple while loop.

LISTING A.13   The *while* Statement

```
int x = 0;
while(x <=10){
    Console.WriteLine("x=" + x++);
}
```

This simple example of a `while` loop achieves the same result as the do loop in Listing A.12. Remember, however, that a do loop always executes at least once.

for

In C#, as in C, C++, and Java, the `for` statement allows for the declaration, initialization, and incrementing of variables used for looping criteria. Listing A.14 shows a `for` loop writing out the value of the integer i 11 times.

LISTING A.14   The *for* Statement

```
for(int i = 0; i <=10; i++){
    Console.WriteLine("i=" + i);
}
```

foreach

A `foreach` statement executes a statement for every item in a collection or an array. The `foreach` statement is useful when the number of items in a collection isn't known ahead of time. Listing A.15 shows the use of a `foreach` statement.

LISTING A.15   The *foreach* Statement

```
String[] fruit = new String[] {"apples", "oranges", "pears"};

foreach(String fruitItem in fruit){
    Console.WriteLine(fruitItem);
}
```

When compiled and run, the code in Listing A.15 writes each string in the array `fruit` to the screen.

CAUTION

Don't use `foreach` statements to alter the contents of a collection because doing so results in unpredictable behavior.

Jump Statements

You can use a jump statement to alter program control. C# supports `break`, `continue`, `goto`, and `return` statements for this purpose.

break

A break statement stops the flow of execution and returns control to the nearest statement following the loop or conditional statement containing it. Inserting an if statement into the while loop from Listing A.13 and a break results in the loop not continuing past the if statement when that condition is met. Listing A.16 shows this statement.

LISTING A.16   The *break* Statement

```
int x = 0;
while(x <=10){
   if(x==2)
      break;
   Console.WriteLine("x=" + x++);
}
```

The outcome of compiling and running this code is x=0 and x=1 printed to the screen.

continue

The continue statement passes control to the next iteration of the looping statement that houses it. Listing A.17 shows a continue statement used to write out the odd numbers between 1 and 11.

LISTING A.17   The *continue* Statement

```
int x = 1;
while (x <=10 ){
   x++;
   if (x%2 ==0)
      continue;
   Console.WriteLine(x);
}
```

goto

In C#, as in many other languages, the goto statement can pass execution control to a specified label somewhere else in the program. Listing A.18 shows the use of a goto statement.

LISTING A.18   The *goto* Statement

```
1: public static void Main(){
2:    for(int i = 0; i <=10; i++){
3:       if(i==3){
4:          goto exitLoop;
```

LISTING A.18 Continued

```
 5:       }
 6:       Console.WriteLine(i);
 7:    }
 8:
 9:    goto exitMain;
10:
11:    exitLoop:
12:       Console.WriteLine("Loop was exited.");
13:    exitMain:
14:       Console.WriteLine("End of Main.");
15: }
```

Listing A.18 shows looping with a for statement until the value of i is 3, at which time the flow of execution is passed to the exitLoop: label on line 11. If the expression in the if statement on line 3 is changed to a value greater than 10, the WriteLine statement on line 12 will never be executed.

> **NOTE**
>
> Because the use of goto statements is frowned upon, C# limits their use.

return

The return statement stops execution of the method containing it and returns control to the calling method. In C#, only methods with a return type of void don't have to implement the return statement. Listing A.19 shows a Main method implemented with a return type of int.

LISTING A.19 The *return* Statement

```
public static int Main(){
   Console.WriteLine("The return statement.");
   return 0;
}
```

Operators

C# supports the usual logical and arithmetic operators in addition to a few others. Table A.2 briefly describes the operators supported by C#.

TABLE A.2 C# Operators

Operator(s)	Description	Overloadable
&	Logical AND	Yes
^	Logical XOR	Yes
|	Logical OR	Yes
&&	Conditional AND	No
||	Conditional OR	No
?:	Conditional	No
=, *=, /=, %=, +=, -=, <<=, >>=, &=, ^=, and |=	Assignments	No
new	Object creation	No
()	Cast	No
true or false	Boolean	Yes
.	Member access	No
++	Increment	Yes
--	Decrement	No
sizeof, typeof, and is	Type information	No
+, -, *, /, and %	Arithmetic	Yes
==, >=, <=, !=, >, and <	Relational	Yes

Comparison operators can be overloaded only in pairs. For example, if the == operator is overloaded, the != operator must also be overloaded.

User-defined types can choose to overload many of the operators in Table A.2.

Operator Overloading

Operator *overloading* is a language feature that permits user-defined classes and structs to redefine the functions of certain operators. Overloading is most often done with operators in which the operation to be performed is fairly obvious. For instance, overloading the relational operators (==, !=, >=, <=, >, <) makes sense because uses are well known. Similarly, overloading the + operator makes sense when used with objects whose constituent parts are commonly added. In other words, if the addition analogy makes sense, overloading the + operator is appropriate. Listing A.20 shows an example of overloading the + operator.

LISTING A.20   Overloading the + *Operator*

```csharp
using System;

class Point{

   private double x = 0;
   private double y = 0;

   public Point(double X, double Y){
      x = X;
      y = Y;
   }

   public double X{
      get{ return x; }
      set{ x = value;}
   }

   public double Y{
      get {return y;}
      set { y = value;}
   }

   public void print(){
      Console.WriteLine("(" + X + ", " + Y + ")");
   }

   public static Point operator +(Point p1, Point p2){
      return new Point(p1.X + p2.X, p1.Y + p2.Y);
   }
}// End of Class

public class PointTest{
   public static void Main(){
      Point p1 = new Point(5,5);
      Point p2 = new Point(6,6);
      Point p3 = p1 + p2;

      p1.print();
      p2.print();
      p3.print();

   }
}
```

Properties

Properties are a convenient, built-in way to access private fields in C#.

You access properties the same way you would access a public field. Listing A.21 illustrates the use of properties to conceal private fields of the Point class.

LISTING A.21   Properties in the *Point* Class

```
class Point{
    private double x=0;
    private double y=0;

    public Point(){
        x = 0;
        y = 0;
    }

    public Point(double X, double Y){
        x = X;
        y = Y;
    }

    public double X {
        get { return x; }

        set { x = value; }
    }

    public double Y{
        get{ return y;  }
        set { y = value; }
    }

    public void print(){
        Console.WriteLine("(" + X + ", " + Y + ")" );
    }
}
```

Attributes

Attributes enable you to provide extra metadata to your classes and methods at compile time. Other programs can access this extra information either at compile time, runtime, or by simply reading the metadata.

The .NET Framework allows C# and other .NET languages to use some built-in attributes. These built-in attributes, derived from `System.Attribute`, are used for everything from conditional compilation to transactional support to specifying Web Services methods.

Using Attributes

To create a Web Services method, use the `WebMethod` attribute. Listing A.22 shows an example of this attribute.

LISTING A.22   The *WebMethod* Attribute

```
[WebMethod]
public String MyMessage(){
    return "This is a Web Service method.";
}
```

When you specify the `WebMethod` attribute, the `MyMessage` method is available from remote Web-based clients.

Creating Attributes

As my friend David puts it, "Metadata does no good if there is nothing there to read it." He means that most reasons for creating custom attributes revolve around a scenario in which a container object houses other objects that implement one or more custom attributes.

If you want to create your own custom attribute, you must create an attribute class that inherits directly or indirectly from `System.Attribute`. Listing A.23 shows creating a custom attribute that allows logging to a file from within a Web service.

LISTING A.23   Creating a Custom Attribute

```
namespace CSharpWebSamples
{
    using System;
    using System.Collections;
    using System.ComponentModel;
    using System.Data;
    using System.Diagnostics;
    using System.Web;
    using System.Web.Services;
    using System.Web.Services.Protocols;
    using System.IO;
    using System.Xml;
```

LISTING A.23   Continued

```
// Create a new custom attribute that will allow
// users to configure the log file. This attribute
// will also tell the ASP.NET system which type to
// load for our extension
[AttributeUsage(AttributeTargets.Method)]
public class SoapLoggerAttribute : SoapExtensionAttribute
{
   private int _priority = 0;
   private string _logFile = @"C:\soap.log";
   public SoapLoggerAttribute() {}
   public SoapLoggerAttribute(string logFile) {_logFile = logFile;}
   public string LogFile {get{return _logFile;}}
   public override Type ExtensionType {get{return typeof(SoapLogger);}}
   public override int Priority {get {return _priority;} set{
➥_priority = value;}}
 }

// Create a new SoapExtension class. When users
// apply the above attribute to a method of their
// web service, this class will be instantiated
// by the ASP.NET system
public class SoapLogger : SoapExtension
{
   private string LogFile = "";
   private Stream SoapStream;
   private Stream TempStream;

   public override object GetInitializer(Type serviceType)
   {
      // we need to read some service configuration from the attribute
      // so differ creating an initializer
      return null;
   }
   public override object GetInitializer(LogicalMethodInfo methodInfo,
      ➥SoapExtensionAttribute attribute)
   {
      // whatever we return here will be passed back to
      // our initialize method every time the ASP.NET system
      // needs to create a new instance of this extension class
      return ((SoapLoggerAttribute)attribute).LogFile;
   }
   public override void Initialize(object initializer)
   {
      // grab the logfile name that we returned in
```

LISTING A.23   Continued

```csharp
            // GetInitializer
        LogFile = (string)initializer;
    }
    public override Stream ChainStream(Stream stream)
    {
        // by overriding ChainStream we can
        // cause the ASP.NET system to use
        // our stream for buffering SOAP messages
        // rather than the default stream.
        // we will store off the original stream
        // so we can pass the data back down to the ASP.NET system
        // in original stream that it created.
        SoapStream = stream;
        TempStream = new MemoryStream();
        return TempStream;
    }
    public void CopyTextStream(Stream src, Stream dest)
    {
        TextReader reader = new StreamReader(src);
        TextWriter writer = new StreamWriter(dest);
        writer.WriteLine(reader.ReadToEnd());
        writer.Flush();
    }
    public override void ProcessMessage(SoapMessage message)
    {
        // this method will be called several times during
        // the processing of a SOAP request. The ASP.NET system
        // tells us which stage the SOAP request is at with the
        // Stage property of the SoapMessage class
        switch (message.Stage)
        {
            case SoapMessageStage.BeforeDeserialize:
                {
                // copy the SOAP request from the network stream
                // into our memory buffer
                CopyTextStream(SoapStream, TempStream);
                FileStream fs = new FileStream(LogFile,
                    ➥FileMode.Append, FileAccess.Write);
                StreamWriter sw = new StreamWriter(fs);
                sw.WriteLine("** BEGIN SOAP REQUEST: {0}", DateTime.Now);
                sw.Flush();
                // copy the mem buffer stream to the log file
                TempStream.Position = 0;
                CopyTextStream(TempStream, fs);
```

A

LISTING A.23   Continued

```
                sw.WriteLine("** END SOAP REQUEST");
                sw.Flush();
                fs.Close();
                // reset the memory buffer position
                // so the ASP.NET system can parse and
                // decode the message
                TempStream.Position = 0;
                }
                break;
            case SoapMessageStage.AfterSerialize:
                {
                FileStream fs = new FileStream(LogFile, FileMode.Append,
➥FileAccess.Write);
                StreamWriter sw = new StreamWriter(fs);
                sw.WriteLine("** BEGIN SOAP RESPONSE: {0}", DateTime.Now);
                sw.Flush();
                TempStream.Position = 0;
                CopyTextStream(TempStream, fs);
                sw.WriteLine("** END SOAP RESPONSE");
                sw.Flush();

                // copy the memory buffered response
                // to the network stream
                TempStream.Position = 0;
                CopyTextStream(TempStream, SoapStream);

                fs.Close();
                }
                break;
        }

        return;
    }
}
[WebService(Namespace="http://technicallead.com/csharpwebsamples")]
public class ExtensionSample : System.Web.Services.WebService
{
    public ExtensionSample()
    {
        //CODEGEN: This call is required by the ASP.NET Web Services
        ➥Designer
        InitializeComponent();
    }
    public override void Dispose()
    {
```

LISTING A.23   Continued

```
        }
        [
         WebMethod,
         SoapLogger
        ]
        public Author GetAuthorInfo()
        {
            Author author = new Author();
            author.FirstName = "Bob";
            author.LastName = "Tabor";
            author.Email = "bob@technicallead.com";
            author.Books = new Book[2];
            author.Books[0] = new Book();
            author.Books[0].Title = "Microsoft .NET WebServices";
            author.Books[0].Publisher = "SAMS Publishing";
            author.Books[1] = new Book();
            author.Books[1].Title = "Microsoft .NET WebServices 2nd Edition";
            author.Books[1].Publisher = "SAMS Publishing";
            return author;
        }
        [
         WebMethod,
         SoapLogger
        ]
        public Author SaveAuthorInfo(Author a)
        {
            return a;
            }
        }
}
```

NOTE

This example came from my friend and colleague David Findley.

Indexers

C# permits the accessing of classes and structs in a manner similar to the way arrays are indexed. You create indexers similarly to the way you create properties. Listing A.24 shows an example of creating an indexer.

LISTING A.24   Indexers

```
 1: using System;
 2:
 3: public class Nonsense{
 4:     private string[] nonsense = new string[] {"foo", "bar", "baz", "quirk"};
 5:
 6:     public string this[int indexer]{
 7:         get{return nonsense[indexer];}
 8:         set{nonsense[indexer] = value;}
 9:     }
10:
11:     public int Length{
12:         get{return nonsense.Length;}
13:     }
14:
15:}
16:
17: class MyClass{
18:
19:     public static void Main(){
20:         Nonsense n = new Nonsense();
21:
22:         for(int i = 0; i< n.Length; i++){
23:             Console.WriteLine(n[i]);
24:         }
25:     }
26: }
```

NOTE

In general, you should refrain from using indexers unless the array analogy adds value to your class design. For simplicity, I broke that rule in Listing A.24 to demonstrate the syntax in action.

Line 6 defines the indexer's signature, whereas lines 7 through 9 show the indexer's actual implementation. Notice how similar in structure it is to the property syntax.

When an instance of the Nonsense class is created (line 20), the class instance can be accessed just like an array would be accessed. Line 23 shows indexing the Nonsense class in order to print the internal nonsense array.

Possible real-world examples would be an order object with an order items collection or any other container object that houses a collection of other objects.

Arrays

Arrays are reference type data structures that can contain a number of other variables. These variables, known as *elements*, are accessed via indexes. C# arrays start with a zero index.

In C# and other .NET languages, arrays are heap allocated, but the storage of each element is dictated by that element's type. In other words, if an array contains objects, the array contains references to those objects, but if the array contains integers, the array actually contains those integers.

Declaring Arrays

You declare arrays by specifying the type of array, brackets ([]), the name of the array variable, and a size. The new operator creates the array and initializes its elements to their default value:

```
String [] sNonsense = new String[4];
```

Initializing Arrays

You can initialize arrays at the same time they are declared:

```
String sNonsense = new String[4];
```

The C# compiler can determine the necessary size based on the number of items specified in the initialization. So,

```
String[] sNonsense = {"foo", "bar", "baz", "quirk"};
```

is equivalent to

```
String[] sNonsense = new String[4] {"foo", "bar", "baz", "quirk"};
```

Working with Multidimensional Arrays

C# supports multidimensional and jagged arrays. The syntax for declaring multidimensional arrays is as follows:

```
int[,] Points = new int[,] {{1,1}, {2,2}, {2,2}, {3,2}};
```

You also can create a three-dimensional version:

```
int[,,] Points = new int[3,3,3];
```

Also, you can declare a multidimensional array without immediately initializing it. However, when you do initialize it, you must use the new keyword:

```
int[,] Points;
Points = new int[,]{{1,1}, {2,2}, {2,2}, {3,2}};
```

Jagged arrays, or arrays of arrays, can also be created in C#:

```
string [][] myStrings = new string[2][];
```

Strings

The .NET Framework represents strings as Unicode characters. In C#, the keyword string is an alias for System.String. Therefore, the following declarations are equivalent in C#:

```
string sMyString = "Some string value";
```

```
System.String sAnotherString = "Some other string value";
```

Because the keyword string is an alias for System.String, strings are technically reference types in .NET. The == and != operators are overloaded regarding strings, so comparison of string values is more intuitive.

One benefit of basing the string type on the System.String class is that you have access to a rich set of static methods for manipulating and comparing strings. Table A.3 shows some of the common String object methods, a description of their use, and scope.

TABLE A.3 *String* Object Methods

Method	Description
Static Scope	
Compare	Compares two string objects
Concat	Combines two or more strings into a single new one
Copy	Creates a new String object from another
Equals	Determines whether two strings have the same value
Join	Joins an array of strings to form a single string
Instance Scope	
Split	Creates an array of strings
ToUpper	Creates a copy of the string in all uppercase letters
ToLower	Creates a copy of the string in all lowercase letters
ToCharArray	Creates an array of characters from the string
Trim	Removes either whitespace or specified characters from the string

The .NET Framework provides many more methods and a few properties for dealing with string values, but Table A.3 gives you some idea of what can be done.

Interfaces

An *interface*, similar to an abstract class, supports interface-based inheritance. Interfaces are declarations for an abstract reference type. Another way to think about interfaces is to consider them to be contracts between the class that implements them and the calling class.

Declaring an Interface

Interfaces can inherit from one or more base interfaces but can't have any access to modifiers or security attributes associated with them. Listing A.25 shows the declaration of a simple interface.

LISTING A.25   A Simple Interface

```
using System;

interface IPerson{

    String Name{
        get;
        set;
    }

    int Age{
        get;
        set;
    }
}
```

This example shows the simple IPerson interface that requires Name and Age properties to be implemented. Notice that the get and set portions of the properties have no implementation and that no access modifier is associated with any part of the interface. By definition, all interface methods and properties must be public.

Implementing an Interface

When a class or struct implements an interface, it must provide implementation details for all properties and methods declared by the interface. To cause a class or struct to inherit from an interface, it uses the same syntax as implementation inheritance. Listing A.26 shows the implementation of an interface.

LISTING A.26 Implementing an Interface

```csharp
using System;
using System.Collections;

class MyClass: ICollection{
   private int count;
   private bool isSynchronized;
   private IEnumerator enumerator;

   public MyClass(){
      this.count++;
      this.isSynchronized = true;
   }

   public void CopyTo(Array dest, int copyBegins){
       // implement copying here
   }

   public int Count{
      get{return count;}
   }

   public bool IsSynchronized{
      get{return isSynchronized;}
   }

   public object SyncRoot{
      get{return this;}
   }

   public IEnumerator GetEnumerator(){
      return enumerator;
   }
}
```

Delegates and Events

Delegates are the type-safe, secure, managed equivalents of C++ function pointers. You can use delegates with instance, virtual, or static methods. Another way to think about delegates is as encapsulating a specific method. In .NET, delegates are also used for events and callback functions.

Delegates are implemented by inheriting from System.Delegate and supporting a list of methods executed when the delegates are invoked. Listing A.27 shows the use of a delegate.

LISTING A.27   Delegates

```
 1: using System;
 2:
 3: delegate void MessageDelegate();
 4:
 5: public class MyClass{
 6:    public void WriteMessage (){
 7:       Console.WriteLine("I made this.");
 8:    }
 9: }
10:
11: public class MyClassTester{
12:    static public void Main (){
13:       MyClass mc = new MyClass();
14:
15:       MessageDelegate md = new MessageDelegate(mc.WriteMessage);
16:
17:       md();
18:    }
19: }
```

Listing A.27 declares the delegate MessageDelegate on line 3. The public class MyClass implements a WriteMessage method on lines 6 through 8, and the MyClassTester class assigns the WriteMessage method to the MessageDelegate instance md. This means that any time the md() delegate is fired, the message I made this. will appear onscreen.

Exception Handling

C# supports a structured exception handling model that's based on an exception object. The exception handling syntax in C# is similar to the try/catch/finally syntax in C++. Listing A.28 shows an example of this syntax.

LISTING A.28   *try/catch/finally* Syntax

```
try{
   int zero = 0;
   int divideByZero = 100/zero;
}catch(DivideByZeroException e){
   Console.WriteLine(e.Message);
}finally{
   Console.WriteLine("This is always executed.");
}
```

The try portion of this block is wrapped around the suspect code. This example is an obvious attempt to create a divide-by-zero exception.

In the catch portion, an error will be dealt with. The catch statement's DivideByZeroException object parameter is the type of exception that will be dealt with; all other exceptions won't.

The optional finally section is always executed. Typically, in this section, you would do object cleanup or other graceful exiting of a function regardless of the outcome.

A more realistic example might be to use a try/catch block around code that opens a database connection and catch a SqlException object.

Method Parameters

In C#, method parameters default to "by value." C# does, however, provide for other types of method parameters. You can specify method parameters by using the keywords out, ref, or params.

out

Values passed as out parameters reflect any changes made to them while inside the method they were passed. This capability can be useful when multiple values need to be returned from a method. Listing A.29 shows the use of out parameters.

LISTING A.29   Using an out Parameter

```
 1: using System;
 2:
 3: class Rectangle{
 4:
 5:     private int Length = 0;
 6:     private int Width = 0;
 7:     private int Height = 0;
 8:
 9:     public Rectangle(int length, int width, int height){
10:         Length = length;
11:         Width = width;
12:         Height = height;
13:     }
14:
15:     public void GetDimensions(out int length, out int width, out int height){
16:         length = this.Length;
17:         width = this.Width;
18:         height = this.Height;
```

LISTING A.29   Continued

```
19:    }
20: }// End of Rectangle Class
21:
22: class RectangleTest{
23:    public static void Main(){
24:       int l, w, h;
25:
26:       Rectangle rect = new Rectangle(5, 10, 12);
27:       rect.GetDimensions(out l, out w, out h);
28:
29:       Console.WriteLine("Length=" + l + "\n" +
30:                "Width=" + w + "\n" +
31:                "Height=" + h);
32:    }
33: }// End of RectangleTest Class
```

The RectangleTest class tries out the out parameters Length, Width, and Height. Line 24 declares the parameters that are passed to the GetDimensions method in the Rectangle class, but notice that they aren't initialized. In C#, you don't need to initialize out parameters.

ref

The ref keyword also is used when the value of the parameter passed to the method needs to be changed. The ref keyword varies from out in that parameters passed using the ref keyword must be initialized before passing them to the method. Listing A.30 shows a simple example of using the ref method parameter keyword.

LISTING A.30   The *ref* Method Parameter Keyword

```
1: using System;
2:
3: class MyClass{
4:
5:    public static void Main(){
6:       String sMessage = "Hello.";
7:       MyClass mc = new MyClass();
8:
9:       mc.refMethod(ref sMessage);
10:
11:       Console.WriteLine(sMessage);
12:    }
13:
14:    public void refMethod(ref String message){
```

LISTING A.30   Continued

```
15:        message = "You said " + message;
16:    }
17: }
```

This example shows a simple method called refMethod that does nothing more than append the string "You said " to a string parameter passed to the function. Notice how both the method declaration on line 14 and the call to the method specify that the parameter is a ref parameter. Notice also, on line 6, the string sMessage is initialized with "Hello.".

params

The params method parameter keyword provides a convenient way to pass a variable number of parameters to a function. Listing A.31 shows the use of the params keyword.

LISTING A.31   The *params* Method Parameter Keyword

```
using System;

class MyClass{

    public void TakeParams(params Object[] thing){
        for(int i = 0; i< thing.Length; i++){
            Console.WriteLine(thing[i].ToString());
        }
    }

    public static void Main(){
        MyClass mc = new MyClass();
        mc.TakeParams("Foobar", "Bazquirk", "Ipsum");
    }
}// End of MyClass Class
```

A parameter that uses the params keyword must be a single-dimensional array. The data type of the array can be any valid data type. I used an Object array because I felt it was the most flexible option.

Function Overloading

C#—and the .NET Common Language Runtime (CLR) in general—enables you to create methods, with the same name, that vary only in their number and/or type of arguments.

Function overloading is one means by which .NET allows for polymorphism which is the notion that a single entity can perform different functions or a single function different ways but appear as only one object. Listing A.32 shows an example of function overloading.

Listing A.32   Function Overloading

```
using System;

class MyClass{

    public int add(int num1, int num2){
        return num1 + num2;
    }

    public double add(double num1, double num2){
        return num1 + num2;
    }

    public string add(string string1, string string2){
        return string1 + string2;
    }

    public static void Main(){
        MyClass mc = new MyClass();

        Console.WriteLine(mc.add(1, 1).ToString());
        Console.WriteLine(mc.add(1.1, 1.1).ToString());
        Console.WriteLine(mc.add("one", "one" ).ToString());
    }
}// End of MyClass Class
```

Inheritance

Inheritance allows objects to assume the properties and methods of other objects. Listing A.33 shows a simple C# inheritance example.

Listing A.33   A Simple Inheritance Example

```
1: using System;
2:
3: class Person{
4:     private string name;
5:     private int age;
6:
```

LISTING A.33 Continued

```
 7:    public Person(string name, int age){
 8:        this.name = name;
 9:        this.age = age;
10:    }
11:
12:    public string Name{
13:        get{return name;}
14:        set{name = value;}
15:    }
16:
17:    public int Age{
18:        get{return age;}
19:        set{age = value;}
20:    }
21: }
22:
23: class Employee: Person{
24:    DateTime hireDate;
25:
26:    public Employee(string name, int age, DateTime hireDate):
27:        base(name, age){
28:        this.hireDate = hireDate;
29:    }
30:
31:    public DateTime HireDate{
32:        get{return hireDate.Date;}
33:        set{hireDate = value;}
34:    }
35: }
36:
37: class Tester{
38:    public static void Main(){
39:        Employee e = new Employee("Jason", 28, new DateTime(2000,12,22) );
40:        Console.WriteLine(e.HireDate);
41:    }
42: }
```

Listing A.33 shows a Person class and an Employee class that inherits from the Person class. The declaration of the Employee class is essentially the same as that of the Person class except for line 23, which tells the .NET Framework to give the Employee class all public and protected properties and methods of the Person class, and the constructor, on lines 26 through 29, that calls the Person class' constructor via the base syntax.

NOTE

You can use the base keyword anytime a method in a parent class needs to be accessed by one of its children. The two most common uses are to call a base class' constructor (as in Listing A.33) or a method in an overridden parent class.

The Tester class, on lines 37 through 42, show that an Employee object can be created and call a method that was created in the Person class.

VB.NET Language Reference

This appendix provides a brief overview of some of the new language features available in Microsoft VB.NET and covers the features most likely to be used to create applications like the one presented in this book. However, VB.NET is a feature-rich, complicated language that can't be fully covered in a single appendix.

This appendix is broken into two fairly large sections. One section discusses language and syntax changes; the other targets VB.NET's new object-oriented features.

> **NOTE**
>
> You can find the code examples for this appendix online.

Syntax Changes and New Language Features

VB.NET has many new language features and syntax changes. It has new data types and operators, a new implementation of arrays; it also introduces structures into the language, structured exception handling, support for multithreading, and true object-oriented functionality.

Data Types

Because VB.NET was built with the Common Language Runtime (CLR) in mind, many data type changes were necessary. These changes include everything being inherited from the base class `Object`, the replacement of the `Variant` type, new size and value ranges for the `Integer` types, changes to the `String` type, and the addition of a `Decimal` type.

`Object` Base Class

One of the more important data type changes for VB.NET is that everything—including simple data types—is derived from the base class `Object`. This means that even though you can still treat native types, such as integers and doubles, as you did in Visual Basic 6.0, you can also treat them as objects.

Why would you want to treat a variable that represents a simple data type as an object? Each data type in VB.NET (and .NET in general) is represented by a base class or structure in the `System` namespace of the .NET Framework. This means that any time you deal with native types, you have at your disposal a rich set of methods and properties for parsing, comparing, and manipulating those data types.

No More `Variant`

One of the most flexible features in previous versions of Visual Basic was the `Variant` data type. With `Variant`, you could create a variable and assign any other type to it at runtime. VB would massage the data behind the scenes, so you didn't have to worry about what data type was needed.

Using Variants had its downside, though. When variables were declared as type Variant, automatic type coercion often caused unintentional bugs. Using Variant data types also meant a performance penalty because VB had to figure out which data type was really supposed to be used.

Because everything in .NET is really an object, you can use variables of type Object where you once used Variant. What about the performance penalty and potential for unwanted bugs? The Object type is implemented totally differently from how Variant was, so although you still might run into some type-mismatch problems, it's unlikely that you'll suffer the same performance problems.

New Integer Sizes

Because VB.NET was built to work with the .NET runtime, many of its native type sizes and ranges have changed to coincide with the other .NET languages. These changes also bring VB.NET data sizes more in line with those used by SQL Server, thus reducing the potential for data-type conversion errors and type mismatches.

Specifically, the Integer data type has changed from 16-bit to 32-bit, whereas Long has changed from 32-bit to 64-bit. Also, the Short data type is now 16-bit. The Byte data type remains 8-bit, as you would expect.

Because Integer is the most common data type used, these changes enhance performance because Integer is now 32-bit. A 32-bit Integer performs better than either a 16-bit or 64-bit Integer on a 32-bit system (such as Windows 2000).

> **NOTE**
>
> Integer values can now range from –2,147,483,648 to 2,147,483,647.

String Changes

The changes to the String data type in VB.NET are subtle. In previous versions of Visual Basic, a String variable could be changed in place. In VB.NET, Strings are *immutable*. This means that any change to a String variable results in a new copy of the variable being created.

The VB.NET String type comes from the .NET type System.String. As with the Integer types, this means that you now have access to a rich set of "baked-in" methods and properties for manipulating and comparing string values. Table B.1 shows some of the properties and methods.

TABLE B.1 *String* Object Methods

Method	Description
Compare	Compares two string objects
Concat	Combines two or more strings into a single new string
Copy	Creates a new String object from another
Equals	Determines whether two strings have the same value
Join	Joins an array of strings to form a single string
Split	Creates an array of strings
ToUpper	Creates a copy of the string in all uppercase letters
ToLower	Creates a copy of the string in all lowercase letters
ToCharArray	Creates an array of characters from the string
Trim	Removes either whitespace or specified characters from the string

Decimal Type

VB.NET supports the new 128-bit data type Decimal. This data type is useful for representing very large floating-point values or currency. A variable of type Decimal can hold values that have between 0 and 28 digits to the right of the decimal point. That's a lot of precision!

> **NOTE**
>
> Bear in mind that the overall range of values you can represent with Decimal is indirectly proportional to the number of digits used to the right of the decimal point. Simply put, the higher the precision, the lower the possible range of values.

VB.NET no longer supports the Currency value type, but you can achieve the same functionality with the Decimal type.

Operators

VB.NET has a few new operators worth mentioning, as described in Table B.2.

TABLE B.2 New VB.NET Operators

Operator	Description
BitAnd	Bitwise AND
BitOr	Bitwise OR
BitNot	Bitwise NOT

VB.NET Language Reference

APPENDIX B

481

B

VB.NET
LANGUAGE
REFERENCE

TABLE B.2   Continued

Operator	Description
BitXor	Bitwise XOR
+=	x = x + *value*
-=	x = x – *value*
*=	x = x * *value*
/=	x = x / *value*
&=	s = s & *StringValue*

Arrays

VB.NET introduces a few changes to arrays. Arrays in VB.NET are reference types of the System.Array class rather than native types as they were in previous versions of VB. This means that you can pass arrays from object to object just like any other reference type in .NET regardless of the language that object was written in.

Another important change with the way .NET handles arrays is that all arrays are now zero based. In VB 6.0, the Option Base keyword allowed developers to specify whether they wanted their array to start at 0 or 1. The Option Base syntax is no longer supported, which has a ripple effect on other previously supported features.

In VB 6.0, you could write Dim aMyStringArray (1 to 10). The To syntax is no longer supported. This means you can no longer specify that an array's index should start at any value other than 0.

VB.NET also simplifies the initialization of arrays by allowing you to prefill an array with data:

```
Dim asMyStringArray() As String = {"foo", "bar", "baz", "quirk"}
```

NOTE

The Array() function provides the same functionality.

One final benefit to arrays being based on the System.Array class is that a rich set of methods and properties for manipulating arrays is built in. Listing B.1 shows this syntax and illustrates how VB.NET implements arrays.

LISTING B.1   Arrays

```
Imports System
Public Module MyModule
   public sub Main()
      Dim asMyStringArray() As String = {"foo", "bar", "baz", "quirk"}
      Dim i as Integer

      For i = 0 To asMyStringArray.Length - 1
         Console.WriteLine(asMyStringArray(i))
      Next i
   End Sub
End Module
```

The only new feature demonstrated in Listing B.1 is the Length property of the Array class.

> **NOTE**
>
> UBound and LBound still work.

Some other new methods and properties include, but aren't limited to, BinarySearch, Copy, Clear, IndexOf, Reverse, Sort, Rank, Length, and SyncRoot.

Structures

VB 6.0 used the Type construct to represent structures. VB.NET no longer supports the Type syntax but uses the new Structure keyword.

Structures support many of the same language features as classes, with a few exceptions. Structures are value types but can't inherit directly from any other class. Listing B.2 shows the new Structure syntax.

LISTING B.2   A Structure

```
Public Structure Customer
   Public ID as Integer
   Public String StreetAddress
   Public String City
   Public String State
   Public String Zip

   Public Function GetDiscountRate() as Double
   '-- Do discount rate lookup here
```

LISTING B.2   Continued

```
      return 0
   End Function


End Structure
```

One obvious aspect to note about structures in VB.NET, as opposed to types in VB 6.0, is that structures support functions and subs as well as raw data. This support aligns VB.NET a little closer with some of the other .NET languages.

Say Goodbye to Set

One of the most commonly maligned features of previous versions of VB was the keyword Set. VB.NET does away with the keyword because it was considered superfluous and confusing. So, assigning an object to a variable looked like this in VB 6.0:

```
Set obj = New Object
```

In VB.NET, the same statement looks like this:

```
obj = New Object()
```

Declaring Properties

Property declaration has changed in VB.NET. The new model is simplified and works more seamlessly with other .NET languages. Listing B.3 shows an example of the new property syntax.

LISTING B.3   New Property Declaration Syntax

```
Private dX as Double
Private dY as Double

Public Property X as Double
   Get
      X = dX
   End Get

   Set
      dX = Value
   End Set
End Property

Public Property Y as Double
```

Listing B.3   Continued

```
Get
    Y = dY
End Get

Set
    dY = Value
End Set
End Property
```

I want to point out a couple of things about the new property syntax:

- All the property routine code is in one code block, with two smaller Get and Set blocks inside.
- The new Value keyword is used even though it's never declared as part of the property method signature.

Exception Handling

VB.NET supports a structured exception-handling model that's based on an exception object. The new exception-handling syntax in VB.NET is similar to the try/catch/finally syntax in C++. Listing B.4 shows an example of this syntax.

Listing B.4   *try/catch/finally* Syntax

```
try
    Throw (new ArgumentNullException())
Catch e as Exception
    Console.WriteLine(e.Message)
Finally
    '-- Do some cleanup
    Console.WriteLine("This is always executed.")
end try
```

The try portion of the block is wrapped around the suspect code. This example simply throws a new ArgumentNullException exception when a Nothing reference is passed to a function or sub that expects an object reference.

An error is dealt with in the catch portion. The Exception object parameter is the type of exception that will be dealt with; all other exceptions won't. In this case, the generic Exception object will catch all exceptions. Typically, you would want to catch the specific exception (ArgumentNullException).

Including the `finally` section in the code is optional; regardless of its inclusion, `finally` is always executed. Typically, in this section, you would do object cleanup or otherwise gracefully exit a function regardless of the outcome.

A more realistic example might be to use a `try/catch` block around code that opens a database connection and catch a `SqlException` object.

The `Return` Keyword

In previous versions of VB, values were returned from functions when the function name was set equal to the value being returned:

```
public function Message() as String
   Message = "Hello."
End Function
```

VB.NET now supports the `Return` keyword, which serves the same purpose as setting the function name equal to some value, as in older versions of VB:

```
Public Function SayHi() as String
   Return "Hello."
End Function
```

By supporting the `Return` keyword, VB.NET is more in line with other .NET languages, such as C# and managed extensions for C++. It also makes changing the name of the function easier because you don't have to find the old name in the function body.

NOTE

VB.NET still supports the old syntax: *FunctionName = SomeValue.*

Delegates and Events

Delegates are the type-safe, secure, managed equivalent of C++ function pointers. You can use delegates with instance, virtual, or shared methods. Another way to think of delegates is as encapsulating a specific method. In .NET, delegates are also used for events and callback functions.

Delegates are implemented by inheriting from `System.Delegate` and supporting a list of methods executed when the delegate is invoked. Listing B.5 illustrates the use of a delegate.

B

LISTING B.5   Delegates

```
 1: Imports System
 2:
 3: Delegate Sub MessageDelegate()
 4:
 5: Public Class MyTestClass
 6:    public Sub WriteMessage()
 7:       Console.WriteLine("I made this.")
 8:    End Sub
 9: End Class
10:
11: public Module MyModule
12:    public Sub Main()
13:       Dim mc as new MyTestClass()
14:       Dim md as New MessageDelegate(AddressOf mc.WriteMessage)
15:          md()
16:    End Sub
17: End Module
```

Listing B.5 declares the delegate `MessageDelegate` on line 3. The public class `MyClass` implements a `WriteMessage` method (lines 6 through 8), and the `MyTestClass` class assigns the `WriteMessage` method to the `MessageDelegate` instance `md`. This means that any time the `md()` delegate is fired, the message `I made this.` will appear onscreen.

Attributes

Attributes enable developers to provide extra metadata to their classes and methods at compile time. Other programs can access this extra information either at compile time, runtime, or by simply reading the metadata.

The .NET Framework allows VB.NET and other .NET languages to use some built-in attributes. These attributes, derived from `System.Attribute`, are used for everything from conditional compilation to transactional support to specifying Web Services methods.

Using Attributes

The `WebMethod` attribute is used to create a Web Services method. When you specify the `WebMethod` attribute, as shown in Listing B.6, the `GetSum` method is available from remote Web-based clients.

Listing B.6   The *WebMethod* Attribute

```
Public Class <WebService> MyWebService : Inherits WebService
    Public Function <WebMethod> GetSum(X as Integer, Y as Integer)
➥As Integer
        Return X + Y
    End Function
End Class
```

In VB.NET, you have to mark the class as using an attribute from a particular class and then mark the method you want to use the attribute with.

Creating Attributes

As my friend David puts it, "Metadata does no good if there is nothing there to read it." He means that most reasons for creating custom attributes revolve around a scenario in which a container object houses other objects that implement one or more custom attributes.

If you want to create your own custom attribute, you must create an attribute class that inherits either directly or indirectly from System.Attribute. Listing B.7 shows how to create your own custom attribute.

Listing B.7   Creating a Custom Attribute

```
<AttributeUsage(AttributeTargets.Method)> Public Class SoapLoggerAttribute
    Inherits SoapExtensionAttribute

    Public Sub New()
    End Sub

    Public Sub New(ByVal logFile As String)
        _logFile = logFile
    End Sub

    Public ReadOnly Property LogFile()
        Get
            LogFile = _logFile
        End Get
    End Property
```

LISTING B.7 Continued

```
Public Overrides ReadOnly Property ExtensionType() As Type
    Get
        ExtensionType = Type.GetType("VBWebSamples.SoapLogger")
    End Get
End Property

Public Overrides Property Priority() As Integer
    Get
        Priority = _priority
    End Get
    Set(ByVal Value As Integer)
        _priority = Value
    End Set
End Property
End Class
```

This custom attribute allows users to configure a log file. This attribute also tells the ASP.NET system which type to load for this SOAP extension.

Free Threading

Free threading is the process of allowing multiple tasks to execute on independent threads. This process prevents other tasks from being held up while a given task is completed. As a result, free threading enables you to write more responsive applications. Listing B.8 shows a simple example of what free threading looks like in VB.NET.

LISTING B.8 Free Threading

```
Imports System
Imports System.Threading

Public Class ClassFoo
    Public Sub Message()
        Console.WriteLine("ClassFoo.Message is running on thread "
➥& AppDomain.GetCurrentThreaedID() & ".")
    End Sub
End Class

Public Class SimpleThreadingVB
    Public Shared Sub Main()
        Dim oMyClass as ClassFoo = new ClassFoo()
        Dim oThread as Thread
            Dim i as Integer
```

LISTING B.8   Continued

```
    For i = 0 To 9
        oThread = new Thread(new ThreadStart(AddressOf oMyClass.Message))
        oThread.Start()
    Next i
  End Sub
End Class
```

> **CAUTION**
>
> Writing free-threaded applications is a risky proposition. You can easily create diffi-
> cult-to-find bugs when writing free-threaded applications. Don't fall into the trap of
> using VB.NET's new free-threaded capabilities simply because you can.

Object-Oriented Features

For years, VB developers have asked for true object-oriented language features. Finally, with VB.NET, they get their wish. VB.NET supports implementation inheritance, constructors and destructors, method overloading, the new Overrides keyword, and shared members.

Inheritance

How long have you been asking for true inheritance? VB.NET supports inheritance by enabling you to extend the properties and methods of a given base class. When you derive a class in VB.NET, you can also override inherited methods with your own implementation. In VB.NET, all classes are inheritable by default. Listing B.9 shows a simple example of inheritance.

LISTING B.9   Simple Inheritance

```
 1: Imports System
 2:
 3: Public Class TwoDPoint
 4:     Public X as Integer = 0
 5:     Public Y as Integer = 0
 6: End Class
 7:
 8: Public Class ThreeDPoint
 9:        Inherits TwoDPoint
10:
11:    Public Z as Integer = 0
12: End Class
```

LISTING B.9 Continued

```
13:
14: Public Module PointTest
15:    public sub Main()
16:       Dim o3DPoint As New ThreeDPoint()
17:
18:       With o3DPoint
19:          .X = 2
20:          .Y = 10
21:          .Z = 12
22:       End With
23:
24:       Console.WriteLine("(" & o3DPoint.X & ", " & o3DPoint.Y & ",
➡" & o3DPoint.Z & ")")
25:    End Sub
26: End Module
```

Listing B.9 declares a simple TwoDPoint class with X and Y public properties (lines 4 and 5). Class ThreeDPoint declares a Z public property (line 11), but notice in the PointTest module that a ThreeDPoint class is created and has access to the TwoDPoint properties X and Y (lines 14 through 22).

To implement inheritance in VB.NET, use the Inherits keyword as shown on line 9. Doing so makes all inheritable properties and methods available to the child class.

Method Overloading

One of the more interesting new features of VB.NET is *method overloading*. With method overloading, you can create more than one function with the same name, as long as those functions have different signatures. In other words, they must have a different number and type of parameters. Listing B.10 shows an example of two overloaded methods in VB.NET.

LISTING B.10 Method Overloading

```
1: Imports System
2: Public Module MyModule
3:    public sub Main()
4:       Dim oMath As New MyMath()
5:       Console.WriteLine(oMath.Add(1, 1))
6:       Console.WriteLine(oMath.Add(1.1, 1.1))
7:       Console.WriteLine(oMath.Add("One","One" ))
8:    End Sub
9: End Module
10:
```

LISTING B.10   Continued

```
11: Public Class MyMath
12:     Overloads Public Function Add(ByVal X As Double, ByVal Y As Double)
➥As Double
13:         Return X + Y
14:     End Function
15:
16:     Overloads Public Function Add(ByVal X As Integer, ByVal Y As Integer)
➥As Integer
17:         Return X + Y
18:     End Function
19:
20:     Overloads Public Function Add(ByVal X As String, ByVal Y As String)
➥As String
21:         Return X & Y
22:     End Function
23: End Class
```

The MyMath class, on line 11, overloads the Add function so that it may be called by passing two integers, two doubles, or two strings.

The Overloads keyword (on lines 12, 16, and 20) tells the compiler that there are other methods with the same name but different parameter lists.

Constructors

VB.NET no longer supports Class_Initialize and Class_Terminate. Instead, VB.NET supports the notion of constructors and destructors. Combined with method overloading (discussed in the preceding section), constructors provide a powerful mechanism for creating an instance of a class and simultaneously initializing property values.

VB.NET uses the reserved method Sub New() as its constructor, as shown in Listing B.11.

LISTING B.11   The *Point Class* Constructor

```
Public Class Point
    Public X As Integer
    Public Y as Integer

    Overloads Public Sub New()
        Me.X = 0
        Me.Y = 0
    End Sub
```

LISTING B.11   Continued

```
Overloads Public Sub New(iX As Integer, iY As Integer)
    Me.X = iX
    Me.Y = iY
End Sub
```

```
End Class
```

Now you can create an instance of the Point class that automatically initializes the X and Y properties:

```
Dim oPoint As New Point(5,6)
```

Overrides

The Overrides keyword tells the compiler that the function it precedes needs to override the functionality of an identically named function in its base class. Listing B.12 shows the Overrides keyword in action.

LISTING B.12   The Overrides Keyword

```
 1: Imports System
 2: Public Module TestModule
 3:    public sub Main()
 4:        Dim oC as Parent
 5:        oC = new Child()
 6:        oC.Print()
 7:    End Sub
 8: End Module
 9:
10: Public Class Parent
11:    Overridable Public Sub Print()
12:        Console.WriteLine("Parent class")
13:    End Sub
14: End Class
15:
16: Public Class Child
17:    Inherits Parent
18:
19:    Overrides Public Sub Print()
20:        Console.WriteLine("Child class")
21:    End Sub
22: End Class
```

In this simple parent-child hierarchy, both the Parent and Child class implement the Print method. Because the Parent.Print method is marked with the Overridable keyword on line 11, the Child class can override the Print method with a version of its own (on line 19).

If this code didn't use the Overridable and Overrides keywords, the call to Print() on line 6 would result in Parent.Print() being called.

Shared Members

VB.NET supports *shared members*, which are properties and methods that all instances of the class can utilize. They are similar to Static members in languages such as C# and C++.

You use the Shared keyword to signify that a function, sub, or property should be available to all instances of that member:

```
Public Shared Function Add(p1 As Point, p2 As Point) As Point
    Return New Point( p1.X + p2.X , p1.Y + p2.Y)
End Function
```

Shared members can be accessed via the class name, not necessarily via a class instance:

```
Dim oPoint3 As Point
oPoint3 = Point.Add(oPoint, oPoint2)
```

B

VB.NET
LANGUAGE
REFERENCE

ASP.NET Object Model

This appendix provides a brief overview of some of the more important aspects of the ASP.NET object model. Specifically, it covers the `HttpContext`, `HttpRequest`, `HttpResponse`, `HttpApplicationState`, `HttpSessionState`, and `HttpServerUtility` objects. Wherever possible, I included only the new or changed features. Properties and methods inherited directly from `Object` aren't discussed here.

HttpContext

The core of the ASP.NET object model starts with the `HttpContext` object. This object encapsulates all the information related to an HTTP request and is used by the Web server to process requests. `HttpContext` also provides access to all other high-level objects commonly used to implement ASP.NET applications. Table C.1 shows some of the more important properties and methods available from the `HttpContext` object.

TABLE C.1   `HttpContext` Properties and Methods

Name	Description
Properties	
Application	Returns `HttpApplicationState` object reference
Cache	Returns a reference to the `Cache` object
Error	Returns a reference to an `Exception` object if an error was thrown during the processing of the last request
Items	Returns a reference to a key-value collection table that implements the `IDictionary` interface
Request	Returns a reference to the current `HttpRequest` object
Response	Returns a reference to the current `HttpResponse` object
Server	Returns a reference to the current `HttpServerUtility` object
Session	Returns a reference to the current `SessionState` object
TimeStamp	Returns a `DateTime` object representing the initial time stamp of the current request
Trace	Returns a reference to the `TraceContext` object
User	Returns a reference to the `IPrincipal` object currently running the application
Methods	
AddError	Adds a new error to the errors collection
ClearError	Clears all errors from the current request
GetConfig	Returns a configuration object representing the current application's `Web.Config`

HttpRequest

The `HttpRequest` object (`Request`) enables ASP.NET applications to read HTTP values sent by a client during a Web request. ASP.NET adds more than 25 new methods and properties. Some new functionality includes file uploading support, text and stream writer support, filter stream support, and write file support. Tables C.2 and C.3 show some of the new `Request` object's properties and methods.

TABLE C.2 New *HttpRequest* Properties

Property	Description
AcceptTypes	Returns an array of the MIME types the client accepts
ApplicationPath	Returns the application's virtual path
Browser	Returns an `HttpBrowserCapabilities` object for gathering information about the client's browser
ContentEncoding	Returns the client's encoding type
ContentType	Returns the MIME content type of the current request
FilePath	Returns the virtual path of the current request
Files	Returns an `HttpFileCollection` object
Filter	Gets or sets a `Stream` object used as a filter for the current request
Headers	Returns a collection of HTTP headers
HttpMethod	Returns a string indicating the transfer method, such as `GET` and `POST`
InputStream	Returns a `Stream` object containing the contents of the incoming body
IsAuthenticated	Returns a Boolean value indicating whether the current user is authenticated
IsSecureConnection	Returns a Boolean value indicating whether the current connection uses HTTPS
Params	Returns a collection object containing a mixed collection of `QueryString`, `Form`, `ServerVariable`, and `Cookies` collections
Path	Returns the virtual path of the current request
PathInfo	Returns additional path info for an URL
PhysicalAppPath	Returns the physical application path
PhysicalPath	Returns the physical application path and filename
Url	Returns information about the URL
UrlReferrer	Returns the URL of the client's previous request

C

ASP.NET
OBJECT MODEL

TABLE C.2   Continued

Property	Description
UserAgent	Returns the user agent string of the client browser
UserHostAddress	Returns the client's IP address
UserHostName	Returns the client's DNS name
UserLanguages	Returns an array of strings representing the client's language preferences

NOTE

You can think of these methods and properties as the simplification of the old `Request.ServerVariables`.

TABLE C.3   New *Request (HttpRequest)* Methods

Method	Description
MapPath	Maps the virtual path of the current request to the physical path
SaveAs	Saves a request to disk

HttpResponse

The HttpResponse (Response) object has more than 15 new properties and methods. Tables C.4 and C.5 show some of the new Response object's properties and methods.

TABLE C.4   New *HttpResponse* Properties

Property	Description
BufferOutput	Gets and sets a Boolean value indicating whether the output to the client is to be buffered after the page is finished
Cache	Returns an HttpCachePolicy object that contains caching information about the current response
ContentEncoding	Gets and sets an Encoding object that contains character set information about the current response

TABLE C.4 Continued

Property	Description
Filter	Gets and sets a Stream object that acts as the output filter
Output	Returns a TextWriter object that enables custom text output to the client
OutputStream	Returns an I/O Stream object that represents the raw binary content going to the client
StatusCode	Gets and sets an integer value representing the status of the HTTP output
StatusDescription	Gets and sets a string value describing the status of the HTTP output
SupressContent	Gets and sets a Boolean value that determines whether to send content to the client

TABLE C.5 New *HttpResponse* Methods

Method	Description
ClearContent	Clears all output to the buffer stream
ClearHeaders	Clears headers from the buffer stream
Close	Closes the socket connection to the client
WriteFile	Specifies the name of the file to write to the HTTP output and optionally allows reading into memory or specifying a file handle, an offset, and a size

HttpApplication

The HttpApplicaton (Application) object allows the sharing of data across all sessions of an ASP.NET application. The ASP.NET Application object adds almost 30 new properties, methods, and events. Compare that to ASP 3.0, where the only events were Application_OnStart and Application_OnEnd, the only methods were Lock() and UnLock(), and the only properties were Contents and StaticObjects. Tables C.6 through C.8 show the new properties, methods, and events.

C

ASP.NET
OBJECT MODEL

Part V

Table C.6 New *HttpApplication* Properties

Property	Description
Application	Returns an instance to an HttpApplication state bag instance
Context	Returns a reference to the HttpRuntime context
Modules	Returns a collection of all the HttpModules for the current application
Request	Returns a reference to the current HttpRequest (Request) object
Response	Returns a reference to the current HttpResponse (Response) object
Server	Returns an HttpServer (Server) utility object
Session	Returns a reference to an HttpSessionState object
Site	Returns an ISite reference
User	Returns an IPrincipal object representing the current user

Table C.7 New *HttpApplication* Methods

Method	Description
Dispose	Cleans up the HttpModule's instance variables
Equals	Determines whether two instances are the same
GetHashCode	Serves as a hash function for use in data structures such as hash tables; returns an integer representing the hash code for the given object
GetString	Returns a human-readable string representation of the object
Init	Initializes instance variables and registers event handlers for the current application

NOTE

The HttpApplication Methods also includes CompleteRequest and GetType.

The HttpApplication class supports a variety of events as well. Table C.8 lists the available events. Note, however, that as of this printing, no documentation is available.

TABLE C.8   New *HttpApplication* Events

Event
AcquireRequestState
AuthenticateRequest
AuthorizeRequest
BeginRequest
Disposed
EndRequest
Error
PostRequestHandlerExecute
PreRequestHandlerExecute
PreSendRequestContent
PreSendRequestHeaders
ReleaseRequestState
ResolveRequestCache
UpdateRequestCache

HttpSessionState

The HttpSessionState (Session) object gives users access to session-scoped data across multiple requests. ASP.NET has greatly enhanced the HttpSessionState object. Tables C.9 through C.10 show the new properties, and methods of the ASP.NET Session object.

TABLE C.9   New *HttpSessionState* Properties

Property	Description
CodePage	Gets and sets the code page identifier (an integer value) for the session
Contents	Returns a reference to the current session state object
Count	Returns an integer value representing the number of items in the session
IsCookieless	Returns a Boolean value indicating whether the session is managed using a cookieless session

TABLE C.9 Continued

Property	Description
IsNewSession	Returns a Boolean value indicating whether the current request created the session
IsReadOnly	Returns a Boolean value indicating whether the session is read only
IsSynchronized	
IsSeparateProcess	Returns a Boolean value indicating whether the session is stored externally
Key	Returns a string representing the current item's key

TABLE C.10 New *HttpSessionState* Methods

Method	Description
Add	Adds a name/value pair to the session
Clear	Removes all name/value pairs from the session
GetDictionaryEnumerator	Returns a DictionaryEnumerator object containing all items in the session
GetEnumerator	Returns an Enumerator object containing all items in the session

HttpServerUtility

ASP.NET's HttpServerUtility object is exposed via ASP.NET's intrinsic Server object. The Server object provides methods and properties for carrying out routine tasks while processing requests.

The HttpServerUtility object supports two public properties and a handful of public methods. Table C.11 shows the server utility object's public properties, and Table C.12 lists its public methods.

TABLE C.11 *HttpServerUtility* Properties

Property	Description
MachineName	Returns a string value representing the server machine name
ScriptTimeout	Gets and sets an integer value representing the number of seconds for requests to timeout

TABLE C.12   New *HttpServerUtility* Methods

Method	Description
ClearError	Clears the last exception thrown.
CreateObject	Creates an instance of a COM object using the object's Programmatic Identifier (ProgID).
CreateObjectFromClsid	Creates an instance of a COM object by using its class identifier (CLSID).
Execute	Executes a request to another .aspx page and returns execution to the original page upon completion. (This works the same in ASP 3.0.)
GetLastError	Returns the last exception thrown.
HtmlDecode	Decodes encoded string values to eliminate invalid HTML characters.
HtmlEncode	Encodes string values to ensure all browsers will correctly transmit text in URL query strings.
MapPath	Returns the physical file path corresponding to a virtual path on the server. (This works the same in ASP 2.0 and higher.)
Transfer	Stops the execution of the current page and begins executing the specified .aspx page. (This works the same in ASP 2.0 and higher.)
UrlDecode	Decodes strings that have been encoded for HTTP transmission. This ensures all browsers transmit the text in URLs correctly and that certain characters and spaces are not truncated.
UrlEncode	Encodes strings for reliable HTTP transmission from server to browser in a URL.
UrlPathEncode	URL-encodes the path portion of URLs to ensure correct transmission of text in URL strings.

NOTE

Equals, GetHashCode, GetType, and ToString are available as well. These methods are inherited from the Object base class.

C

ASP.NET
OBJECT MODEL

ADO.NET Quick Reference

This appendix provides a brief overview of the features available in ADO.NET and covers the features most likely to be used in this book. ADO.NET is a feature-rich component of the .NET Framework and cannot be fully covered in an appendix. For a more complete approach, I suggest the .NET help or the ADO.NET section on `http://msdn.microsoft.com`.

ADO.NET

ADO.NET is Microsoft's latest technology for accessing data within the .NET platform. ADO.NET gives you a method of accessing data from within your application. It was specifically designed for accessing data within Web applications but still maintaining the functionality necessary to work in other types of applications. It's the predecessor of ADO but with a much stronger feature set. Your .NET application will use ADO.NET to display data on a Web form or manipulate the data source's data. Figure D.1 shows the general components of ADO.NET.

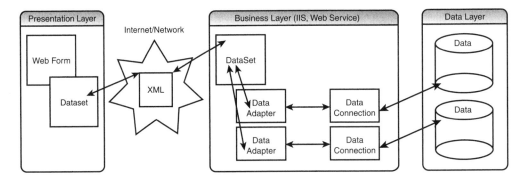

Figure D.1
Components of ADO.NET.

To access the classes that make up ADO.NET from your application, you must reference the correct namespace. Table D.1 describes the namespaces and provides a few samples of the available classes.

Table D.1   ADO.NET Namespaces

Namespace	Description
System.Data	Contains classes that build the .NET architecture, including DataTable, DataColumn, DataRow, DataRelation, and so on
System.Data.Common	Contains shared classes for accessing a data source, including DataAdapter, DataTableMapping, and so on

TABLE D.1   Continued

Namespace	Description
System.Data.OleDb	OLE DB .NET provider; contains classes such as `OleDbCommand`, `OleDbConnection`, `OleDbDataAdapter`, and so on
System.Data.SqlClient	SQL .NET provider; contains classes such as `SqlCommand`, `SqlConnection`, `SqlDataAdapter`, `SqlDataReader`, and so on
System.Data.SqlTypes	Contains classes for SQL Server data types, including `SqlBit`, `SqlDateTime`, `SqlInt32`, `SqlDouble`, `SqlGuid`, and so on

ADO.NET Architecture

ADO.NET's architecture is based on two main concepts: disconnected data and the eXtensible Markup Language (XML). Having these items at the core of ADO.NET makes for a powerful and flexible data access object.

ADO.NET is based on an XML format, which provides for richer data types, sharing of data, and improved performance. All these topics will be discussed in this appendix.

The main components that make up ADO.NET include the Connection, Command, DataAdapter, and DataSet objects. We'll also look at XML Schema Definition (XSD) schemas and the role they play with datasets.

Connections and `SqlConnection` Objects

Connecting to the database will be our starting point. You connect to a database by using a data connection object. When you're connecting to SQL Server, be sure to use the `SqlConnection` object.

Listing D.1 shows how to create and open a connection to a SQL Server. Remember to use the `Close()` method to close the connection when you are done.

LISTING D.1   Connecting to SQL Server

```
1: SqlConnection conn = SqlConnection("server=localhost;uid=sa;pwd=;
➥ database=MyGolfGear");
2: conn.Open();
3: //
4: // Do some work
5: //
6: conn.Close();
```

> **NOTE**
>
> In a Web application where you are using a connection string in multiple places, having to find all the connection strings is a maintenance nightmare when you need to change something. Listing D.2 has two parts. The first part stores the connection string in web.config; then a snippet of code reads the connection string from web.config to open a new connection. Note that you must use the namespace System.Collections.Specialized.

LISTING D.2   Storing a Connection String in *web.config* and Then Using It

```
<configuration>
    <appSettings>
    <add key="ConnectString" value="Data Source=localhost; User ID=sa;
➥ Password=; Initial Catalog=MyGolfGear" />
    </appSettings>
</configuration>

NameValueCollection config = NameValueCollection)HttpContext.Current.
➥GetConfig("appSettings");
SqlConnection conn = SqlConnection((String)config["ConnectString"]);
conn.Open();
//
// Do some work
//
conn.Close();
```

> **NOTE**
>
> You can find the complete listing for the web.config file online.

Command Object

After you create a connection, you can use the Command object to execute commands against the data source and return results. When creating a command, you must specify a SQL statement and a connection. Listing D.3 creates a new MyGolfGear.NET order using the Command object based on a stored procedure with parameters.

LISTING D.3   Storing a Connection String in *web.config* and Then Using It

```
1:   NameValueCollection config = NameValueCollection)HttpContext.Current.
➥GetConfig("appSettings");
2:   SqlConnection con = new SqlConnection((String)config["ConnectString"]);
3:   SqlCommand com = new SqlCommand("spCreateNewOrder", con);
4:   com.CommandType = CommandType.StoredProcedure;
5:   com.Parameters.Add(new SqlParameter("@UserID", SqlDbType.UniqueIdentifier,
➥16,"UserID"));
6:   com.Parameters["@UserID"].Value = UserID;
7:   com.Parameters.Add(new SqlParameter("@OrderID", SqlDbType.UniqueIdentifier,
➥16,"OrderID"));
8:   com.Parameters["@OrderID"].Value = OrderID;
9:   con.Open();
10:  com.ExecuteNonQuery();
11:  con.Close();
```

NOTE

You can find the code for Listing D.3 in `MyGolfGearDP.cs` online.

Table D.2 shows the different `Execute` methods available from the `Command` object and the reason to use one rather than another.

TABLE D.2   The *Command* Object's *Execute* Methods

Execute *Method*	*Description*
ExecuteNonQuery	Use when no rows will be returned.
ExecuteScalar	Use only when you need to return the value of the first column of the first row.
ExecuteReader	Use when you need a `DataReader` object returned.

ADO.NET `DataAdapters`

`DataAdapters` are an important part of ADO.NET. They transfer data from any data source to a `DataSet`, as well as from the `DataSet` back to the data source. Usually, the data source is a database, but it could also be an XML file.

When you use DataAdapters, you can specify the portions of the data required from the data source by using a SQL statement or stored procedure. The same logic applies when you are trying to implement the changes from the DataSet into the data source.

The two types of DataAdapters are OleDbDataAdapter and SqlDataAdapter. OleDbDataAdapter can be used with any data source that has an OLE DB provider, whereas SqlDataAdapter is only for SQL Server. Additionally, because SqlDataAdapter doesn't have to go through the OLE DB layer, it is much more efficient. SqlDataAdapter is compliant only with SQL 7.0 and higher. If you are using SQL 6.5, therefore, you have to use OleDbDataAdapter. SqlDataAdapter is in the System.Data.SqlClient namespace. (The rest of this section is based on your using SQL 7.0 and higher.)

Usually, you use a DataAdapter to populate a single table within your DataSet. The same strategy applies to using your DataAdapter to apply the changes from the DataSet to the data source.

Listing D.4 uses the DataAdapter to populate a DataSet from a stored procedure. Notice that you use SelectCommand of the DataAdapter to specify the CommandType property as a stored procedure. The stored procedure spGetCompleteCatalog has several selects in it, so you can grab all the data necessary in one call. Then you use TableMappings to tie the source's data table name, the first parameter, to the name of the table in the DataSet you want to map to. Last, you use the data adapter to fill the DataSet on Line 14. At this point, all the data returned from the stored procedure is populated into the specified DataTables within the DataSet.

LISTING D.4   Using a *DataAdapter* to Fill a *DataSet, MyGolfGearDP.cs.*

```
1: public void FillCatalog(CatalogDS ds) {
2:     NameValueCollection config = NameValueCollection)HttpContext.Current.
➥GetConfig("appSettings");
3:     SqlConnection con = new SqlConnection((String)config["ConnectString"]);
4:     SqlDataAdapter sda = new SqlDataAdapter("spGetCompleteCatalog", con);
5:     sda.SelectCommand.CommandType = CommandType.StoredProcedure;
6:     con.Open();
7:
8:     sda.TableMappings.Add("Table", "Category");
9:     sda.TableMappings.Add("Table1", "Product");
10:    sda.TableMappings.Add("Table2", "CategoryProductMapping");
11:    sda.TableMappings.Add("Table3", "ProductPrice");
12:    sda.TableMappings.Add("Table4", "ProductOptions");
13:    sda.TableMappings.Add("Table5", "ProductSpecial");
14:    sda.Fill(ds);
15     con.Close();
16: }
```

> **NOTE**
>
> You can find the complete listing for the `MyGolfGearDP.cs` file online.

Now that we have looked at the retrieval of data using a `DataAdapter`, let's look at one that takes the changes within a `DataSet` and updates the data source. The `DataAdapter` in Listing D.5 initiates the `Delete`, `Insert`, or `Update` command for each row in the `DataTable` only if that row is marked as being new, changed, or deleted. After the `Update` method is executed, the data source is immediately updated.

LISTING D.5   Using a `DataAdapter` to Update a Data Source, *MyGolfGearDP.cs*.

```
1:   public void UpdateCatalog(CatalogDS ds)
2:   {
3:       NameValueCollection config = NameValueCollection)HttpContext.Current.
➥GetConfig("appSettings");
4:       SqlConnection con = new SqlConnection((String)config["ConnectString"])
➥;
5:       SqlDataAdapter sda = new SqlDataAdapter("spGetCompleteCatalog", con);
6:       con.Open();
7:       SqlTransaction t = con.BeginTransaction();
8:       try{
9:           sda.DeleteCommand = new SqlCommand("spDeleteCategory", con, t);
10:          sda.DeleteCommand.Parameters.Clear();
11:          sda.DeleteCommand.CommandType = CommandType.StoredProcedure;
12:      sda.DeleteCommand.Parameters.Add("@CategoryID",
➥SqlDbType.UniqueIdentifier,4,"CategoryID");

13:          sda.InsertCommand = new SqlCommand("spInsertCategory", con, t);
14:          sda.InsertCommand.CommandType = CommandType.StoredProcedure;
15:          sda.InsertCommand.Parameters.Clear();
16:      sda.InsertCommand.Parameters.Add("@CategoryID",
➥SqlDbType.UniqueIdentifier,4,"CategoryID");
17:          sda.InsertCommand.Parameters.Add("@Name", SqlDbType.VarChar, 25,
➥"Name");
18:      sda.InsertCommand.Parameters.Add("@ParentCategoryID",
➥SqlDbType.UniqueIdentifier,4,"ParentCategoryID");
19:          sda.InsertCommand.Parameters.Add("@Description", SqlDbType.VarChar,
➥100,"Description");
20:          sda.InsertCommand.Parameters.Add("@DisplaySeq", SqlDbType.SmallInt,
➥2,"DisplaySeq");
21:          sda.InsertCommand.Parameters.Add("@Display", SqlDbType.SmallInt,
➥2,"Display");
```

Listing D.5   Continued

```
22:          sda.UpdateCommand = new SqlCommand("spUpdateCategory", con, t);
23:          sda.UpdateCommand.CommandType = CommandType.StoredProcedure;
24:          sda.UpdateCommand.Parameters.Clear();
25:      sda.UpdateCommand.Parameters.Add("@CategoryID",
➥SqlDbType.UniqueIdentifier,4,"CategoryID");
26:          sda.UpdateCommand.Parameters.Add("@Name", SqlDbType.VarChar, 25,
➥"Name");
27:      sda.UpdateCommand.Parameters.Add("@ParentCategoryID",
➥SqlDbType.UniqueIdentifier,4,"ParentCategoryID");
28:          sda.UpdateCommand.Parameters.Add("@Description",
SqlDbType.VarChar,100,"Description");
29:          sda.UpdateCommand.Parameters.Add("@DisplaySeq", SqlDbType.SmallInt,
➥2,"DisplaySeq");
30:          sda.UpdateCommand.Parameters.Add("@Display", SqlDbType.SmallInt,2,
➥"Display");

31:          sda.Update(ds, "Category");
32:          t.Commit();
33:            }
34:      catch( Exception e )
35:        {
36:          t.Rollback();
37:          throw new Exception("SQL Update Failed" + e.ToString());
38:            }
39: finally
40:        {
41:          con.Close();
42:            }
43: }
```

Note

You can find the complete listing for the `MyGolfGearDP.cs` file online.

Note

Notice how we wrapped the update in a *transaction* in Listing D.5 by sending the transaction as a parameter for each `SqlCommand`. We needed to do so because we wanted to make sure that all updates successfully made it to the data source; otherwise, we wanted to roll back any changes made. This way, we can keep the data in the data source valid.

ADO.NET DataSets

`DataSets` are the core of ADO.NET. They are the reason ADO.NET works in a disconnected environment. Basically, a `DataSet` is an in-memory representation of some data. The representation is in the form of `DataTables` with columns and rows, just like a table in your database. In most situations, your `DataSet` will have a similar structure to your database schema; however, this is not a requirement for a `DataSet` schema. This also holds true for the data source of the `DataSet`. In most cases, the data source will be your database; however, because `DataSets` are data-source independent, it could be a non-database source such as an XML file.

In ADO, data was represented as a single table in a *recordset*. In ADO.NET, the data is represented as a `DataSet`. Within that `DataSet` class, you can work with the `Tables` and `Relations` collections. The `DataTable` class uses the `Rows`, `Columns`, `ParentRelations`, and `ChildRelations` collections. They are all self-explanatory. For example, the `Rows` collection contains every row within a `DataTable`, and the `Relations` collection contains relationships between two `DataTables`.

DataSet Schemas and XML

One thing that makes `DataSets` so powerful is that they are stored and transferred as XML. The native serialization format of a `DataSet` is XML. Therefore, if you try to persist a `DataSet`, it will be serialized as an XML file. However, the actual data within the `DataSet` is not XML but can be serialized as XML.

Even though `DataSets` are based on XML, you don't need to be an XML expert to work with them. You just need to be comfortable with the normal programming model. For example, Listing D.6 shows how to access the name of a category within the category data table for a specified row.

LISTING D.6 Accessing a value within a *DataSet*

```
1: string catname;
2: catname = ds.Category[0].CategoryName;
```

Because `DataSets` are transmitted as XML, they can be shared with any component that can understand an XML schema. This capability adds great interoperability to your application if you are using `DataSets`.

Another important role that XML plays in `DataSets` is in the `DataSet` schema, which defines the content and data structure of a `DataSet`. The schema defines the tables, columns, and data types for those columns, constraints, and data table relationships. This schema is called an *XSD schema*.

XSD schemas contain two types of definitions: complex and simple. A simple type element can contain only text values, whereas a complex type allows you to specify a set of attributes and content of the element. XSD has base data types such as integer and string but also allows you to define new data types by using simpleType and complexType elements. This way, DataSets can have complex views of data, with easy access. Listing D.7 is a snippet of MyGolfGear.NET's CatalogDS schema.

LISTING D.7   XSD Schema

```
1: <?xml version="1.0" encoding="utf-8"?>
2: <xsd:schema id="DataSet1" targetNamespace=http://tempuri.org/DataSet1.xsd
➥ elementFormDefault="qualified" xmlns=http://tempuri.org/DataSet1.xsd
➥xmlns:xsd="http://www.w3.org/2001/XMLSchema" xmlns:msdata=
➥"urn:schemas-microsoft-com:xml-msdata">
3: <xsd:element name="CatalogDS" msdata:IsDataSet="true">
4:     <xsd:complexType>
5:         <xsd:choice maxOccurs="unbounded">
6:                 <xsd:element name="Category">
7:                     <xsd:complexType>
8:                         <xsd:sequence>
9:                             <xsd:element name="CategoryID" msdata:DataType=
➥"System.Guid"msdata:DefaultValue="NULL" type="xsd:string"
➥ msdata:Ordinal="0" />
10:                             <xsd:element name="Name" msdata:DefaultValue=
➥"NULL" type="xsd:string" minOccurs="0" msdata:Ordinal="1" />
11:                             <xsd:element name="ParentCategoryID"
➥msdata:DataType="System.Guid"msdata:DefaultValue="NULL"
➥ type="xsd:string" minOccurs="0" msdata:
➥Ordinal="2" />
12:                             <xsd:element name="Description" msdata:
➥DefaultValue="NULL"
➥ type="xsd:string" minOccurs="0" msdata:Ordinal="3" />
13:                             <xsd:element name="DisplaySeq" msdata:
➥DefaultValue="NULL"
➥type="xsd:short" minOccurs="0" msdata:Ordinal="4" />
14:                             <xsd:element name="Display" msdata:
➥DefaultValue="NULL"
➥type="xsd:short" minOccurs="0" msdata:Ordinal="5" />
15:                         </xsd:sequence>
16:                     </xsd:complexType>
17:                 </xsd:element>
18:                 <xsd:element name="CategoryProductMapping">
19:                     <xsd:complexType>
20:                         <xsd:sequence>
21:                             <xsd:element name="ID" msdata:ReadOnly="true"
➥msdata:AutoIncrement="true" type="xsd:int" msdata:Ordinal="0" />
```

LISTING D.7   Continued

```
22:                                <xsd:element name="CategoryID" msdata:DataType=
➡"System.Guid"
➡ msdata:DefaultValue="NULL" type="xsd:string" minOccurs="0" msdata:
➡Ordinal="1" />
23:                                <xsd:element name="ProductID" msdata:DataType=
➡"System.Guid"
➡msdata:DefaultValue="NULL" type="xsd:string" msdata:Ordinal="2" />
24:                          </xsd:sequence>
25:                      </xsd:complexType>
26:                  </xsd:element>
27:              </xsd:choice>
28:          </xsd:complexType>
29:          <xsd:key name="NewDataSetKey1" msdata:PrimaryKey="true">
30:              <xsd:selector xpath=".//Category" />
31:              <xsd:field xpath="CategoryID" />
32:          </xsd:key>
33:          <xsd:key name="NewDataSetKey11" msdata:PrimaryKey="true">
34:            <xsd:selector xpath=".//CategoryProductMapping" />
35:              <xsd:field xpath="ID" />
36:          </xsd:key>
37:          <xsd:keyref name="CategoryProductMapping" refer="NewDataSetKey1">
38:              <xsd:selector xpath=".//CategoryProductMapping" />
39:              <xsd:field xpath="CategoryID" />
40:          </xsd:keyref>
41:  </xsd:element>
42: </xsd:schema>
```

> **NOTE**
>
> You can find the complete listing for the `CatalogDS.xsd` file online.

Data Relationships

To get the most out of `DataSets`, you will probably use more than one `DataTable` in a `DataSet`. Usually, you need to create a relationship between two of these tables. Your ability to create these relationships makes `DataSets` versatile. The relationship between two `DataTables` is called a `DataRelation`. However, this relationship must be created. Even if you base your `DataSet` on a data source that has two tables with an already-defined relationship, you still have to define that relationship within your schema by creating a keyref, a primary key reference, in the XSD schema. This keyref is shown on lines 37 to 40 in Listing D.7. The power of this feature is evident when you are coding. Any time you are on a row in the `Category` table, which is the parent table, you can retrieve all the related child rows in the `CategoryProduct Mapping` table. The same is true when you try to determine the parent of a specified child row. An example is the parent/child relationship shown in Listing D.8. This listing shows how easily you can retrieve related data in a `DataSet`. In the this example, notice how the programming logic is very readable. Here, we created a typed `DataSet` that will be explained later in this appendix. However, you do not have to have a strongly typed `DataSet` to be able to work with related tables.

LISTING D.8   Accessing Related Data in a *DataSet*

```
//Find a specific category row
CatalogDS.CategoryRow CatRow = catalogds.Category.FindByCategoryID
➥(CategoryID);
// Retrieve all related CategoryProductMapping Rows related to this
➥Category Row
CatalogDS.CategoryProductMappingRow[] cpmr =
➥CatRow.GetCategoryProductMappingRows();
```

> **NOTE**
>
> You can find the complete listing for the preceding code in the `CategoryAdmin.aspx.cs` file online.

Constraints

Another feature that makes `DataSets` so powerful is your ability to create constraints. You can create constraints to keep the integrity of the data. They can be applied any time a row is altered (inserted, updated, or deleted). Keep in mind that constraints are specific to a single table.

The two types of constraints are unique and foreign-key constraints. A unique constraint verifies that new values in a column are unique within a `DataTable`. You can apply this constraint either by setting a `DataColumn`'s unique property to `true` or specifying that a `DataColumn` is the primary key. The latter approach is shown on line 29 in Listing D.7.

A foreign-key constraint determines what should occur to a child row when a parent row in a related table is altered. You can create a constraint by altering the attributes defined in the `DataRelation`. On line 37 of Listing D.7 , you could add `msdata:ConstraintOnly="true"` to the keyref to state that this relationship is for constraint purposes only.

Programming with DataSets (Typed Versus Untyped)

An untyped DataSet is one that is not based on a schema. Therefore, it is simply a collection of tables, columns, rows, and so on. This means that you cannot create a class that simplifies the programmatic access of the data within a DataSet. For example, Listing D.9 creates an untyped DataSet and then accesses one of its elements. However, even though this example is not a strongly typed DataSet, accessing data is not very difficult because you are just working with collections.

LISTING D.9   Accessing Related Data in a *DataSet*

```
1:  DataSet catalog= new DataSet();
2:  DataTable category = new DataTable("Category")
3:  category.Columns.Add("CategoryID");
4:  category.Columns.Add("Name");
5:  category.Columns.Add("Description");
6:  DataRow catrow = category.NewRow();
7:  catrow["CategoryID"] = 1;
8:  catrow["Name"] = "Woods";
9:  catrow["Descriptions"] = "Individual and sets of woods";
10: category.Rows.Add(catrow);
11: catalog.Tables.Add(category);
12: // access that categoryID value
13: int i = (int) catalog.Tables["Category"].Rows[0]["CategoryID"];
```

> **NOTE**
>
> You can find the complete listing for the preceding code in the CategoryAdmin. aspx.cs file online.

A typed DataSet is one that is derived from the base DataSet class and then based on an XSD schema that creates a class simplifying the programmatic access of all the contents within the DataSet. The contents of the schema are compiled into a class that contains objects and properties. We created MyGolfGear.NET's catalog and order DataSet this way. In a typed DataSet, line 13 of Listing D.9 would look like this:

```
int i = (int) catalogds.Category[0].CategoryID;
```

You'll find some other benefits to creating and using typed DataSets. For one thing, the code is easy on the eyes. Also, VisualStudio.NET supports intelliSense, so type checking is done at compile time. Therefore, the majority of user errors will be identified before the code is executed.

To create this class from a typed `DataSet`, you could use either VS.NET or `xsd.exe`. To create a class based on a `DataSet` schema, execute the code line in Listing D.10. The class will be created with C# code and inserted into the current directory as `CatalogDS.cs`.

LISTING D.10   Creating a Class from an XSD Schema

```
xsd / dataset / language:C# CatalogDS.xsd
```

> **NOTE**
>
> When you create a class from a typed `DataSet`, that class is tied to the specified XSD schema. Therefore, whenever the schema is changed in any way, you must rerun the `xsd.exe` tool to generate a new class that will work with the updated XSD schema.

Binding to a `DataGrid`

`DataSet`s tie seamlessly into Web forms and the controls within them. You can bind most ASP.NET controls, such as `DataGrid`, `DataList`, or even `ListBox`, to a table in a `DataSet`. Listing D.11 creates a `DataView` from a table, sorts the data by a specified column, and then binds it to a `DataList`. If you don't need to sort the data, you can simply bind the `DataGrid` to `catalogds.Category.DefaultView`.

LISTING D.11   Creating a *DataView* and Setting a Sort Column

```
1:  // Create the catalog dataset first, then continue w/ the following
2: DataView dv = catalogds.Category.DefaultView;
3: dv.Sort = "DisplaySeq";
4: DataGrid1.DataSource = dv;
5: DataGrid1.DataBind();
```

> **NOTE**
>
> You can find the complete listing for the preceding code in the `CategoryAdmin.aspx.cs` file online.

A `DataView` is a customized view of a `DataTable`. It allows you to filter out rows based on certain criteria, sort on specific columns, and do much more. You can manipulate the `DataView` without harming the original data in the `DataSet`. The best thing about a `DataView` is that it can be bound to ASP.NET controls.

INDEX

X-Z

Other Related Titles